Michael K.W. Suh
Power and Peril

Beihefte zur Zeitschrift
für die neutestamentliche
Wissenschaft

Edited by
Matthias Konradt, Judith Lieu, Laura Nasrallah,
Jens Schröter and Gregory E. Sterling

Volume 239

Michael K.W. Suh

Power and Peril

Paul's Use of Temple Discourse in 1 Corinthians

DE GRUYTER

ISBN 978-3-11-077810-6
e-ISBN (PDF) 978-3-11-067894-9
e-ISBN (EPUB) 978-3-11-067897-0
ISSN 0171-6441

Library of Congress Control Number: 2019957124

Bibliographic information published by the Deutsche Nationalbibliothek
The Deutsche Nationalbibliothek lists this publication in the Deutsche Nationalbibliografie;
detailed bibliographic data are available on the Internet at http://dnb.dnb.de.

© 2021 Walter de Gruyter GmbH, Berlin/Boston
This volume is text- and page-identical with the hardback published in 2020.
Printing and binding: CPI books GmbH, Leck

www.degruyter.com

Preface

This book is a revised version of the doctoral dissertation written at Emory University, and so my committee deserves many thanks. Professor Carl Holladay has instilled in me a deep appreciation of the Jewish milieu of the New Testament. His words of encouragement and tales of his travels around the world (always with tantalizing details that make for such great stories!) have provided me with much needed laughter and energy during the completion of this project. His embodiment of the consummate professional and scholar will always remain a model. Professor Walter Wilson's incisive questions have driven me to be clear and efficient in my argumentation, and this project stands better because of his critical eye. Professor Cynthia Patterson, from the Department of History, has graciously welcomed into her office a dilettante in the world of Greek historiography. Her enthusiasm concerning all my sophomoric questions have opened up an avenue of historical inquiry of which I have only begun to scratch the surface in this project. Finally, the biggest thanks are due to Professor Luke Timothy Johnson. When I think of Luke, an old Korean idiom comes to mind, one that can roughly be translated: "Leader, teacher, and parent are one." Luke truly embodies this idiom, and without his support and guidance as a leader, teacher, and Doktorvater, this project would never have seen the light of day, still less come to its eventual completion. His excitement concerning this project since the beginning to its end is a testimony to his unwavering commitment to see his students succeed from day one. If I can replicate even a tenth of his energy as a scholar and teacher, I will consider my academic career to have been a success.

Earlier portions of chapter 2 first appeared in *Vigiliae Christianae* as "Τὸ πνεῦμα in 1 Corinthians 5:5: A Reconsideration of Patristic Exegesis," *VC* 72 (2018): 121–141. I am grateful to Brill and the editors of *VC* for providing permission to republish this work. Many thanks to Albrecht Döhnert, Alice Meroz, Jana Fritsche, and Florian Ruppenstein of De Gruyter for accepting this work and for their guidance through the editorial process. I am also honored that the editors of BZNW have accepted this work for their prestigious series.

There are also many friends and family who have watched the progress of this project from both near and far. My wonderful colleagues at Emory University deserve many thanks: Tony Alonso, David Carr, Collin Cornell, Chris Holmes, Eric Moore, Jenny Pietz, Devin White, and Jennifer Wyant. Above all, Jonathan Potter has been a great friend and valuable conversation partner. Special thanks are also due to my colleague and friend, Johann Choi, and his wife, Jina Choi, for sharing their life together with my family and me.

I would also like to thank the Undergraduate Research Programs at Emory University for providing the final year of funding and support. Our directors, Folashade Alao, Rachel Diamond, and Pat Marsteller, provided sage guidance to our cohort of graduate fellows (Michael Thees, Aimée Vester, Signe White, and Julian Whitney) as we met weekly to discuss classroom strategies, research translation, and professional development. I will always be grateful for the opportunity I had to learn from such a talented and diverse group of scholars. Thanks are also due to Dean Lisa Tedesco, Associate Dean Rosemary Hynes, and Professor Walter Melion (Art History) of Emory's Laney Graduate School, whom I have had the pleasure of working with through the Andrew W. Mellon Humanities Ph.D. Interventions Project. They have been immensely supportive of my own research and writing even as they have taught me the value of interdisciplinary dialogue and the difficult but rewarding work of advancing graduate education in the 21st century.

Also, much thanks are due to my mother, In-Young Suh and my sister, Mina Suh. My father, Yoon-Suk Suh, passed away many years before I had even begun this chapter of my life, but I hope that he would have been proud of this accomplishment. Special thanks also to my other parents (in-law), David Kang and Jean Kang, who have been one of my biggest supporters from afar.

Last, but certainly not least, my deepest gratitude is due to my wife, Janice Kang. She has watched me pursue this passion from the earliest days prior to our marriage, to the eventual completion of this project many years later. She is truly my better-half and I am undoubtedly a better thinker, writer, and most importantly, a better person because of her. Thank you.

Contents

Abbreviations —— XI

1	**Experiencing Power and Peril in Corinth —— 1**
1.1	Introduction —— 1
1.2	History of Interpretation —— 5
1.2.1	Reading 1 Corinthians 5, 10, and 11 —— 6
1.2.2	The Corinthians as Temple of God —— 8
1.3	Avenues of Inquiry —— 13
1.4	*Table 1:* Temple Themes in 1 Corinthians 5:1–13, 10:1–22, and 11:17–34 —— 19
2	**Constructing Temple and Identity in 1 Corinthians —— 21**
2.1	Reading 1 Corinthians 5:1–13, 10:1–22, and 11:17–34 in Literary Context —— 21
2.2	Reading 1 Corinthians 5:1–13, 10:1–22, and 11:17–34 as Temple Discourse —— 25
2.3	The Exodus Tradition and Christological Connection —— 29
2.3.1	Exodus 12–13 in 1 Corinthians 5:1–13 —— 31
2.3.2	Exodus 13–17 in 1 Corinthians 10:1–22 —— 38
2.3.3	Exodus 24 in 1 Corinthians 11:17–34 —— 42
2.3.4	Exodus in 1 Corinthians 5:1–13, 10:1–22, and 11:17–34 —— 44
2.4	Power in 1 Corinthians —— 45
2.4.1	Power in 1 Corinthians 12 and 14 —— 49
2.4.2	Power in 1 Corinthians 5:1–13 —— 51
2.4.3	*Excursus:* Early Christian Interpretations of τὸ πνεῦμα in 1 Corinthians 5:5 —— 58
2.4.4	Power in 1 Corinthians 10:1–22 —— 77
2.4.5	Power in 1 Corinthians 11:17–34 —— 85
2.4.6	Power in 1 Corinthians 5:1–13, 10:1–22, and 11:17–34 —— 88
2.5	Peril in 1 Corinthians —— 88
2.5.1	Peril in 1 Corinthians 5:1–13 —— 89
2.5.2	Peril in 1 Corinthians 10:1–22 —— 96
2.5.3	Peril in 1 Corinthians 11:17–34 —— 100
2.6	Meals within the Temple of God —— 104
2.7	A Synthetic Summary of Temple Discourse —— 106
2.8	Chart I: Components of the Lord's Supper Tradition in the Synoptic Gospels and 1 Corinthians 11 —— 109

3 Accessing Sacred Spaces in Greek and Roman Contexts — 110
- 3.1 Introduction — 110
- 3.2 Transgressions in the Greek Context — 111
- 3.2.1 Prescriptions Regarding the Sacred — 112
- 3.2.2 Divine Power — 117
- 3.2.3 Participation in Rituals — 119
- 3.2.4 Penalties for Transgressions — 125
- 3.3 Transgressions in the Roman Context — 132
- 3.3.1 Divine Power — 133
- 3.3.2 Participations in Rituals — 145
- 3.3.3 *Excursus:* Aelius Aristides and Divine Power — 147
- 3.4 Summary of Evidence from Greek and Roman Contexts — 151

4 Accessing Sacred Spaces in Jewish Contexts — 154
- 4.1 Introduction — 154
- 4.2 The Hebrew Bible and Other Related Writings — 154
- 4.3 Philo — 166
- 4.4 Material Culture — 168
- 4.5 Qumran — 171
- 4.5.1 (Im)purity of the Temple — 176
- 4.5.2 Maintenance of Membership — 179
- 4.5.3 *Excursus:* Spirit in the Qumran Community — 183
- 4.5.4 Penalties for Transgressions — 189
- 4.6 Summary of Evidence from Jewish Contexts — 191

5 Temple Discourse in 1 Corinthians — 195
- 5.1 Broad Outlines — 195
- 5.2 Specific Issues — 197
- 5.2.1 Location of the Temple: Corinth — 197
- 5.2.2 Inclusion and Exclusion — 200
- 5.2.3 Divine Spirit and Power — 202
- 5.2.4 Use of Scripture — 205
- 5.2.5 Penalties for Transgressions — 208
- 5.2.6 Presence of Christ — 211
- 5.3 Constructing Temple in 1 Corinthians — 212

6 Conclusion — 214

Bibliography — 216
- B.1 Primary Sources — 216

B.2	Commentaries —— **220**	
B.2.1	Ancient to Pre-Modern —— **220**	
B.2.2	Modern —— **221**	
B.3	Secondary Literature —— **222**	

Index of Ancient Citations —— 241

Index of Bible Citations —— 261

Index of Names —— 273

Index of Subjects —— 275

Abbreviations

Agora XVI	Woodhead, A.G. *The Athenian Agora XVI. Inscriptions: The Decrees.* Princeton: American School of Classical Studies at Athens, 1997.
BGU	*Aegyptische Urkunden aus den Museen zu Berlin:* Griechische Urkunden I–VIII, 1895–1933.
BIWK	Petzl, Georg. *Die Beichtinschriften Westkleinasiens* (special issue, *EpAnat* 22). Bonn: 1994.
CID	*Corpus des inscriptions de Delphes.* 4 vols. Paris: de Boccard, 1977–2002.
	I: G. Rougemont, ed (1977). *Lois sacrées et règlements religieux.*
	II: J. Bousquet, ed (1989). *Les comptes du quatrième et du troisième siècles.*
	III: A. Bélis, ed. (1992). *Les hymnes à Apollon.*
	IV: D. Lefèvre, D. Laroche, and O. Masson, ed. (2002). *Documents Amphictioniques.*
CIL	Mommsen, Theodore et al. *Corpus Inscriptionum Latinarum.* 17 vols. in 78. Berglin: 1863–.
CMRDM	Lane, Eugene N. *Corpus monumentorum religionis dei Menis.* 4 vols. Leiden: Brill, 1971–1978.
CPJ	Tcherikover, Victor A., Alexander Fuks, and Menahem Stern, ed. *Corpus Papyrorum Judaicarum.* 3 vols. Cambridge: Harvard University Press, 1957–1964.
Edelstein	Edelstein, Emma J. and Ludwig Edelstein. *Asclepius: Collection and Interpretation of the Testimonies.* 2 vols. Baltimore: The Johns Hopkins Press, 1975 [1945].
F. Delphes III,3	*Fouilles de Delphes III.* 2 vols. Paris: de Boccard, 1932–1943.
	1: G. Daux, ed. (1932). *Du trésor des Athéniens jusqu'aux bases de Gélon.*
	2: G. Daux, ed. (1943). *Du trésor des Athéniens jusqu'aux bases de Gélon.*
Halikarnassos	Migeotte, L. *L'emprunt public dans les cités grecques.* No. 102 (pp. 319–22). Paris: Les Belles Lettres, 1984.
IC	Guarducci, M. *Inscriptiones Creticae.* 4 vols. Rome: 1935–1960.
IDelos	Durrbach, Félix, André Plassart, Pierre Roussel, Marcel Launey, et al. *Inscriptiones de Délos.* 7 vols. Paris: 1926–2008.
IEph	Börker, Christoph, Helmut Engelmann, Dieter Knibbe, Reinhold Merkelbach, et al. *Die Inscriften von Ephesos.* 8 vols. in 10. Bonn: 1978–1984.
IG	Dittenberger, Wilhelm, Adolf Kirchhoff, Johannes Kirchner, Ulrich Koehler, et al. *Inscriptiones Graecae.* 11 vols. in 57. Berlin: 1873–.
IGUR	Moretti, Luigi. *Inscriptiones Graecae Urbis Romae.* 4 vols. Rom: 1968–1990.
Ilasos	Blümel, Wolfgang. *Die Inschriften von Iasos.* 2 vols. Bonn: 1985.
IJO	*Inscriptiones Judaicae Orientis.* 3 vols. Tübingen: Mohr Siebeck, 2004.
	I: D. Noy, A. Panayotov, and H. Bloedhorn. *Eastern Europe.*
	II: W. Ameling. *Kleinasien.*
	III: D. Noy, A. Panayotov, and H. Bloedhorn. *Syria and Cyprus.*
IK 57	Horsley, G. H. R. and S. Mitchell. *The Inscriptions of Central Pisidia.* Bonn: Rudolf Habelt GMBH, 2000.
IKibyra	Corsten, T. *Die Inschriften von Kibyra.* Bonn: Rudolf Habelt GMBH, 2002.

ILS	Dessau, Hermann. *Inscriptiones Latinae Selectae*. 3 vols. in 5. Berlin: 1982–1916.
ILydiaHM	Herrmann, Peter and Hasan Malay. *New Documents from Lydia*. Vienna: Verlag der Österreichischen Akademie der Wissenschaften, 2007.
Iscr. di Cos	Segre, Mario, ed. *Iscrizioni di Cos*. Rome: "L'Erma" di Bretschneider, 1995, 2007.
ISmyrna	Petzl, Georg. *Die Inschriften von Smyrna*. 2 vols. in 3. Bonn: 1982–1990.
IStratonikeia	Sahin, Mehmet C. *Die Inschriften von Stratonikeia*. 3 vols. in 4. Bonn: 1981–2010.
IvP III	Habicht, Christian. *Die Inschriften von Pergamon 3: Die Inschriften des Asklepieion*. Berlin: 1969.
LGS	*Leges Graecorum Sacrae*. 2 vols. Leipzig: 1896, 1906. I: J. von Prott: *Fasti Sacri*. II: L. Ziehen: *Leges Graeciae et Insularum*.
Livadie	Ridder, A. de and A. Choisy. "Devis de Livadie." *BCH* 20 (1896): 318–335.
LSAM	Sokowlowski, Franciszek. *Lois sacrées de l'Asie Mineure*. Paris: 1955.
LSCG	Sokowlowski, F. *Lois sacrées des cités grecques*. Paris: 1969.
LSS	Sokowlowski, F. *Lois sacrées des cités grecques: supplement*. Paris: 1962.
NewDocLyd	Herrmann, P. and H. Malay. *New Documents from Lydia: With 103 Figures and a Map*. Vienna: Österreichischen Akademie der Wissenschaften, 2007.
OGIS	Dittenberger, W. *Orientis Graeci Inscriptiones Selectae*. 2 vols. Leipzig: 1903–1905.
PECS	Stillwell, Richard, ed. *Princeton Encyclopedia of Classical Sites*. Princeton: Princeton University Press, 1976.
PG	Migne, J.P. et al., ed. *Patrologia Graeca*. 161 vols. in 166. Paris: 1857–1866.
PL	Migne, J.P. et. al., ed. *Patrologia Latina*, 221 vols. Paris: 1844–1865.
P. Gen.	Nicole, J. *Les papyrus de Genève*. Vol. 1, 3 fascicles. Genève: 1896, 1900, 1906.
P. Oxy.	Grenfell, Bernard P., Arthur S. Hunt, et al. *The Oxyrhynchus Papyri*. 80 vols. London: 1898–.
SEG	*Supplementum epigraphicum graecum* (vols. 1–25, Leiden; vols. 26–27, Alphen aaa den Rijn; vols. 28–51, Amsterdam; vols. 52–, Leiden & Boston: 1923–).
Syll.[3]	Dittenberger, Wilhelm. *Sylloge Inscriptionum Graecarum*. 4 vols. Leipzig: 1915–1920.
TAM	Kalinka, Ernst, Rudolf Heberdey, Friedrich K. Dörner, Peter Herrmann, and George Petzl. *Tituli Asiae Minoris*. 5 vols. in 9. Vienna: 1901–.

1 Experiencing Power and Peril in Corinth

1.1 Introduction

In 1 Corinthians 3:16–17, Paul writes: "Do you not know (Οὐκ οἴδατε) that you are the temple of God and that the Spirit of God dwells among you? If anyone destroys the temple of God, God will destroy that person. For the temple of God is holy, and you are that temple." This statement is striking for two reasons, reasons that remain obscure in secondary literature that discuss this concept of the Corinthians as the temple of God. First, Paul's formulation of the question with the interrogative particle, οὐκ, expects a positive answer. The expectation of an affirmative response is actually unexpected: ancient texts, both literary and epigraphical, rarely map the concept of sacred space upon a group of religious adherents, so why should Paul expect the Corinthians to respond affirmatively to his question? Second, Paul's assumption that God's temple can be corrupted, even destroyed (φθείρω), highlights the danger that lies in proximity to the temple. This project probes the significance of these two reasons by analyzing Paul's various statements about the Corinthian assembly in his first letter to the Corinthians.

What distinguished the Corinthian assembly as God's temple? In his seminal book, *The Sacred and the Profane*, Mircea Eliade observed that "[e]very sacred space implies a hierophany, an irruption of the sacred that results in detaching a territory from the surrounding cosmic milieu and making it qualitatively different."[1] That is, a divine power is what set something apart as sacred. In contrast, Jonathan Z. Smith saw the contingent nature of sacredness, the idea that human beings themselves can sacralize certain spaces or places.[2] A helpful terminology to describe the human activity of sacralization is what Jorunn Økland refers to as "ritually constructed space." The ritually constructed space described in 1 Corinthians 5, 10, 11, and 14 sets these sections apart from a regular household space.[3] This idea can be traced to influential theorists of religion, such as Catherine Bell and Jonathan Z. Smith, who have described the process of ritual action within

---

[1] Mircea Eliade, *The Sacred and the Profane: The Nature of Religion*, trans. Willard R. Trask (New York: Harcourt, 1959), 26.
[2] Jonathan Z. Smith, *To Take Place: Toward Theory in Ritual* [Chicago: University of Chicago Press, 1987, 76–95.
[3] Jorunn Økland, *Women in Their Space: Paul and the Corinthian Discourse of Gender and Sanctuary Space* (London: T&T Clark, 2004), 143–149.

sacred space.⁴ When the Corinthians gather together, there is a "partitioning and enclosing" that takes place, marking this assembly as temple. Jeanne Halgren Kilde observes, "places are sacred because they are made so by human beings."⁵ It is not, however, simply human activity that distinguished the Corinthians as a type of sacred space.⁶ Moreover, it is unnecessary to create a false dichotomy between an Eliadian versus Smithian perspective. In 1 Corinthians, Paul describes a dynamic relationship between the Corinthians' ritual activity as well as divine power and presence in their midst that undergirds his belief that the Corinthian assembly is the temple of God.

In 1 Corinthians, Paul provides snapshots of the practices and beliefs of both Paul and the Corinthians. Within the Corpus Paulinum, only 1 Corinthians contains explicit references to their "gathering together" to engage in ritual, and that, only in chapters 5, 10, 11, and 14.⁷ 1 Cor 14 is an important and highly interesting section concerning Paul's instructions about glossolalia and prophecy, though it will be apparent that the concerns one finds in 5:1–13, 10:1–22, and 11:17–34 are distinctive from those of 14:1–40. The latter chapter remains largely instructional in form and content (i.e. how should Corinthians engage in glossolalia and prophecy in their assembly).⁸ The sections under inquiry from 1 Cor 5, 10, and 11, however, are quite different in that something more is at stake than the 'order' of worship (1 Cor 14:26–33a). One finds in these earlier chapters a fascinating set of themes concerning the power and peril that lies within close prox-

---

4 See Catherine Bell's discussion of Arnold van Gennep in *Ritual: Perspectives and Dimensions* (Oxford: Oxford University Press, 1997), 36–37.
5 Jeanne Halgren Kilde, *Sacred Space: An Introduction to Christian Architecture and Worship* (Oxford: Oxford University Press, 2008), 7.
6 Ronald L. Grimes, *Rite out of Place: Ritual, Media, and the Arts* (Oxford: Oxford University Press, 2006), 95.
7 συνάγω: 1 Cor 5:4 and συνέρχομαι: 1 Cor 11:17, 18, 20, 33, 34; 14:23, 26. 1 Corinthians 10 technically does not contain these terms, but it will be argued that this chapter contains within it many—if not all—of the important details that Paul describes in the other two chapters. There are other places that scholars usually mine to gain insight into the Corinthians' communal activities such as singing hymns, prophesying, and speaking in tongues (e.g. 1 Cor 12 and 14), but what I am after in this study is different, as the following chapters will show. The importance of "coming together" for the meal is noted by Andreas Lindemann, *Der Erste Korintherbrief* (Tübingen: Mohr Siebeck, 2000), 248 in his comments regarding συνέρχομαι in 1 Cor 11:17. Wolfgang Schrage names συνέρχομαι as the "*terminus technicus* für die gottesdienstliche Versammlung," and observes its use by Philo to describe the meetings of Therapeutae in *Contempl.* 66 and Essenes in *Hypoth.* 7.13 (*Der Erste Brief an die Korinther*, EKKNT 7/1–4 [Zurich: Benzinger, 1991–2001], 3:18 and 3:18n386).
8 1 Cor 14:20–25, however, will be of particular interest because of what Paul states there concerning the effect upon outsiders due to the order and disorder within the assembly.

imity to the community as the temple. As the *Forschungsbericht* shows, no full treatment has yet put these sections together so as to consider the nature of the Corinthian ἐκκλησία as the temple, with its concomitant practices, and surrounding language about death and destruction that exist within this ritually constructed space.

What is distinctive in these passages? In 1 Corinthians 5:1–13 and 11:17–34, there is the gathering of the ἐκκλησία and a ritual that is to take place within the assembly: in 1 Cor 5, the expulsion of the incestuous man,[9] and in 1 Cor 11, the taking of the δεῖπνον κυριακόν. Both sections presuppose the dangers that lurk nearby, and both use the language of death and destruction (e.g., 5:5 and 11:30).[10] In 1 Cor 10, there are warnings concerning participation in other rituals, such as in the table of demons. One also finds the demonstrable presence of power that is larger than the energy generated by any single individual—in other words, Paul assumes that something happens in the gathering of the Corinthian community beyond the simple pronuncence of words or an outward set of actions. Furthermore, it is striking that the activities condemned in 1 Cor 10:1–22—acts of sexual immorality and faulty participation in meals—are the very issues that are of main concern in 5:1–13 and 11:17–34. There are also references to various evil forces that lie in wait to destroy God's people: serpents and more curiously, "the destroyer" (10:9–10).[11] All three sections contain within

---

9 1 Corinthians 5 points to their taking of the meal together, specifically in 1 Cor 5:8 (ἑορτάζωμεν: "let us celebrate the feast") and more generally, with the language about yeast and unleavened bread in 5:6–8. See further discussion in chapter 2.

10 "Assembly" will be the favored translation of ἐκκλησία. The common translation, "church," is largely avoided, since this word primes the reader to think in modern terms, both in its sociological character and its structural circumscription within a physical building. For a recent study on the use of the term, ἐκκλησία, in antiquity, see Ralph J. Korner, *The Origin and Meaning of* Ekklēsia *in the Early Jesus Movement* (Leiden: Brill, 2017).

11 According to TLG, the term ὀλοθρευτής ("destroyer") is not found anywhere in Greek literature prior to this occurrence in Paul. Its cognate noun, ὄλεθρος ("destruction") is found in 1 Cor 5:5; 1 Thess 5:3; 2 Thess 1:9; 1 Tim 6:9 in the NT and in 1 Kgs 13:34; Jud 11:15; 2 Macc 6:12; 13:6; 3 Macc 6:30, 34; 4 Macc 10:15; Prov 1:26, 27; 21:7; Wisd 1:12, 14; 18:13; Sir 39:30; Pss. Sol. 8:1; Hos 9:6; Obad 13; Jer 28:55; 31:3, 8, 32; 32:31; Ezek 6:14; 14:16 in the LXX. The cognate verb, ὀλοθρεύω ("to destroy") occurs only in Heb 11:28 in the entire NT/LXX. The other two related terms are: ὀλεθρεύω ("to destroy"; Exod 12:23; 22:19; Num 4:18; Josh 3:10; 7:25; Jud 2:3; 8:15; 1 Macc 2:40; 3 Macc 6:21; Wisd 18:25; Pss. Sol. 4:12; 15:5; 17:24; Hag 2:22; Jer 2:30; 5:6; 22:7; 32:36) and ὀλεθρία ("destruction"; Esth 16:21; 3 Macc 4:2; 3 Macc 5:5).

In Jewish and Christian literature outside the canon: ὀλοθρεύω in Philo, *Leg.* 2.34; Sib. Or. 5.304; T. Levi 13:7; T. Jud. 6:5; 7:3; Hist. Rech. 8.2; ὀλεθρεύω in Liv. Pro. 4.7; ὀλεθρία in Josephus, *Ant.* 11.282 (ὀλέθριος in *War* 5.35); ὄλεθρος in 1 Clem. 57:4; Ign. *Eph.* 13.1; T. Reub. 4:6; Ezek. Trag. 241; 60x in Josephus; 41x in Philo; 13x in the Sibylline Oracles.

their respective arguments allusions to the exodus tradition that also inform Paul's concerns about the need to uphold communal purity.¹² Therefore, by putting these three sections in conversation, this project aims to investigate how Paul conceives of the Corinthian assembly and its boundaries, including the manifestation of power in its midst and peril that lies at its outskirts.

The most important and related concept to the foregoing discussion is Paul's pronouncement to the Corinthians that they are "the temple of God" (ὁ ναὸς τοῦ θεοῦ in various forms in 1 Cor 3:16–17; 6:19; and 2 Cor 6:16). This is a highly unusual way to describe a group of worshippers of a deity, and is one that Paul does not use ever again with respect to other early Christian communities that he founded or with whom he corresponds. This project aims to draw out this relationship between temple and power/peril that tends to be discussed separately in current scholarship on 1 Corinthians. The thesis of this study is that 1 Corinthians 5:1–13, 10:1–22, and 11:17–34 can be read as a cohesive and coherent set of passages that parallel temple discourse found throughout the ancient Mediterranean world, and that such discourse serves not just as symbolic metaphor but

---

There is also an interesting inscription from Corinth that contains language of "Satan" coming into the home and "destroying the people" (Σατανάς αὐτῶν εἰς τὸν οἶκον εἰσέλθοιτο καὶ ἐξολεθρεύσαιτο αὐτούς). See Benjamin Dean Meritt, ed., *Corinth 8.1. Greek Inscriptions: 1896–1927* (Cambridge: Harvard University Press, 1931), 92–93 (no. 136). The editor of this volume marks this inscription to be from the Byzantine period, though they also note that the "exact provenance [is] unknown."

Modern commentators remain puzzled by "the destroyer" figure and sometimes make the tentative connection to Satan in 1 Cor 5 or the similarly named figure of Exod 12:23 (LXX: ὁ ὀλοθρεύων / MT: המשחית). E. g., C.K. Barrett, *A Commentary on The First Epistle to the Corinthians*, 2ⁿᵈ ed. (London: Adam & Charles Black, 1971 [1968]), 226; Hans Conzelmann, *Der erste Brief an die Korinther*, KEK 5 (Göttingen: Vandenhoeck & Ruprecht, 1969), 206n36; Gordon D. Fee, *The First Epistle to the Corinthians*, NICNT (Grand Rapids: Eerdmans, 1987), 457n38; Joseph A. Fitzmyer, *First Corinthians: A New Translation with Introduction and Commentary*, AB 32 (New Haven: Yale University Press, 2008), 387; Schottroff, *Der erste Brief*, 182.

It is also noteworthy that patristic interpreters often conflate verses 9 and 10 together by taking the first half of verse 10 ('do not complain') with the second half of verse 9 ('destroyed by serpents'). The apparatus criticus of the NA²⁸ does not reveal any significant variants here, so this may be an intentional way to make sense of these two strange verses. See, for example: Origen, *Hom. Exod.* 7.3–4; *Hom. Num.* 21.1; Eusebius, *Comm. Ps.* 58:16; Jerome, *Epist.* 51. Furthermore, near verbatim quotations of 1 Cor 10:10 are found in Theodoret of Cyrus, *Interpretatio in epistulas Paulinas* (PG 82:304); Basil of Caesarea, *Asceticon magnum* 1.29; 2.133; *Regulae morales* 11.3; John Chrysostom, *Exp. Ps.* 141; *Hom. 1 Cor.* 23, so it may be safe to posit that the instability of the text is not the main cause of these conflations.

12 It almost appears as if Paul is narrating and interpreting Exodus in sequential order: 1 Cor 5 (Exod 12, Passover); 1 Cor 10 (Exod 16, manna and quail; Exod 17, water from the rock); and 1 Cor 11 (Exod 24, blood and covenant).

describes their present experiences.¹³ Thus, these sections of Paul's letter unpack in greater detail what Paul meant by his earlier statement that the Corinthian assembly is ὁ ναὸς τοῦ θεοῦ.

By reading the relevant sections of 1 Corinthians side by side and reflecting upon the language that Paul uses therein, it is clear that all three chapters are undergirded by the same assumptions about the Corinthian assembly. Table 1 at the end of this chapter shows a host of themes that occur only in 1 Cor 5:1–13, 10:1–22, an 11:17–34. As the table shows, there is a complex network of themes that bind these three sections together. The following chapters will show that these themes can be found in other temple discourse in antiquity. Also, placing these sections of Paul's letter in conversation will reveal important details about Paul's perspective of the assembly in Corinth. More specifically, it reveals the inner workings of the community-as-temple. While many studies have addressed some of the issues that Paul mentions in these paragraphs, none have drawn a comprehensive comparison across all three chapters. This project sets out with two initial questions concerning these three passages. First, what is the import of the language found in these texts? Second, where did such language come from? To restate these questions, the first question aims to understand and interpret the rhetorical force of Paul's language in 1 Corinthians 5, 10, and 11, and the second question pursues evidence from the broader ancient Mediterranean culture or from the logic of Paul's own experience that may be important in providing insight into Paul's perception of the gathered community.

1.2 History of Interpretation

The *Forschungsbericht* shows that there are very few works that have dealt comprehensively with all three passages in question. I begin by reviewing important works that tried to assess 1 Corinthians 5, 10, and 11, together. These studies do not address Corinthians as temple per se. But since they remain influential studies of these sections of Paul's letter, they merit discussion. This overview will be followed by the more relevant history of research concerning Corinthians and the temple.

---

13 By "temple discourse," I mean any discursive evidence concerning temples, other types of sanctuaries, deities housed within these spaces, sacred objects, and performed or prescribed rituals related to sacred spaces.

1.2.1 Reading 1 Corinthians 5, 10, and 11

The following works are fairly broad in their scope and more thematic rather than exegetical in their approach. In 1986, Jerome Neyrey published an essay in *Semeia* 35 that used a model from cultural anthropology to understand Paul's "body language" in 1 Corinthians.[14] He borrowed heavily from the anthropologist Mary Douglas and her understanding that human concern for "body" reflects broader social concerns.[15] Neyrey concluded that Paul's various strictures about body control should be understood as ciphers for proper social control/stability that the apostle wanted the Corinthians to uphold. Neyrey analyzed all three passages in question (1 Cor 5, 10, and 11)[16] and argued that disagreements over the proper control of bodily orifices had become a significant point of contention between Paul and his opponents.[17] Neyrey's study is an interesting interpretation of these texts, though it seems, at times, unnecessarily encumbered by the use of anthropological categories. In other words, it may not be necessary to import an entire foreign apparatus from another discipline in order to reach the same conclusions as Neyrey does in his essay. Nevertheless, his interaction with Mary Douglas marks a significant milestone in the history of interpretation of 1 Corinthians.

In *The Corinthian Body* (1995[18]), Dale Martin analyzed the ideological positions of "the body" taken by members of the Corinthian community. Similar to Neyrey's portrayal of the groups in Corinth, Martin asserted that a "fault line" split the wealthier Christians from their poorer counterparts.[19] Some scholars have criticized the strong class-based ideology underlying Martin's interpretation (i.e. as driven by Marxist tendencies),[20] but his inclusion of 1 Corinthians 5, 10,

---

[14] Jerome H. Neyrey, "Body Language in 1 Corinthians: The Use of Anthropological Models for Understanding Paul and His Opponents," *Semeia* 35 (1986): 129–170. An expanded version of this essay is found in his *Paul, in Other Words: A Cultural Reading of His Letters* (Louisville: Westminster John Knox Press, 1990), 102–146.

[15] See the chart Neyrey concerning strong/weak group and high/low grid in Neyrey, *Paul, in Other Words*, 133–134, adapted from Mary Douglas, *Natural Symbols: Explorations in cosmology*, 3rd ed. (New York: Routledge, 2003 [1970]), 57–71.

[16] Neyrey also includes interpretations of 6:12–20; 7:1–38; and 8:1–9:27 (including chapter 10 here as 1 Cor 8–10) in his essay.

[17] In his later work *Paul, in Other Words*, Neyrey also delved into the notion of boundaries. See Neyrey, *Paul, in Other Words*, 75–101.

[18] Dale B. Martin, *The Corinthian Body* (New Haven: Yale University Press, 1995).

[19] Martin, *Corinthian Body*, 69.

[20] See the various published critiques of Martin's *Corinthian Body*, many of which Martin had already anticipated in *Corinthian Body*, xiv–xv.

and 11 in his study makes Martin's work relevant for the present inquiry. He pointed out that other interpreters have erroneously treated issues of incest (1 Cor 5), prostitutes (6:12–20), meat eating (8–10), and impropriety toward the meal (11:17–34) as separate and unrelated questions. In contrast, Martin argues that all of these sections are "particular instances of what is essentially a single conflict regarding the boundaries of the body,"[21] and treats 1 Cor 5, 10, and 11 in chapters 6 and 7 of his book.[22] He uses the category of "pollution," bringing into the discussion medical literature (both ancient and modern) and medical anthropology in order to understand the etiologies of disease as they are represented by the divided members of the Corinthian community. Martin's use of the term "pollution" is, however, sometimes confusing because it draws upon ideas that extend far beyond the medical field, as he himself is certainly aware.[23] His study of medical literature is vast and measured, but his ignorance of Mary Douglas's discussion of purity and pollution in the context of religions and ritual is unfortunate.[24]

These seminal works remain influential in the current study of 1 Corinthians 5:1–13, 10:1–22, and 11:17–34. Both Neyrey and Martin address the three chapters in question, but their aims are quite different from the ones proposed here. Their investigations only tangentially touch upon the questions posed at the outset of this project. Neyrey adopts anthropological categories of group cohesion in his essay and Martin works with medical anthropology to create a two-level scheme

---

[21] Martin, *Corinthian Body*, 163.
[22] In *Corinthian Body*, "The Body, Disease, and Pollution" and "Sex, Food, and the Pollution of the Corinthian Body," respectively.
[23] In contrast to Jerome Neyrey, who had already discussed the issue of pollution from an anthropological perspective, Martin refers only to one work by Mary Douglas (*Rules and Meanings* [Harmondsworth: Penguin Education, 1973]) and completely ignores any discussions vis-à-vis ritual purity/pollution that could figure significantly in Paul's language about the body in 1 Corinthians. Furthermore, Martin's discussion of "pollution" remains strictly in the realm of "disease" as it concerns the body (i.e. pollution = infection).
[24] Martin's class-based analysis also creates a rather facile dichotomy in the Greek and Roman perceptions about bodies: anxieties about purity/pollution remained on the side of the poor and the critique of such things as "superstition" (*deisidaimonia*) was the posture of the upper-class. This easy categorization is possible because Martin leaves behind discourse about body, disease, and pollution found in the context of religion. Contra Martin (e.g. *Corinthian Body*, 160–162), plenty of "educated" figures of antiquity seemed concerned enough about purity and sacred boundaries, particularly in the context of ritual or urban religion, and these figures do not hold to an "etiology of balance" that Martin seems to believe reflects the attitude of those occupying the higher levels of society. See, e.g. Cicero, *Div.* 1.121; *Har. resp.* 9; *Leg.* 2.19–24; *Nat. d.* 2.28; Vergil, *Aen.* 6.258–9; *Ecl.* 4.11–14; Gaius (jurist), *Inst.* 2.1–10; Horace, *Carm.* 2.13.1; Livy, *Ab urbe cond.* 1.45; 3.18.10; Varro, *De lingua latina* 6.30.

reflecting ideologies of body. Moreover, the texts adduced in their studies include much more than an intentional focus on 5:1–13, 10:1–22, and 11:17–34. Neyrey is interested in "body language," so these and other texts are analyzed to discover what they have to say about the control of bodily orifices, and Martin is interested in class-based ideologies about "body," so he includes a variety of other texts in his discussion.

Neither study differentiates between texts that talk about body(s) in the abstract and texts that describe the Corinthian assembly gathering together to engage in a particular activity (which makes 1 Cor 5:1–13; 10:1–22; and 11:17–34 distinctive; see chapter 2). Above all, the concept of assembly as temple has no bearing in their accounts. In contrast to Neyrey and Martin, this study establishes that the various issues concerning bodily consumptions, boundaries, and pollution in these passages of Paul's letter can be interpreted in the context of temple discourse, bringing greater clarity and cohesion to these texts.

1.2.2 The Corinthians as Temple of God

Within scholarship concerning temple language in 1 Corinthians, interpreters often focus on one of two ways of understanding this imagery, discussed either as separate issues or as mutually informed ideas: spiritualization and substitution. The interpretative lens of spiritualization became influential in 1932 with Hans Wenschkewitz's *Die Spiritualisierung der Kultusbegriffe*.[25] He argued that Paul was not thinking in a concrete sense of the Jerusalem temple or its related cult, but was performing what C. F. D. Moule later referred to as "sublimating [the temple] ... into purely spiritual senses."[26] The next generation of scholars in the 1960s and 70s took this one step further, by looking at Qumran literature and the New Testament more broadly.[27] There are also other studies that reflect upon the utility of the term "spiritualization," though for all intents and purpos-

---

[25] Hans Wenschkewitz, *Die Spiritualisierung der Kultusbegriffe: Tempel, Priester und Opfer im Neuen Testament* (Leipzig: E. Pfeiffer, 1932). See also C. F. D. Moule, "Sanctuary and Sacrifice in the Church of the New Testament," *JTS* 1 (1950): 29–41; J. C. Coppens, "The Spiritual Temple in the Pauline Letters and Its Background," in *Studia Evangelica VI: Papers Presented to the Fourth International Congress on New Testament Studies Held at Oxford*, ed. E. A. Livingstone (Berlin: Akademie-Verlag, 1973), 53–66.
[26] Moule, "Sanctuary and Sacrifice," 36.
[27] E.g., Bertil Gärtner, *The Temple and the Community in Qumran and the New Testament*, SNTSMS 1 (Cambridge: Cambridge University Press, 1965); R. J. McKelvey, *The New Temple: The Church in the New Testament* (Oxford: Oxford University Press, 1969). See chapter 4 for discussion of texts at Qumran.

es, the overall agenda remains quite similar to that set by Wenschkewitz decades prior.²⁸ This spiritualization concept then becomes further actualized in the belief that more than just ignoring the centrality of the Jerusalem temple,²⁹ Paul is purposefully turning his back towards it. For example, G. K. Beale (2004) saw Malachi 3–4 as *the* background text for Paul in 1 Corinthians 3:10–17 that "points to the church being the actual beginning fulfillment of the end-time temple ... the inaugurated fulfillment of the expected latter-day temple."³⁰

Various scholars have also expanded the scope of study beyond Paul and the Corinthians. Devorah Dimant (1986) accepted the spiritualization of the temple concept at Qumran, though she denied the view that the language of the Scrolls functioned to substitute the temple at Jerusalem.³¹ More recently, George Brooke (1999) and Lawrence Schiffman (1999 and 2016) continued to work within the framework of spiritualization and substitution in their study of the Dead Sea Scrolls.³²

To turn back to Paul and early Christianity, Christfried Böttrich (1999) pushed back against the spiritualization and substitution idea.³³ In the concluding

---

28 For example, Georg Klinzing preferred the term "Umdeutung" and devoted a section of chapter six of his book on the term "spiritualization." In Georg Klinzing, *Umdeutung des Kultus in der Qumrangemeinde und im Neuen Testament* (Göttingen: Vandenhoeck & Ruprecht, 1971), 143–147. See also Elisabeth Schüssler Fiorenza, "Cultic Language in Qumran and in the NT," *CBQ* 38.2 (1976): 159–177, and esp. 161 where she opts for the term "transference" over "spiritualization."
29 As recently as 2006, some continued to argue for ignorance, with the following comments concerning 1 Cor 3:16–17: "The Corinthians need not be concerned about the Jerusalem Temple or pilgrimage or whatever is bound up with Israelite Temple, since what that temple offers can be experienced in their gathering." In Bruce J. Malina and John J. Pilch, *Social Science Commentary on the Letters of Paul* (Minneapolis: Fortress Press, 2006), 75.
30 G. K. Beale, *The Temple and the Church's Mission: A Biblical Theology of the Dwelling Place of God* (Downers Grove, IL: InterVarsity Press, 2004), 253.
31 Devorah Dimant, "4QFlorilegium and the Idea of the Community as Temple," in in *Hellenica et Judaica: Hommage à Valentin Nikiprowetzky*, ed. A. Caquot, et al. (Leuven: Peeters, 1986), 165–189, esp. 187. See also Elisabeth Schüssler Fiorenza, "Cultic Language in Qumran and in the NT," *CBQ* 38.2 (1976): 159–177.
32 George J. Brooke, "Miqdash Adam, Eden and the Qumran Community," in *Gemeinde ohne Tempel = Community Without Temple: zur Substituierung und Transformation des Jerusalemer Tempels und seines Kults im Alten Testament, antiken Judentum und frühen Christentum*, ed. B. Ego, A. Lange, and P. Pilhofer (Tübingen: Mohr Siebeck, 1999), 285–301; Lawrence H. Schiffman, "Community Without Temple: The Qumran Community's Withdrawal from the Jerusalem Temple," in *Gemeinde ohne Tempel*, 267–284; idem, "Qumran Temple? The Literary Evidence," *JAJ* 7.1 (2016): 71–85.
33 Christfried Böttrich, "'Ihr seid der Tempel Gottes'. Tempelmetaphorik und Gemeinde bei Paulus," in *Gemeinde ohne Tempel: Zur Substituierung und Transformation des Jerusalemer Tempels*

section of his essay, he avers: "Deshalb läßt sich die Tempelmetaphorik auch nicht durch Begriffe wie Spiritualisierung oder Substituierung erfassen, die vor allem auf einen Kontrast zum Jerusalemer Heiligtum abzielen."[34] Albert Hogeterp (2006) also rejected the substitution of the contemporary Jewish cult as holding explanatory power for Paul's use of the temple metaphor in 1 Corinthians.[35] Both Jürgen Becker (2006) and Timothy Wardle (2010), however, remain convinced that the Jerusalem temple should be regarded as pivotal for interpreting early Christian ideas about the community as the temple.[36]

The efforts to incorporate Jewish material such as precursors from the Hebrew Bible and texts from Qumran demonstrate a move towards a more nuanced comparative inquiry, leading to scholarship that brought ancient comparanda and Paul into conversation. Michael Newton (1985) used the concept of purity to interrogate the temple concept at Qumran and Paul, while John Lanci (1997) brought to bear archaeology and material evidence upon Paul's letter.[37] This focus on archaeology is further refined in Annette Weissenrieder's essay (2012) which is informed by Vitruvius's *De architectura* and the physicality of a temple structure.[38] More recently, Kar Yong Lim (2010 and 2017) has convincingly argued

---

und seines Kults im Alten Testament, antiken Judentum und frühen Christentum, ed. B. Ego et al. (Tübingen: Mohr Siebeck, 1999), 411–425.

34 Böttrich, "'Ihr seid der Tempel Gottes,'" 422. See also Økland, *Women in Their Space*, 164–166.

35 Albert L. A. Hogeterp, *Paul and God's Temple: A Historical Interpretation of Cultic Imagery in the Corinthian Correspondence* (Leuven: Peeters, 2006), 6–8. He rightly cites E. P. Sanders, who has shown the error in simple dichotomies such as faith versus works; liberty versus law; a spiritual religion versus a materialistic one, and so forth. See his *Paul and Palestinian Judaism: A Comparison of Patterns of Religion* (Philadelphia: Fortress Press, 1977), 12–13.

36 Jürgen Becker, "Die Gemeinde als Tempel Gottes und die Tora," in *Das Gesetz im frühen Judentum und im Neuen Testament: Festschrift für Christoph Burchard zum 75. Geburtstag*, ed. Dieter Sänger and Matthias Konradt (Göttingen: Vandenhoeck & Ruprecht, 2006), 9–25 (on page 10, he succinctly states: "Der Bildspender ist der [noch nicht zerstörte] Jerusalemer Tempel, in dem nach jüdischer Auffassung Gott wohnt."); Timothy Wardle, *The Jerusalem Temple and Early Christian Identity* (Tübingen: Mohr Siebeck, 2010).

37 Michael Newton, *The Concept of Purity at Qumran and in the Letters of Paul* (Cambridge: Cambridge University Press, 1985); John R. Lanci, *A New Temple for Corinth: Rhetorical and Archaeological Approaches to Pauline Imagery* (New York: Peter Lang, 1997). The issue of purity and the Corinthian correspondence is developed further in Yulin Liu, *Temple Purity in 1–2 Corinthians* (Tübingen: Mohr Siebeck, 2013). See chapter 3 for my analysis and discussion of material evidence from Greek and Roman contexts.

38 Annette Weissenrieder, "'Do you not know that you are God's temple?' Towards a new perspective on Paul's temple image in 1 Corinthians 3:16," in *Contested Spaces: Houses and Temples in Roman Antiquity and the New Testament*, ed. David L. Balch and Annette Weissenrieder (Tübingen: Mohr Siebeck, 2012), 377–411.

that for an audience such as the Corinthians, their immediate context (i.e. the religious landscape of Corinth) must play a major role in how interpreters consider Paul's temple terminology in 1 Corinthians.[39] He asserts, "Hence, it is reasonable to assume that any mention of 'God's temple' would naturally conjure up the reality that was closest and most familiar to the gentile Christ-followers."[40]

The above studies have clarified Paul's use of temple language in several ways: navigating the Pauline material concerning temple; collecting relevant parallel texts from Jewish literature; and reflecting upon the value of archaeological data for comparative inquiry. These positives notwithstanding, there are areas that require further elaboration. First, a majority of studies about Paul's use of temple language are second-order reflections. They often focus on the substitution versus spiritualization dichotomy as the possible critique that Paul held towards the Jerusalem temple.[41] Whether implicitly or explicitly, the Jerusalem cult remains *the* background structure that informs their interpretations of Paul. These works also describe the socially unifying role of temple imagery, which is an overly simplified understanding of Paul's temple discourse. By this logic, all of Paul's language regarding temple is just one more rhetorical tool Paul employs to fight *stasis* à la the arguments laid out by Margaret Mitchell in her influential study of 1 Corinthians.[42]

The present study, however, addresses the more fundamental questions. What kinds of experiences were tied to temples? What were the rules that governed temples, and how were boundaries of such spaces maintained? What types of divine benefit or power did people encounter or expect to encounter when they entered within a temple? And how was such power mediated? Are there punishments, if any, for misbehavior within sacred spaces? These questions address the experiential dimension of the Corinthians as temple that tend to go unanswered in the scholarship surveyed above. Since Paul unequivocally states that the Corinthian assembly is "the temple of God," such experien-

---

39 Kar Yong Lim, "Paul's Use of Temple Imagery in the Corinthian Correspondence: The Creation of Christian Identity," in *Reading Paul in Context: Explorations in Identity Formation: Essays in Honour of William S. Campbell*, ed. Kathy Ehrensperger and J. Brian Tucker (London: T&T Clark, 2010), 189–205 and *Metaphors and Social Identity Formation in Paul's Letter to the Corinthians* (Eugene, OR: Pickwick Publications, 2017), 137–158.
40 Kar Yong Lim, *Metaphors*, 146.
41 The danger here is the potential for allowing supersessionism in through the backdoor; the present study militates against this type of reading vis-à-vis temple discourse in antiquity.
42 Margaret M. Mitchell, *Paul and the Rhetoric of Reconciliation: An Exegetical Investigation of the Language and Composition of 1 Corinthians* (Louisville: Westminster/John Knox Press, 1991). See chapter 2 for further discussion about her contribution to the passages in question.

tial dimensions of temples must be taken into account in our understanding of Paul's temple discourse.

Second, this project builds upon earlier scholarship, but also depart from them in their readings of certain texts in isolation. For instance, others have interpreted various combinations of 1 Corinthians 3:16–17, 5:7–8, 6:19, and 10:18, in order to consider Paul's temple language, but none have engaged in a full exegesis of the relevant texts within their broader literary context, and still less in relation to the other. I focus on the variety of themes that appear to be concentrated in these sections of Paul's letter that explore in greater detail the idea that the Corinthians are the temple of God. Additionally, if 1 Cor 3:16–17 is as important for Paul's view of the Corinthians as I argue, then other texts can be interpreted in light of this essential text.[43] In 1991, Brian S. Rosner published a brief essay that engaged in a reading of 1 Corinthians 5 vis-à-vis the Corinthians as the temple of God. As far as I can tell, this reading of Paul's letter in light of the concept of Corinthians as the temple of God had little to no impact on Pauline scholarship. This study expands the scope of Rosner's project to incorporate other relevant texts.[44]

Third, in terms of ancient comparanda, the overdependence on literary texts, to the minimization or exclusion of relevant material evidence, is a method that is eschewed in this study. Since the literary evidence tends to represent the beliefs and practices of the socio-political elite, the employment of material evidence can function to counterbalance the literary accounts concerning temples in antiquity. Thus, the following chapters include as much epigraphical and archaeological data as possible, many of which remain untranslated or difficult to access for non-specialists. Fourth and finally, current scholarship does not fully examine the peril that is inherently tied to temples. For example, scholars often discuss in abstract the rhetorical nature of Paul's language, his internal attitudes toward the Jerusalem temple, or connections to the archaeological data from Roman Corinth. But, the actual experience of visits to temples and the nature of such sacred spaces are rarely, if at all, discussed to any significant degree in the secondary literature. That is to say, visits to temples were never benign events, and that such is the reality is not fully appreciated within the secondary literature.

---

[43] Martin Vahrenhorst investigates the tradition-history of this temple motif in 1 Corinthians 3:16–17 in the excursus "Zur Herkunft des Tempelmotivs und der kultischen Begrifflichkeit bei Paulus," in *Kultische Sprache in den Paulusbriefen*, WUNT 230 (Tübingen: Mohr Siebeck, 2008), 216–219. See the relevant discussion in chapter 2.

[44] Brian S. Rosner, "Temple and Holiness in 1 Corinthians 5," *TynBul* 42.1 (1991): 137–145.

1.3 Avenues of Inquiry

A few lines of inquiry will aid this investigation of Paul's view of the Corinthian assembly in 1 Corinthians 5, 10, and 11. First, a database needs to be established with which to compare Paul's temple discourse in 1 Corinthians. This involves, at the outset, a contextualizing of 1 Corinthians 5, 10, and 11 in the overall form and function of the letter. Here, one can quickly observe themes such as power, Spirit, boundaries, rituals, and punishments that must be accounted for in any reading of 5:1–13, 10:1–22, and 11:17–34. Furthermore, the following assessment is required: whether or not similar language is found elsewhere within the Pauline corpus. Is the language found in 1 Corinthians a particularly distinct moment in Paul's writing? Or is how he conceives of the Christian assembly fairly consistent throughout his letters? The foregoing project will then involve research into Mediterranean culture, to find significant or helpful comparanda for what is recounted in 1 Corinthians. Here, Greek, Roman, and Jewish contexts of sacred spaces and gathered groups, with their concomitant rituals, will be important data for research.[45] The data includes investigations into associations and religious organizations,[46] as well as traditions from the Hebrew Bible (MT and LXX), Jewish material culture, midrashic material,[47] and Qumran literature.

In order to properly contextualize Paul's view, I survey ancient evidence spanning roughly six centuries (ca. 400 BCE–200 CE) across the Mediterranean basin. This includes engagement with epigraphical data to supplement the avail-

---

[45] In this survey, one could potentially add other religious architecture such as Egyptian, Mesopotamian, and Hittite temples. Chronology and geography place these structures further out from Paul's purview, but they may form yet another layer background information useful for interrogating Paul's ideas. For introduction to these structures, see Michael B. Hundley, *Gods in Dwellings: Temples and Divine Presence in the Ancient Near East* (Atlanta: Society of Biblical Literature, 2013).

[46] For a recent survey of literature on "associations," see Richard S. Ascough, "What Are They Now Saying about Christ Groups and Associations?" *CBR* 13.2 (2015): 207–244.

[47] The term "midrash" remains highly debated and could either be narrowly defined generically or broadly understood as a process/product of interpretation. Here, I am using the term more loosely in the latter sense and make no claim about a generic category. See James Kugel, "Introduction," in *Midrash and Literature*, ed. G. H. Hartman and S. Budick (New Haven: Yale University Press, 1986), 77–103, esp. 91; Gary G. Porton, "Midrash, Definitions of," in *Encyclopaedia of Midrash: Biblical Interpretation in Formative Judaism*, Volume I, ed. Jacob Neusner and Alan J. Avery-Peck (Leiden: Brill, 2005), 520–534; Carol Bakhos, "Recent Trends in the Study of Midrash and Rabbinic Narrative," *CBR* 7.2 (2009): 272–293. While some of the literature considered "Jewish midrash" will postdate 1 Corinthians, the use of this material will nevertheless help triangulate the religious experience and language concerning temples from the perspective of ancient Judaism.

able literary evidence. As alluded to earlier, the employment of material culture is important because it provides on-the-ground ideas within a specific locale over against the views of the socioeconomic elite that tends to be reflected in the literary evidence.[48] Inscriptions are, to be sure, as ideological as all other texts, often paid for by important patrons who likely had their own agenda in providing the funds for such a project. Nevertheless, the available material data can enhance one's interrogation of ideas about sacred spaces, pollution, purity, and punishments that are discussed by Paul in 1 Corinthians.

Second, having established an important baseline of data for my research, the present study is informed by various methods that cross disciplinary boundaries, enhancing the interpretation of the vast evidence collected: social sciences, religious phenomenology, and the historical/comparative approach. Within the social sciences, discussions from anthropology will be brought to bear on how the dynamic between communal integrity, power, and pollution functioned within ancient discourse of a gathered community. In other words, this methodological lens will make important contributions to understanding boundaries and systems that permitted and/or prohibited certain acts, and why transgressions of prescribed limits yielded disastrous results.[49]

---

[48] Given the nature of their primary subject of interest, scholars of the New Testament tend to gravitate towards *literary* texts as their prime source of background information, and my own conviction is that nothing should replace the Greek *New Testament* in *New Testament* studies as the most important primary source material. But, it would serve scholars well to consider the wealth of other non-literary texts that are still being collected, translated, and published by specialists and related institutions. John Scheid, a scholar of Roman religion, affirmed as much when he wrote, "the study of Roman religion cannot do without epigraphy any more than it can do without archaeology." In John Scheid, "Epigraphy and Roman Religion," trans. J Davies, in *Epigraphy and the Historical Sciences*, ed. John Davies and John Wilkes (Oxford: Published for the British Academy by Oxford University Press, 2012), 37.

See the helpful review of literature in Pieter van der Horst, "Jewish–Greek epigraphy in antiquity," in *The Jewish–Greek Tradition in Antiquity and the Byzantine Empire*, ed. James K. Aitken and James Carleton Paget (Cambridge: Cambridge University Press, 2014), 215–228. See also B. H. McLean, *An Introduction to Greek Epigraphy of the Hellenistic and Roman Periods from Alexander the Great down to the Reign of Constantine (323 B.C.–A.D. 337)* (Ann Arbor: University of Michigan Press, 2011); Alison E. Cooley, *The Cambridge Manual of Latin Epigraphy* (Cambridge: Cambridge University Press, 2012); Christer Bruun and Jonathan Edmonson, eds., *The Oxford Handbook of Roman Epigraphy* (Oxford: Oxford University Press, 2015). See the utility of inscriptions for New Testament studies in Paul Trebilco, "Epigraphy and the Study of Polis and Ekklēsia in the Greco-Roman World," in *The First Urban Churches 1: Methodological Foundations*, ed. James R. Harrison and L. L. Welborn (Atlanta: Society of Biblical Literature, 2015), 89–109.

[49] On this point, the notion of "pollution" in the context of religion/ritual will be a significant concept to be analyzed this project. An important sub-discipline within anthropological studies is ritual studies. As noted in the introduction, 1 Corinthians refers to a gathering and something

Along this line of inquiry, Mary Douglas (1921–2007) remains a supremely influential figure, whose early publication, *Purity and Danger* (1966), became the pioneering work on the question of impurity.[50] Her oeuvre has spawned many and diverse studies on this topic,[51] with both classical and religious studies following suit.[52] In the study of ritual impurity in the Hebrew Bible, Mary Douglas stands as the sole foundation upon which all succeeding scholarship

---

akin to a 'ritual' broadly defined. It will be important to consider the meaning of these rituals in 1 Corinthians and elsewhere when appropriate. Ritual study maintains a long history within scholarship, stretching from Émile Durkheim with his *Les Formes élémentaires de la vie religieuse: Le system totémique en Australie* (1912) to more recently, Catherine Bell's *Ritual Theory, Ritual Practice* (1992). On the application of ritual studies on one of the passages analyzed in the present study, see Peter-Ben Smit, "Ritual Failure, Ritual Negotiation, and Paul's Argument in 1 Corinthians 11:17–34," *JSPL* 3.2 (2013): 165–193.

The following paragraphs will describe the methods that inform this project, but it is important to reiterate the point that I am not following specific parameters of any of the methods I outline below. Perhaps the historical/comparative approach is the one most often used throughout this project, but the discussion and notes show that scholarship from anthropology and religious phenomenology have also influenced the way that I read and interpret the primary sources.

50 Douglas, *Purity and Danger* (1966). Other works that belong to this earlier phase of her conceptuality are: "Deciphering a Meal," *Daedalus* 101.1 (1972): 61–81; "Self-Evidence," *Proceedings of the Royal Anthropological Institute of Great Britain and Ireland [PRAIGBI]* (1972): 27–43; *Natural Symbols: Explorations in Cosmology* (Middlesex, UK: Penguin Books, 1973).

51 E.g., Anna S. Meigs, "A Papuan Perspective on Pollution," *Man: New Series* 13.2 (1978): 304–318; Cyrus C. M. Mody, "A Little Dirt Never Hurt Anyone: Knowledge-Making and Contamination in Materials Science," *Social Studies of Science* 31.1 (2001): 7–36; Astrid Blystad et al., "Seclusion, Protection and Avoidance: Exploring the metida Complex among the Datoga of Northern Tanzania," *Africa: Journal of the International African Institute* 77.3 (2007): 331–350; Byron Ellsworth Hamann, "Chronological Pollution: Potsherds, Mosques, and Broken Gods before and after the Conquest of Mexico," *Current Anthropology* 49.5 (2008): 803–836; Arden Rowell, "Allocating Pollution," *The University of Chicago Law Review* 79.3 (2012): 985–1049.

52 *Classical studies:* e.g., Robert Parker, *Miasma: Pollution and Purification in Early Greek Religion* (Oxford: Clarendon Press, 1983); Andreas Bentlin, "Purity and Pollution," in *A Companion to Greek Religion*, ed. Daniel Ogden (Malden, MA: Blackwell Publishing, 2007), 178–89; Mark Bradley, ed., *Rome, Pollution and Propriety: Dirt, Disease and Hygiene in the Eternal City from Antiquity to Modernity* (Cambridge: Cambridge University Press, 2012); Jack J. Lennon, *Pollution and Religion in Ancient Rome* (Cambridge: Cambridge University Press, 2014).

Religious studies: e.g., Jacob Neusner and Jacob Milgrom (see note below); Jonathan Klawans, "Notions of Gentile Impurity in Ancient Judaism," *AJSR* 20.2 (1995): 285–312; idem, "Idolatry, Incest, and Impurity: Moral Defilement in Ancient Judaism," *JSJ* 29.4 (1998): 391–415; Eyal Regev, "Moral Impurity and the Temple in Early Christianity in Light of Ancient Greek Practice and Qumranic Ideology," *HTR* 97.4 (2004): 383–411.

was built.⁵³ Her works have shown that purity rules are both *systemic* and *symbolic*. Anomalous entities cannot be isolated and analyzed apart from the system(s) of defilement to which they belong.⁵⁴ These systems can thus be understood symbolically: certain attitudes and strictures are evidence of an underlying symbolic system and one must discern the correspondence between the symbol and the signified to find coherence.⁵⁵ Despite her prominence in OT scholarship insofar as it is concerned with ritual purity and related concepts,⁵⁶ NT scholarship has only scratched the surface in its interaction with Mary Douglas's ideas.⁵⁷

---

53 This does not mean however that Douglas's entire critical apparatus was brought wholesale into the study of ancient Israelite culture without critique. Her unique role as the theoretical *fons* meant that her works came under close scrutiny and that some aspects of her theory were rejected.

54 Douglas, *Purity and Danger*, 36: "Dirt then, is never a unique, isolated event. Where there is dirt there is a system. Dirt is the by-product of a systematic ordering and classification of matter, in so far as ordering involves rejecting inappropriate elements."

55 For example, some scholars have insisted on viewing ancient Israelite system of impurity as arbitrary as its very core (e.g. Jonathan Z. Smith in *To Take Place: Toward Theory in Ritual*), but Mary Douglas has attempted to understand the rules symbolically, to find both meaning and coherence behind them. Douglas would be the first to acknowledge, however, that it would be erroneous to speak generally of purity rules or systems—there are no universally valid concepts of pollution, taboo, and purity. What is required here is a specific analysis of *Paul's* language vis-à-vis these concepts and attempt to understand what kind of system underlies his own proscriptions for the Corinthian assembly.

56 Two scholars of the Hebrew Bible, Jacob Neusner and Jacob Milgrom, stand as exemplary figures who have taken on Mary Douglas as an important interlocutor for their respective works. See, for example, Jacob Neusner, *The Idea of Purity in Ancient Judaism* (Leiden: E. J. Brill, 1973) and Jacob Milgrom, *Leviticus: A New Translation with Introduction and Commentary*, 3 vols. (New York: Doubleday, 1992–2001).

57 As far as I can tell, no works have considered the question of purity and pollution in 1 Corinthians 5, 10, and 11 with Mary Douglas's system as an important methodological lens. The only publication I could find that deals with Mary Douglas—and somewhat superficially at that—is Yulin Liu, *Temple Purity in 1–2 Corinthians* (Tübingen: Mohr Siebeck, 2013). However, Liu only cites *Purity and Danger* and fails to note that Douglas herself has significantly revised her position since 1966.

The only other major work in recent scholarship that interacts with Mary Douglas is Jerome H. Neyrey, though the questions that he seeks to answer and the theoretical framework he borrows from Douglas are completely different from the issue at hand. See his *Paul, in Other Words*, 102–46 and the review of his work above.

Other later works are: Mary Douglas, "The Forbidden Animals in Leviticus," *JSOT* 59 (1993): 3–23; "Atonement in Leviticus," *JSQ* 1.2 (1993–94): 109–30; "The Glorious Book of Numbers," *JSQ* 1.3 (1993–94): 193–216; *In the Wilderness: The Doctrine of Defilement in the Book of Numbers* (Sheffield: JSOT Press, 1993); *Leviticus as Literature* (Oxford: Oxford University Press, 1999).

If the anthropological lens signifies an etic approach to ancient discourse of power and danger, then religious phenomenology can serve as its helpful emic counterpart.[58] That is to say, rather than dismissing the strange language one finds in 1 Corinthians 5, 10, and 11 concerning death, destruction, and so forth, as remnants of an antiquated past, this mode of interpretation insists on taking Paul's words seriously at face value. This is not to suggest that we revive the older methods of religious phenomenology that received much criticism by scholars for its perceived lack of conceptual precision and methodological rigor.[59] As Jason Blum recently argued,[60] however, a more responsible phenomenology of religion can (1) interpret religious experience without necessarily implying the existence or absence of a transcendent reality;[61] (2) operate in con-

---

These later publications bear witness to some changes (or developments) that can be identified briefly thus: (1) the move away from the broadly comparative study of earlier publications; (2) the understanding that Israel's system of purity was distinctive in its own right; (3) the different ideas concerning the function of ritual impurity in Israelite society. See Jonathan Klawans, *Impurity and Sin in Ancient Judaism* (Oxford: Oxford University Press, 2000), 18–19.

[58] For a helpful review of the history of study on the phenomenology of religion, see the "Introduction" in Sumner B. Twiss and Walter H. Conser, Jr., eds. *Experience of the Sacred: Readings in the Phenomenology of Religion* (Hanover, NH: Brown University Press, 1992), 1–74; James K.A. Smith, "Liberating religion from theology: Marion and Heidegger on the possibility of a phenomenology of religion," *International Journal for Philosophy of Religion* 46.1 (1999): 17–33; James L. Cox, *A Guide to the Phenomenology of Religion: Key Figures, Formative Influences and Subsequent Debates* (London: T&T Clark, 2006).

[59] The most famous proponent of the phenomenology of religion in this mode could be considered Mircea Eliade who argued at length about the irreducible "essence" of religious phenomena. See his *The Sacred and the Profane: The Nature of Religion*, trans. by Williard R. Trask (Orlando, FL: Harcourt Brace & Company, 1959). See also Gerardus van der Leeuw, *Phänomenologie der Religion* (Tübingen: Mohr Siebeck, 1933). For recent critiques of this type of phenomenology of religion, see Robert Segal, "In Defense of Reductionism," *Journal of the American Academy of Religion* 51.1 (1983): 97–124; Ingvild Sælid Gilhus, "The Phenomenology of Religion and Theories of Interpretation," *Temenos* 20 (1984): 26–39 (27); Robert McCutcheon, *Manufacturing Religion: The Discourse on Sui Generis Religion and the Politics of Nostalgia* (Oxford: Oxford University Press, 1997).

[60] Jason N. Blum, "Retrieving Phenomenology of Religion as a Method for Religious Studies," *Journal of the American Academy of Religion* 80.4 (2012): 1025–1048.

[61] Smith, "Liberating religion from theology," 18–19: "The phenomenology of religion, as a *Religionswissenschaft* distinct from theology, 'brackets' committed participation in a faith community and analyzes the intentions or 'meanings' of a religious community or tradition. As such, it stands in contrast to theology, which investigates religious existence *from within* the commitments of the community; but is [sic] also stands in contrast to a traditional 'philosophy of religion' (if there is one) which generally becomes linked to a particular theism."

junction with the available historical evidence for this interpretative function;[62] and (3) reconsider the claim that the study of religion in this mode necessarily leads to reductionism.[63] In other words, one can be attentive to both the social/historical/ideological *and* the experiential dimensions of Paul's language in 1 Corinthians rather than positing an either/or dichotomy from the start.[64] This is an important contribution of the present study that remains largely ignored in modern scholarship concerning Paul's temple discourse.

Finally, the historical/comparative analysis will serve as a familiar and essential method that balances out the more theoretical approaches from the social sciences and the phenomenology of religion. On one hand, it is difficult to conclude at this point whether or not Paul was dependent on an antecedent understanding of gathered communities that came in close contact with entities of power and/or danger in relation to temples, but this study aims to delve deeper into this question. On the other hand, the situation might be more complex than historians or phenomenologists have been willing to consider: it may not be possible to draw a straight line from the practices and beliefs found in the ancient Mediterranean to those expounded by Paul in 1 Corinthians, but it may also be the case that Paul's ideas are not entirely distinctive either. Having established a vast database from the Pauline, Greek, Roman, and Jewish con-

---

It should also be made clear that some recent studies that are quick to ascribe any evidence of the divine or transcendent to naturalistic causes and to dismiss the religious significance of such language do so unfairly and uncritically. See, for example, the critique of Jonathan Z. Smith in Johnson, *Religious Experience*, passim.

62 In other words, *contra* the older phenomenologists of religion, "religion" need not be viewed strictly as autonomous and ahistorical. Furthermore, as Twiss and Conser have shown, many earlier practitioners of this method had "deeper (and somewhat hidden) agenda governed by normative aims of one sort or another" (*Experience of the Sacred*, 8). Also Gilhus, "Phenomenology of Religion," 32; Blum, "Retrieving Phenomenology of Religion," 1035–1036. Blum rightly states (1038):

Acknowledgement of 'politics' as a synthetic and contingent category does not suggest that individuals do not in fact have significant and valid beliefs or experiences which inform the ways in which they believe nations should be governed. In like manner, acknowledging religion as a constructed category does not invalidate (or validate) the beliefs or experiences that inform the varied religious practices, groups, and identities that have powerfully shaped human history and culture.

63 Blum, "Retrieving Phenomenology of Religion," 1025–1048. A classic proponent of "reductionism" in the study of religion is, of course, Jonathan Z. Smith. See his various works cited in the bibliography below.

64 Johnson, *Religious Experience*, 164. See also, Francisca Cho and Richard K. Squier, "'He Blinded Me With Science': Science Chauvinism in the Study of Religion," *Journal of the American Academy of Religion* 76.2 (2008): 420–448.

texts, a historical reading of each of these moments, as well as a careful comparison of their rhetoric, base assumptions, and prescribed boundaries, will help draw a better and more sensible distinction and connection between what is found in 1 Corinthians with other comparanda from the ancient Mediterranean.

1.4 Table 1: Temple Themes in 1 Corinthians 5:1–13, 10:1–22, and 11:17–34

Theme	1 Cor 5:1–13	1 Cor 10:1–22	1 Cor 11:17–34
The Assembly	Gathering together (5:4)	Paul addresses the community (10:1)	Gathering together (11:17, 18, 20, 33, 34)
Language of Power/Spirit	Paul's presence in spirit (5:3); the spirit with power of Lord Jesus (5:4)	Reference to God's presence by the pillar of cloud (10:1); the spiritual drink (10:4); God's power (10:22)	Inappropriate participation produces negative power (11:27)
Exodus Tradition	Exodus/Passover/Unleavened Bread (5:6–8)	Exodus (10:1–13)	Exodus/Passover/Unleavened Bread (11:17–24)
Ritual	Expulsion of the polluting individual from the community (5:2–5); the celebration of the feast (5:8)	Eating and imbibing of certain foods and drinks (10:19–21)	Consumption of the Lord's supper (11:17–34)
Evil forces	Satan (5:5); leaven of malice and evil (5:8)	Serpents (10:9); the destroyer (10:10); demons (10:20–21)	Demons (which 1 Cor 10:20–21 seems to make clearer)
*κρινω	Judgment of insiders and outsiders (5:3, 12–13)	Judgment of foods (10:14–22)	Judgment of foods (11:29), oneself (11:31)
Danger	Danger present in associating with polluted people	Danger present in partaking of certain foods and drinks	Danger present in taking the meal unworthily
Consequence #1	Save "the spirit" (5:5)	Falling (10:12)	Sickness (11:30)
Consequence #2	Destroy the flesh (5:5)	Destruction; hurting others (10:9–10)	Death (11:30)
Action	Cast out wicked (5:5, 7, 11, 13)	Avoid certain activities (10:7–10); right judgment (10:15)	Discernment (worthily) of the body (11:27, 29); avoid judgment (11:31–32)

continued

Theme	1 Cor 5:1–13	1 Cor 10:1–22	1 Cor 11:17–34
Christological	Name of the Lord Jesus (5:4a) and power of the Lord Jesus (5:4b); reference to paschal lamb (5:7b)	Sharing in the body/blood of Christ (10:16)	Body/blood of Lord, proclaiming his death (11:23–26); one could even be "liable" for his body/blood (11:27).

2 Constructing Temple and Identity in 1 Corinthians

2.1 Reading 1 Corinthians 5:1–13, 10:1–22, and 11:17–34 in Literary Context

This section is a close reading of 1 Corinthians 5:1–13, 10:1–22, and 11:17–34,[1] in order to establish a rationale for why these three passages should be read in conversation, and how doing so reveals further details about Paul's construction of Corinthian identity as the temple of God.[2] Prior to a thick exegetical analysis of the texts in question, however, these passages must be contextualized within Paul's first letter to the Corinthians and in view of the idea of the Corinthian assembly as temple that Paul broached in 1 Cor 3:16–17.

---

1 In the following analyses of 1 Cor 5:1–13, 10:1–22, and 11:17–34, it is necessary to read the three passages from various angles because the themes that are found therein are numerous and diverse. While it may seem repetitive, these multi-readings lift up the richness of these three sections and show why they deserve to be read in conversation. These details are not incidental to these sections of Paul's letter but are carefully crafted in such a way that parallel the concerns found in temples in other ancient Mediterranean contexts (see chapters 3 and 4). While 10:23–33 (+11:1) could potentially be added to this discussion, since Wayne Meeks's influential 1982 article ("'And Rose up to Play': Midrash and Paraenesis in 1 Corinthians 10:1–22," *JSNT* 16 [1982]: 64–78), scholars have generally been content to read verses 1–22 as a discrete unit. See, e.g., Hays, Lietzmann, Lindemann, Smit, and Weiss (or others even more narrowly vv. 1–13: e.g., Barrett, Bruce, Collins, Conzelmann, Fee, Garland, Héring, Murphy-O'Connor [2009], Robertson–Plummer, Schrage, and Thiselton). In my view, the prohibition against participating in two "temple" meals from 10:1–22 remains in 10:27–28. Regardless, the details found in 10:23–33 are less about boundaries and activities surrounding the "temple of God," and focuses more on marketplace foods.

2 Various scholars have discussed Paul's use of temple-imagery that begins in 1 Cor 3 in light of topics such as spiritualization of the temple, substitution of the Jerusalem cult, and rhetorical criticism, though in my view these discussions are second-order reflections on temple discourse in 1 Corinthians. There are other studies that have investigated Paul's use of temple imagery in his first letter to the Corinthians, though they differ from the present study in two important respects: (1) 1 Cor 5:1–13; 10:1–22; and 11:17–34 are never read together in conversation; and (2) the dimensions of religious experience are rarely discussed. See R. J. McKelvey, *The New Temple: The Church in the New Testament* (Oxford: Oxford University Press, 1969), 92–124; John R. Lanci, *A New Temple for Corinth: Rhetorical and Archaeological Approaches to Pauline Imagery* (New York: Peter Lang, 1997); Jorunn Økland, *Women in Their Place: Paul and the Corinthian Discourse of Gender and Sanctuary Space* (London: T&T Clark, 2004); Albert L.A. Hogeterp, *Paul and God's Temple: A Historical Interpretation of Cultic Imagery in the Corinthian Correspondence* (Leuven: Peeters, 2006).

The first four chapters of the letter depict various points of dispute within the Corinthian community (1:10–4:21). In 1 Cor 1:5–7, Paul regards the present situation of the Corinthian assembly as one that is full of spiritual gift and enrichment. Unfortunately, it also appears that through their positive experiences of the Spirit and of the power of God (1:18; 2:4–5, 12), the Corinthians have become overenthusiastic in their pursuit of such encounters and have even become divisive and arrogant in their supposed maturity.³ The problem is indeed dire, as Paul considers the following grotesque imagery: μεμέρισται ὁ Χριστός (1:13).⁴ In response to these issues, Paul sent Timothy ahead of him (4:17–18) and reminds the Corinthians of who they are, a people who had nothing to show in terms of worldly standards (1:26). They were deficient in their education (οὐ πολλοὶ σοφοὶ κατὰ σάρκα), lacked clout (οὐ πολλοὶ δυνατοί), and did not come from respectable lineage (οὐ πολλοὶ εὐγενεῖς).

Paul has been notified by Chloe's people of the split within the Corinthian community (1:11), wherein some have proclaimed allegiance to Paul, with others to Apollo, some to Cephas, and still yet others to Christ (1:12–13).⁵ They have for-

---

3 E.g., 1 Cor 3:1–4; 4:6–8; 6:1–8. Note the unique use of φυσιόω in 1 Corinthians among the undisputed Pauline letters, likely evidence that arrogance was particularly a problem in Corinth: 1 Cor 4:6, 18, 19; 5:2; 8:1; 13:4. The only other occurrence in the LXX/NT is Col 2:18. This word is not common prior to its use by Paul, and it is found in less than a dozen times in earlier Greek literature, though with a very different meaning (= "snorting; breathing out; blowing"). See Homer, *Il.* 4.227; 16.506; *Homeric Hymns To Hermes* (Hymn 4) 118; Sophocles, *Ant.* 1238; Aristotle, *Cat.* 9a.2; Apollonius of Rhodes, *Argon.* 2.87; 3.410, 496, 1303; Chrysippus, *Frag. mor.* 233.5.

Closer to the time of Paul's writing, φυσιόω occurs with similar semantic range only in T. Levi 14:7–8 and in other texts after Paul. E.g., Ign. *Magn.* 12.1; *Pol.* 4.3; *Smyrn.* 6.1; *Trall.* 4.1; 7.1; *Diogn.* 12.5; Clement of Rome, *Epistulae de virginitate* 1.11; Clement of Alexandria, *Paed.* 1.6; 3.1; *Strom.* 1.11; 2.11; 7.7, 16; Oppian, *Hal.* 1.570; 2.325, 545; Origen, *Cels.* 3.64; 5.8; Eusebius, *Praep. ev.* 3.17.

4 While the NA²⁸ interprets this sentence as a question, the earliest Greek manuscripts did not contain such punctuations. Ambrosiaster (fl. 366–384 CE), the author of the earliest complete Latin commentary on the thirteen Pauline letters, understood Paul's phrase in 1 Cor 1:13 as a statement rather than as a question. See Ambrosiaster, *Commentary*, CSEL 81/2.10–13; Gregory Nazianzus, *Or.* 6.3 For a brief introduction to Ambrosiaster, see David G. Hunter, "Fourth-Century Latin Writers: Hilary, Victorinus, Ambrosiaster, Ambrose," in *The Cambridge History of Early Christian Literature*, ed. Frances Young, Lewis Ayres, and Andrew Louth (Cambridge: Cambridge University Press, 2004), 302–317. John Chrysostom, however, interpreted 1 Cor 1:13 as Paul's use of the rhetorical question to demonstrate the absurdity of this imagery (*Hom. 1 Cor.* 3.5: γὰρ μὴ κατασκευάζῃ, ἀλλ' ἐρωτᾷ μόνον). Whether or not the sentence is read as a rhetorical question has no ultimate bearing on the fact that for Paul, the mere *image* of a divided Christ is cause for great alarm.

5 A classic study on opposing parties existing in the earliest period of the Christian movement is Ferdinand Christian Baur, "Die Christuspartei in der korinthischen Gemeinde, der Gegensatz des

gotten the message of the cross (1:18) that negates confidence in human wisdom or power (1:22–25). Furthermore, Paul intimates that his ministry among the Corinthians was marked by demonstration of the Spirit and of power (2:4, ἀποδείξει πνεύματος καὶ δυνάμεως[6]), so it is fairly certain that from the perspectives of both Paul and the Corinthians, the apostle's message involved more than just a proclamation of truth-claims.[7] If the terms "Spirit" and "power" are nearly synonymous for Paul,[8] then it is also relevant to note that power is an important concept throughout Paul's Corinthian correspondence. The following are the var-

---

paulinischen und petrinischen Christentums in der ältesten Kirche, der Apostel Petrus in Rom," *Tübinger Zeitschrift für Theologie* 4 (1831): 61–206. According to Baur, what one finds in 1 Cor 1:12 concerning the parties of Paul, Apollo, Cephas, and Christ was really an indicator of two major and opposing parties: of Paul (+ Apollos) and of Cephas (+ Christ). This scheme is augmented further by Baur's reading of the apparent conflict between the two apostles in Galatians 2, and Baur asserted that Christianity "took its stand as a new form of religious thought and life, *essentially different from Judaism*, and freed from all its national exclusiveness, is the point of next greatest importance in the primitive history of one Christianity" (*Paul: The Apostle of Jesus Christ*, trans. Eduard Zeller, 2nd ed. [London: Williams & Norgate, 1876], 3; emphasis added).

Unfortunately, Baur himself failed to recognize that this interpretation was borne out of broader contemporary discussions on the relationship between "Judaism" and "Christianity" which was fueled by an Orientalist perspective that scholars now understand as inherently racist. Despite the many errors in his reading of early Christian history, F. C. Baur's influence upon subsequent scholarship is undeniable. At the very least, there seems to be a measure of rivalry between Paul and Apollos in Corinth, and Baur rightly pushed back against readings that ignore this dynamic in 1 Corinthians. See Nils A. Dahl, "Paul and the Church at Corinth," in *Studies in Paul: Theology for the Early Christian Mission* (Minneapolis: Augsburg, 1977), 40–61. See also the recent volume interacting with Baur's ideas in Martin Bauspieß, Christof Landmesser, and David Lincicum, eds. *Ferdinand Christian Baur und die Geschichte des frühen Christentums* (Tübingen: Mohr Siebeck, 2014).

6 Ἀπόδειξις ('proof'): This word is a *hapax legomenon* in NT (LXX: 3 Macc 4:20; 4 Macc 3:19). Conzelmann (*1 Corinthians*, 55) notes that ἀπόδειξις is a technical term in Greek literature and Gordon D. Fee (*The First Epistle to the Corinthians*, NICNT [Grand Rapids: Eerdmans, 1987], 95) suggests that the word means something "more than simply 'manifestation.'"

7 See Origen, *Comm. Jo.* 1.10; *Princ.* 1.2, 62; 3.68; *Cels.* 6.2 (Φησὶ δ' ὁ θεῖος λόγος οὐκ αὐτάρκες εἶναι το λεγόμενον [κἂν καθ'αὑτὸ ἀληθές καὶ πιστικώτατον ᾖ], πρὸς τὸ καθικέσθαι ἀνθρωπίνης ψυχῆς, ἐὰν μὴ καὶ δύναμίς τις θεόθεν δοθῇ τῷ λέγοντι, καὶ χάρις ἐπανθήσῃ τοῖς λεγομένοις, "For the divine word says that preaching [although itself true and most trustworthy] is not sufficient to reach the human heart, unless a certain power be imparted to the speaker from God, and a grace appears upon his words"); Chrysostom, *Hom. 1 Cor.* 6.

8 Fee, *First Epistle to the Corinthians*, 95. This claim is expanded in the analysis of "power" in 1 Corinthians in 2.4 below. See also the section, "The Claims of the First Christians," in Luke Timothy Johnson, *The Writings of the New Testament: An Interpretation*, 3rd ed. (Minneapolis: Fortress Press, 2010), 85–94, esp. 91–93.

ious ways in which Paul foregrounds "power" in 1 Corinthians: (1) the message of the cross is viewed as "the power of God" (1:18); (2) the identification of Christ as "the power of God" (1:24); (3) the necessity of faith to rest only on "the power of God" (2:5); (4) the warning that Paul will assess "the power" of the arrogant ones in Corinth because God's kingdom consists of "power" (4:19–20); (5) the authorization of expulsion by "the power of the Lord Jesus" (5:4); (6) the resurrection through "power" (6:14); and (7) the manifestation of spiritual "powers" in the community (12:10, 28–29). Lexical use aside, we also find various places in 1 Corinthians that contact with power is presupposed in Paul's argument, including 5:1–13, 10:1–22, and 11:17–34 (see 2.4 below).

In 1 Cor 1:10–4:21, Paul brings to the Corinthians' attention various critiques about their faulty understanding of the assembly. They quarrel among one another along party lines (1:11–17; 3:1–9, 21–23), fail to acknowledge their status as recipients of God's gift rather than as earners of it (1:26–31; 2:12–14; 4:6–8), and remain ignorant about the nature of their assembly as God's building and temple (3:9, 16–17). The subsequent chapters (5:1–14:40) then address more specific and alarming cases that are symptoms of these fundamental maladies of the Corinthian community,[9] followed by a lengthy discourse on the reality of the resurrection (15:1–58),[10] and concluded by final epistolary remarks

---

[9] 5:1–13, on the incestuous figure // 6:1–11, on litigation // 6:12–20, on prostitutes // 7:1–40, on marriage // 8:1–11:1, on food and idols // 11:2–16, on women and men // 11:17–34, on the Lord's supper // 12:1–31, on spiritual gifts // 13:1–13, on love // 14:1–25, on tongues and prophecy // 14:26–40, on various gifts.

I am not attempting to revive the interpretation that Paul addresses factionalism only in chapters 1–4 while other issues are at stake for the apostle in chapters 5–16. For representatives of this older reading, see Conzelmann, *1 Corinthians*, 93: "The discussion of the σχίσματα, 'divisions,' has reached its conclusion. There follows a loosely connected string of topics arising from community life in Corinth."; Paul W. Schmiedel, *Die Briefe an die Thessalonicher und an die Korinther*, HKNT 2.1 (Tübingen: J. C. B. Mohr [Paul Siebeck], 1893²), 58: "Nur 1¹⁰–4²¹ ist gegen die Parteien oder vielmehr gegen die Parteiung gerichtet."; Weiss, *Korintherbrief*, 123: "Hiermit ist nun die Erörterung über das Parteiwesen endgültig abgeschlossen." See Mitchell for the argument that in fact 1 Corinthians as a whole is filled with rhetoric that attacks division in the community (*Paul and the Rhetoric of Reconciliation*, esp. 111–183).

[10] For classic interpretations of this chapter in the context of the entire letter, see Karl Barth, *Die Auferstehung der Toten. Eine akademisch Vorlesung über I Kor. 15* (München: Chr. Kaiser, 1924; English translation: *The Resurrection of the Dead*, trans. H. J. Stenning [London: Hodder and Stoughton, 1933]); Rudolf Bultmann, "Karl Barth, "Die Auferstehung der Toten,'" *Theologische Blatter* 5 (1926): 1–14 (English translation now as "Karl Barth, *The Resurrection of the Dead*," in *Faith and Understanding I*, trans. Louise Pettibone Smith [London: SCM Press, 1969], 66–94); Hendrikus W. Boers, "Apocalyptic Eschatology in I Corinthians 15: An Essay in Contemporary Interpretation," *Interpretation* 21.1 (1967): 50–65.

(16:1–24).¹¹ Of these cases, chapters 5, 10, and 11 contain important and explicit information about communal activities and the maintenance of boundaries that will be the subject of the following analysis.

2.2 Reading 1 Corinthians 5:1–13, 10:1–22, and 11:17–34 as Temple Discourse

As alluded to in chapter 1, these passages unpack in greater detail the concept of the assembly as the temple of God that is first noted in 1 Corinthians 3:16. Before analyzing these texts as temple discourse, however, it is necessary to locate 1 Cor 3:16 within its broader literary context. The paragraph reads thus:

> ⁵What then is Apollos? And what then is Paul? Servants through whom you came to believe, as the Lord gave to each. ⁶I planted, Apollos watered, but God caused the growth. ⁷So neither the one who plants nor the one who waters is anything, but God the one who gives growth. ⁸The one who plants and the one who waters have one purpose, and each will receive his own reward according to his own labor. ⁹For we are God's fellow workers, you are God's field, God's building. ¹⁰According to the grace of God given to me, as a wise master builder (σοφὸς ἀρχιτέκτων) I laid a foundation, and another builds upon it. But let each watch how he builds on it. ¹¹For no one can lay another foundation other than the one that has been laid, which is Jesus Christ. ¹²Now if any builds on the foundation with gold, silver, previous stones, wood, hay, straw (χρυσόν, ἄργυρον, λίθους τιμίους, ξύλα, χόρτον, καλάμην), ¹³the work (τὸ ἔργον) of each builder will become visible, for the day will make it clear, because it will be revealed in the fire. And the fire will test what sort of work (τὸ ἔργον) of each one. ¹⁴If any work (τὸ ἔργον) remains which was built up, the builder will receive a reward. ¹⁵If any work (τὸ ἔργον) is burned up, the builder will suffer loss, but he will be preserved, but as through fire. ¹⁶Do you not know that you are the temple of God and the Spirit of God dwells among you? (Οὐκ οἴδατε ὅτι ναὸς θεοῦ ἐστε καὶ τὸ πνεῦμα τοῦ θεοῦ οἰκεῖ ἐν ὑμῖν;) ¹⁷If any destroys the temple of God, God will destroy such a one. For the temple of God is holy, and you are that temple.

1 Corinthians 3:5–17 contains a host of images and intertextual links that are important for thinking about Paul's temple discourse throughout the letter.

The first obvious characteristic of this paragraph is the use of visual imagery such as the field, building, and temple. It may appear at first that Paul is quickly changing registers as he moves from one concept to another. Within ancient Is-

---

For a recent review of the possible issues that 1 Corinthians 15 might have addressed, see Fee, *First Epistle to the Corinthians*, 713–809; Anthony Thiselton, *The First Epistle to the Corinthians: A Commentary on the Greek Text*, NIGTC (Grand Rapids: Eerdmans, 2000), 1169–1314.
11 16:1–4, on the collection // 16:5–12, on Paul's (and Apollos's?) travel plans // 16:13–18, closing exhortations // 16:19–24, final greetings.

raelite and early Jewish traditions, however, there is a tight connection between a field (or a garden) and sacred space (see chapter 4 for further discussion). In other words, Paul's comments about planting, watering, and growing are not separate from his comments about the Corinthians as a building and the temple of God. Rather, they are all directly related. Thus, when Paul tells the Corinthians in general terms that they are God's field and God's building in 1 Cor 3:9, he is pointing towards the explicit identification of the Corinthians as God's temple in 3:16–17. The importance of this temple motif throughout this paragraph is made even clearer when Paul describes himself as the σοφὸς ἀρχιτέκτων in 1 Cor 3:10. Ἀρχιτέκτων is a term found in Exodus 35:31–33 that describes the builder of the tabernacle. This worker is filled with "divine spirit" (πνεῦμα θεῖον) that provides him with "wisdom" (σοφίας) in his work as a master builder (ἀρχιτεκτονεῖν). Such tasks involved working with materials such as "gold" (χρυσίον), "silver" (ἀργύριον), "stone" (λίθον), and "wood" (ξύλα), the very same materials specified by Paul in 1 Cor 3:12.[12] It is not without significance that Paul recalls traditions from Exodus in only three other places in his letter, namely, in 1 Corinthians 5:1–13, 10:1–22, and 11:17–34.

A second detail about this paragraph is the nature of the building material itself. Standard interpretations understand these materials to be referring to acts of Christian ministry, such as preaching and teaching, but the overall tenor of the paragraph militates against this reading.[13] In Paul and in other NT texts (e.g., Eph 2:19–22; 1 Pet 2:4–8), the temple of God never refers to human activities, but to the people of God. It does not make sense to suggest that the Corinthian assembly is the temple of God, but imply that somehow the materials that make up this temple are not the Corinthians but their actions. Instead, as Kirk argues, the building materials of 1 Cor 3:12 and τὸ ἔργον of 3:13–15 should be understood as "the 'product' of those activities in the form of *human persons*," which in this case would be the Corinthian Christians.[14] I find this to be a convincing argument, especially in light of Paul's immediate words thereafter in 3:16–17 that equate the Corinthians as God's property, or more specifically

---

[12] See Daniel Frayer-Griggs, "Neither Proof Text nor Proverb: The Instrumental Sense of διά and the Soteriological Function of Fire in 1 Corinthians 3.15," *NTS* 59 (2013): 521. In the LXX, cognates of ἀρχιτεκτον* occur only in: Ex 31:4; 35:32, 35; 37:21; 2 Macc 2:29; Sir 38:27; Isa 3:3.
[13] E.g., Dieter Zeller, *Der erste Brief an die Korinther*, KEK 5 (Göttingen: Vandenhoeck & Ruprecht, 2010), 163: "der jeweiligen *missionarischen* 'Werkes'" (emphasis added).
[14] Alexander N. Kirk, "Building with the Corinthians: Human Persons as the Building Materials of 1 Corinthians 3.12 and the 'Work' of 3.13–15," *NTS* 58.4 (2012): 549–570 (552; emphasis original).

God's temple.¹⁵ This tight connection between human beings and temple can best explain Paul's concerns about communal integrity and boundaries in 1 Cor 5:1–13, 10:1–22, and 11:17–34.

To turn now to Paul's question in 1 Cor 3:16, it is worth thinking about this sentence afresh. The interrogative particle, οὐκ, suggests the expectation of a positive answer. That is, Paul expected the Corinthians to reply, "Yes, we know we are the ναὸς θεοῦ."¹⁶ Additionally, the rhetorical force of this question serves as warning that one's ignorance of the Corinthian assembly as God's temple would not exempt a transgressor from punishment (1 Cor 3:17). The fact that ancient authors and other extant epigraphy rarely, if ever, map the concept of sacred space upon a group of religious adherents should give us pause.¹⁷ To put it another way, because the idea that an assembly of people *is* the temple of a deity is not a common one in the ancient Mediterranean world, it is all the more remarkable that Paul expected the Corinthians' response to his question to be an affirmative "yes." This signals that Paul's ministry in Corinth included instilling upon the Corinthians this important understanding of the assembly.¹⁸

---

15 In his study of the temple metaphor in Paul, Christfried Böttrich asserts that scholars have focused on the wrong question with regard to the building materials: "Für die christliche Gemeinde wird so in Anspruch genommen, daß sie Gottes Eigentum ist und zu seinem Machtbereich gehört. In ihrer Mitte ist Gott durch seinen Geist gegenwärtig. Deshalb eignet der Gemeinde in ihrer Gesamtheit die Qualität einer tabuisierten Größe. Wer sie zu vernichten versucht, zieht die Vernichtung durch Gott auf sich. Nicht graduelle Unterschiede des Erfolges von Mitarbeitern sind dabei im Blick, sondern der grundsätzliche Versuch, die Einheit der Gemeinde, die durch das gemeinsame Fundament begründet ist, auseinanderzureißen." In Christfried Böttrich, "'Ihr seid der Tempel Gottes'. Tempelmetaphorik und Gemeinde bei Paulus," in *Gemeinde ohne Tempel: Zur Substituierung und Transformation des Jerusalemer Tempels und seines Kults im Alten Testament, antiken Judentum und frühen Christentum*, ed. B. Ego et al. (Tübingen: Mohr Siebeck, 1999), 416–417.
16 BDF §440. See also Martin Vahrenhorst, *Kultische Sprache in den Paulusbriefen*, WUNT 230 (Tübingen: Mohr Siebeck, 2008), 145–146 (145: "das ihnen schon bekannt ist"). At the same time, however, Vahrenhorst argues that the temple discourse introduced in 3:16 is surprising because it does not follow from the previous arguments. See the prior discussion that shows why he is incorrect on this point.
17 The only exception is Qumran. See discussion in chapters 4 and 5. On the development of this temple concept, Vahrenhorst suggests, "Möglich wäre auch, dass die Qumrangemeinde und Paulus unabhängig voneinander auf dem Hintergrund biblischer Tempeltheologie in unterschiedlichen Situationen zu ähnlichen Denkmodellen gefunden haben" (*Kultische Sprache*, 149n60). Vahrenhorst also rightly recognizes that this temple motif is particularly suited to bridge the gap between those of Jewish heritage and those of non-Jewish backgrounds in the Corinthian community.
18 Christfried Böttrich observes: "Alle expliziten Belege der Tempelmetapher bei Paulus begegnen im Rahmen der Korintherkorrespondenz." In "'Ihr seid der Tempel Gottes,'" 413. Also John

How else can Paul expect the Corinthians' answer to his question in 1 Cor 3:16 to be in the affirmative? If contemporaneous evidence from the ancient Mediterranean is any indication, then the default answer to Paul's question would easily be one of confusion at best (i.e. "we do not understand"), or a negative one (i.e. "no, we are not the temple") at worst. This would render the entirety of 1 Cor 3:5–17 as highly ineffective rhetoric. While interpreters of Paul often consider the body of Christ as the central motif to describe the Corinthians, Paul does not provide any strong indication that this was an emphasized part of his teaching to the Corinthians.[19] He never once asks, Οὐκ οἴδατε ὅτι σῶμα Χριστοῦ ἐστε;: the closest he comes to this way of addressing the Corinthian assembly is found in 1 Cor 12:27, Ὑμεῖς δέ ἐστε σῶμα Χριστοῦ καὶ μέλη ἐκ μέρους.[20] This is to suggest that if body discourse is one topic in which scholars have engaged in fruitful discussions about Paul's view of the Corinthian assembly,[21] then

---

R. Levison, "The Spirit and the Temple in Paul's Letters to the Corinthians," in *Paul and His Theology*, ed. Stanley E. Porter (Leiden: Brill, 2006), 189–215. Vahrenhorst investigates the intriguing tradition-historical question of the origin of this temple motif in Paul (see the excursus, "Zur Herkunft des Tempelmotivs und der kultischen Begrifflichkeit bei Paulus," in *Kultische Sprache*, 216–219). He concludes that despite resonances with other early Christian tradition, the fact that Paul does readily apply the "ganze Repertoire kultischer Begrifflichkeit" in his earlier letters implies that this tradition was not firmly developed earlier in Antioch or Jerusalem (*Kultischer Sprache*, 219). I agree with Vahrenhorst's assessment and show how Paul develops and applies this temple motif to the community in Corinth.

19 The closest indicator may be 1 Cor 6:15 (οὐκ οἴδατε ὅτι τὰ σώματα ὑμῶν μέλη Χριστοῦ ἐστιν;) but even this is undergirded by Paul's description of the relationship between human bodies and the temple of God in 6:19 (ἢ οὐκ οἴδατε ὅτι τὸ σῶμα ὑμῶν ναὸς τοῦ ἐν ὑμῖν ἁγίου πνεύματός ἐστιν οὗ ἔχετε ἀπὸ θεοῦ, καὶ οὐκ ἐστὲ ἑαυτῶν;). This latter sentence is commonly accepted as the *individualization* of the *corporate* temple concept that Paul began in 1 Cor 3:16, but such bifurcation is unnecessary. In 1 Cor 5, for example, Paul's view of the Corinthian assembly blurs the line between the individual body/spirit with that of the corporate body/Spirit, and so also here in 1 Cor 6. See Levison, "The Spirit and the Temple," 202–207. For the argument that 1 Cor 6:19 must be read beyond the traditional individual versus communal divide, see Nijay K. Gupta, "Which 'Body' Is a Temple (1 Corinthians 6:19)? Paul beyond the Individual/Communal Divide," *CBQ* 72.3 (2010): 518–536. In any case, even if one grants that body discourse was an emphasized part of Paul's teaching, it does not make temple discourse any less important.

20 Notice how many translations opt to read δέ as "now," which implies a different connotation than asking affirmation of a previously accepted fact. See NRSV, NIV, NASB, ESV, ASV, NKJV; Barrett; Ciampa and Rosner; Fee; Fitzmyer; Robertson-Plummer.

21 E.g., Yung Suk Kim, *Christ Body in Corinth: The Politics of a Metaphor* (Minneapolis: Fortress Press, 2008); Michelle V. Lee, *Paul, the Stoics, and the Body of Christ* (Cambridge: Cambridge University Press, 2006); Dale B. Martin, *The Corinthian Body* (New Haven: Yale University Press, 1995); Margaret M. Mitchell, *Paul and the Rhetoric of Reconciliation: An Exegetical Investigation of the Language and Composition of 1 Corinthians* (Louisville: Westminster/John Knox Press,

my argument is that temple discourse can serve as another important context to interpret his letter. 1 Cor 3:16 should not be read as an isolated statement that has no bearing on Paul's comments elsewhere, but given its curious formulation and the implications of his emphasized teaching therein, it should be acknowledged as an essential text underlying Paul's subsequent exhortations to the Corinthians. Thus, the burden of this study is to show how 1 Corinthians 5:1–13, 10:1–22, and 11:17–34 explain further what it means for the Corinthians to be the temple of God.

To be sure, there are other places in the letter that reveal Paul's ideas concerning the Corinthian ἐκκλησία, but these three passages in particular serve as the best examples for close analysis. All three chapters address similar fundamental issues, even if the specific practices mentioned by Paul in each instance may differ. I have already hinted at the various themes found only in these three passages (see chart in chapter 1), many of which reflect concerns found in other temples in antiquity. Additionally, the participation in the Lord's meal described in these texts indicates the reality of the Corinthian assembly as a ritually constructed space (1 Cor 5:7–8, 11; 10:16–21; 11:17–34). In order to show how these passages construct Christian identity vis-à-vis the temple of God, the discussion will unfold first by a general description of important themes within Paul's temple discourse, second, by a close reading of each section in light of these themes, then finally, by a synthetic summary of the evidence.

2.3 The Exodus Tradition and Christological Connection

Apart from 1 Corinthians 3:16–17, specific allusions to Exodus occur only in 1 Corinthians 5:6–8, 10:1–22, and 11:25.[22] What is more, a close reading of these texts

---

1991). Typical of privileging "body of Christ" as the dominant theme in studying Paul's ecclesiology is David J. Downs, "Pauline Ecclesiology," *PRSt* 41.3 (2014): 243–255. He devotes three full pages to a subsection titled, "Ἐκκλησία as Σῶμα Χριστοῦ," with everything else (including temple imagery) falling under the subsection, "Other Ecclesiological Images," which runs a total of two short paragraphs.

22 The editors of NA[28] agree with this assessment, indicated by the margins in the Greek text with "Ex" in only the following three passages in 1 Corinthians: 1 Cor 5:6–7 (Exod 12:19, 21; 13:7); 1 Cor 10:1–13 (Exod 13:21; 14:22; 16:2, 4–35; 17:6; 32:6); and 1 Cor 11:27 (Exod 24:8). I make no claim here on the continuing and complex debate about what constitutes allusions and how intertextuality is applied to NT studies. I only demonstrate in the following analysis that Paul is clearly referencing the exodus tradition in the three passages. Whether he does so elsewhere in the letter is a possibility that I leave open. For an introduction to Paul's relationship to and appropriation of the Hebrew Bible, see Richard B. Hays, *Echoes of Scripture in the*

suggests that Paul read through Exodus sequentially: 1 Corinthians 5 (Exodus 12–13), 1 Cor 10 (Exod 13–14; 16–17; 32[23]), and 1 Cor 11 (Exod 24). For now, it is unclear whether or not this is intentional, though I will consider the implication of this phenomenon with regard to how Paul constructs the Corinthian assembly as the temple of God.

The story of the exodus asserted significant influence upon Israel, and subsequently upon early Christian identity. In the introduction to her commentary, Carol Meyers asserts:

> Although it is not the first book of the Bible, Exodus arguably is the most important ... First and foremost are memories of a past marked by persecution and hard-won, if not miraculous escape. As it is recounted in Exodus, this past is inextricably linked with a theophany on a national level at Sinai, the initiation of a binding covenant with the god whose name is revealed to Moses, and the establishment of community life and guidelines for sustaining it.[24]

The exodus theme is referenced in the Hebrew Bible approximately 120 times, a remarkable number that attests to "its centrality in the religion of Israel."[25] In the three sections of 1 Corinthians, Paul also recalls the exodus tradition, particularly as it has been ignored or misunderstood by the Corinthian assembly.[26] And in his use of Exodus, Paul foregrounds a connection to Christ that puts further emphasis on what is being said (1 Cor 5:7; 10:9, 16; 11:27). In each case, Paul warns the Corinthians about their improper practices, all interpreted through the con-

---

Letters of Paul (New Haven: Yale University Press, 1989); Christopher D. Stanley, *Paul and the Language of Scripture: Citation technique in the Pauline Epistles and contemporary literature*, SNTSMS 69 (Cambridge: Cambridge University Press, 1992).

23 The quotation of Exod 32:6 in 1 Cor 10:7 may be the sole exception to my suggestion that Paul is reading through and utilizing Exodus in sequential order in his letter.

24 Carol Meyers, *Exodus*, NCBC (Cambridge: Cambridge University Press, 2005), xv.

25 Nahum M. Sarna, "Exodus, Book of," *ABD* 2:689–700 (698). The exodus tradition continued to be a source of authority and contention among later writers such as Apion (1st CE), Artapanus (early 1st BCE), Chaeremon (1st CE), Hecataeus of Abdera (ca. 300 BCE), Lysimachus (1–2nd BCE), and Manetho (3rd BCE). For background, text, and translation of these writers, consult Carl R. Holladay, *Fragments from Hellenistic Jewish Authors*, 4 vols. (Chico, CA; Atlanta: Scholars Press, 1983–96). See also John J. Collins, "Reinventing Exodus: Exegesis and Legend in Hellenistic Egypt," in *For a Later Generation: The Transformation of Tradition in Israel, Early Judaism, and Early Christianity*, ed. R. A. Argall, B. Bow, and R. Werline (Harrisburg, PA: Trinity Press International, 2000), 52–62.

26 See the issue of ignorance that is repeated throughout 1 Corinthians and other Pauline letters by the use of the following two phrases: οὐκ οἴδατε: Rom 6:16; 11:2; 1 Cor 3:16; 5:6; 6:2, 3, 9, 15, 16, 19; 9:13, 24 and οὐ θέλω (or θέλομεν) δὲ ὑμᾶς ἀγνοεῖν: Rom 1:13; 11:25; 1 Cor 10:1; 12:1; 2 Cor 1:8; 1 Thess 4:13. Dieter Zeller understands these phrases as rhetorical tools used in diatribe (e.g. Epictetus, *Diatr.* 1.4.16). See Zeller, *Der erste Brief*, 165n457.

text of the exodus: including the πόρνος in the assembly and participating in the paschal lamb in 1 Cor 5; partaking of temple meals and Lord's meal in 1 Cor 10; and sharing in the Lord's supper in 1 Cor 11.

The tabernacle theme from Exodus that featured earlier in 1 Cor 3:16 is brought to bear on the idea of the Corinthians as the temple of God. The Exodus material does not occur anywhere else besides 1 Cor 5, 10, and 11, and there are good reasons to believe there is a special connection between the material from Exodus and temple discourse in 1 Corinthians. Exodus not only highlights the tabernacle, but contains related issues such as sacrifices/meal-eating, the presence of God, and divine punishments, which are all topics of concern within these sections of Paul's letter as well as in temples and other sacred spaces in antiquity.

2.3.1 Exodus 12–13 in 1 Corinthians 5:1–13

The account of the Passover[27] from Exodus 12–13 found new contexts for its observance and retelling throughout the Hebrew Bible and in other Jewish literature during the Hellenistic period.[28] For example, a late 5th century BCE letter to the Jewish community in Elephantine emphasizes the importance of keeping Passover,[29] and the 2nd century BCE book of Jubilees recounts the Passover event in

---

[27] Technically speaking, Exodus 12–13 contain descriptions of two celebrations that are thought to have been combined at a later time: פֶּסַח and מַצּוֹת. Scholars posit that these festivals must have been distinct and separate celebrations initially, but also accept their linkage in the scriptural accounts. See Baruch M. Bokser, "Unleavened Bread and Passover, Feasts of," *ABD* 6:755–765.

[28] See Lev 23:4–8.; Num 9:1–15.; 28:16–25; 33:3; Deut 16:1–8; Josh 5:10–15; 2 Kgs 23:21–3; 2 Chr 30; 35:1–19; Ezra 6:19–22; Ezek 45:21; Wis 18:5–25.

[29] See now "The Passover Letter" dated to 419 BCE, in Bezalel Porten and Ada Yardeni, *Textbook of Aramaic Documents from Ancient Egypt, Volume 1: Letters* (Jerusalem: Hebrew University, 1986), 53–54. The relevant portion of this document as reconstructed is as following:

Recto

4. ...שמשיא פסחא אב[דו ומן יום ל[ניסן חגא]
5. [זי פטיריא עבדו שבעת יומן פטירן אכלו כעת]דכין הוו ואזדהרו עבידה א[ל תעבדו]
6. [ביום וביום לניסן כל שכר]אל תשתו וכל מנדעם זי חמיר אל [תאכלו

Recto

4. ...ob]serve [the Passover] and from the 15th day until the 21st day of [Nisan observe the
5. Festival of Unleavened Bread. Seven days eat unleavened bread. Now,] be pure and take heed. [Do] n[ot do] work
6. [on the 15th day and on the 21st day of Nisan.] Do not drink [any fermented drink. And do] not [eat] anything of leaven.

greater detail than the broader story of the exodus itself (Jub 49:1–13 and 48:12–19, respectively).[30] Around the same time period, Ezekiel the tragedian's *Exagoge* (ca. 2nd BCE) also provides more information about the Passover than about the Israelites' departure out of Egypt.[31] It is clear that this meal-event recounted in the book of Exodus made an indelible impression in Jewish memory.

Closer to the time of Paul, both Philo and Josephus interpreted the Passover for their own particular aims.[32] For example, Philo spends the first book of his *Questions and Answers on Exodus* answering 23 questions rising from a reading of Exodus 12, in order to find both the literal and deeper meaning of this text. In question #4, Philo observes that the literal meaning (τὸ ῥητόν) of the Passover refers to the favorable acts of God on Israel's behalf, resulting in the changing of their physical dwelling-place, while the deeper meaning (τὸ πρὸς διάνοιαν) recalls the changing of their inward condition from that of disorder (στάσιν), ignorance (ἀνοίας), and intemperance (ἀκρασίας) to that of education (παιδεία), wisdom (σοφίαν), and patience (ὑπομονήν).[33] Paul echoes this type of physical-ethical transformation wrought by the Passover.

1 Corinthians 5:1–13 is the first specific problem after Paul's opening discourse concerning factions and wisdom (1:10–4:21). The situation is dire. The Corinthian community is, in Paul's view, ignoring a type of πορνεία that "does not even exist among the pagans" (5:1, ἥτις οὐδὲ ἐν τοῖς ἔθνεσιν).[34] Paul does

---

[30] See also the preserved statement of Aristobulus (ca. 2nd BCE) concerning the Passover, in Eusebius, *Hist. eccl.* 7.32.16–19. See Carl R. Holladay, *Fragments from Hellenistic Jewish Authors, Volume III: Aristobulus* (Atlanta: Scholars Press, 1995), 72–75; 117–119.

[31] Ezek. Trag. 150–192. For a thorough discussion about the dating and provenance of the *Exagoge*, see Howard Jacobson, *The* Exagoge *of Ezekiel* (Cambridge: Cambridge University Press, 1983), 5–17.

[32] See Philo, *Congr.* 106; *Heir* 192; 255; *Migr.* 25; *Sacr.* 63; *Spec.* 2.145–9; Josephus, *Ant.* 2.312–3; 3.248; 11.109–10; *J.W.* 2.10.

[33] Philo, *QE* 1.4 (Marcus, LCL) : "Not only do men make the Passover sacrifice when they change their places but so also and more properly do souls when they begin to give up the pursuits of youth and their terrible disorder and they change to a better and older state. And so our mind should change from ignorance and stupidity to education and wisdom (ἐξ ἀπαιδευσίας καὶ ἀνοίας εἰς παιδείαν καὶ σοφίαν), and from intemperance and dissoluteness to patience and moderation (ἐξ ἀκρασίας καὶ ἀκολασίας εἰς ὑπομονὴν καὶ σωφροσύνην), and from fear and cowardice to courage and confidence (ἐκ φόβου καὶ δειλίας εἰς ἀνδρείαν καὶ θάρσος), and from avarice and injustice to justice and equality (ἐκ πλεονεξίας καὶ ἀδικίας εἰς δικαιοσύνην καὶ ἰσότητα)."

[34] The clause lacks a finite verb, though some manuscripts contain ονομαζεται, which the editors of NA[28] leave in the apparatus criticus as a later addition. The earliest witness for this addition is the 7th century mss P[68] with other witnesses such as ℵ[2] L P Ψ 104 365 630 1241 1506 1739 1881 2464 𝔐 latt. There is also the possibility of scribal borrowing from Eph 5:3 (Πορνεία δὲ καὶ ἀκαθαρσία πᾶσα ἢ πλεονεξία μηδὲ ὀνομαζέσθω ἐν ὑμῖν, καθὼς πρέπει ἁγίοις).

not mean that such incidents did not occur in the broader Mediterranean world. Numerous anecdotes[35] and recorded legislations[36] demonstrably prove that both

---

To address this awkward grammar, translators have provided various glosses on what Paul must mean in 1 Cor 5:1 (emphasis added): NIV ("of a kind that even pagans *do not tolerate*"); CEB ("isn't even *heard of* among the Gentiles"); NRSV ("of a kind *that is not found* even among pagans"); NLT ("something that even pagans *don't do*"); NASB ("of such a kind as *does not exist* even among the Gentiles"); John Calvin, *Commentary on First Corinthians* 5:1–5 (*quae ne inter Gentes quidem nominatur*, "which is *not even named* among the Gentiles"); Collins, *First Corinthians*, 209 ("such as *does not exist* among the Gentiles"); Fee, *First Epistle to the Corinthians*, 198 ("of a kind that *does not occur* even among pagans"); Fitzmyer, *First Corinthians*, 228 ("of such a kind *found not* even among pagans"); Hans Lietzmann, *An Die Korinther I–II* (Tübingen: Verlag von J.C.B. Mohr, 1949), 22 ("wie sie nicht einmal bei den Heiden [*vorkommt*]"); Robertson–Plummer, *First Epistle*, 96 ("And of so monstrous a character as *does not exist* even among the heathen"). I argue that Paul is using a rhetorical device, and therefore, it is unnecessary for this clause to be laden with such specific terms such as "found," "tolerated," or "named."

35 Andocides, *On the Mysteries* 124–129; Plato, *Laws* 838a–39a; Sophocles, *Oed. tyr.*; Euripides, *Hippolytus*; Valerius Maximus, 5.9.1; Diodorus Siculus, *Bib. hist.* 20.33.5; Cicero, *Clu.* 14–15 (*Nubit genero socrus, nullis auspicibus, nullis auctoribus, funestis omnibus omnium. O mulieris scelus incredibile et praeter hanc unam in omni vita inauditum! o libidinem effrenatam et indomitam!*, "And so the mother-in-law marries the son in law, with none to bless, none to sanction the union, and amid nought but general foreboding. Oh! To think of the woman's sin, unbelievable, unheard of in all experience save for this single instance! To think of her wicked passion, unbridled, untamed!"); Seneca, *Phaed.* 165–73; Quintus Curtius Rufus, *Hist. Alex.* 8.2.19 (on Persians: *quippe apud eos parentibus stupro coire cum liberis fas est*, "For among those people it is right for parents to cohabit with their children"); Tatian, *Or. Graec.* (Νομίζουσι γοῦν Ἕλληνες φευκτὸν εἶναι τὸ συγγίνεσθαι μητρί· κάλλιστον δὲ τὸ τοιοῦτόν ἐστιν ἐπιτήδευμα παρὰ τοῖς Περσῶν μάγοις., "The Greeks consider intercourse with a mother as unlawful, but this practice is esteemed most becoming by the Persian Magi."); Catullus, 90; Martial, *Epigr.* 4.16; Iamblichus, *Vit. Pyth.* 31.210; Aelian, *Nat. an.* 3.47; Plutarch, *Demetr.* 38; Apuleius, *Metam.* 10.2–12; Artemidorus, *Onir.* 4.20; Tacitus, *Ann.* 6.49; Juvenal, *Sat.* 6.133–4.

For stories of other shameful incestuous relationships, see Dio Cassius, *Hist. rom.* 58.22; Tacitus, *Ann.* 6.19; Catullus, 74,, 88–9,. There are also stories from the Hebrew Bible and other Jewish and rabbinic texts that describe similar cases: Gen 35:22; 49:4; 1 Chr 5:1; 2 Sam 16:20–2; Ezek 22:10–11; Sir 23:23; 26:9; b. Sanh. 103b.

36 Gaius, *Inst.* 1.63: "Neither can I marry her who has before been my mother-in-law or stepmother, or daughter-in-law or stepdaughter. I say 'before'; for if the marriage that created the affinity still subsists, I cannot take her to wife for this other reason,—that neither can the same woman have two husbands, nor can the same man have two wives" (adapted from *The Institutes of Gaius and Rules of Ulpian*, ed. and tr. James Muirhead [Edinburgh: T&T Clark, 1880], 24–5). See also Gaius, *Inst.* 1.59, 61; *Pauli Sententiae* 2.26; D.23.2.14 (Paulus; D = *The Digest of Justinian*, ed. Th. Mommsen [Berlin: Weidmann, 1868]; repr. with English trans., ed. A. Watson [Philadelphia: University of Pennsylvania Press, 1985]); D.23.217.2 (Gaius); D.23.2.8 (Pomponius); D.23.2.56 (Ulpian); D.48.5.39 (Papinian); Tacitus, *Ann.* 12.7; *Mosaicarum et Romanarum Legum Collatio* VI.4 (295 CE); Cod. Theod. 3.12.1 (342 CE).

Greeks and Romans acknowledged the possibility of such shameful unions. Rather, Paul is utilizing hyperbole in order to illustrate the depth of depravity now infecting the Corinthian assembly.[37] The scandal noted in 1 Cor 5:1–2 is twofold: (1) the man presently engaging[38] in an incestuous relationship prohibited by both Jewish and Roman laws,[39] and (2) the members of the community arrogantly continuing to associate with said offender in plain sight. Paul chastises the Corinthians for their misplaced pride that condoned such behavior from a member of their community. He exclaims that they should be grieving over this shameful deed instead.[40]

---

[37] Paul's near contemporary, Seneca the Younger, used similar rhetoric in *Phaedra* 165–6 to describe the horror of an incestuous relationship between a son and his stepmother: *nefasque quod non ulla tellus Barbara commisit umquam*, "a crime which no barbaric land has ever committed."

[38] The present tense ἔχειν in 1 Cor 5:1 implies that the shameful relationship remains intact, and was not a one-time affair. Conzelmann, *1 Corinthians*, 96; Fee, *First Epistle to the Corinthians*, 200; Fitzmyer, *First Corinthians*, 233.

[39] For Jewish strictures, see Lev 18:7–8; 20:11; LXX Deut 23:1; 27:20; Amos 2:7b; 11Q19 66:12; Philo, *Spec.* 3.12–21 (in 3.13 Philo echoes the Greek/Roman sources in attributing the practice of marriage or intercourse with one's own mother to Persians); Josephus, *Ant.* 3.274; T. Reu. 1:6–10; 3:10, 14–15; Jub. 33:1–13; Ps.-Phoc. 179–80; b. Sanh. 54a; m. Sanh. 7.4; 9.1; m. Ker. 1:1; m. Yebam. 1.3; b. Yebam. 13a; t. Sanh. 10.1–2; y. Sanh. 7.6; Str-B, 3:347–50. For Roman law, see footnote #35.

[40] The tacit approval of the incestuous relationship by the Corinthians likely stemmed from a misunderstanding of their status as οἱ πνευματικοί (1 Cor 2:15–3:3; 4:17–21). Fee, *First Epistle to the Corinthians*, 201; Fitzmyer, *First Corinthians*, 235. See the personal use of πνευματικός in 1 Cor 2:15; 3:1; 14:37; Gal 6:1. See Paul's use of arrogance language (φυσιόω) in 1 Corinthians in footnote #3. The "grieving" or "mourning" (πενθέω) that Paul envisions in 1 Cor 5:2 could be the result of two different causes: (1) mourning in shame over the transgression present in their own community (scholars often cite the following parallels: 1 Esd 8:69; 9:2; 2 Esd 10:6; Dan 10:1; T. Reu. 1.10; Matt 5:4; 2 Cor 12:21; see Collins, *First Corinthians*, 210; Conzelmann, *1 Corinthians*, 96; Fee, *First Epistle to the Corinthians*, 202n31; Fitzmyer, *First Corinthians*, 235) or (2) mourning over the impending judgment/loss of the transgressor (Robertson–Plummer, *First Epistle*, 97). One of the earliest commentators of this passage, Tertullian of Carthage (ca. 160–225 CE), understood 1 Cor 5:2 in the latter sense, with the further caveat that the incestuous figure would have faced physical death. In *De Pudicitia* 14.16, Tertullian quotes 1 Cor 5:2 and comments simply: *Pro quo lugerent? Vtique pro mortuo*, "For whom would they mourn? Surely for a dead person." For further arguments against interpreting πενθέω as an internal psychological disposition, see Richard E. DeMaris, "Contrition and Correction or Elimination and Purification in 1 Corinthians 5?" in *The Social Sciences and Biblical Translation*, ed. Dietmar Neufeld (Atlanta: Society of Biblical Literature, 2008), 42–4. DeMaris provides an important parallel from antiquity concerning the ritual connection between mourning and expulsion in Tacitus, *Hist.* 4.45 (incorrectly identified as *Annales* on p. 44).

2.3 The Exodus Tradition and Christological Connection — 35

In 1 Cor 5:6–8, Paul recalls the exodus tradition with his rhetorical question, "Do you not know (οὐκ οἴδατε) that a little yeast leavens the whole dough?"⁴¹ He then commands the Corinthians to "clean out the old yeast" (5:7a, ἐκκαθάρατε τὴν παλαιὰν ζύμην), referring to the incestuous man of 5:1. These statements are subtle references to the Passover account from Exodus 12 that prohibits the presence and consumption of leaven by the Israelites.⁴² Coincidentally, this proscription is applied even to those beyond traditional social boundaries (Exod 12:19, "aliens": גֵּר/γειώρας), opening up the possibility for Paul's present application to a largely Gentile audience. According to Fee, the allusion to the removal of leaven then "prompts an allusion to the most important event of all, the sacrifice of the Paschal Lamb (Exod 12:6)."⁴³

This emphasis on Christ is an interpretative move that Paul also makes in 1 Cor 10 and 11. For the only time in his entire corpus, Paul notes that Christ is "our Passover lamb" (1 Cor 5:7, πάσχα ἡμῶν), and utilizes the cultic imagery of "sacrifice" for his death (θύω; see Exod 12:21; Deut 16:2).⁴⁴ Rather than a simple reference to *the* Passover lamb, Paul's use of ἡμῶν connects the experience of the Israelites closely to that of the Corinthians, a motif he will develop further in 1 Cor 10. This connection to Christ is important, because the issue concerns not just behavior (i.e. incest), but also what defaces their new identity provided through Christ. The Corinthians' status is one grounded in Christ's sacrifice and

---

41 See Exod 12:15, 19; 13:3, 7; Deut 16:3–4. For Paul's use of οὐκ οἴδατε in his letters, see footnote #26 above. The form of the question "do you not know" implies that the following details are something the Corinthians should have known.

42 Exod 12:19–20 (NRSV), "For seven days no leaven shall be found in your houses for whoever eats what is leavened shall be cut off from the congregation of Israel, whether an alien or a native of the land. You shall eat nothing leavened; in all your settlements you shall eat unleavened bread."

LXX generally agrees with the MT here, though it takes the punishment one step further in Exod 12:19 (also Exod 13:6–8): "For seven days no leaven shall be found in your houses. Everyone who eats what is leavened, that soul will be destroyed from the congregation of Israel, both among the aliens and the natives of the land (ἑπτὰ ἡμέρας ζύμη οὐχ εὑρεθήσεται ἐν ταῖς οἰκίαις ὑμῶν· πᾶς, ὃς ἂν φάγῃ ζυμωτόν, ἐξολεθρευθήσεται ἡ ψυχὴ ἐκείνη ἐκ συναγωγῆς Ισραηλ ἔν τε τοῖς γειώραις καὶ αὐτόχθοσιν τῆς γῆς)." See 2.5 below.

43 Fee, *First Epistle to the Corinthians*, 216.

44 In the NT, θύω + πάσχα: Mark 14:12; Luke 22:7; 1 Cor 5:7. Conzelmann (*1 Corinthians*, 99; also Fitzmyer, *First Corinthians*, 241) suggests that similar tradition can also be found in: John 1:29, 36; 19:36; 1 Pet 1:19; Rev 5:6, 9, 12; 12:11. There is a textual variant, "For the Passover lamb was sacrificed *for us*" (υπερ ημων), which has some attestation but is trumped by the better witnesses to the main reading.

thus, Paul emphasizes this reality in his exhortation to the Corinthians.⁴⁵ Additionally, the purposeful reversal of events from Exodus puts further emphasis on the priority of Christ for the life of the Corinthian assembly.⁴⁶

The moral implications of the Passover that Philo described in his *Questions and Answers on Exodus* Book 1 are paralleled by Paul in 1 Corinthians 5:1–13. Paul admonishes not only the incestuous deed of the individual offender but also the moral disposition of the assembly with regard to this shameful relationship.⁴⁷ He asserts that the Corinthians must be a "new dough" since they are now the "unleavened bread" (5:7b, ἵνα ἦτε νέον φύραμα, καθώς ἐστε ἄζυμοι).⁴⁸ This identification of the Corinthians as ἄζυμοι is noteworthy, since ἄζυμος in the Hebrew Bible is the object of Israelite consumption and never the Israelites themselves.⁴⁹ This attribution raises the ethical standards. It is not simply the presence of an external substance that affects the purity of the Corinthians; what each individual does affects the constitution of the whole.⁵⁰ Paul exhorts the Corinthians to celebrate the festival "not with the yeast of evil and wickedness" (5:8, μηδὲ ἐν ζύμῃ κακίας καὶ πονηρίας) but "with the unleavened bread of purity and truth" (ἐν ἀζύμοις εἰλικρινείας καὶ ἀληθείας).⁵¹ His use of the verb ἑορτάζω in

---

45 Joachim Jeremias suggests that the "casual way" that Paul writes γὰρ τὸ πάσχα ἡμῶν ἐτύθη Χριστός means "that this comparison was already familiar to the Corinthian church." There is no way to be certain of this, but Paul does assume a level of familiarity with the exodus tradition and Passover by the Corinthians in all three sections under investigation. *TDNT* 5:900.
46 In Exodus, the dwelling place is cleansed of all leaven *prior* to the sacrifice of the Passover lamb, but in 1 Corinthians 5, this procedure is reversed, as the sacrifice of Christ (the Passover lamb) is chronologically prior to the imperative to remove the leaven.
47 Many of the characteristics of the former life (pre-Passover) and of the renewed life (post-Passover) that Philo describes in his *Questions and Answers in Exodus* are the very things that Paul himself notes throughout 1 Corinthians. For example, as Margaret Mitchell has shown (*Paul and the Rhetoric of Reconciliation*, passim), στάσις in Corinth was of particular concern for Paul. Paul also argues at length about "wisdom" (σοφία) particularly in chapters 1–4 and points out the Corinthians' ignorance on important issues throughout the letter (see note above).
48 Interpreters try to highlight the indicative statement by translating καθώς ἐστε ἄζυμοι by using words such as "indeed" or "as really."
49 Gen 19:3; Exod 12:8, 15, 18, 20, 39; 34:18; Lev 10:12; 23:6; Num 9:11; 28:17; Deut 16:3; Judg 6:21; 2 Kgs 23:9; Ezek 45:21; Ezek. Trag. 171, 189; Philo, *Congr.* 162; *Contempl.* 81; Josephus, *Ant.* 3.249, 321.
50 Paul uses similar language in Gal 5:9. See Exod 12:34; 13:6–8.
51 Various English translations translate εἰλικρίνεια as "sincerity" (NIV, NRSV, NLT, NASB, ASV, NKJV, NET) though this obscures the concern for purity in Paul's exhortation. This interpretation may have been influenced by pairing the term with "truth" in 1 Cor 5:8, but this almost seems redundant. The translation ("sincerity") remains in the conceptual field of truth telling as opposed to falsehood, but εἰλικρίνεια can mean something more than this, as it is derived from the adjective, εἰλικρινής. BDAG, s.v. εἰλικρινής: "unmixed, then pure in moral sense" (εἰλικρί-

1 Cor 5:8 concludes Paul's appropriation of Exodus, which is linked to his earlier reference to Christ as the paschal lamb in 5:7.⁵²

The connection to the tabernacle may not be noticeable at first glance, since the Israelites are yet located in Egypt in Exod 12. Closer scrutiny, however, reveals important details that presage the tabernacle. The story of Passover includes graphic details of the gathered Israelites slaughtering an unblemished lamb, eating it with unleavened bread, and marking the doorposts and lintel of their homes with its blood. Dozeman concludes: "the blood on the doorpost invites comparison to the tabernacle altar."⁵³ The Israelites' homes can thus be understood as a type of protected, even sacred, space: such is possible by the apotropaic function of blood. Moses warns in Exod 12:22, "None of you shall go outside the door of your house until morning."⁵⁴ He then describes the process when YHWH God will come upon the Egyptians when "the destroyer" (Exod 12:23 MT: הַמַּשְׁחִית; LXX: τὸν ὀλεθρεύοντα) is prevented from entering the homes

---

νεια: "sincerity, purity of motive"); *TDNT*, s.v. εἰλικρινής, εἰλικρίνεια: "derives from εἴλη (ἀλέα, ἥλιος), meaning 'warmth or light of the sun,' and κρίνω, so that the full sense is 'tested by the light of the sun,' 'completely pure,' 'spotless. The derived subst. εἰλικρίνεια means 'purity.'"; LSJ, s.v. εἰλικρινής: "unmixedness, without alloy, pure" (εἰλικρίνεια: I. "unmixedness, purity"; II. "sincerity, uprightness").

Unfortunately, there are less than a handful of occurrences of εἰλικρίνεια prior to the first century CE, so it is difficult to establish a firm semantic range for this term: Philolaus (ca. 5ᵗʰ BCE), *Testimonia* A16b ("[Philolaus] calls the uppermost part of the surrounding, in which [he says] is the purity of the elements [τὴν εἰλικρίνειαν εἶναι τῶν στοιχείων], Olympus"); Aristotle, *De coloribus* 793a ("in their mixture with each other and in their purity" [τὴν πρὸς ἄλληλα μίξιν καὶ εἰλικρίνειαν αὐτῶν]); Chrysippus, *Fragmenta logica et physica* Fr. 1105 ("pureness of the air" [τὴν εἰλικρίνειαν τοῦ ἀέρος]).

See also, Plato (εἰλικρινής), *Phaed.* 66a; 81c; *Symp.* 211e; Wis 7:25 (εἰλικρινής); T. Benj. 6:5 (εἰλικρινής); Phil 1:10; Philo (εἰλικρινής), *Opif.* 31; *Leg.* 1.88; *Ebr.* 101, 189; *Her.* 98; *Congr.* 143; *Somn.* 2.74, 134; Acts John 29; Clement of Alexandria, *Strom.* 4.22; 6.7. Some early Christians also interpreted this use of εἰλικρίνεια with connections to purity: Justin, *Dial.* 14.2; Origen, *Comm. Matt.* 12.5; Athanasius, *Ep. fest.* 3; 6 (*azymis puritatis et veritatis*).

52 ἑορτάζω, NT: *hapax legomenon*. In the OT, it often refers to the Feast of Unleavened Bread, though also used in other ways: Exod 5:1; 12:14; 23:14; Lev 23:39, 41; Num 29:12; Deut 16:15; 1 Sam 30:16; Ps 41:5; 75:11; Nah 2:1; Zech 14:16, 18, 19; Isa 30:29. The significance of the reference to feasting is described below.

53 Thomas B. Dozeman, *Commentary on Exodus* (Grand Rapids: Eerdmans, 2009), 267.

54 Later Jewish interpreter understood the space itself to have provided protection. Mek. Exod. 12:21–24 (Pisha 11) on the phrase "and none of you shall go out": "This tells that the angel, once permission to harm is given him, does not discriminate between the righteous and the wicked." Translation from Jacob Z. Lauterbach, *Mekhilta De-Rabbi Ishmael: A Critical Edition, Based on the Manuscripts and Early Editions, with an English Translation, Introduction, and Notes*, 2 vols. (Philadelphia: The Jewish Publication Society, 2004), 57–62.

marked with blood. This reference to a mysterious agent of destruction is mentioned also by Paul in 1 Cor 10:10.⁵⁵ Just as the sacrifice of the paschal lamb in Exodus protected the Israelites from "the destroyer" within their homes, so too the sacrifice of "our paschal lamb" protects the Corinthians through their identity as the temple of God. Additionally references to the Corinthians' gathering, sacrifice, and participation in a feast are best understood in light of ritual activities connected to temples.

2.3.2 Exodus 13–17 in 1 Corinthians 10:1–22

In 1 Cor 10:1, Paul again underscores the Corinthians' neglect of the exodus tradition: "I do not want you to be unaware (οὐ θέλω γὰρ ὑμᾶς ἀγνοεῖν), brothers and sisters, that all our fathers were under the cloud and all passed through the sea." The cloud refers to God's presence that led the Israelites through the wilderness (Exod 13:21–22).⁵⁶ The introductory allusion to Exodus is followed by a catena of Israelite activities: passing through the sea (1 Cor 10:2; see Exod 14:19–22), consuming manna (1 Cor 10:3; see Exod 16:4–35), drinking water from the rock (1 Cor 10:4; see Exod 17:1–7), crafting the golden calf (1 Cor 10:7; see Exod 32:1–6), engaging in sexual immorality (1 Cor 10:8; see 5:1–13; Exod 32:25–29; Num 25:1–15),⁵⁷ and dying in the wilderness (1 Cor 10:5, 9, 10; see

---

55 See further discussion in 2.5.2.
56 Exod 40:34 recalls that "the cloud covered the tent of meeting ... [and] the glory of the Lord filled the tabernacle" (see also Exod 40:38; Num 9:15–17). Origen even likened the cloud to the Holy Spirit in *Hom. Exod.* 5: "What the Jews supposed to be a crossing of the sea, Paul calls baptism; what they supposed to be a cloud, Paul asserts is the Holy Spirit." Translation from Origen, *Homilies on Genesis and Exodus*, trans. Ronald E. Heine (Washington, D.C.: Catholic University of America Press, 1982), 276. See Origen, *Comm. Cant.* 2.8; *Hom. Num.* 7.2.
57 While Numbers 25 is often understood as the source of Paul's allusion in 1 Cor 10:8, there are various reasons to view Exodus 32 as a complementary source. First, Paul cites directly from Exod 32:6 just one verse prior in 10:7. Second, there is already precedence in Jewish interpretation that connected both accounts from the Hebrew Bible. For example, see Philo, *Mos.* 1.302 (i.e. the addition of "sacrifice" that fits with the idolatry of Exodus 32); *Spec.* 3.126 and *Mos.* 2.170–2, 273 (i.e. the killing of family members, Exod 32:27); *Spec.* 3.126 (i.e. the substitution of the 3,000 killed by the Levites in Exodus with the fallen 24,000 in Numbers). Commentaries generally ignore this connection. But see more recently Bart J. Koet, "The Old Testament Background to 1 Cor 10,7–8," in *The Corinthian Correspondence*, ed. R. Bieringer (Leuven: Leuven University Press, 1996), 607–615; David Lincicum, "Philo on Phinehas and the Levites: Observing an Exegetical Connection," *BBR* 21.1 (2011): 43–50. Some commentators attribute the difference in the numbers of the dead between 1 Cor 10:8 and Exod 32:28/Num 25:9 to Paul's faulty

Exod 16:2; Num 14:16; 16; 21:4–9; 25:1–9).[58] This is a highly concentrated utilization of Exodus material. There are three characteristics concerning these verses that require further elaboration.

First, just as in 1 Corinthians 5, Paul highlights the presence of Christ in the assembly. The rock from which the Israelites drank (Exod 17:1–7; see Num 20:1–13; Ps 78:15–20; Isa 48:21; Wis 11:4) is interpreted thus in 1 Cor 10:4b: "The rock was Christ (ὁ Χριστός)." This is a powerful Christological statement that implies a specific type of divine presence through the ages.[59] Paul goes one step further by identifying God (YHWH) in Exodus with Christ in 1 Cor 10:9: "We must not put Christ to the test, as some of them did and were destroyed by serpents."[60] This is very unusual since there are no indications in the Hebrew Bible that Christ was present anywhere in the story of the exodus, and it would be obvious to any reader that the target of Israelite grumbling was God (YHWH) and not a messianic figure (Christ). Yet Paul emphasizes that

---

memory. See Weiss, *Korintherbrief*, 225 ("Gedächtnisfehler"); C. K. Barrett, *First Epistle to the Corinthians* (New York: Harper & Row, 1968), 225 ("lapse of memory").

58 While Paul explicit cites (ὥσπερ γέγραπται) Exodus 32 in 1 Cor 10:7, it is apparent that narratively speaking, Exod 13–17 does the most work for Paul in 1 Corinthians 10. Exodus 15 (Exod 15:1–21, "Song of the Sea") does not figure significantly in Paul's narrative of 1 Cor 10, though that may be due to its formal difference in genre from the other chapters surrounding it. Generic differences aside, what is evoked as poem in Exod 15 is described as prose in Exod 14. Meyers, *Exodus*, 116–17; Nissim Amzallag and Mikhal Avriel, "Responsive Voices in the *Song of the Sea* (Exodus 15:1–21)," *JBQ* 40.4 (2012): 211; Anja Klein, "Hymn and History in Ex 15: Observations on the Relationship between Temple Theology and Exodus Narrative in the Song of the Sea," *ZAW* 124.4 (2012): 516–527. It is also worth noting that the Song of the Sea contains various references to sacred space (v. 13: "holy abode"; v. 17: "mountain of your own possession," "place ... that you made your abode," and "sanctuary"), even though chronologically speaking, Israelites have yet to enter the promised land or to build any temple structure.

59 Matthew Thiessen, "'The Rock Was Christ': The Fluidity of Christ's Body in 1 Corinthians 10.4," *JSNT* 36.2 (2013): 103–126. Thiessen mentions prior, contemporary, and subsequent Jewish interpreters to make his case, but he does not mention the connection that some interpreters make between the rock (= divine presence) and the temple. Also McKelvey, *The New Temple*, 136–137.

60 The text traditions diverge somewhat on this identification, as some witnesses read κυριον (ℵ B C P 33 104 326 1175 2464 sy^hmg) while few others read θεον (A 81). Scholars now generally agree that Χριστον is the *lectio difficilior* with good external witnesses (𝔓^46 D F G K L Ψ 630 1241 1505 1739 1881 𝔐 latt sy co; Ir^lat Or^1739mg; Clement of Alexandria, *Ecl.* 49.2; Marcion [also Epiphanius, *Pan.* 42.11–12]); Ambrosiaster, CSEL 81/2.110. See Collins, *First Corinthians*, 372; Fee, *First Epistle to the Corinthians*, 457n34; Fitzmyer, *First Corinthians*, 386. *Contra* Robertson-Plummer, *First Epistle*, 205–6. While θεον is very weakly attested, it is possible that κυριον could have been the original reading. This does not effect Paul's Christological interpretation, however, since κυριος for him generally means the risen Christ.

it was indeed Christ present during the exodus, bringing great continuity to the story of the Israelites and their relationship to YHWH with the present experiences of the Corinthians and their relationship to Christ.

The second characteristic of Paul's reading of Exodus is related to the connection just noted, with his various statements that the experience of the Israelites echoes the current experience of the Corinthians. He begins the narration in 1 Cor 10:1 by naming the subjects of Exodus as "all our fathers" (οἱ πατέρες ἡμῶν πάντες), a rare construction in Paul. This is similar to his earlier reference to Christ as "*our* paschal lamb" in 1 Cor 5:7.[61] According to Carla Works, this terminology is significant because "[it] does not merely instruct the Gentile Corinthians, but tailors the story to mirror the believers' experience and to draw them into a heritage that had not been theirs by birth."[62] It is no small matter that the Corinthians' ignoble heritage—insofar as most of them were concerned—is now replaced with a rich Jewish heritage that stretches back to the time of Moses. Paul also maps onto this story language that would have been familiar, though technically anachronistic, to the Corinthians. In 10:2a, Paul calls the Israelites' passage through the sea as a type of baptism (πάντες εἰς τὸν Μωϋσῆν ἐβαπτίσθησαν). The importance of this sacrament in Christian theology notwithstanding, the language of baptism does not occur often beyond 1 Corinthians in Paul's letters, and not at all in connection to the Israelites.[63] This interpretation of the people and circumstances of Exodus is remarkable for the way it connects his present auditors and their experiences with the Israelites of Exodus.[64]

---

[61] This sort of rhetorical solidarity between audience and the Israelites occurs elsewhere in the NT though always with a strictly *Jewish* audience. Acts 3:11–16; 5:27–32; 7; 13:13–17; 15:1–11; 22:12–16; 26:1–8; Jas 2:21. Paul uses such language elsewhere only in his letter to the Romans (4:12, 16; 9:10). Carla Works notes that "the reference to Christ as 'our πάσχα' in 1 Cor 5:7 provides the rationale not only for the Corinthians' invitation to feast (5:8) but also for the lesson from 'our ancestors' (10:1)." In Carla Swafford Works, *The Church in the Wilderness: Paul's Use of the Exodus Tradition*, WUNT II/379 (Tübingen: Mohr Siebeck, 2014), 161. It is interesting to find that Works reads Paul's use of the Exodus exclusively only in 1 Cor 5 and 10. While she discusses 11:17–34 in various places throughout her work, not once does she mention the possibility of the Exodus tradition as the background of 11:17–34 and Exod 24:8 is excluded entirely from consideration (see her Index of Ancient Sources). Against her reading, see my analysis below as well as Conzelmann, *1 Corinthians*, 199n73; Fee, *First Epistle to the Corinthians*, 554; Fitzmyer, *1 Corinthians*, 443.
[62] Works, *Church in the Wilderness*, 52.
[63] Βαπτίζω in the Pauline epistles: Rom 6:3; 1 Cor 1:13, 14, 15, 16, 17; 10:2; 12:13; 15:29; Gal 3:27.
[64] Zeller, *Der erste Brief*, 327.

2.3 The Exodus Tradition and Christological Connection — 41

Indeed, Paul pushes his interpretation of past events yet one step further by claiming that these events from Exodus are instructive for the Corinthians' current situation:[65]

1 Cor 10:6a,   ταῦτα δὲ τύποι ἡμῶν ἐγενήθησαν
1 Cor 10:11a, ταῦτα δὲ τυπικῶς συνέβαινεν ἐκείνοις, ἐγράφη δὲ πρὸς νουθεσίαν ἡμῶν

Paul then provides instructions about the maintenance of certain behaviors. In 1 Cor 10:6b–10, Paul repeats various forms of the statement, 'Do not x as some of them, and so y happened,' with x denoting a negative behavior and y denoting the consequence of such misconduct.[66] It is not by accident that earlier transgressions from Israel parallel the problems in Corinth, since Paul has carefully crafted his appropriation of Exodus.[67] In light of these examples from Exodus, Paul concludes with a stern warning: "So if you think you are standing, watch out, lest you fall!" (10:12)[68] In other words, if the Corinthians believed their assembly was safe, the example of the Israelites should serve as sober warning that they remained vulnerable.

---

[65] The wilderness account also served as a paradigm in other Jewish and Christian contexts. E. g., Pss 78; 105; 135; 136; Ezek 20:1–31; 4 Ezra 14.29–30; John 6:31, 48–50; Acts 7:23–51; Hebrews 3:7–19; CD 3.7–13. Luke Timothy Johnson, *Hebrews: A Commentary*, NTL (Louisville: Westminster John Knox Press, 2006), 111–22; Thomas B. Dozeman, Craig A. Evans, and Joel N. Lohr, eds., *The Book of Exodus: Composition, Reception, and Interpretation* (Leiden: Brill, 2014), esp. 305–562.

[66] The following table demonstrates Paul's repeated use of the stock statement:

	'Do not x …	as some of them …	and y …'
1 Cor 10:6	εἰς τὸ μὴ εἶναι ἡμᾶς ἐπιθυμητὰς κακῶν	καθὼς κἀκεῖνοι ἐπεθύμησαν	
10:7	μηδὲ εἰδωλολάτραι γίνεσθε	καθώς τινες αὐτῶν	
10:8	μηδὲ πορνεύωμεν	καθώς τινες αὐτῶν ἐπόρνευσαν	καὶ ἔπεσαν μιᾷ ἡμέρᾳ εἴκοσι τρεῖς χιλιάδες
10:9	μηδὲ ἐκπειράζωμεν τὸν Χριστόν	καθώς τινες αὐτῶν ἐπείρασαν	καὶ ὑπὸ τῶν ὄφεων ἀπώλλυντο
10:10	μηδὲ γογγύζετε	καθάπερ τινὲς αὐτῶν ἐγόγγυσαν	καὶ ἀπώλοντο ὑπὸ τοῦ ὀλοθρευτοῦ

[67] Richard Hays, *1 Corinthians*, Interpretation (Louisville: John Knox, 1997), 164–165.
[68] Multiple times throughout the Corinthians correspondence, Paul charges the Corinthians to 'watch out!' (βλέπετε): 1 Cor 1:26; 8:9; 10:12 (βλεπέτω) 10:18; 16:10; 2 Cor 10:7. The phrase occurs infrequently elsewhere in the Pauline corpus: Gal 5:15; Eph 5:15; Phil 3:2; Col 2:8.

The third and final characteristic of Paul's use of Exodus in 1 Cor 10 is his emphasis on the presence of God and the idea of sacred or protected space. Beginning with the reference to God's presence (10:1) to the appearance of Christ as the rock (10:4), the well-being of the Israelites was assured due to the presence of God within their midst. Throughout the exodus, the divine presence in "the cloud" functioned in several important ways: it covers Mount Sinai, marking it as a special place (Exod 24:15); it descends upon the entrance of the tent when Moses would enter to speak with God (33:9); and it dictated when the Israelites would continue on their journey (40:36–37). If divine presence led God's people and energized God's dwelling-place (i.e. tabernacle), then likewise Christ's presence among the Corinthians as the temple of God.

2.3.3 Exodus 24 in 1 Corinthians 11:17–34

In 1 Corinthians 11:23–26, Paul refers to the "handing on" of tradition, which he purportedly "received from the Lord," with similarities to the Synoptic tradition.[69] There are four components of this tradition that exist across the witnesses, the last component being the most relevant for analysis: (1) Jesus's action concerning the bread, (2) Jesus's words about the nature of the bread, (3) Jesus's action concerning the cup, and (4) Jesus's words about the cup and drink. In all four versions, Jesus connects the cup with the establishment of the new covenant *through blood*, language that is found in Exodus 24:8 ("This is the blood of the covenant that the Lord has made with you").[70] There is also a connection to Jer 38:31 LXX ("I will make a new covenant"), but one should not dismiss the importance of Exod 24, since it is only there one finds the sealing of covenant with blood and the partaking of a covenant meal (Exod 24:11). In 1 Cor 11:25, Paul quotes Jesus, "This cup is the new covenant in *my blood*." The direct link between what Jesus institutes in the supper and what God established in Exodus 24 elevates the sanctity of this event above a simple Roman *convivium*.

---

[69] For the variations in the Synoptic tradition + Paul, see Chart 1 at the end of this chapter.
[70] This is especially true for three out of the four versions (Matt, Mark, and 1 Cor), though the longer ending of Luke 22:19b–20 is now accepted as the better reading (these verses are omitted in D and it). See also Heb 9:15–22. Joel B. Green, *The Gospel of Luke*, NICNT (Grand Rapids: Eerdmans, 1997), 761–764; François Bovon, *Luke 3: A Commentary on the Gospel of Luke 19:28–24:53* (Minneapolis: Fortress Press, 2012), 158–160. See also Jer 39:40 LXX; Zech 9:11. On the importance of Exod 24:8 here see Wolfgang Schrage, *Der Erste Brief an die Korinther*, EKKNT 7/1–4 (Zurich: Benzinger, 1991–2001), 3:40. The language of blood in reference to covenant also occurs in Zech 9:11.

2.3 The Exodus Tradition and Christological Connection — 43

Just as in 1 Cor 5 and 10, Paul emphasizes the centrality of Christ in the assembly. Paul is aided by the presence of the Jesus tradition in 11:23–26, but the emphasis is not on the earthly Jesus but on the risen Lord. The ritual that is instituted and repeated in these verses does not necessarily lead to the ὥστε of 11:27 that bridges the two sections together.[71] That is, it is not immediately clear how recounting the Jesus tradition becomes the basis for strictures regarding proper participation in the Lord's supper. But it is here that Paul makes the relationship clear: the improper (ἀναξίως) eating of the bread and drinking of the cup meant that an offender "will be guilty of the body and blood of the Lord" (ἔνοχος ἔσται τοῦ σώματος καὶ τοῦ αἵματος τοῦ κυρίου).[72] The radical nature of Paul's statement is confirmed by the experience of the Corinthian assembly since many of them have been struck by disease, or even death, due to their offense (11:30, διὰ τοῦτο ἐν ὑμῖν πολλοὶ ἀσθενεῖς καὶ ἄρρωστοι καὶ κοιμῶνται ἱκανοί; see 2.5.3 below).

What is the context of Exod 24:8? It occurs just after the Lord's invitation to Moses "to come near" (24:2). According to Carol Meyers, this chapter contains extraordinary features, including the construction of an altar, an experience of God or divine power, reference to God's dwelling place and body, and a sacred meal.[73] These elements all point toward interpreting Moses's statement about the blood of the covenant within the context of sacred space. The different zones of holiness described in Exod 24 also confirm this idea: all Israelites are present in the general vicinity; Moses, Aaron, and other elders of Israel are called to wor-

---

[71] In other words, it is not immediately clear how the exhortation to take the bread and drink the cup as a "proclamation of the Lord's death" (11:26) is related to the issue of offense and judgment in 11:27–34. Scholars have rightly highlighted the horizontal dimension of the cruciform manner of life here that would connect the two sections together, but it remains just that, a social problem that existed within the Corinthian assembly. See 2.5.3 below.

[72] Commentators do not elaborate on the meaning of ἔνοχος here. They tend to follow the lexicon in defining it as something akin to "guilty," "liable for x," or "answerable for x," but do not explain what this entails for Paul's understanding of what is happening in Corinth. E. g., Collins, *First Corinthians*, 438 ("'Answerable' [enochos, hapax in Paul], is primarily a judicial term, used in reference to the court, the punishment, the crime, or the person against whom the crime is committed, as here); Fitzmyer, *First Corinthians*, 445 ("the fut. *enochos estai* is to be understood eschatologically"); Schrage, *Korinther*, 3:49 ("Schuldig wird der unwürdig Essende und Trinkende vielmehr gegenüber dem am Kreuz dahingegebenen Leib und Blut Christi, weil er sich an der Gemeinde vergeht"); Zeller, *Der erste Brief*, 376 ("es handelt sich nicht um ein – gar von Propheten angesagtes – eschatologisches Futur, sondern um die logische Rechtsfolge wie in anderen Fällen").

[73] Meyers, *Exodus*, 205.

ship from afar; and finally Moses alone is given permission to draw near to God and come up to Mount Sinai where God speaks to him from the "cloud." Thus, when Paul alludes to Exod 24:8, all the similar elements are found: a sacred meal, Christ's body, and an experience of divine power. Also notice that Paul distinguishes the Corinthian ἐκκλησία as a different kind of space from a regular οἰκία (1 Cor 11:22).[74]

2.3.4 Exodus in 1 Corinthians 5:1–13, 10:1–22, and 11:17–34

The foregoing analysis shows that Exodus plays a significant role in all three of these sections in 1 Corinthians. There is much to commend the earlier suggestion that Paul is interpreting the Exodus narrative in sequential order in 1 Corinthians 5, 10, and 11, though the evidence is more suggestive than definite. In any case, just as Exodus is the narration of Israelite experiences of power and danger within proximity to a sacred space known as the tabernacle, so also 1 Corinthians 5:1–13, 10:1–22, and 11:17–34 stand as important moments of encounters with power and peril within proximity to God's temple. The accounts from Exodus recall the tabernacle as a sacred space within Israelite history that parallel the idea of Corinthians currently existing as the temple of God. God powered the tabernacle in Exodus, and likewise God provides energy to his temple in Corinth.[75]

In addition, the allusions to Exodus become occasions for Paul to make connections to Christ, elevating the problems discussed in each chapter to matters central to the constitution of the assembly. That is to say, since the events of the exodus were watershed moments in the formation of Israel's relationship to YHWH, Paul draws a tight connection between the activities of the Israelites and those of the Corinthians, in order to emphasize the need to acknowledge Christ who is Lord over this community. Sexual promiscuity, improper eating habits, and misconduct in sacred meals are not isolated incidents that have no ultimate bearing on the community. Rather, these problems are symptoms of their overall misunderstanding of the nature of the Corinthian assembly, one that is brought into existence through the sacrifice of their Lord (i.e. the pas-

---

[74] Økland, *Women in Their Place*, 143 notes the "possibility of reading *ekklesia* as a *place*" and also "that for Paul there exists two different patterns of performing a meal that belong to two different spaces—*ekklesia* space, and *oikia* space" (144–45).

[75] In his study of the theme of divine power in Exodus, Thomas Dozeman remarks, "In fact, it is only through God's exerting power that other characters acquire a place in the story as either opponents or allies of God." In Thomas B. Dozeman, *God at War: Power in the Exodus Tradition* (Oxford: Oxford University Press, 1996), 5.

chal lamb), and one in which the Spirit of God dwells, not just within autonomous individuals, but also corporately within the temple of God. Just as in Exodus, their actions have ramifications for both the individual and group, and in 1 Cor 5:1–13, 10:1–22, and 11:17–34, Paul rebukes the Corinthians for failing to understand this.[76]

2.4 Power in 1 Corinthians

In the introduction of this chapter, I noted the various ways in which "power" is foregrounded by Paul and hinted at the subtle connections between power and Spirit in 1 Corinthians. In that discussion, I purposely did not provide a detailed analysis of how this theme functions throughout the letter. I now address this issue more fully. Modern studies of power in 1 Corinthians are often exercises in ideological criticism that adopt etic postures toward Paul's language.[77] They are primarily concerned with how power functions as a factor of persuasion in Pauline discourse. They are not concerned with the emic dimension of what

---

[76] Brian S. Rosner, "'ΟΥΧΙ ΜΑΛΛΟΝ ΕΠΕΝΘΗΣΑΤΕ': Corporate Responsibility in 1 Corinthians 5," NTS 38 (1992): 470–473.

[77] E.g., Elizabeth A. Castelli, "Interpretations of Power in 1 Corinthians," Semeia 54 (1991): 197–222; idem, Imitating Paul: A Discourse of Power (Louisville: Westminster John Knox Press, 1991); Ronald Charles, "The Report of 1 Corinthians 5 in Critical Dialogue with Foucault," Journal for Cultural and Religious Theory 11.1 (2010): 142–158; Bengt Holmberg, Paul and Power: The Structure of Authority in the Primitive Church As Reflected in the Pauline Epistles (Lund: Gleerup, 1978); Sandra Hack Polaski, Paul and the Discourse of Power (Sheffield: Sheffield Academic Press, 1999; NB: Polaski's work is focused on Paul's letter to the Galatians.). It should also be noted here that Michel Foucault, particularly his analysis of power relations, heavily influenced Castelli and Polaski as did also Max Weber's sociological understanding of leadership and institutions. See, e.g., Michel Foucault, Discipline and Punish: The Birth of the Prison, trans. Alan Sheridan Smith (Harmondsworth: Penguin, 1977); idem, The History of Sexuality, Vol. 1: Introduction, trans. Robert Hurley (New York: Vintage, 1980); idem, Power/Knowledge: Selected Interviews and Other Writings, 1972–1977, ed. Colin Gordon; trans. Colin Gordon et al. (New York: Pantheon, 1980); idem, "The Subject and Power," in Hubert L. Dreyfus and Paul Rabinow, Michel Foucault: Beyond Structuralism and Hermeneutics (Chicago: University of Chicago Press, 1982), 208–226; Max Weber, Economy and Society: An Outline of Interpretive Sociology, ed. G. Roth and C. Wittich, trans. E. Fischoff et al., 2 vols. (Berkeley: University of California Press, 1978). The only recent works not driven by such ideological interests may be Petrus J. Gräbe, The Power of God in Paul's Letters, WUNT II/123 (Tübingen: Mohr Siebeck, 2000) and Kathy Ehrensperger, Paul and the Dynamics of Power: Communication and Interaction in the Early Christ-Movement, LNTS 325 (London: T&T Clark, 2007). Gräbe's work, however, is broader in scope (it analyzes 1 Cor, 2 Cor, Rom, 1 Thess, Phil, and Eph) and primarily lexical in method, and Ehrensperger's work is focused on what she calls "the network of power" (i.e. aspects of group dynamics).

power means for Paul in 1 Corinthians, still less how this is related to πνεῦμα and temple. They focus only on the horizontal dimension of power language: power is an element within the struggle between the superior apostle and the subordinate Corinthians,[78] or as an element within the general system of Roman patronage.[79] Seldom is the vertical dimension of Paul's language explored in such studies.[80] A handful of German scholars, however, engaged in this research, though without much influence upon subsequent scholarship.[81] More recently, several scholars have focused on the apparent paradox between "weakness" and "power" in 2 Corinthians.[82] With the exception of two recent works, little interest is shown in further exploring Paul's view of Spirit and power in 1 Corinthians.[83]

---

78 Castelli, *Imitating Paul*; Charles, "Report of 1 Corinthians 5"; Holmberg, *Paul and Power*; Rick F. Talbott, *Jesus, Paul, and Power: Rhetoric, Ritual and Metaphor in Ancient Mediterranean Christianity* (Eugene, OR: Cascade Books, 2010), esp. 128–161. More positively (with respect to Paul's horizontal exercise of power), see Ehrensperger, *Paul and the Dynamics of Power*.
79 E. g., John K. Chow, *Patronage and Power: A Study of Social Networks in Corinth*, JSNTSS 75 (Sheffield: JSOT, 1992); Joshua Rice, *Paul and Patronage: The Dynamics of Power in 1 Corinthians* (Eugene, OR: Pickwick Publications, 2013).
80 There are also other, more discrete investigations of smaller sections of 1 Corinthians though they too remain silent about how power is variously understood by Paul, and none sufficiently investigate—if at all—1 Corinthians 5, 10, and/or 11. E. g., Timothy H. Lim, "'Not in Persuasive Words of Wisdom, But in the Demonstration of the Spirit and Power,'" *NovT* 29.2 (1987): 137–149; William David Spencer, "The Power in Paul's Teaching (1 Cor 4:9–20)," *JETS* 32.1 (1989): 51–61.
81 E. g., Otto Schmitz, "Der Begriff ΔΥΝΑΜΙΣ bei Paulus: Ein Beitrag zum Wesen urchristlicher Begriffsbildung," in *Festgabe für Adolf Deissmann zum 60. Geburtstag 7. November 1926*, ed. K. L. Schmidt (Tübingen: J. C. B. Mohr, 1926), 139–167; Walter Grundmann, *Der Begriff der Kraft in der neutestamentlichen Gedankenwelt* (Stuttgart: W. Kohlhammer, 1932); Erich Fascher, "Dynamis," *RAC* 4 (1959): 415–458; Karl Prümm, "Dynamis in griechisch-hellenistischer Religion und Philosophie als Vergleichsbild zu göttlicher Dynamis im Offenbarungsraum," *ZKT* 83 (1961): 393–430; G. Friedrich, "δύναμις, εως, ἡ," *EDNT* 1:355–58; Helge Kjaer Nielsen, "Paulus' Verwendung des Begriffes Δύναμις. Eine Replik zur Kreuzestheologie," in *Die Paulinische Literatur und Theologie*, ed. Sigfried Pedersen (Göttingen: Vandenhoeck & Ruprecht, 1980), 137–158.
82 David E. Garland, "Paul's Apostolic Authority: The Power of Christ Sustaining Weakness (2 Corinthians 10–13)," *Review & Expositor* 86.3 (1989): 371–389; Ulrich Heckel, *Kraft in Schwachheit: Untersuchungen zu 2. Kor 10–13*, WUNT II/56 (Tübingen: Mohr Siebeck, 1993); Timothy B. Savage, *Power Through Weakness: Paul's Understanding of the Christian Ministry in 2 Corinthians*, SNTSMS 86 (Cambridge: Cambridge University Press, 1996); Margareta M. Gruber, *Herrlichkeit in Schwachheit: Eine Auslegung der Apologie des Zweiten Korintherbriefs 2 Kor 2,14–6,13* (Würzburg: Echter, 1998); Alexandra R. Brown, "The Gospel Takes Place: Paul's Theology of Power-in-Weakness in 2 Corinthians," *Interpretation* 52.3 (1998): 271–285; Sze-kar Wan, *Power in Weakness: Conflict and Rhetoric in Paul's Second Letter to the Corinthians* (Harrisburg, PA: Trinity Press International, 2000).

2.4 Power in 1 Corinthians — 47

In the Pauline epistles, δύναμις occurs far more frequently in the Corinthian correspondence than in anywhere else.[84] In the opening section of 1 Corinthians, Paul highlights the importance of power, by equating the "message of the cross" as the "power of God" (1:18, Ὁ λόγος γὰρ ὁ τοῦ σταυροῦ ... δύναμις θεοῦ ἐστιν). Just a few verses later, Paul states that Christ is this power (1:24, Χριστὸν θεοῦ δύναμιν).[85] Paul even asserts that his own ministry involved a demonstration of Spirit *and* power (2:4, ἀποδείξει πνεύματος καὶ δυνάμεως) with the aim that the faith of the Corinthians would rest solely upon the power of God (2:5, ἵνα ἡ πίστις ὑμῶν μὴ ᾖ ἐν σοφίᾳ ἀνθρώπων ἀλλ' ἐν δυνάμει θεοῦ). This suggests that there was some visible and real experience of power in the eyes of the Corinthians.

One must not ignore the subtle hints that Paul provides in these opening chapters of 1 Corinthians with respect to what power *is*, particularly its conceptual proximity to πνεῦμα,[86] Χριστός,[87] and ναός. In the most recent and thorough study of the "power of God" in Paul's letters, Petrus Gräbe writes the following:

> [Paul] did not rely on his own wise and persuasive words to make his message effective, but relied on the power of God which he interprets *pneumatologically* (1 Cor 2,4–5). Since the message about the crucified Christ is *contrary to the wisdom of this world* it can only be be-

---

83 Gräbe, *Power of God* and Gordon D. Fee, *God's Empowering Presence: The Holy Spirit in the Letters of Paul* (Peabody, MA: Hendrickson, 1994).
84 Per 1000 words, the frequencies of δύναμις in 1 and 2 Corinthians are 1.78 (15x) and 1.84 (10x) respectively. The only other undisputed letter that comes close to this level is Romans (0.93; 8x). In other letters: Gal (1x); Eph (5x); Phil (1x); Col (2x); 1 Thess (1x); 2 Thess (3x); and 2 Tim (3x).
85 2 Cor 12:9b, ἵνα ἐπισκηνώσῃ ἐπ' ἐμὲ ἡ δύναμις τοῦ Χριστοῦ.
86 Paul is not alone in making the connection between πνεῦμα and δύναμις. Philo also hints at this connection in *Questions and Answers on Genesis* 2.28 (Marcus, LCL), when he asks, "What is the meaning of the words, 'He brought a spirit (πνεῦμα) over the earth and the water ceased'?" His answer reads: "Some would say that by 'spirit' is meant the wind through which the flood ceased. But I myself do not know of water being diminished by a wind. Rather it is disturbed and seethes ... Accordingly, (Scripture) now seems to speak of the spirit of the Deity (τὸ τοῦ θείου πνεῦμα) ... That such (an amount of water) should be cleared out by the wind is not fitting, likely or right; but, as I said (it must have been done) by the invisible power of God (ὑπὸ τῆς ἀοράτου δυνάμεως τῆς τοῦ θεοῦ)." See Carl R. Holladay, "Spirit in Philo of Alexandria," in *The Holy Spirit and the Church according to the New Testament: Sixth International East-West Symposium of New Testament Scholars, Belgrade, August 25 to 31, 2013*, ed. Predrag Dragutinovic, Karl-Wilhelm Niebuhr, and James Buchanan Wallace, with Christos Karakolis, WUNT 354 (Tübingen: Mohr Siebeck, 2016), 356–357.
87 Commenting on 1 Cor 1:24, Conzelmann calls this "die christologische Fassung" (*Der erste Brief*, 68).

lieved and thus be God's δύναμις through the powerful activity of the Spirit. The charismatic-thaumaturgical dimension of the δύναμις of the Spirit is here not to be excluded.[88]

This important observation can elucidate Paul's conception of power and spirit, since Paul does not tend to provide a specific definition of πνεῦμα in his letters.[89] Gräbe prematurely concludes that δύναμις is "essentially a pneumatological category," though I am not fully convinced that this exhausts the relationship between δύναμις and πνεῦμα, especially given the other important link to Χριστός.[90] Moreover, divine power can be interpreted in the context of temple, which Gräbe ignores. Paul sometimes refers to the spirit in present terms (e.g., 1 Cor 4:21; 5:5; 7:34; 14:14; 16:18) or in eschatological terms (e.g. 1 Cor 15); sometimes he means the human spirit (e.g., 1 Cor 4:21; 16:18) and sometimes the Holy Spirit (2:10, 12; 6:19; 12:3). Despite such variety, Paul's use of πνεῦμα in 1 Corinthians most often refers to God's Spirit (2:11–12, 14; 3:16; 6:11; 7:40; 12:3) or the Holy Spirit (6:19; 12:3), particularly when he does not provide qualifications indicating he means otherwise.[91]

Other Pauline terms for power can also be considered, such as δυνατός, δυνατέω, (ἐν)δυναμόω, ἐνέργ- words, ἐξουσία, and ἐξουσιάζω. Paul reminds the Corinthians that they are, in worldly terms, without power (1 Cor 1:26, οὐ πολλοὶ δυνατοί), while stating in other places that that God and Christ exercise or provide power and authority to believers through the Spirit (δυνατός: Rom 9:22; 11:23; 2 Cor 10:4; 12:10; 13:3; [ἐν]δυναμόω: Rom 4:20; Phil 4:13; ἐξουσία: Rom 13:1–2; 1 Cor 15:24,; 2 Cor 10:8,; 13:10,).[92] There are also "energies" that surround various activities within the assembly that Paul attributes to the power of the Spirit (ἐνεργήματα: 1 Cor 12:6,, 10, 11; Gal 3:5,; 5:6; 1 Thess 2:13; Phlm 6;).[93] Though the situation described in each of these instances is not exactly parallel to that of 1 Corinthians, the data supports the supposition that the power man-

---

88 Gräbe, *Power of God in Paul's Letters*, 66 (emphasis original). See also pages 245–55 ("Chapter 24: Pneumatological emphasis"); Rudolf Bultmann, *Theology of the New Testament*, 2 vols., trans. Kendrick Grobel (Baylor: Baylor University Press, 2007), 1:155–157.
89 Luke Timothy Johnson, "Life-Giving Spirit: The Ontological Implications of Resurrection," *Stone-Campbell Journal* 15.1 (2012): 85. See also 2 Cor 3:17.
90 Gräbe does concede that "[w]ithin a soteriological context Paul's theological use of δύναμις (δύναμις θεοῦ, 1,18; also 1,24) is interpreted *Christologically*. In 1,23.24.30.31 and 2,2 the supreme centrality of Christ in the whole process of salvation becomes very clear" (*Power of God*, 66).
91 This observation is important for my analysis of "spirit" in 1 Corinthians 5. Johnson, "Life-Giving Spirit," 85.
92 See also Eph 1:21; 6:10; Col 1:11, 16; 2:10, 15; 1 Tim 1:12; 2 Tim 2:1; 4:17.
93 See also Eph 3:20–21; Col 1:29.

ifested within the ἐκκλησία is for Paul, above all, a manifestation of God's presence through the Spirit.

The relationships between power, spirit, and Christ are complex. And even when Paul does not draw explicit connections between these terms, his exhortations to the Corinthians throughout the letter presuppose the reality of such power within their assembly. For example, Paul reminds the Corinthians that they have been called into fellowship with Christ (1 Cor 1:9; 10:16), whose presence as the Lord is mediated by the Spirit (1 Cor 3:16–17; 12:13), and that their assembly —or the ναὸς θεοῦ, as so named in 1 Cor 3:16—is the place within which the Spirit of God dwells. The community is the locus of God's display of power, the place where one can find positive and powerful experiences from the Spirit, or negative and dangerous consequences of misbehavior when they stray beyond the limits of the assembly. That divine power is housed within a temple is not a novel concept: visitants to temples throughout the Mediterranean fully expected to encounter various forms of divine power (see especially chapter 3).

2.4.1 Power in 1 Corinthians 12 and 14

For Paul's descriptions of power and Spirit, 1 Corinthians 12 and 14 are understandably taken as the *loci classici*, and therefore demand brief analysis.[94] In 1 Cor 12, there are references to the Spirit (12:1–13), the God-given and Spirit-activated πνευματικά, ἐνεργήματα, and χαρίσματα (12:1–10, 28–31), and above all, the well-known concept of the ἐκκλησία as body of Christ through the Spirit (12:12–27).[95] In 1 Cor 14, there are practices of πνευματικά (14:1–37) and the presence of the Spirit (14:2, 14–16). Like 1 Cor 5:1–13, 10:1–22, and 11:17–34, 1 Cor 12 and 14 both presuppose the activities of the "gathered" assembly.[96]

---

[94] Even more so than discussions about power, 1 Cor 12–14 (and Rom 12) tend to be the dominant texts for Paul's "ecclesiology." The typical symbolism that comes to mind for many Pauline interpreters vis-à-vis Paul's view of the Corinthian assembly is "body" not "temple." See, for example, the classic work by Lucien Cerfaux, *The Church in the Theology of St. Paul*, trans. G. Webb and A. Walker (New York: Herder and Herder, 1963), esp. 262–286.
[95] On the assembly as "body," Christopher Tuckett writes: "For those who would argue that this motif is *the* central idea in his ecclesiology, there is thus a potential problem of seeking to explain why it occurs relatively *in*frequently in the undisputed letters." In "The Church as the Body of Christ," in *Paul et l'unité des chrétiens*, ed. J. Schlosser (Leuven: Peeters, 2010), 163.
[96] More explicitly in 1 Cor 14:23, 26 (συνέρχομαι [v. 23: + ἐπὶ τὸ αὐτό]). See 1 Cor 5:4; 11:17–18, 20 (+ ἐπὶ τὸ αὐτό), 33–34. In the latter two chapters (1 Cor 12 and 14), Paul describes the Corinthian assembly less under threat.

In Paul's discussion in 1 Cor 12–14 we do not find any evidence that the Corinthians have breached the "temple of God," nor do we find any discussions of, or even subtle allusions to, the Corinthians' participation in the Lord's meal, in contrast to the central role played by meals in communal life in 1 Cor 5, 10, and 11. That is not to say, however, that Paul exhibits two mutually exclusive visions of the Corinthian assembly, one espoused in 1 Cor 5, 10, and 11, and another in 1 Cor 12 and 14. As already noted, the latter two chapters contain various elements of what constitutes the nature of the Corinthian assembly that Paul describes in the earlier chapters.

As in 1 Cor, 10, and 11, Paul sets up clear boundaries for the community in 1 Cor 14. In 1 Cor 14:20–25, one can see hints of the insider-outsider dynamic. On the one hand, when outsiders, or the ἰδιῶται ἢ ἄπιστοι, witness the activity of the gathered community in 1 Cor 14:23 (Ἐὰν οὖν συνέλθῃ ἡ ἐκκλησία ὅλη ἐπὶ τὸ αὐτὸ καὶ πάντες λαλῶσιν γλώσσαις), their reaction is negative: "You are mad" (οὐκ ἐροῦσιν ὅτι μαίνεσθε;). On the other hand, when such outsiders are not only made privy to ritual activity, but are, as Paul describes it, "convicted" and "examined" by the assembly in 1 Cor 14:24–25 (ἐλέγχεται ὑπὸ πάντων, ἀνακρίνεται ὑπὸ πάντων), a different reaction occurs. In contrast to 1 Cor 14:23 when the outsiders remain outsiders, 14:25 describes a revelatory process through which such individuals are brought from their position of external observation (negative) to that of an internal participant of the community (positive). In both cases the people do not suffer any harm. Furthermore, not only are secrets laid bare, but also the participants prostrate themselves before God and make an important declaration. The earlier reaction was ὅτι μαίνεσθε, though now it is ὅτι ὄντως ὁ θεὸς ἐν ὑμῖν ἐστιν, a brief, though powerful statement affirming the manifestation of God's presence in the Corinthian assembly.[97]

The two chapters, 1 Corinthians 12 and 14, contain many elements about power and spirit that are found in 1 Cor 5, 10, and 11. Also, 1 Cor 12:3 includes the important statement concerning confession by the Spirit of God. What the later chapters of Paul's letter are missing is the flipside of the same coin, namely the peril that also lies in proximity to the community. Paul does not refer to any practices that impinges upon one's (in)correct Christology nor does he describe the presence of hostile powers that can endanger the community. In 1 Cor 12 and 14, there is the insider-outsider distinction as well as the exclusionary principle concerning the self-proclaimed prophet who does not abide by the law of the Lord. But, his descriptions of what are at stake for the Corinthian assembly re-

---

[97] Kevin A. Muñoz, "How Not to Go out of the World: First Corinthians 14:13–25 and the Social Foundations of Early Christian Expansion" (Ph.D. diss., Emory University, 2008), 23.

main far more benign than what was shown to be present in 1 Cor 5:1–13, 10:1–22, and 11:17–34. And above all, there are no discussions about the Corinthians' participation in sacred meals, whether the Lord's or otherwise in chapters 12 and 14 of the letter.

2.4.2 Power in 1 Corinthians 5:1–13

In 1 Corinthians 5, Paul expresses surprise that the Corinthians have callously accepted the incestuous relationship of one of their members. In Paul's instruction about the transgressor, there are various declarations vis-à-vis spirit and power in the assembly. The following is an exegetical analysis of the various statements about divine power or spirit that occur throughout 1 Cor 5. Because Paul uses each term or phrase with careful distinction, it is necessary to analyze his language in discrete units.

Spirit in 1 Cor 5:3–4. Paul tells the Corinthians that though he is absent in body, he is present in the spirit (5:3, ἀπὼν τῷ σώματι παρὼν δὲ τῷ πνεύματι). The meaning of "spirit" here is ambiguous. Unfortunately, secondary literature is not particularly helpful, since many interpreters tend to minimize the strength of Paul's assertion. Johannes Weiss, for example, avers that the phrase παρὼν δὲ τῷ πνεύματι is said in "ganz populärem Sinne," though apart from Col 2:5, he adduces no further evidence for his opinion.[98] Furthermore, his appeal to Col 2:5 does not help, since there too the s/Spirit distinction is unclear.[99] C. K. Barrett appeals directly to Weiss and concludes that Paul is using the term "psychologically rather than theologically."[100] Joseph Fitzmyer argues that "it is not a matter of God's Spirit being present with them; it is Paul's spirit ... His body is not in

---

[98] Weiss, *Korintherbrief*, 126. Also Robertson–Plummer, *First Epistle*, 97–98.
[99] The use of Col 2:5 to anchor this interpretation is not only circular but also neglects recent scholarship on Colossians that has problematized readings based on Cartesian dualism. Fee, *God's Empowering Presence*, 645–6; James D. G. Dunn, *The Epistles to the Colossians and to Philemon*, NIGTC (Grand Rapids: Eerdmans, 1996), 134–135; Douglas Moo, *The Letters to the Colossians and to Philemon*, PNTC (Grand Rapids: Eerdmans, 2008), 173. *Contra* J. B. Lightfoot, *Saint Paul's Epistles to the Colossians and to Philemon* (London: Macmillan, 1890 [1875]), 173 ("the common antithesis of flesh and spirit"); Joachim Gnilka, *Der Kolosserbrief*, HTKNT 10.1 (Freiburg: Herder, 1980), 114 ("*floskelhaften Aussage*"); F.F. Bruce, *The Epistles to the Colossians, to Philemon, and to the Ephesians*, NICNT (Grand Rapids: Eerdmans, 1984), 92 ("spiritually present"). In fact, the Colossian text in question suggests a type of presence mediated through the s/Spirit: εἰ γὰρ καὶ τῇ σαρκὶ ἄπειμι, ἀλλὰ τῷ πνεύματι σὺν ὑμῖν εἰμι.
[100] Barrett, *First Epistle to the Corinthians*, 123.

Corinth ... yet he is with them 'in spirit,' i.e., psychologically."[101] Wolfgang Schrage cites Weiss and Barrett and concludes that Paul's language is "ein bekannter Brieftopos."[102]

Some scholars have investigated the so-called "Greek epistolary style" that informed Paul's use of "spirit."[103] Hans-Josef Klauck describes this concept of "a mediated presence" that is similar to Paul's language in 1 Cor 5:3, though the language found in the adduced sources is not exactly parallel to that in Paul.[104] The only evidence with corresponding Greek expression that also occurs in 1 Corinthians postdates Paul by several centuries. For example, a mid-4th century CE letter reads: εἰ κὲ(*) ἐν σώματι οὐκ ἴκα(*) παρὰ τοὺς πόδας σ[ο]υ ἐν πνεύματι εἶκα(*) πρὸς τοὺς πό[δ]ας σου (P.Lond. 6 1926, lines 17–19). In fact, the phrase "present in spirit," insofar as it is used in modern parlance (i.e. 'you are in my thoughts'), is not attested in Greek literature prior to Paul's letters, if the latter should even be construed in this way.[105] A few other scholars since Rudolf Bultmann have detected a more nuanced view of Paul's use of "spirit" in this text. The following interpretation builds upon these earlier works.[106]

Paul's use of "spirit" in 1 Corinthians most often refers to "the Holy Spirit." To properly identify τῷ πνεύματι in 1 Cor 5:3, this position requires elaboration.

---

101 Fitzmyer, *First Corinthians*, 236.
102 Schrage, *Korinther*, 1:373. He does concede, however, that a clear decision remains difficult.
103 Conzelmann, *1 Corinthians*, 97n33. See also Gustav Karlsson, "Formelhaftes in Paulusbriefen?" *Eranos* 54 (1956): 138–141; Hans-Josef Klauck, *Ancient Letters and the New Testament: A Guide to Context and Exegesis*, trans. Daniel P. Bailey (Baylor: Baylor University Press, 2006), 188–194.
104 Contra Klauck see Bultmann, *Theology*, 1:208; Thiselton, *First Epistle to the Corinthians*, 390–392.
105 This phrase is basically limited to Christian use, often in their quotation of 1 Cor 5:3. E.g., Origen, *Comm. Jo.* 13.18; Eusebius, *Hist. eccl.* 7.11.12. The primary sources Klauck mentions in his *Ancient Letters* use the language of presence or absence of the letter writer, but such language is never used in conjunction with someone's "spirit." On P.Lond. cited above, Karlsson ("Formelhaftes," 140) acknowledges: "Die Paulinische Ausgestaltung ist natürlich ihrerseits von christlichen Briefschreibern ausgenützt worden. Ein Brief aus der sog. Paphnutius-Korrespondenz (Mitte des 4. Jh.) gibt die briefliche Formel in folgender Art, wahrscheinlich nach dem Muster des Kolloserbriefes."
106 The comments found within the following works remain brief with regard to Paul's language; my analysis attempts to elaborate upon these earlier reflections. See Bultmann, *Theology*, 1:208–9; Ernest Best, *One Body in Christ: A Study in the Relationship of the Church to Christ in the Epistles of the Apostle Paul* (London: SPCK, 1955), 58–59; Fee, *First Epistle to the Corinthians*, 204; David E. Garland, *1 Corinthians* (Grand Rapids: Baker Academic, 2003), 165; Jacob Kremer, *Der Erste Brief an die Korinther*, Regensburger Neues Testament (Regensburg: Friedrich Pustet, 1997), 102; Thiselton, *First Epistle to the Corinthians*, 390–391.

2.4 Power in 1 Corinthians — 53

In the Corpus Paulinum, there are 146 references to πνεῦμα, with the greatest number of occurrences found in 1 Corinthians (40x). Of these occurrences, there are a handful of dative articular forms without other qualifications that can usually aid the reader in identifying the type of "spirit" being referred to:[107]

Rom 12:11,	τῇ σπουδῇ μὴ ὀκνηροί, τῷ πνεύματι ζέοντες, τῷ κυρίῳ δουλεύοντες
1 Cor 5:3,	ἐγὼ μὲν γάρ, ἀπὼν τῷ σώματι παρὼν δὲ τῷ πνεύματι
1 Cor 7:34,	καὶ ἡ γυνὴ ἡ ἄγαμος καὶ ἡ παρθένος μεριμνᾷ τὰ τοῦ κυρίου, ἵνα ᾖ ἁγία καὶ τῷ σώματι καὶ τῷ πνεύματι
1 Cor 14:15,	τί οὖν ἐστιν; προσεύξομαι τῷ πνεύματι, προσεύξομαι δὲ καὶ τῷ νοΐ· ψαλῶ τῷ πνεύματι, ψαλῶ δὲ καὶ τῷ νοΐ
Col 2:5,	εἰ γὰρ καὶ τῇ σαρκὶ ἄπειμι, ἀλλὰ τῷ πνεύματι σὺν ὑμῖν εἰμι

In two of the five verses above, the identification of the spirit is rather straightforward. Since John Calvin, various interpreters have suggested that Paul is likely describing the activity of "the Spirit" in Rom 12:11,[108] and 1 Cor 7:34 is consistently understood as referring to the human spirit.[109] The other three verses, however, have remained problematic for Pauline interpreters, as seen in the cases of 1 Cor 5:3 and Col 2:5. Given Paul's statements elsewhere in the letter concerning the indwelling Spirit, the Corinthians' drinking from the one Spirit, and the idea of even becoming one Spirit with the Lord (see 1 Cor 3:16; 6:17; 12:13), there is find sufficient reason to believe that Paul is thinking about a fundamental connection between his spirit and the Spirit in 1 Cor 5:3. Therefore, the usual bifurcation becomes unnecessary. The remaining verse where τῷ πνεύματι occurs, 1 Cor 14:15, gives further support for this position, since the context there directly links the activity of the human spirit with that of the Holy Spirit.[110] In other words, it may be better to think of πνεῦμα in 1 Cor 5:3 functioning in a *both/and* rather than in an *either/or* manner. Since πνεῦμα in Pauline thought often encapsulates more

---

[107] "Qualifications" refer to noun constructions such as "of God" (e. g., Rom 8:9, 14; 1 Cor 12:3; 2 Cor 3:3) or "of Christ" (e. g., Rom 8:9; Phil 1:19), and adjectives such as "holy" (e. g., Rom 5:5; 9:1; 1 Cor 12:3; 2 Cor 6:6; 1 Thess 1:5).

[108] John Calvin, *Commentary on Romans* 12:11. See Gregory of Nazianzus (NB: it is possible he is borrowing the language from Rom 12:11 than an actual interpretation of it), *Or.* 6.4; 17.1; Douglas J. Moo, *The Epistle to the Romans*, NICNT (Grand Rapids: Eerdmans, 1996), 778–9; Frank J. Matera, *Romans* (Grand Rapids: Baker Academic, 2010), 291.

[109] Conzelmann, *1 Corinthians*, 134n32; Fee, *First Epistle to the Corinthians*, 346; Fitzmyer, *First Corinthians*, 320. Conzelmann notes variants for τῷ σώματι καὶ τῷ πνεύματι on 131n5. See also Clement of Rome, *Ad uirgenes epistulae duae* 1.7.2; Origen, *Hom. Exod.* 9.4 where there are some ambiguities about the identification of spirit.

[110] See the translations of τό πνεῦμα in 1 Cor 14:15 and in 14:16 in the commentary tradition.

than that which is confined to an individual body, I do not think it too difficult to accept this interpretation.

This reading of "s/Spirit" in 1 Cor 5:3a also presents a better connection to Paul's words in 5:3b–4 where he indicates the reality of his presence in the community and qualifies his own πνεῦμα with the emphatic possessive ἐμοῦ when *his* spirit is being described. The phrase ὡς παρών in 1 Cor 5:3b is often given a concessive gloss in translations—"as if (I were) present" (NRSV, CEB, ESV; Barrett, Collins, Fee, Fitzmyer, Keener, Lindemann) or "as though present" (NLT, NASB, NKJV, GNT, ASV, NET; Conzelmann, Perkins)—but these translations only make sense if one assumes a body/spirit dualism that is not native to Pauline thought.[111] Also, this reading runs afoul of Paul's various statements about πνεῦμα throughout the letter, and more immediately, is contrary to Paul's use of πάρειμι in 5:3a that emphasizes his presence in the assembly.[112] Since one major problem in Corinth was division, where some members held other leaders in higher regard than Paul, then it would have been an ineffective rhetorical tool indeed to highlight his absence and ask his auditors to mentally pretend that he was somehow present in their "minds." The implication of Paul's "real presence" is clear: his body may be across the Aegean Sea in Ephesus but in the Spirit, he is present within the gathered assembly, urging them to expel the incestuous individual.[113]

Power of the Lord in 1 Cor 5:3–5. The modern edited Greek text (NA[28]) creates a break between 1 Cor 5:4 and 5:5 by adding a comma between the two verses, with the implication that the phrase σὺν τῇ δυνάμει τοῦ κυρίου ἡμῶν Ἰησοῦ

---

[111] In the Pauline letters, πάρειμι is used to indicate Paul's real, physical presence (2 Cor 10:2; 11; 11:9; 13:2, 10; Gal 4:18, 20). The only exception to this rule is Col 1:5–6, when the subject of the verb is the gospel. In the NT, the phrase ὡς + πάρειμι is found only here and in 2 Cor 13:2 (his actual presence). While the typical translation ('as if/though...') is not impossible, this phrase in Greek literature usually describes the actual presence of the subject. See Thucydides 5.46; Euripides, *Orest.* 1104; Sophocles, *El.* 882; *Oed. tyr.* 445; *Phil.* 1420; Demosthenes, *Symm.* 25.5; *3 Aphob.* 7.4; Theophrastus, *Char.* 23.4; Diodorus Siculus, *Bib. hist.* 10.27.1; Philo, *Virt.* 30; Josephus, *Ant.* 4.309; Clement of Alexandria, *Paed.* 2.2.33.

[112] Jerome Murphy-O'Connor, *Keys to First Corinthians: Revisiting the Major Issues* (Oxford: Oxford University Press, 2009), 15n20: "The note of unreality thus implied is contradicted by the initial *parôn*."

[113] On 1 Cor 5:3a, John Chrysostom explains (*Hom. 1 Cor.* 15.3): Τοῦτο γάρ ἐστι παρεῖναι τῷ πνεύματι, ὥσπερ ὁ Ἐλισσαῖος παρῆν τῷ Γιεζῇ ... βαβαί! πόση τοῦ χαρίσματος ἡ δύναμις, ὅταν πάντας ὁμοῦ καὶ κατ'αὐτὸ εἶναι ποιῇ, καὶ τὰ πόρρωθεν εἰδέναι παρασκευάζῃ! = "For this is the meaning of being present in spirit as Elisha was present with Gehazi ... Amazing! How great the power of the gift, since it makes all things as one and together, and provides one to know the things far off!" See Chrysostom, *Hom. Col.* 1. The reference to Elisha and Gehazi is found in 2 Kings 5.

should be taken with the participle συναχθέντων from 5:4. The phrase becomes somewhat superfluous in the edited text, however, since the earlier break between 5:3 and 5:4 suggests that ἐν τῷ ὀνόματι τοῦ κυρίου [ἡμῶν] Ἰησοῦ also modifies συναχθέντων. The NA²⁸ text of 1 Cor 5:3–5 is as follows: ³ἐγὼ μὲν γάρ, ἀπὼν τῷ σώματι παρὼν δὲ τῷ πνεύματι, ἤδη κέκρικα ὡς παρὼν τὸν οὕτως τοῦτο κατεργασάμενον· ⁴ἐν τῷ ὀνόματι τοῦ κυρίου [ἡμῶν] Ἰησοῦ συναχθέντων ὑμῶν καὶ τοῦ ἐμοῦ πνεύματος σὺν τῇ δυνάμει τοῦ κυρίου ἡμῶν Ἰησοῦ, ⁵παραδοῦναι τὸν τοιοῦτον τῷ σατανᾷ εἰς ὄλεθρον τῆς σαρκός, ἵνα τὸ πνεῦμα σωθῇ ἐν τῇ ἡμέρᾳ τοῦ κυρίου. If one were to translate 5:4 as punctuated, it would read something like, "When you are gathered together and my spirit *in the name of the Lord Jesus, with the power of our Lord Jesus* ..." This construction is repetitive. Consequently, many scholars opt to interpret just one of the two prepositional phrases as modifying συναχθέντων. Their rationale for this interpretation is often left unstated while others leave this Greek construction ambiguous and underinterpreted.[114]

The cumulative effect of the inserted punctuations and the verse divisions is that interpreters are led to make erroneous conclusions regarding Paul's words in 1 Cor 5:3–5.[115] In fact, *neither* prepositional phrase is best read in relationship to συναχθέντων, though one need not deny that their gathering together is connected to the power of the Lord. Several scholars have already noted the formal and solemn nature of the penalty for the incestuous man in 1 Cor 5:1–13, and therefore, it makes this reality most explicit when the two prepositional phrases, "in the name of the Lord Jesus" and "with the power of our Lord Jesus," are understood as divine authorizations of what is to be exacted upon the transgressor. If this is accepted, then it may be appropriate to forgo the punctuation and verse divisions and to translate the relevant parts of 1 Cor 5:3–5 in the following way:

---

[114] There are three ways that scholars have opted to interpret these verses:
(i) "Gathered in the name of the Lord Jesus": ESV; NEB; NJB; Barrett; Fee; Fitzmyer; Schottroff.
(ii) "Gathered with the power of our Lord Jesus": NRSV; NET; RSV; Robertson–Plummer.
(iii) Ambiguous or connect both prepositional phrases to the participle: CEB; KJV; ASV; NASB; NKJV; NLT; Calvin; Ciampa and Rosner; Collins; Lietzmann.
  It is, however, very unlikely that both qualifications will be attached to either συναχθέντων or παραδοῦναι, leaving the other without qualification. This makes the third option the least likely solution to the problem posed by the Greek. Jerome Murphy-O'Connor, "1 Corinthians 5:3–5," *RB* 84.2 (1977): 239; Robertson–Plummer, *First Epistle*, 98.
[115] While it critically rejects the verse division, the least convincing translation may be to read 1 Cor 5:3–4a as "I have already pronounced judgment on the man who has done such a thing *in the name of the Lord Jesus*." For further bibliography and arguments against, see Fee, *First Epistle to the Corinthians*, 206n49.

1 Cor 5:3a,	"For I, on one hand absent in body, but on the other hand present in s/Spirit,"
1 Cor 5:3b–4a,	"As one present[116] I have already pronounced judgment *in the name of the Lord Jesus* on the man who has done such a thing. When you and my spirit are assembled together,"
1 Cor 4b–5a,	"*With the power of our Lord Jesus* hand over such a one to Satan."

This interpretation forms a better parallel structure between Paul's statement about judgment upon the offender and his command to the Corinthians concerning the communal act of handing over this individual to Satan.[117]

The gravity of the situation is made clearer when these grammatical issues are settled: the Corinthians' extended association with the incestuous man has put the entire assembly at peril. This kind of corruption in one of its own members requires a powerful excision, demanding the invocation of the name and power of the Lord Jesus for its efficacy.[118] Having been informed of the πορνεία, Paul tells the Corinthians that they need not wait for him to arrive physically to pass judgment upon this individual. Already, he has judged as one present (κέκρικα ὡς παρών) in the name of the Lord Jesus, and the Corinthians are to follow suit by handing him over immediately to Satan with the power of the Lord.

---

116 The participle παρών is best interpreted as an anarthrous substantive participle rather than as a circumstantial participle. See my earlier argument on Paul's use of πάρειμι.

117 Adela Yarbro Collins, "The Function of 'Excommunication' in Paul," *HTR* 73 (1980): 256–257. This is not entirely novel as many translations already connect one of the two phrases ("in the name/with the power of the Lord Jesus") either to Paul's judgment language in 1 Cor 5:3 or to communal handing over in 5:5. E.g., GNT; NIV; NLT; NRSV; RSV; Ciampa and Rosner; Fitzmyer; Havener; Robertson-Plummer.

118 The invocation of name as a source of power was not uncommon in both the Greek/Roman and Jewish/Christian contexts. 1 Kgs 18:24–26; 2 Kgs 2:24; 5:11; Ps 43:6; 53:3; 123:8; Acts 3:6; 4:7–10; 16:18; 1 Cor 16:22; *IG* III App. 108; PGM IV. See Collins, "Function,"256; Adolf Deissmann, *Light from the Ancient Near East: The New Testament Illustrated by Recently Discovered Texts of the Graeco-Roman World*, trans. Lionel R. M. Strachan (1927; reprint, Peabody, MA: Hendrickson, 1995), 305n2; Fitzmyer, *First Corinthians*, 238; John Fotopoulos, "Paul's Curse of Corinthians: Restraining Rivals with Fear and *Voces Mysticae* (1 Cor 16:22)," *NovT* 56 (2014): 275–309. Some scholars have criticized Deissmann's use of the Great Magical Papyrus of Paris as anachronistic, since the papyrus is likely of early 4th century CE origin. To his credit, it is now understood that the traditions found therein range from the first to third centuries CE. For a recent discussion of this papyrus, see Pieter W. van der Horst, "The Great Magical Papyrus of Paris (PGM IV) and the Bible," in *A Kind of Magic: Understanding Magic in the New Testament and its Religious Environment*, ed. Michael Labahn and Bert J. L. Peerbolte (London: T&T Clark, 2007), 173–183. For an excellent discussion of the milieu within which such formulae were conceived, see Christopher A. Faraone, "The Agonistic Context of Early Greek Binding Spells," in *Magika Hiera: Ancient Greek Magic and Religion*, ed. Christopher A. Faraone and Dirk Obbink (Oxford: Oxford University Press, 1991), 3–32.

Spirit in 1 Cor 5:5. In 1 Cor 5:5, Paul mentions "spirit" for the third time: ἵνα τὸ πνεῦμα σωθῇ ἐν τῇ ἡμέρᾳ τοῦ κυρίου. Again, translators are not entirely in agreement, opting for one of two ways to read this clause:

Reading #1: "so that *his spirit* may be saved..."[119]
Reading #2: "so that *the spirit* [i.e. the Spirit] may be saved..."[120]

Despite what many take to be a foregone conclusion that Paul must be talking about the spirit of the offending individual (Reading #1), I want to reconsider the viability of other alternative readings (Reading #2; and Reading #3, which will be explained below), paying special attention to patristic interpretations of this passage.

---

119 E.g., NRSV; NIV; NASB; CEB; NKJV; NLT; Fee; Robertson–Plummer; Horsley; Schottroff; Barrett; Hays. The English translation of Conzelmann's commentary (*1 Corinthians*, 94: "that *his spirit* may be saved...") is interesting since the original German allows for some ambiguity (*Der erste Brief*, 121: "damit *der Geist* am Tage des Herrn gerettet werde." [emphasis added]), also Lietzmann, *Korinther*, 22). It is possible, however, that the German article is functioning as a possessive pronoun, though in his comments that follow, Conzelmann himself seems somewhat unsure about the identity of the πνεῦμα in 1 Cor 5:5 (*1 Corinthians*, 97–98 and 98n40–41). A different German translation avoids this ambiguity: "damit sein Geist am Tag des Gerichtes gerettet werden kann" (Hoffnung für Alle translation).
See also, Ivan Havener, "A Curse for Salvation—1 Corinthians 5:1–5," in *Sin, Salvation, and the Spirit: Commemorating the Fiftieth Year of The Liturgical Press*, ed. Daniel Durken (Collegeville, MN: The Liturgical Press, 1979), 334–344; S. D. MacArthur, "'Spirit' in Pauline Usage: 1 Corinthians 5.5," in *Studia biblica 1978, III: Papers on Paul and Other New Testament Authors*, ed. E. A. Livingstone (Sheffield: JSOT Press, 1980), 249–256; James T. South, "A Critique of the 'Curse/Death' Interpretation of 1 Corinthians 5.1–8," *NTS* 39 (1993): 539–561; Robert E. Moses, "Physical and/or Spiritual Exclusion? Ecclesial Discipline in 1 Corinthians 5," *NTS* 59 (2013): 172–191.
120 E.g., Geneva Bible, ASV, KJV; Collins, *First Corinthians*, 213. Fitzmyer makes this reading even more explicit by capitalizing the word in *First Corinthians*, 239 ("so that *the Spirit* may be saved..."). One of the first scholars who argued for this position in the modern period is Karl P. Donfried, "Justification and Last Judgment in Paul," *Interpretation* 30.2 (1976): 140–152. See also, Collins, "Function," 259 ("The reference to the spirit in v 5 is best understood in terms of the Holy Spirit of God and Christ which dwells in the community."); James Benedict, "The Corinthian Problem of 1 Corinthians 5:1–8," *Brethren Life and Thought* 32.2 (1987): 70–73; Barth Campbell, "Flesh and Spirit in 1 Cor 5:5: An Exercise in Rhetorical Criticism of the NT," *JETS* 36.3 (1993): 331–342; Richard E. DeMaris, "Elimination," 39–50.

2.4.3 *Excursus:* Early Christian Interpretations of τὸ πνεῦμα in 1 Corinthians 5:5

In his commentary on 1 Corinthians, Gordon Fee concludes the following regarding early Christian interpretations of 1 Corinthians 5:5 (παραδοῦναι τὸν τοιοῦτον τῷ σατανᾷ εἰς ὄλεθρον τῆς σαρκός, ἵνα τὸ πνεῦμα σωθῇ ἐν τῇ ἡμέρᾳ τοῦ κυρίου):

> What Paul was desiring by having this man put outside the believing community was the destruction of what was "carnal" in him, so that he might be "saved" eschatologically … Apart from Tertullian (*pudic.* 13–15), who knew his view was contrary to common opinion, this was *the standard* view in the early church, being found explicitly in Origen, Chrysostom, and Theodore of Mopsuestia.[121]

Fee is referring to the fact that τὸ πνεῦμα of 1 Cor 5:5 should be read as "his spirit," namely, the spirit of the offender, and not of another entity as Tertullian proposed in *De pudicitia*. Tertullian identified "spirit" as the Spirit of God that dwelled within the church and not in an individual. Fee's conclusion that patristic exegesis of 1 Cor 5:5 was generally uniform is commonly repeated in modern scholarship.

Modern interpreters of 1 Corinthians 5:5 who mention precedents in patristic exegesis do so haphazardly. Observe the following examples: Robertson-Plummer and Thiselton only mention Origen; Collins and Campbell only Tertullian; Fitzmyer and Schrage note Tertullian and Ambrosiaster; and Shillington discusses Origen and Tertullian.[122] After reading the secondary literature that is supposed to provide modern readers with a better understanding of the patristic exegesis of 1 Cor 5:5, one may not be faulted for believing that the only early Christians who commented on this text were Origen, Tertullian, and Ambrosiaster.

This excursus was published earlier as "Τὸ πνεῦμα in 1 Corinthians 5:5: A Reconsideration of Patristic Exegesis," *VC* 72 (2018): 121–141. I would like to thank Brill and the editors of *Vigiliae Christianae* for providing permission to republish this article.

121 Fee, *First Epistle to the Corinthians*, 212 and 212n82 (emphasis added).
122 Robertson-Plummer, *First Epistle*, 100 n. * (Origen without proper primary source citation); Thiselton, *First Epistle to the Corinthians*, 396 (Origen); Fitzmyer, *First Corinthians*, 240 (Tertullian and Ambrosiaster); George T. Montague, SM, *First Corinthians* (Grand Rapids: Baker Academic, 2011), 93–94 (Theodore of Mopsuestia and Severian of Gabala); Schrage, *Korinther*, 1:378n63 (Tertullian and Ambrosiaster); Lindemann, *Korintherbrief*, 128 (Tertullian); Collins, "Function," 260 (Tertullian); Campbell, "Flesh and Spirit," 333 (Tertullian); V. George Shillington, "Atonement Texture in 1 Corinthians 5.5," *JSNT* 71 (1998): 29–50, esp. 30–31 (Origen and Tertullian); Fee, *First Epistle to the Corinthians*, 212n81 (Origen, Chrysostom, Theodore of Mopsuestia, and Tertullian, but only provides a citation from Tertullian).

2.4 Power in 1 Corinthians — 59

The actual evidence from patristic exegesis demonstrates that there were many other early Christians who read and interpreted 1 Corinthians 5:5. Moreover, it is patently wrong to accept any reading as "the standard view in the early church" and neglect other interpretations, even if it may be correct to acknowledge Origen as an important proponent of one particular reading.[123] Also, some recent scholarship has misrepresented the available data on 1 Cor 5, making a fair evaluation of the patristic exegesis of 1 Cor 5:5 more difficult still.[124] Several patristic interpreters disagreed with Origen are conveniently left out of modern discussions of this text. The excursus will first discuss Origen and other proponents of Reading #1, then turn to Tertullian and others of Read-

---

123 Fee, *First Epistle to the Corinthians*, 212n82. Fee does mention John Chrysostom and Theodore of Mopsuestia, but his references are problematic for two reasons. First, the lack of primary source citations renders his references to both figures impossible to assess (i.e. what text[s] from Chrysostom and Theodore are being referred to?). Second, while Theodore's comments on 1 Corinthians approximate Reading #1 (*PG* 66:881: τὸ μὲν, παραδοῦναι τῷ Σατανᾷ, οὐκ ὡς αὐτὸς τοῦτο γενέσθαι ὁρίζων εἶπεν = "So on one hand, 'to hand over to Satan,' he did not say this to mean literally."), it does not fully reveal how the Antiochene exegete understood τὸ πνεῦμα in 1 Cor 5:5. The following subsection shows where the evidence from Theodore of Mopsuestia precludes Fee's facile conclusion.

124 Laura L. Brenneman's dissertation ("Corporate discipline and the people of God: a study of 1 Corinthians 5.3–5," [Ph.D. diss., University of Durham, 2005]) is one example of recent scholarship that muddies the waters by providing false data and making wrong conclusions. In the opening section of her *Forschungsbericht*, she states on page 6: "A majority of the Church fathers believed that the punishment of the offender of 1 Corinthians was intended to bring about his remorse, repentance, and eventual reintegration into the Corinthian body." She then provides in n. 14 the following primary sources to justify her conclusion: Clement of Alexandria, *Strom.* 2.13; Athanasius, *Ep. mort. Ar.* 4.13; Origen, *Hom. Ps. 37* 1; Ignatius, *Phld.* 8.1; Polycarp, *Phil.* 11.4; and John Chrysostom, *Diab.* 2. With the exception of Origen and Chrysostom, the other interpreters do not have any stake in 1 Corinthians 5. Clement of Alexandria is describing repentance in general, not the incestuous man of 1 Cor 5:5, and the same goes for Ignatius. So also Polycarp, though more specific in his reference to a wayward presbyter named Valens. Athanasius is not talking about the offender in 1 Cor 5, but about whether Arius was in communion with the Church prior to his death. Brenneman completely ignores all early interpreters who follow the alternative readings (see my analysis to follow). Also, if these figures constitute the "majority," then who belonged to the "minority"? She only cites Tertullian. Even in chapter 8 where she specifically addresses patristic views about this passage, the same mode of argumentation is repeated.

In another recent dissertation (Jeremy M. Kimble, "'That His Spirit May be Saved': Church Discipline as a Means to Repentance and Perseverance," [Ph.D. diss., Southeastern Baptist Theological Seminary, 2013]), it is remarkable to find that the author never discusses the ambiguity of the Greek text of 1 Cor 5:5 and not once does he mention patristic exegesis. The author assumes that his interpretation (à la Reading #1) is axiomatic as seen by the title of the dissertation.

ing #2, and finally, to other early Christian exegetes who do not quite fit into either category (Reading #3).

Reading #1: τὸ πνεῦμα as "his spirit"
In the works of Origen (ca. 185–254 CE) we encounter the first explicit interpretation of τὸ πνεῦμα in 1 Corinthians 5:5 as "his spirit" (i.e. of the incestuous man). This reading influenced many other interpreters in early Christianity, to whom I will return below. The power of Origen's influence is clear even in modern interpretations: many scholars simply cite Origen, and often Origen only, as their patristic justification for their preference for Reading #1. The preserved Latin translation of Origen's commentary on Romans and the Greek fragments of his commentary on 1 Corinthians are the best examples of his interpretation of 1 Cor 5:5 and are worth quoting at length:

> [On Rom 6:23]: There is even a praiseworthy kind of death, namely, that by which someone dies to sin and is buried together with Christ, through which correction comes to the soul and eternal life is attained (*per quam emendation fit animae et uita aerna conquiritur*). Since then so many shades of meaning are contained in this single word, "death," when you hear God saying, "I shall kill and I shall also make alive," you need to understand what kind of death it is that befits God to inflict (*intelligere debes quae sit mors quam decet inferre Deum*). Doubtless, it is that sort of death that confers life (*conferat vitam*), i.e., that a person should die to sin and live to God... It is also in this sense that the Apostle was handing over the sinner for the destruction of the flesh in order that his spirit might be saved; that is to say, in order that he would die to sin and live to God (*Sic et Apostolus peccatorem tradebat in interitum carnis, ut spiritum faceret salvum, hoc est, ut moreretur peccato, et viveret Deo*).[125]
>
> [On 1 Cor 5:3–5]: He is handed over not for the destruction of the soul or of the spirit, but for the destruction of the flesh. He is handed over so that his spirit may be saved (τὸ πνεῦμα σωθῇ) in the day of the Lord. Paul expelled such a person without knowing if he would turn and repent but wishing to educate him (θέλων αὐτὸν παιδεῦσαι) ... Therefore, let those with evil lives be treated (θεραπευέσθωσαν) by being put outside of the flock, let them confess and lament their own sins and show evidence of repentance (τῆς μετανοίας) by fasting, mourning, weeping, and the like. They are handed over in order to be educated (παραδίδονται γὰρ ἵνα παιδευθῶσιν), so that the flesh might be destroyed, that is, the way of thinking characteristic of the flesh (τοῦτ'ἔστι τὸ φρόνημα τῆς σαρκός) ... By naming the man's superior part, Paul refers to his entire salvation (ὅλην ... τὴν σωτηρίαν); he does not say, "so that his spirit and soul and body might be saved on the day of the Lord," but that his spirit might be saved, referring to the salvation of the whole person by that of his most important

---

[125] Origen, *Comm. Rom.* 6.6.5–6 (=*PG* 14:1068; trans. Scheck). See also *Hom. Ps.* 37(38) 1.2 (= *PG* 12:1375), where Origen refers multiple times to the *sensus carnis* and argues that the destruction is *pro salute eius*.

faculty (τοῦ κρείττονος ὀνομάσας ὅλου τοῦ ἀνθρώπου τὴν σωτηρίαν). In his Second Letter Paul gives orders that this man be taken back into the church in order that he may be saved (σωθησόμενον αὐτόν) [2 Cor 2:7].[126]

A few comments should be made about Origen's interpretation and influence that his reading had upon subsequent readers of Paul.

Rather than reading 1 Corinthians 5:5 within the context of the chapter—still less within the letter—Origen depends on other texts beyond 1 Corinthians to make sense of what is described in this section of Paul's letter.[127] In his commentary on Romans, Origen borrows from the paradoxical 'dead-but-alive' concept found in Rom 6:11 ("Consider yourselves dead to sin but alive to God in Christ Jesus") as the lens through which to interpret 1 Cor 5:5. Twice he refers to Rom 6:11 and explains that this death is the only kind of death that "befits" God to bestow (*decet inferre Deum*) upon human beings. By the same token, Paul must be following a similar pattern in 1 Corinthians 5: by consigning the transgressor to destruction (=death), Paul is actually bringing about life. This interpretation may not be surprising since it is a commentary on Romans after all, but even Origen's commentary on 1 Corinthians displays a similar tendency.

In his comments on 1 Corinthians 5:5, Origen uses παιδεύω several times in order to explain the purpose of Paul's exhortation concerning the incestuous

---

126 Origen, *Fr. 1 Cor.* 24.93.1–19. The numbering of Origen's commentary follows Claude Jenkins, "Origen on 1 Corinthians," *JTS* 9 (1908): 231–247; 353–372; 500–514; and *JTS* 10 (1909): 29–51. Translation modified from Judith L. Kovacs, ed., *1 Corinthians: Interpreted by Early Christian Commentators* (Grand Rapids: Eerdmans, 2005), 84–85. My translation of the verb παιδεύω differs from that of Kovacs (see below for explanation).

127 On one hand, the initial turn to 2 Corinthians 2 is a faulty interpretative move that modern scholars sometimes make in their reading of 1 Cor 5:5. For example, even though Hays, *First Corinthians*, 86 admits that 2 Cor 2:5–11 is not about the same person from 1 Cor 5:1–13, the 2 Cor text is still brought through the backdoor, so to speak, when he insists that "Paul's belief that stern community discipline can lead to transformation and reintegration." For the same error, see Fee, *First Epistle to the Corinthians*, 212; and E. Von Dobschütz, *Die urchristlichen Gemeinden* (Leipzig: J. C. Hinrichs, 1902) 41–42: "Der Fluch ward ausgesprochen. Freilich, das Strafwunder blieb aus. Der selbstverständlich mit Exkommunikation verbundene Fluch hatte aber offenbar eine andere Wirkung: der Schuldige selbst kam zum Bewusstsein seiner Schuld und that Busse ... was uns vor allem deutlich an dem Beispiele Ninivehs die Jonaserzählung klar macht, das gilt auch für den Apostel und seine Zeit: die Wirkung des Fluches kann aufgehoben werden durch bussfertige Abkehr von der Sünde. Daraus aber ergiebt sich als praktische Konsequenz, dass in dem Ausbleiben des Gottesgerichtes eine göttliche Bestätigung der Busse des Sünders zu sehen ist." On the other hand, recent scholarship has problematized this connection between 1 Cor 5:1–13 and 2 Cor 2:5–11. Collins, *First Corinthians*, 211; Fitzmyer, *First Corinthians*, 235; David Raymond Smith, *'Hand This Man Over to Satan': Curse, Exclusion and Salvation in 1 Corinthians 5*, LNTS 386 (London: T&T Clark, 2008), 41.

man. Although Paul himself does not use παιδεύω in 1 Cor 5, Origen's reference purposefully brings to mind another text, 1 Tim 1:19b–20.[128] In this latter text, Paul[129] writes: "By rejecting conscience, certain persons have suffered shipwreck in the faith; among them are Hymenaeus and Alexander, whom I handed over to Satan, so that they may learn not to blaspheme (οὓς παρέδωκα τῷ σατανᾷ, ἵνα παιδευθῶσιν μὴ βλασφημεῖν)." For someone of Origen's educational background, for whom scriptural interpretation was a way of life, it would have been natural to bring the slight linguistic similarity of 1 Cor 5:5 and 1 Tim 1:19b–20 into conversation, i.e., the language about handing over someone to Satan.[130] Apart from this image of handing over to Satan, however, there is not much, if at all, that connects the two passages together: in 1 Timothy 1, there is nothing about the destruction of the flesh, the saving of his/the spirit, or the action of the community, and conversely, there is nothing about being taught not to blaspheme in 1 Corinthians 5.[131]

To elaborate further on παιδεύω, Origen's use of this educational terminology from 1 Tim 1:19b–20 in his comments on 1 Cor 5:1–5 is striking because this concept is not found at all in the context of the latter passage. Judith Kovacs translates Origen's use of παιδεύω as "discipline," though this is only partially correct because it misses the educational valence of παιδεύω, especially in light of what Origen says here and elsewhere in his works concerning education.[132] In other words, by focusing on "discipline," one may fail to note how Ori-

---

128 The verb παιδεύω is not a preferred term in Pauline vocabulary: 1 Cor 11:32; 2 Cor 6:9; 1 Tim 1:20; 2 Tim 2:25; Titus 2:12.
129 I make no claim about the (deutero-)Pauline authorship of 1 Timothy, but merely use the name "Paul" for the sake of simplicity. Origen accepts the Pauline authorship of 1 Tim to construct his interpretation of 1 Cor 5, so I include this exegetical move by Origen in my analysis.
130 On Origen and the dynamic relationship between biblical interpretation and the Christian life, see Peter W. Martens, *Origen and Scripture: The Contours of the Exegetical Life* (Oxford: Oxford University Press, 2012). A *TLG* search shows that in Greek literature the phrase παραδίδωμι τῷ σατανᾷ occurs for the first time in 1 Cor 5:5 and is found only one other time in the NT in 1 Tim 1:20. After the NT, the phrase is found for the first time in Origen's writings, for example, in *Philoc.* 27.8; *Schol. Apoc.* 30.39; *Fr. Ps.* 118:121; *Hom. Jer.* 1.3; 19.14; *Fr. Jer.* 48.7; and *Comm. Matt.* 16.8; 17.14.
131 Scholars now rightly conclude that these two passages are not parallel. E.g., Hays, *First Corinthians*, 86; Lindemann, *Korintherbrief*, 126; and Collins, "Function," 258. The contrast between the two texts is sharpened by the currently held view that differentiates the authentic Pauline letters from the deutero-Pauline letters.
132 In three other works, Origen puts great emphasis on the value of education for the Christian life that subsequently found both supporters and detractors. To illustrate, in *Contra Celsum* Book 3, Origen endorses the value of education and responds to Celsus's critique that Christians only recruit the vulnerable and the young when their authority figures such as fathers or teachers are

gen develops, or more precisely, creatively infuses into the text of 1 Cor 5 an educational motif. The upshot of this innovative reading is clear. First, in the rest of his comments on 1 Cor 5:1–5, Origen assumes that there is a *mental/moral* correction that must take place, and so he interprets Paul's use of σάρξ in 1 Cor 5:5 as "the mind of the flesh" (τοῦτ'ἔστι τὸ φρόνημα τῆς σαρκός).[133] Second, Origen's comments throughout portray an educational setting wherein the offending individual is taught his error and is rehabilitated back into the Corinthian assembly through a process of instruction and discipline.

We can observe here two related concepts informing Origen's exegesis, ideas that will continue to be found in other interpreters of 1 Cor 5:5: (a) a focus on the individual person; notice Origen's references to individual repentance and other ascetic duties; and (b) an emphasis on the individual's recovery.[134] This latter point is conspicuous since Paul himself never presents this idea in 1 Corinthians 5, or anywhere in the entire letter. Origen is able to forcefully argue for such a reading by infusing into his interpretation the educational aspect imported from 1 Timothy 1:20.

Origen is also a pioneer in working out the anthropological problem that presents itself once an interpreter accepts that τὸ πνεῦμα in 1 Cor 5:5 must belong to the individual offender. If the person is eventually rehabilitated and

---

absent (3.55, 58). Origen argues that if one falters in his discipline (read: education), then it would lead to behavioral issues as can be seen in 1 Cor 5. See also Origen's *Epistula ad Gregorium Thaumaturgum* and *Philocalia* 14.

133 Origen, *Fr. 1 Cor.* 24.93.12–13. This interpretation of "flesh" is one that Rudolf Bultmann would famously take up, and it continues to influence modern scholarship on this verse. Bultmann, *Theology*, 1:208–209; and Thiselton, *First Epistle to the Corinthians*, 396. The following examples are typical: Barrett, *First Epistle to the Corinthians*, 127 ("the man's essential self will be saved with the loss not only of his work but of his flesh"); Fee, *First Epistle to the Corinthians*, 212 ("the destruction of what was 'carnal' in him"); Fisk, *First Corinthians*, 27 ("His 'flesh' or 'sinful nature' will be chastened"); Klaus Thraede, "Schwierigkeiten mit 1Kor 5,1–13," *ZNW* 103.2 (2012): 177–212 (205: "Tatsächlich kann es kein Zufall sein, dass Paulus hier zwar mit seiner Dichotomie σῶμα-πνεῦμα arbeitet").

134 See, for example, Origen, *Fr. 1 Cor.* 24.93.19, where he concludes that the offender is eventually παραληφθῆναι εἰς τὴν ἐκκλησίαν. In the most exhaustive study of 1 Cor 5:5 to date, Bruce A. McDonald observes: "Origen finds it impossible to think of I Cor. 5 without thinking of the penitential structure of the Church of his day, and this has been echoed by subsequent writers." In "Spirit, Penance, and Perfection: The Exegesis of I Corinthians 5:3–5 from A.D. 200–451" (Ph.D. diss., The University of Edinburgh, 1993), 184–85. Although McDonald's work is still the most thorough study of early Christian exegesis of 1 Cor 5:5, his scope is larger (i.e. on 1 Cor 5:3–5) than that of the present essay and the identity of "spirit" in 1 Cor 5:5 is not the main question addressed in his work. Unfortunately, his dissertation is unpublished and remains difficult to access.

saved as Origen's readings of 1 Cor 5 and 2 Cor 2 tell us, what does it mean for his flesh to be "destroyed"? According to Origen, this destruction must function at the metaphorical level because the person is disciplined/educated so that they may "confess and lament their own sins ... showing evidence of repentance."[135] The flesh to be destroyed is not flesh *qua* flesh, but what he calls τὸ φρόνημα τῆς σαρκός. Origen then identifies τὸ πνεῦμα as man's "most important faculty" that subsequently becomes the object of salvation.[136] Origen is, therefore, able to argue that it is both "his flesh" and "his spirit," but only the redeemable part will be saved on the day of the Lord.

The foregoing analysis of Origen's interpretation of 1 Cor 5:5 is important because of his great influence upon subsequent interpreters of this passage. Others who subscribe to Reading #1 basically repeat Origen's arguments concerning the individual and his rehabilitation. The patristic interpreters of 1 Cor 5:5 that agree with Origen are the following: Eusebius of Caesarea, Didymus the Blind, Hilary of Poitiers, Basil the Great, Ambrose of Milan, John Chrysostom, Jerome, and Procopius of Gaza.[137]

---

135 Origen, *Fr. 1 Cor.* 24.93.9–11: ἐξομολογούμενοι καὶ πενθοῦντες τὰ ἴδια ἁμαρτήματα ... τὰ τῆς μετανοίας προσάγοντες.

136 Origen, *Fr. 1 Cor.* 24.93.18: ἀπὸ τοῦ κρείττονος ὀνομάσας ὅλου τοῦ ἀνθρώπου τὴν σωτηρίαν. Many other interpreters follow a similar path in resorting to metaphor when Paul's language does not fit into a preconceived interpretative framework.

137 Eusebius of Caesarea, *Comm. Ps.* 38:8–12 (=*PG* 23:349; note his use of ἐξομολόγησις as well as the educational valence of punishment); Didymus the Blind, *Frg. 2 Cor. 2:10* (note his use of πορνεία in reference to the figure in 2 Cor 2 that recalls 1 Cor 5); Hilary of Poitiers, *Tractatus super psalmos* 51 (§5); 59 (§3); 68 (§22); Basil the Great, *Moralia* 6.72 (notice the way he connects λύπη to μετάνοια to σωτηρία); *Ep.* 188.7; *Enarratio in prophetam Esaiam* 13.261; *Homilies on Psalms* 17.7; Ambrose of Milan, *De fuga saeculi* 2.8; *De officiis ministrorum* 3.18.109 (notice the flesh/spirit dichotomy and the following sentence: *Denique exterior corrumpitur, sed renovator interior*); *De paenitentia* 1.13 §60, 62, 65, 77, 78, and 95; 2.2 §7; John Chrysostom; *Stag.* 1.3; *Theod. laps.* 1.8 (according to Chrysostom, Paul, by destroying the flesh and saving the spirit, βουλόμενος δὲ ἡμῖν δεῖξαι, ὅτι οὐκ ἔστιν ἁμάρτημα, ὃ μὴ δύναται ἰαθῆναι. Note his use of 1 Cor 2:6 thereafter); *Adv. Jud.* 8.6–7 (note the use of θεραπεία to refer to Paul's admonition in 1 Cor 5:5); *Hom. 1 Cor.* 15.4–9; *Hom. Jo.* 57.3; *Hom. Matt.* 9.2 (note his statement that μειζόνως κερδαίνουσιν whether one is smitten by God or whipped by the devil following his citation of 1 Cor 5:5); Jerome, *Jov.* 1.8; *Lucif.* 5; *Comm. Joel* 2:25–27 (*CCL* 76.191; note his use of 1 Tim 1:20); *Ruf.* 2.7; and Procopius of Gaza, *Catena in Esaiam* (=*PG* 87.2:2073–75). Even Augustine (354–430 CE), who one might assume to be distant from Origen, agrees with the latter's reading of 1 Cor 5:5 in many ways. In two places, Augustine links 1 Tim 1:20 and 1 Cor 5:5 together: *Ep.* 93.7 and *Exp. Gal.* 32.9–10. In the letter, Augustine argues that Paul deemed it a "bonum opus" to correct wayward individuals by using the evil one, and in his commentary on Galatians, Augustine asserts that Satan is used "*ad correptionem ... ad salutem.*" In *Parm.* 3.3, Augustine interprets τὸ πνεῦμα of 1 Cor 5:5 basically as "*his* spirit." In the dialogues of Adamantius (fl. 4th century CE), *De recta*

This is an impressive list of patristic thinkers, and one cannot resort to a simple Antiochene/Alexandrian dichotomy to make sense of the data. More important for the present discussion, however, is that their exegeses of 1 Cor 5:5 present nothing innovative compared to what Origen already argued.[138] For example, in his *Homilies on 1 Corinthians*, John Chrysostom (a) identifies τὸ πνεῦμα as the "soul"; (b) names Satan as "instructor" (παιδαγωγός) who would play a disciplinary role to the errant sinner; and (c) leaves open the possibility that the repentant person would be accepted back "with all earnestness."[139] These are all hallmarks of Origen's exegesis that I analyzed above. Margaret Schatkin has argued that while Chrysostom was not an Origenist in the strict sense, he was nevertheless "profoundly influenced" by Origen including his scriptural exegesis.[140] Ambrose of Milan also focuses on the positive value of penance by stating that "the destruction of the flesh leads to gain for the spirit" and follows this observation with a quotation of 1 Cor 5:5.[141] Moreover, what

---

in *Deum fide* 2.825d–826b, one can also find some resonance of Origen, which is not surprising since the latter is credited with "paternity of the dialogue." Ilaria L.E. Ramelli, "The *Dialogue of Adamantius*: A Document of Origen's Thought? (Part Two)," StPatr 56 (2013): 268; idem, "Origen in Augustine: A Paradoxical Reception," *Numen* 60 (2013): 380–307.

138 See footnote #137 with included commentary on how the interpretations of 1 Cor 5:5 by these patristic exegetes recall Origen's exegesis of this text.

139 John Chrysostom, *Hom. 1 Cor.* 15.4–9 (=*PG* 61:123–26): καὶ ὥσπερ παιδαγωγῷ τὸν τοιοῦτον παραδιδούς ... ἵνα τὸ πνεῦμα σωθῇ ἐν τῇ ἡμέρᾳ τοῦ Κυρίου Ἰησοῦ. Τουτέστιν, ἡ ψυχή ... Ἐπειδὴ δὲ μετενόησε, μετὰ πάσης αὐτὸν εἰσήγαγε πάλιν τῆς σπουδῆς = "And as to an instructor delivering up such a one ... so that the spirit may be saved on the day of the Lord Jesus. That is, the soul ... And as soon as he [the sinner] repented, he [Paul] brought him [the sinner] in again with all earnestness." Chrysostom is somewhat more careful than Origen in his interpretation because he admits in *Hom. 1 Cor.* 15.9 (=*PG* 61:126): Ἐν τῇ προτέρᾳ Ἐπιστολῇ οὐ δίδωσιν ἐλπίδας ἐπανόδου τῷ πεπορνευκότι, ἀλλὰ πάντα αὐτοῦ τὸν βίον ἐν μετανοίᾳ κελεύει γενέσθαι = "In the first letter [1 Cor], he does not give to the fornicator hope of return, but commands his entire life to be [spent] in repentance." Despite this recognition, Chrysostom still insists on the possibility of the sinner's reincorporation into the Corinthian community, and elsewhere emphasizes the restorative nature of punishment: *Laud. Paul.* 3; 6; *Hom. Act. 9:1* 3.1; *Hom. 2 Cor.* 15.2; *Hom. Jo.* 38.1 (specific reference to 1 Cor 5:5); *Hom. Rom.* 13.6; *Paenit.* 1.3; *Ep. Olymp.* 2.3 (specific reference to 1 Cor 5:5).

140 Margaret A. Schatkin, "The Origenism of St. John Chrysostom in the West: From St. Jerome to the Present," in *Origeniana Undecima: Origen and Origenism in the History of Western Thought. Papers of the 11th International Origen Congress, Aarhus University, 26–31 August 2013*, ed. Anders-Christian Jacobsen (Leuven: Peeters, 2016), 136.

141 Ambrose of Milan, *De officiis ministrorum* 3.18.109: *Denique exterior corrumpitur, sed renovator interior. Nec solum in baptismate sed etiam in paenitentia fit carnis interitus ad profectum spiritus, sicut apostolica docemur auctoritate dicente sancto Paulo: Iudicavi ut praesens eum qui sic operatus est, tradere huiusmodi Satanae in interitum carnis, ut spiritus salvus sit in die Domini*

is noteworthy about the above list of interpreters is that most of them were loyal followers or admirers of Origen, and/or the latter's reading of Scripture heavily influenced their own interpretations.¹⁴² Therefore, to borrow an analogy from

---

nostri Iesu Christi. = "Then, the outer human is destroyed, but the inner human is renewed. And it is not only in baptism that the destruction of the flesh leads to gain for the spirit: the same is also true of penance, as we are taught by apostolic authority, as Saint Paul says: 'As if I was present with you, I have judged the person who did this deed: deliver such a person to Satan for the destruction of the flesh, so that his spirit may be saved on the day of our Lord Jesus Christ.'"
142 It should be acknowledged that just because an interpreter was influenced by Origen's reading of x, it does not follow that they were dependent on the latter's reading of 1 Corinthians 5:5. From the survey of literature (see note below), however, it is very probable that many of these early Christian interpreters were privy not just to fragments of Origen's writings, but were exposed to a large part of Origen's diverse corpus, and were very much indebted to his overall mode of interpretation. Furthermore, the fact that Origen expounds upon 1 Cor 5:5 in the same manner in numerous extant works is yet more proof that subsequent interpreters were likely exposed to Origen's interpretation of this passage in one way or another. Origen, *Comm. Matt.* 16.8; *Comm. Matt.* (Lat.) 65; *Comm. Rom.* 6.6.5–6; *Hom. Ps.* 37 1.2; *Fr. 1 Cor.* 24.93; *Fr. Jer.* 48; *Fr. Ps.* 37:4; *Hom. Jer.* 1.3–4; *Hom. Ezech.* 3.8; *Hom. Lev.* 14.4.

On early accounts of Origen's influence, see Eusebius, *Hist. eccl.* 6.2; Jerome, *Epist.* 39; *Vir. ill.* 61, 75. For scholarship on these patristic interpreters and their various relationship to and being influenced by Origen, see: George Lewis, trans., *The Philocalia of Origen, A Compilation of Selected Passages from Origen's Works Made by St. Gregory of Nazianzus and St. Basil of Caesarea* (Edinburgh: T&T Clark, 1911); Emile Goffinet, *L'utilisation d'Origène dans le commentaire des Psaumes de Saint Hilaire de Poitiers* (Louvain: Publications universitaires, 1965); Margaret A. Schatkin, "The Influence of Origen Upon St. Jerome's Commentary on Galatians," *VC* 24 (1970): 49–58; Philip Sellew, "Achilles or Christ? Porphyry and Didymus in Debate over Allegorical Interpretation," *HTR* 82.1 (1989): 79–100; Christoph Markschies, "Ambrosius und Origenes: Bemerkungen zur exegetischen Hermeneutik zweier Kirchenväter," in *Origeniana Septima: Origenes in den Auseinandersetzungen des 4 Jahrhunderts*, ed. W. A. Bienert and U. Kühneweg (Louvain: Leuven University Press, 1999), 545–70; Richard A. Layton, "Propatheia: Origen and Didymus on the Origin of the Passions," *VC* 54.3 (2000): 262–82; Peter W. Martens, "Interpreting Attentively: The Ascetic Character of Biblical Exegesis According to Origen and Basil of Caesarea," in *Origeniana Octava: Origen and the Alexandrian Tradition* (Leuven: Leuven University Press, 2003), 1115–21; Yves-Marie Duval, *L'affaire Jovinien. D'une crise de la société romaine à une crise de la pensée chrétienne à la fin due IVe et au début du Ve siècle* (Roma: Instututum Patristicum Augustinianum, 2003), 112–43, 162–3; Bas ter Haar Romeny, "Procopius of Gaza and His Library," in *From Rome to Constantinople: Studies in Honour of Averil Cameron*, ed. H. Amirav and B. ter Haar Romeny (Leuven: Peeters, 2007), 173–90; Blossom Steaniw, *Mind, Text, and Commentary: Noetic Exegesis in Origen of Alexandria, Didymus the Blind, and Evagrius Ponticus* (Frankfurt am Main: Lang, 2010); Ilaria Ramelli, "Origen's Anti-Subordinationism and its Heritage in the Nicene and Cappadocian Line," *VC* 65.1 (2011): 21–49; Albert-Kees Geljon, "Didymus the Blind: Commentary on Psalm 24 (23 LXX): Introduction, Translation, and Commentary," *VC* 65.1 (2011): 50–73; Andrew Radde-Gallwitz, "The Holy Spirit as Agent, not Activity: Origen's Argument with Modalism and its Afterlife in Didymus, Eunomius, and Gregory of Nazianzus," *VC*

New Testament textual criticism, their interpretations of 1 Cor 5:5 should not be accepted as independent witnesses for Reading #1, but more likely as those that belong to the same family, with Origen as the *fons et origo*. But even if I may be wrong on this specific point, the following sections prove my overall thesis: many early Christian exegetes presented very diverse ways of reading 1 Cor 5:5.

Reading #2: τὸ πνεῦμα as "the Spirit"

If Origen is the earliest exemplar of Reading #1 (τὸ πνεῦμα = "his spirit"), then Tertullian is the earliest exemplar of Reading #2 (= "the Spirit"), though we will see that he was not alone in proposing this reading. This reading sharply diverges from Reading #1, since it interprets the phrase τὸ πνεῦμα in 1 Corinthians 5:5 as referring to the Spirit of God dwelling in the church and not to the individual human spirit. In *De pudicitia*, Tertullian helpfully lays out the logic behind his interpretation of 1 Cor 5:5:

> And on this question, it may be asked whether or not it is the spirit of this individual who will be saved (*si spiritus hominis ipsius saluus erit*). But can a spirit defiled by such a terrible crime be saved, when the flesh is delivered to destruction for this crime? Will he be saved through punishment? If so, the interpretation of the other side must acknowledge that there is a punishment without the flesh. But then the resurrection of the flesh is lost (*Sic resurrectionem carnis amittimus*). It remains only to conclude that he [Paul] wanted to speak about the spirit which is supposed to dwell in the church and which must be presented safe and sound on the day of the Lord, i.e., pure from all the contamination of such impurity, once this incestuous fornicator is thrown out (*Superest igitur ut eum spiritum dixerit, qui in ecclesia censetur, saluum id est integrum praestandum in die Domini ab immunditiarum contagione eiecto incesto fornicatore*). For he has continued, "Do you not know that a little leaven leavens the whole dough?" And the incestuous fornication, however, was not a little, but a large leaven (*grande fermentum*).[143]

After this section, Tertullian discusses 2 Corinthians 2 and rejects the argument that this later passage concerns the same individual from 1 Corinthians 5, an astute observation that eventually became thoroughly argued in modern Pauline

---

65.3 (2011): 227–248; Christopher A. Beeley, *The Unity of Christ: Continuity and Conflict in Patristic Tradition* (New Haven: Yale University, 2012), esp. 3–104; Ashish J. Naidu, *Transformed in Christ: Christology and the Christian Life in John Chrysostom* (Eugene, OR: Pickwick Publications, 2012), 40; Matthew R. Crawford, "Scripture as 'One Book': Origen, Jerome, and Cyril of Alexandria on Isaiah 29:11," *JTS* 64.1 (2013): 137–153; Grant D. Bayliss, *The Vision of Didymus the Blind: A Fourth-Century Virtue-Origenism* (Oxford: Oxford University Press, 2015), esp. 17–29.
143 Tertullian, *Pud.* 13.24–26.

scholarship.¹⁴⁴ In Tertullian's comments, we can notice various details that distinguish his interpretation from that of Origen and other proponents of Reading #1.

First, Tertullian takes seriously the immediate context of 1 Corinthians 5:5 that remains ignored in Origen's interpretation. Tertullian recognizes the import of Paul's reference to the exodus tradition in 1 Cor 5:6b that shows that the apostle's concern was not with reincorporating the undesirable agent back into the dough, but precisely the opposite: save the dough by ejecting what Tertullian calls the *grande fermentum*. This emphasis is made explicit when he states unequivocally: *Sic igitur et incestum fornicatorem non in emendationem, sed in perditionem tradidit satanae.*¹⁴⁵ To miss this immediate context of 1 Cor 5:5 is a serious oversight by Origen and by others who follow Reading #1: they do not discuss the implication that 1 Cor 5:6b–7 holds for 5:5. Second, Tertullian's ecclesiocentric reading of τὸ πνεῦμα is an important counterpoint to the individualistic one of Reading #1. Third, rather than an educational setting envisaged by Origen, Tertullian draws a more precarious picture of pollution and purity that corresponds with the overall tenor of Paul's language in 1 Cor 5:1–13.

There are also other patristic interpreters who arrived at similar conclusions to those of Tertullian: Epiphanius of Salamis and Ambrosiaster.¹⁴⁶ In *Panarion* 66.86, Epiphanius inveighs against Mani's teaching that the spirit is saved without the body. Like Tertullian, Epiphanius is troubled by the mechanism of the resurrection if the man's spirit is saved yet his flesh is destroyed (66.86.2).¹⁴⁷ Epiphanius explains further:

---

144 Tertullian, *Pud.* 14.1–3. See C. K. Barrett, "Ο ΑΔΙΚΗΣΑΣ (2 Cor 7.12)," in *Essays on Paul* (Philadelphia: Westminster, 1982), 111; Derek R. Brown, *The God of this Age: Satan in the Churches and Letters of the Apostle Paul* (Tübingen: Mohr Siebeck), 163; Rudolf Bultmann, *The Second Letter to the Corinthians*, ed. E. Dinkler, trans. R. A. Harrisville (Minneapolis: Augsburg, 1985), 48; Campbell, "Flesh and Spirit," 342n35; Fitzmyer, *First Corinthians*, 235; Murray J. Harris, *The Second Epistle to the Corinthians: A Commentary on the Greek Text* (Grand Rapids: Eerdmans, 2005), 7; Hays, *First Corinthians*, 86; W. G. Kümmel, *Introduction to the New Testament*, trans. H. C. Kee, rev. ed. (Nashville: Abingdon, 1975), 283–284; Smith, *Curse*, 41.

145 Tertullian, *Pud.* 13.22: "Therefore, it was not for his improvement, but for his destruction that the incestuous fornicator was delivered to Satan."

146 Unlike Origen et al., these interpreters likely came to similar conclusions independent of the other. The only work that connects Tertullian with Epiphanius or Ambrosiaster is Marie-Pierre Bussières, "Les *quaestiones* 114 et 115 de l'Ambrosiaster ont-elles été influencées par l'apologétique de Tertullien?" *Revue de Études Augustiniennes* 48 (2002): 101–130.

147 Epiphanius, *Pan.* 66.86.2 (trans. Williams): "But the destruction of the flesh is its entire reduction to nothing. If the flesh is reduced to nothing by the devil's agency, and the spirit is saved, how can there still be a resurrection of bodies or flesh, and a salvation of spirit?"

> Then again, in place of the illustration of our own bodies, he introduces the illustration of the body of Christ, "As we are the body of Christ and members in particular" [1 Cor 12:27] … Now if God's church is a body, it is one spirit when it is joined to the Spirit, that is, to the Lord [1 Cor 6:17], then a member who sins ceases to be spirit and becomes entirely flesh, in his soul and body, and everything in him. Otherwise, how could part of someone be delivered to Satan and part not delivered (ἐπεὶ πῶς ἐδύνατο μέρος παραδοθῆναι τῷ σατανᾷ καὶ μέρος μὴ παραδοθῆναι;)? Paul did not say that the man's flesh was delivered to Satan, but ordered the delivery of "such a one" … If he has delivered him whole, however, he has declared that he is entirely flesh. But he said that "the spirit" is saved at the day of the Lord, so that the church would not be held responsible for the fault of the man who fell, and the whole church polluted by the transgression of the one. Thus what he means is, "Deliver the one who has fallen, that the spirit, that is, the whole church, may be saved (ἵνα τὸ πνεῦμα, τουτέστιν ὅλη ἡ ἐκκλησία, σωθῇ)."[148]

Epiphanius's interpretation parallels Tertullian's, though "spirit" is identified here as "the whole church," rather than simply as "the spirit of the church" as Tertullian argued in *De pudicitia*.

Ambrosiaster is another interpreter who understood τὸ πνεῦμα in 1 Corinthians 5:5 as a reference to something more than the human spirit. In his comments on this verse, Ambrosiaster writes:

> This corrupt man is being handed over to Satan so that the Holy Spirit can be preserved in the members of the congregation on the day of judgment (*ut spiritus sanctus salvus sit in hominibus ecclesiae in die iudicii*) … Paul says to the Romans: "Whoever does not have the spirit of Christ does not belong to him," and in another epistle he writes: "Do not grieve the Holy Spirit of God." For if the Holy Spirit is grieved he will depart and is not protected (*si enim contristatur, deserit et non est salvus*). Of course, he is not unprotected from his own standpoint, since he is incapable of suffering, but he is unprotected as far as we are concerned (*et non est [erit] salvus, non utique sibi, qui impassibilis est*), who need him to prove that we children of God. Something that is lost is not protected, not from its own point of view, but from the standpoint of the person who loses it (*res enim quae amittitur, salva non est, non utique sibi, quae ubicunque sit necesse est sit, sed ei a quo amittitur*).[149]

The above comments are helpful because they show an attempt to negotiate the tension between the two readings represented by Origen and Tertullian. Ambrosiaster asserts that while it is *the* Holy Spirit that will be preserved among the members of the Corinthian assembly, this does not mean that human activity

---

148 Epiphanius, *Pan.* 66.86.7–10 (trans. Williams).
149 Ambrosiaster, *In Epistulas ad Corinthios I* 5:5 (trans. Bray). Ambrosiaster's commentary was wrongly attributed to Ambrose of Milan for many centuries, though now understood to be written by Ambrosiaster because the style and content of this writing differs substantially from the genuine writings of Ambrose. See "Ambrosiaster," in *Oxford Dictionary of the Christian Church*, ed. F. L. Cross and E. A. Livingstone, 3rd ed. (Oxford: Oxford University Press, 2005), 1:51.

can bring about the destruction of the Spirit of God. To be fair, Tertullian did not state explicitly that the Holy Spirit could be harmed, but his comments above show that he did not fully consider the ramification of his argument that "the spirit ... must be presented safe and sound on the day of the Lord."[150] Ambrosiaster understood the problem posed by such a reading when stating unequivocally that the Spirit "is incapable of suffering" (*qui inpassibilis est*), though it is also true that it remains vulnerable (*si enim contristatur, deserit, et non est [erit] salvus, non utique sibi*) from the standpoint of humans. This is an ingenious way to protect the nature of the Holy Spirit while simultaneously taking seriously Paul's words in 1 Cor 5:5 and elsewhere.[151]

Reading #3: Τὸ πνεῦμα as gift

There are several interpretations of 1 Corinthians 5:5 that do not fit neatly into either reading, and therefore belong to a third category that has, to my knowledge, never been articulated as such in modern scholarship. These interpreta-

---

[150] Tertullian, *Pud.* 13.25.

[151] Andreas Lindemann basically repeats Ambrosiaster: "für Paulus damit das Ziel verbindet, den in der Gemeinde präsenten Geist Gottes so zu bewahren" (*Korintherbrief*, 128). One aspect of patristic interpretation of τὸ πνεῦμα that remains ignored is early Christian discussions of Pauline grammar. For example, in his *Letters to Serapion*, Athanasius observes: "Tell us, then, is there any passage in the divine Scripture where the Holy Spirit is found simply referred to as 'spirit' without the addition of 'of God,' or 'of the Father,' or 'my,' or 'of Christ' himself, and 'of the Son,' or 'from me (that is, from God), or with the article (μετὰ τοῦ ἄρθρου) so that he is called not simply 'spirit' but 'the Spirit' (μὴ ἁπλῶς λέγηται πνεῦμα, ἀλλὰ τὸ Πνεῦμα) ... that, just because you heard the word 'spirit,' you take it to be the Holy Spirit? ... To sum up, unless the article is present (ἄνευ τοῦ ἄρθρου) or the above-mentioned addition, it cannot refer to the Holy Spirit ... there is no doubt that it is the Holy Spirit who is intended; especially when it has the article (ὅτι τὸ Πνεῦμα τὸ ἅγιον σημαίνεται, ἔχον μάλιστα τὸ ἄρθρον)." *Ep. Serap.* 1.4 (trans. C. R. B. Shapland). See also Didymus the Blind, *On the Holy Spirit* 3 (the paragraph numbering follows *PG* 39; trans. DelCogliano et al.): "This is why Paul also speaks of him using the definite article (*articulo*), attesting that he is unique and one. Paul says, 'And as the Holy Spirit said' [ref: Heb 3:7], not with an unmodified (*non simpliciter*) Πνεῦμα ἅγιον, that is, 'a holy spirit,' but he adds the definite article (*articuli*), τὸ Πνεῦμα τὸ ἅγιον, that is, 'the Holy Spirit.' Paul also signals that Isaiah prophesied using the definite article (*articulata*): διὰ τοῦ ἁγίου Πνεύματος, that is, 'through the Holy Spirit' [ref: Acts 28:25], and not with an unmodified (*non simpliciter*) διὰ ἁγίου Πνεύματος, that is, 'through a holy spirit.'" Didymus later argues that "articulo" in discussions of the Holy Spirit is the "singularitatis significator" (*On the Holy Spirit* 15). Unfortunately, the Greek original of Didymus's text is lost: our extant copy is Jerome's Latin translation, *Liber Didymi de Spiritu Sanctu* (ca. 385 CE). The Fifth Ecumenical Council in Constantinople condemned Didymus in 553 CE for being an "Origenist," though on this point regarding τὸ πνεῦμα he diverges from Origen.

tions propose an understanding of "spirit" as gift that prevents reading τὸ πνεῦ-μα in 1 Cor 5:5 as a synonym for, or as an inherent part of, the incestuous man. A Syriac manuscript of Theodore of Mopsuestia's *Commentary on Baptism and Eucharist* contains an interesting elaboration about the vulnerability of the Holy Spirit that echoes what Ambrosiaster said, though not quite the same either:

> He ordered him to be delivered to Satan ... the purpose of this by saying, "for the destruction of his flesh (*pgrh*), that he may live in spirit (*brwḥ'*) in the day of our Lord Jesus Christ." As if he were saying: I order this so that he may suffer and be conscious of his sins, and receive reproof ... and after he has thus moved away from sin, he will receive full salvation in the next world, because at his baptism, he had received the gift of the Spirit, which left him when he sinned and persisted in his sin. He undoubtedly calls the salvation of the spirit the turning away from sins and the full reception of the Holy Spirit (*rwḥ' dqwdš'*), who will cause him to revert to his previous state.[152]

In his citation of 1 Cor 5:5, there is the possessive pronoun "his" with "flesh" (*pgrh*) but Theodore does not add the same pronoun to "spirit" (*rwḥ'*) when he could have very easily done so to clearly identify its subject. Some may argue that he is merely taking over the citation from the Syriac Peshitta but this raises the question: why does the Syriac text not simply refer to "his spirit" and why does it contain the preposition *bet* that appears to distinguish the person from "spirit"?[153] Subsequently, the identity of this spirit is made clearer by his reference to "the holy spirit" (*rwḥ' dqwdš'*). On one hand, Theodore's concept of

---

[152] Theodore of Mopsuestia, *Commentary on the Eucharist and Liturgy* in A. Mingana, *Woodbrooke Studies*, vol. 6 (Cambridge: W. Heffer & Sons, Ltd., 1933), 121–2 (translation), 263 (Syriac). The introduction to the excursus observed Fee's reference to Theodore of Mopsuestia as a proponent of Reading #1, but the foregoing evidence clearly demonstrates that such a conclusion needs to be nuanced. Another figure that may belong to this third category may be Thomas Aquinas, but because he postdates the patristic era by several centuries, I do not place him within a specific category. Aquinas tries to bridge the gap between Readings #1 and #2 by arguing that "the spirit may be saved, i.e., that the sinner, recognizing his vileness, may repent and thus be healed ... this can also mean that his Spirit, namely, the Church's Holy Spirit, may be saved for the faithful in the day of judgment, i.e., that they not destroy it by contact with the sinner" (*ut spiritus salvus sit, ut scilicet peccatorum turpitudinem cognoscens confundatur et poeniteat, et sic sanetur ... potest etiam intelligi, ut Spiritus eius, scilicet Ecclesiae, id est Spiritus Sanctus Ecclesiae salvus sit fidelibus in diem iudicii, ne scilicet perdant eum per contagium peccatoris*). In Commentary on the Letters of Saint Paul to the Corinthians, trans. Larcher, Mortensen, and Keating, ed. Mortensen and Alarcón (Lander, WY: The Aquinas institute for the Study of Sacred Doctrine, 2012), 90–91.

[153] In other words, even if Theodore of Mopsuestia took over the Syriac Peshitta directly, then someone before him clearly made an interpretative move that gave this Syriac version a different gloss from the Greek text.

"(Holy) spirit" as "gift/grace" (*tybwt'*) obviously diverges from Reading #1 that read τὸ πνεῦμα of 1 Cor 5:5 simply as "his spirit." On the other hand, the exhortation towards repentance is focused on individual rehabilitation, and does not fit with Reading #2.

There are two other figures that also interpret 1 Cor 5:5 in ways that do not belong to the earlier categories. Theodoret of Cyrus writes in his commentary on 1 Corinthians:

> So to instruct/discipline the body only, furnishing to the soul a beneficial remedy out of instruction. And here by "spirit" he refers not to the soul but to the gift of grace. For I do all these things, he says, so that this (i.e. spirit) may be preserved in him until the coming of our savior.[154]

Just as in Theodore, the distinction here made between "spirit" and "soul" is an interesting interpretation, and militates against the anthropological concern of Reading #1.[155] This contrast between the human being and spirit is further noticeable in Theodoret's last comment that "this (spirit)" would be preserved in the person, which means that he is reading τὸ πνεῦμα differently from "his spirit." And above all, we can notice his emphatic statement that that spirit refers to τὸ χάρισμα. This is a highly loaded term in the New Testament, occurring most frequently in the Pauline letters: Paul never uses this term to refer to something that belongs inherently to the human being.[156] Finally, besides Theodore of Mopsuestia and Theodoret of Cyrus, Severian of Gabala also read this text similarly. In two fragmentary recensions of his work, he asserts:

Recension #1 = The spirit is not the soul, but he was speaking about the gift.
Recension #2 = That the man may be handed over to sufferings of life; for this is the destruction of the flesh, not the destruction of the soul, in order that through the things that occur in the body, he may repent being awoken and the spirit may be preserved in him, which is the gift.[157]

---

154 Theodoret of Cyrus, *Comm. 1 Cor.* on 5:5 (= *PG* 82:261): ὥστε μόνον παιδεῦσαι τὸ σῶμα· τῇ γὰρ ψυχῇ τὸ ἐκ τῆς παιδείας κατασκευάζει φάρμακον ἀλεξίκακον. Πνεῦμα δὲ ἐνταῦθα οὐ τὴν ψυχὴν καλεῖ, ἀλλὰ τὸ χάρισμα. Ταῦτα γάρ, φησί, πάντα ποιῶ, ἵνα τοῦτο ἐν αὐτῷ φυλαχθῇ ἕως τῆς τοῦ Σωτῆρος ἡμῶν ἐπιφανείας.
155 See earlier examples of this interpretation in John Chrysostom's *Homilies on 1 Corinthians*.
156 E.g., Rom 1:11; 11:29; 12:6; 1 Cor 1:7; 7:7; 12:4, 9, 28, 30, 31; 2 Cor 1:11; 1 Tim 4:14; 2 Tim 1:6.
157 Recension #1: τὸ πνεῦμα οὐ τὴν ψυχήν, ἀλλὰ τὸ χάρισμα ἔφασαν / Recension #2: ταῖς τοῦ βίου κακώσεσι παραδίδωσιν· τοῦτο γάρ ἐστιν τὸ εἰς ὄλεθρον τῆς σαρκός, οὐκ εἰς ἀπώλειαν ψυχῆς, ἵνα ἐκ τῶν συμβαινόντων τῷ σώματι διεγερθεὶς μετανοήσῃ καὶ σωθῇ τὸ ἐν αὐτῷ πνεῦμα ὅπερ ἐστι τὸ χάρισμα. The Greek fragments of Severian are found in Karl Staab, *Pauluskommentare aus der Griechischen Kirche* (Münster: Aschendorffschen, 1933), 244.

Again, the evidence from Severian shows that some exegetes did not want to read "spirit" as a cypher for the human being or soul. Furthermore, this interpretation of spirit as gift is one that could not be found in Readings #1 and #2 yet occurs several times in these various interpreters. In summary, the foregoing exegeses from Theodore of Mopsuestia, Theodoret of Cyrus, and Severian of Gabala show that Readings #1 and #2 were not the only possible options for early Christian interpretations of 1 Cor 5:5.

Conclusion

Recent scholarship on the question of patristic exegesis of 1 Corinthians 5:5 has severely minimized or misrepresented the data. Modern scholars are free to evaluate the explanatory power or weaknesses of each of the readings presented above, but they can no longer assume that there was any kind of consensus among early Christians regarding their interpretations of this text. Reading #1 is well represented, with Origen and a number of other well-known patristic exegetes, but the alternatives #2 and #3 also have on their side interpreters such Tertullian, Epiphanius, Ambrosiaster, and Theodore of Mopsuestia, many of whom remain ignored in current literature. In light of the data presented, there was indeed no such thing as "the standard view" when it came to early Christian interpretations of τὸ πνεῦμα in 1 Corinthians 5:5, but only a variety of exegesis that display robust understandings of "spirit" variously construed.

What are some implications for reading 1 Cor 5:5 in view of these various interpretations of τὸ πνεῦμα in 1 Cor 5:5? First, both Readings #2 and #3 show that many exegetes imagined that the presence of God's spirit was a fragile entity within the Christian assembly. This interpretation does not cohere well with Reading #1, but remains plausible as seen in Epiphanius and Ambrosiaster. Such an ecclesial understanding of "spirit" is one that Paul himself hinted at in 1 Cor 3:16–17 and 6:17–19, and accords well with Paul's concern for the preservation of the pure whole in 1 Cor 5:1–13. Second, I have introduced a third category (Reading #3) that has, to my knowledge, never been investigated as a different mode of interpretation from other patristic exegetes. The concept of Spirit as gift is an important marker of this reading that has no parallel in the other readings. Third, this excursus has shown that patristic exegetes read this text in far more diverse ways than is usually assumed in modern scholarship, and simply the recognition of such alternative readings may provide scholars with new ways to interpret this text.

Returning to 1 Corinthians 5, there are two other reasons besides the patristic exegesis of this passage that contribute to my reading of "the Spirit" in 1 Corinthians 5:5: Paul's grammar and the context of 1 Cor 5 itself (anticipated by Tertullian). First, it is unusual for Paul to use the articular form, τὸ πνεῦμα, without qualification to describe human spirit(s), and more importantly, he never uses the nominative articular form to describe anything other than *the* Holy Spirit.[158] I also noted above that early interpreters analyzed Paul's grammatical tendencies in their own readings of his letters.[159] Paul's use of the articular form is not just a Pauline characteristic, but a practice that seems to have been adopted at a very early stage in Christian theology, since other New Testament writers and early Christians all follow the same pattern.[160] Interpreting τὸ πνεῦμα as "the Spirit," however, is not without its own problems since the Spirit is never described as the object of σῴζω in Paul and the rest of the NT. Contrary to the argument of some scholars, I do not believe this to be nearly as fatal for reading "the Spirit" in 1 Cor 5:5 as they make it out to be.[161]

The fact that this may be an anomaly in Pauline language is something to take into account, though there are other related statements in 1 Corinthians also quite rare in the Pauline corpus that can help alleviate the pressure to interpret 1 Cor 5 in only one way.[162] For example, consider what Paul says in

---

158 Rom 8:16, 26; 1 Cor 5:5; 2 Cor 3:17.

159 See the primary source references in footnote #151.

160 Mark 1:12; John 6:63; Acts 2:4; 8:18, 29; 10:19; 11:12; Jas 4:5; 1 John 5:6, 8; Rev 2:7, 11, 17, 29; 3:6, 13, 22; 14:13; 22:17; Ign. *Phld.* 7.1; Did. 4:10; Barn. 12:2; 19:7. NB: These are not just *some* of the texts that use τὸ πνεῦμα in reference to the Holy Spirit, but the *only* texts wherein the authors use the unqualified nominative articular form of "spirit." The only exception to this rule found in the NT and early Christian literature is Mark 9:20.

161 E.g., Hays, *First Corinthians*, 86; Moses, "Ecclesial Discipline." Moses ("Ecclesial Discipline," 176) creates a false dichotomy between the traditional reading and the one proposed here, namely that the latter would imply "ascribing atoning significance to the death of the incestuous man" though it is clearly shown here that one can re-interpret "the spirit" of 1 Cor 5:5 anew without freighting it with such a theological construct that Moses describes. He is arguing against a reading proposed in Shillington ("Atonement Texture"), but one need not adopt the Shillington's position. Against these readings, Luke Timothy Johnson convincingly detected the "social dimension" of salvation in the Pauline letters without jettisoning the individual aspect of such language ("The Social Dimensions of Sōtēria in Luke-Acts and Paul," in *Contested Issues in Christian Origins and the New Testament* [Leiden: Brill, 2013], 183–204; originally published in *Society of Biblical Literature Seminar Papers*, ed. E.H. Levering [Atlanta: Scholars Press, 1993], 520–536).

162 If Paul's words are taken at face value and in their proper context—important points that are explained below—his statement about "the Spirit" in 1 Cor 5:5 would not be all that difficult to accept. The issue arises when one reads through Paul's letters, formulates a preconceived construct of what is or is not "Pauline," and then performs *Sachkritik* on Paul's own words to make it mean what one would like it to mean rather than taking Paul on his own terms. 1 Cor 6:16–17 is yet another passage where Paul makes reference to the Spirit/power dynamic that he makes

1 Cor 3:16–17: "Do you not know that you are the temple of God and the Spirit of God dwells in you? If anyone destroys the temple of God, God will destroy such a one. For God's temple is holy and you are that temple." This concept of the community as the temple of God is not found elsewhere besides 2 Cor 6:16 and Eph 2:19–22, and while scholars seem quite comfortable with accepting this statement at face value, they miss the import of Paul's language, especially the relationship between 1 Cor 3:16–17 and 1 Cor 5:5. This is puzzling since Paul's view of the assembly in 3:16–17—which has implications for 5:5—is rather straightforward: the Corinthian assembly is the temple of God → the Spirit of God dwells within this temple → someone *could* destroy this temple[163] → in that instance, God will destroy such a person.

The same scholars who object to reading "the Spirit" in 1 Cor 5:5 interpret Paul's vivid imagery of destroying the temple in 3:17 in several ways. This destruction is understood to be related to: (1) an ambiguous judgment[164]; (2) an apocalyptic understanding of the community[165]; (3) a "sentence of holy law"[166] to be exacted in the future; or (4) the adoption of Jewish customs in the church.[167] What is problematic about these interpretations is that none of them takes seriously Paul's idea that someone can in fact "destroy" (φθείρω) the temple and in that process even damage the presence of the Spirit of God dwelling within it. The apodosis of Paul's conditional statement ("God will destroy...") is meaningless if the protasis ("If anyone destroys the temple of God...") is contrary-to-fact, which it is not. As just noted, many scholars either blunt the force of Paul's rhetoric or turn his words into metaphor because their understanding of Paul's ecclesiology and pneumatology is predeter-

---

nowhere else in his letters, particularly the notion of becoming "one spirit" (ἓν πνεῦμά) with the Lord, but these verses are not rejected on that account.

163 The Greek construction in 1 Cor 3:17 best resembles the first-class conditional (with no textual variants in this regard) and therefore, at the very least, Paul assumes the reality of the protasis for the sake of argument. See BDF §371; Smyth §2298–2300. Ernst Käsemann even referred to 1 Cor 3:17 as an "inscription on the new divine sanctuary." In Käsemann, "Sätze Heiligen Rechts," 70.

164 Hays, *First Corinthians*, 58.

165 Conzelmann, *1 Corinthians*, 78.

166 Fee, *First Epistle to the Corinthians*, 148; Robertson–Plummer, *First Epistle*, 67. Fee's quotation refers back to the classic article by Ernst Käsemann, "Sätze Heiligen Rechts im Neuen Testament," *NTS* 1 (1954/55): 248–260; reprinted in ET, *New Testament Questions of Today*, trans. W. J. Montague (London: SCM Press, 1969), 66–81. Fee makes reference to this law without much further elaboration on what this destruction means, apart from a quotation of Robertson–Plummer in Fee, *Corinthians*, 148n16.

167 Barrett, *First Epistle to the Corinthians*, 91–92.

mined.¹⁶⁸ The unfortunate consequence is the short-circuiting of the connection between Paul's words in 1 Cor 3:16–17 and in 5:5. In other words, since scholars have already accepted the axiom that the community or the Spirit cannot be in any real danger or be "saved," Paul must mean something else in each context. In light of a proper reading of these passages, however, there is good reason to question the axiom and correctly trace the line of thought from 1 Cor 3:17 to 5:5 by interpreting the phrase, ἵνα τὸ πνεῦμα σωθῇ, as "so that the Spirit [within this assembly] may be preserved."¹⁶⁹

Second, the context of 1 Corinthians 5 provides yet further proof that Paul's main concern lies not with the individual but with the well-being of the Corinthian assembly. When reading 1 Cor 5:5 in the context of the entire chapter, there is nothing that leads one to believe that Paul had expectations of repentance, rehabilitation, or anything of that sort with respect to the incestuous individual. If Paul was referring to the man's spirit being saved, then should we not expect to find at least *something* about this process of personal repentance and redemption? And yet, Paul remains completely silent on this issue. This is where the Origenist reading and other modern interpretations that follow Origen falter. Notice that 1 Cor 5:5 is followed by discussions of the leaven and dough (5:6–8), the need to draw boundaries of association (5:9–11), and the process of right judgment (5:12–13), all concepts that are solely concerned with the wholeness of the assembly.¹⁷⁰ All these ideas are given a final summation with the closing

---

168 The Old Latin also contributes in part to this misreading by translating the two uses of φθείρω in 1 Cor 3:17 differently. E. g. Augustine, *Sermon* 82.13 (PL 38:512): "*Quisquid templum Dei violaverit, disperdet illum Deus*" = "Whoever *violates* the temple of God, God will *destroy* him." The apparatus of the NA²⁸ lists no textual variant that could have contributed to this translation.

169 The concept of "preservation," as it refers to the presently dwelling Spirit in the assembly, is my preferred translation of the verb σῴζω. Similarly to the usual translation of ἐκκλησία (="church"), "to save" is a heavily loaded term with a strictly soteriological valence that distorts Paul's illustration of the fragility of the Corinthian assembly in 1 Cor 5.

170 There is absolutely nothing in this entire section (1 Cor 5:1–13) that presents itself as evidence that Paul had individual discipline and rehabilitation as a goal for his exhortation. This is all the more evident when considering the fact that Paul refers to an earlier letter in which he prohibited associations with the immoral (5:9, μὴ συναναμίγνυσθαι πόρνοις) now clarified as an insider of their community (5:10–11). The verb συναναμίγνυμι is rare in the LXX/NT, found only in Hos 7:8; 1 Cor 5:9, 11; and 2 Thess 3:14. Coincidentally, Hosea 7 contains various elements that overlap with those of 1 Cor 5: (1) judgment in the context of adultery (7:4); (2) leaven as metaphor for transgressions (7:4, 8); (3) mixture with unwanted elements that defile the whole (7:8); (4) loss of power/strength (7:9); and (5) arrogance before God (7:10).

Robert Moses ("Ecclesial Discipline," 176) wonders why others who have indulged in sexual immorality and idolatry (he cites 1 Cor 6:9–20 and 10:19–22) are accepted without penalty if

remark in 1 Cor 5:13 ("Drive out the wicked person from among you"), an exhortation to preserve the assembly through the expulsion or even death of corrupting members, if necessary.[171]

What are the implications of this analysis for understanding Paul's view of the Corinthian assembly? First, as Paul hinted in 1 Cor 3:16–17 and now made explicit in 5:5, the assembly is not only the dwelling place of the Spirit, but is an entity that can be endangered, at least in regards to the presence of the Spirit that resides among the assembly. Paul's imagery of the destruction of the temple and the preservation of the Spirit both point to the idea that the Corinthian assembly is a fragile entity and that the members must take care in order for it to endure. Second, the peril posed by "leaven" within the assembly required a significant act (i.e. the appeal to divine power) in order to preserve the presence of the Spirit in the Corinthian assembly. Later in 1 Cor 6, Paul also warns the Corinthians that because they are joined to the Lord and are one spirit with him (6:17; also 10:17), πορνεία is not just evidence of individual moral failing, but a serious breach of the ναὸς θεοῦ within which the Spirit of God dwells (6:19). Likewise, the situation in 1 Cor 5 is dire enough that the invocation of "the power of the Lord" was necessary to properly expel the corrupting agent. Why was the maintenance of purity so paramount? Rosner concludes, "Surely the best explanation is given only 27 verses before chapter 5 in the solemn affirmation: 'Do you not know that you are God's temple … If anyone destroys God's temple, God will destroy him. For God's temple is holy, and that is what you are' (3:16–17)."[172]

2.4.4 Power in 1 Corinthians 10:1–22

The review of secondary literature on this section reveals the tendency of scholars to highlight the horizontal dimension of Paul's power language and downplay the significance of the vertical dimension. For example, though Margaret Mitchell's work is highly commendable for analyzing Paul's use of deliberative rhetoric in 1 Corinthians, the emphasis on the social dimension of Paul's language results in a somewhat unbalanced perspective. Her comments on the

---

death is envisaged for a similar activity in 1 Cor 5:5. These are red herrings since in 1 Cor 6, it is not certain that such acts are currently happening and accepted by the assembly, and in 1 Cor 10, a correct reading would show that it is parallel to 1 Cor 5 in terms of the threat of destruction. See the following section on death and destruction in 1 Corinthians for further elaboration.
171 The theme of destruction and death is analyzed below in 2.5.
172 Brian S. Rosner, "Temple and Holiness in 1 Corinthians 5," *TynBul* 42.1 (1991): 139–140.

three sections of 1 Corinthians 10 are instructive: on 10:1–13, the Exodus stories "demonstrate the chosen people's *destructive divisiveness* after its 'baptismal' exodus event"; on 10:14–22, Paul's reference to "cultic unity here in the argument is to the *social unity*"; and on 10:23–11:1, "*factionalism* is, at its very heart, tied up in the issue of τὸ συμφέρον."[173] I am not arguing here that factionalism was not a problem in Corinth. Mitchell has clearly shown it to be a major issue. In contrast to Mitchell, however, I highlight the vertical dimension of Paul's language about power.

Paul's discussion of the dangers of idolatry and immorality in 1 Corinthians 10 finds its climax in verses 14–22. Though not obvious at first, these verses are bookended by two related statements.[174] The first bracketing statement is Paul's emphatic command for the Corinthians to abstain from idolatry (10:14b, Διόπερ, ἀγαπητοί μου, φεύγετε ἀπὸ τῆς εἰδωλολατρίας) and the second statement is actually two rhetorical questions regarding God's jealousy and power (10:22, ἢ παραζηλοῦμεν τὸν κύριον; μὴ ἰσχυρότεροι αὐτοῦ ἐσμεν;). Paul's questions in 10:22 are somewhat puzzling since it is not immediately clear what the strength or power of God has to do with idolatry and with verses prior. The following comments on 10:22b show the various ways it is interpreted:

Fitzmyer:	"One wonders what the comparison of the strength of believers with God's strength has to do with idolatry."[175]
Conzelmann:	"Is ἰσχυρότεροι, 'stronger,' an ironical allusion to the 'strong'? No! The rhetorical question must be related to the Corinthian mentality as a whole (see 4:8); cf. v 12."[176]

---

173 Mitchell, *Paul and the Rhetoric of Reconciliation*, 140, 142, and 143, respectively (emphasis added). Mitchell's points are well taken, though I am not sure that 1 Cor 10:1–13 is a demonstration of the Israelite's "divisiveness" as much as it is about their inability to maintain certain boundaries that were delineated by God.

174 See chapter 1 for the division of 1 Corinthians 10 in the history of interpretation, which has wrongly separated 10:14–22 from 10:1–13. *Contra* Conzelmann, for example, who begins his analysis of 10:14–22: "Der Gedankengang des Abschnitts ist in sich geschlossen" (*Der erste Brief*, 209). Such observations are surprising given the emphatic conjunction, διόπερ, which begins 10:14.

175 Fitzmyer, *First Corinthians*, 394. Fitzmyer then suggests that Paul may be thinking of a passage from the Hebrew Bible such as Qoh 6:10b; Job 9:32; 37:23; Isa 45:9, though he also admits that none of them talk about divine jealousy or idolatry. Finally, he considers Exodus 32 as a possible background.

176 Conzelmann, *1 Corinthians*, 174. This is basically the entirety of his comments on this verse, though he does note that God watches over his honor as described in Deut 32:21.

Hays:	"Paul leaves the 'strong' with a final ominous question: 'Are we stronger than he?'"[177]
Fee:	"Those who would put God to the test by insisting on their right to what Paul insists is idolatry are in effect taking God on, challenging him by their actions, daring him to act."[178]
Horsley:	"The second rhetorical question also makes a not-so-subtle criticism of the enlightened Christians who thought of themselves as 'strong' in their spiritual status (1:25–27; 4:10)."[179]

Some of these comments interpret Paul's question as if it were directed only to a particular group (the so-called "strong"[180]), though this would be unusual given Paul's use of the first-person plural twice in 10:22 (παραζηλοῦμεν ... ἐσμεν).[181] If Paul were addressing a specific group in Corinth, then one could expect to read παραζηλοῦτε and ἐστε.[182] It is more logical to interpret Paul's words as a general exhortation to the entire assembly in Corinth.

The second rhetorical question elicits a negative answer (μὴ ἰσχυρότεροι αὐτοῦ ἐσμεν;): "We are not more powerful than he is, are we?" and in the context of 1 Cor 10:1–22, this query explains that involvement in idolatry in its various forms will provoke the display of God's power. Such divine response is necessary because there are both vertical and insidious dimensions of the Corinthians' participation in local temple dining that are alarming. It is vertical because, like the Israelites' actions in 10:1–13, incorrect behavior is not just a transgression of hor-

---

[177] Hays, *First Corinthians*, 170.
[178] Fee, *First Epistle to the Corinthians*, 474.
[179] Horsley, *1 Corinthians*, 142.
[180] "So-called" because this is actually not Paul's terminology for any particular group in Corinth. He does not use the term "the strong" in 1 Corinthians, though some scholars point to 1 Cor 1:26 (δυνατοί) and 4:10 (ἰσχυροί) as relevant parallels. It is likely, however, that they were influenced by a reading of Romans 14:1–15:1, where Paul discusses the positions of the weak and strong (15:1, οἱ δυνατοί), particularly with respect to purity and food consumption. See Fee, *First Epistle to the Corinthians*, 474n59; Brian S. Rosner, "'Stronger than He?' The Strength of 1 Corinthians 10:22b," *TynBul* 43.1 (1992): 171–179.
[181] Paul does not use the first-person plural in his letter to address any specific group of individuals. 1 Cor 2:16; 3:9; 5:8; 8:1; 10:8, 9; 11:16, 32; 12:23; 13:12; 15:19. Rosner rightly notes that in 1 Cor 8–10, the two groups may be more appropriately called "the weak" and "the knowledgeable" as γνῶσις is a leitmotif in this section of the letter ("Strength," 172).
[182] Despite writing the letter from a distance, Paul does not assume the posture of a disinterested observer, but rather that of an affected member of the community. Even if Paul did not intend to address a specific group in Corinth, the use of the second person plural would be perfectly acceptable. Yet multiple times throughout this section, Paul assumes that he is integrally connected to the community. 1 Cor 10:8 (μηδὲ πορνεύωμεν), 9 (μηδὲ ἐκπειράζωμεν), 17 (μετέχομεν).

izontal social boundaries, but is an act that tests God himself.[183] It is also insidious because what appears to be harmless at first (10:19, Τί οὖν φημι; ὅτι εἰδωλόθυτόν τί ἐστιν ἢ ὅτι εἴδωλόν τί ἐστιν;) can potentially disqualify a member of the Corinthian community from partaking in the blood and body of Christ (10:16, 21).

As for rhetorical structure, Wayne Meeks proposed that 1 Cor 10:1–22 be read as a Christian midrash.[184] Some scholars have criticized the use of this terminology to explain Paul's exegetical practice, though it is certain that the Hebrew Bible influenced Paul's logic in 1 Corinthians 10.[185] The presence of the exodus tradition is undeniable, and further connections to Deuteronomy 32 establish the importance of power in this section.[186] The Song of Moses in Deut 32 begins with the call to heaven and earth as witnesses in the proclamation of the great-

---

[183] In one of the few studies devoted explicitly to 1 Cor 10:14–22 (Harm W. Hollander, "The Idea of Fellowship in 1 Corinthians 10.14–22," *NTS* 55.4 [2009]: 456–470), Paul's language is misconstrued. Hollander insightfully marshals various primary sources to show that κοινωνία should be understood "ecclesiologically," but apart from his introduction of the context of 10:14–22, not once does he mention 10:1–13. These earlier verses must figure in one's interpretation of 10:14–22, since Paul's statement about idolatry and God's power only makes full sense if it is related to his description of the Israelites in the wilderness. The error of the Israelites was not that they were crossing social taboos and were "partners" (to use Hollander's term) with other forbidden groups, but that they were putting God himself to the test through their fornication, idolatry, grumbling, and ultimately involvement with powers that were harmful. While Hollander's study is certainly helpful in illuminating the horizontal dimension of κοινων-terms, it need not be accepted at the cost of minimizing or even ignoring the vertical dimension of the Corinthians' participation in meals. In his excursus on the problem of meat offered to idols, Dieter Zeller rightly concludes, "die Mähler nicht nur soziale, sondern auch religiöse Bedeutung hatten" (*Der erste Brief*, 282).

[184] Wayne A. Meeks, "'And Rose up to Play': Midrash and Paraenesis in 1 Corinthians 10:1–22," *JSNT* 16 (1982): 64–78.

[185] E.g. Richard Hays is quite critical of the use of this terminology in *Echoes*, 13: "The term *midrash* can serve as a convenient cover for a multitude of exegetical sins. One frequently finds Christian commentators explaining away their embarrassment over some piece of fanciful Pauline exegesis by noting solemnly that this is midrash, as though the wholesome Hebrew label could render Paul's arbitrariness kosher" (emphasis original). To be fair, Hays (196n31) commends Meeks for his insights in "Midrash and Paraenesis." For a recent critique of Hays and his method, see Bryan J. Whitfield, *Joshua Traditions and the Argument of Hebrews 3 and 4*, BZNW 194 (Berlin: De Gruyter, 2013), 51–84; Paul Foster, "Echoes without Resonance: Critiquing Certain Aspects of Recent Scholarly Trends in the Study of the Jewish Scriptures in the New Testament," *JSNT* 38.1 (2015): 96–111.

[186] For a general overview of Deuteronomy in the Corinthian correspondence, see Brian S. Rosner, "Deuteronomy in 1 and 2 Corinthians," in *Deuteronomy in the New Testament*, ed. Maarten J. J. Menken and Steve Moyise (London: T&T Clark, 2007), 118–135; Thiessen, "'The Rock Was Christ.'" Wayne Meeks also anticipated some of these connections in his "Midrash and Paraenesis."

ness of God, and addresses God as "the Rock," a leitmotif throughout the chapter (Deut 32:1–4).[187] It is not by accident that this song is composed and recited within proximity to the tent of meeting where YHWH God appears to Moses and Joshua (Deut. 31:14–15). The song contains various concepts that fuel Paul's language and logic in 1 Cor 10, including its narration of Israel's provocation of God's anger and power.[188] First, the song recounts God's sustenance of Israel in the wilderness in Deut 32:10–14 (see 1 Cor 10:1–4). Second, it describes Israel's inability to remain faithful to God with their sacrifice to demons in Deut 32:15–18 (see 1 Cor 10:20). Third, the provocation of God's anger leads to the destruction of many Israelites in Deut 32:19–27 (see 1 Cor 10:5–10, 22). Fourth, there is the discussion of idols and their noxious sacrifices in Deut 32:31–33, 37–38 (see 1 Cor 10:14, 19–20, 28). Fifth and finally, the song concludes with extolling God's power in Deut 32:28–30, 34–36, 39–43 (see 1 Cor 10:21–22).

A major problem of the Israelites in Deuteronomy 32, and likewise of the Corinthians in 1 Corinthians 10, is their inability to accurately perceive and acknowledge God's power that has sustained them thus far. In part, this is due to their forgetfulness of God's acts in the past, resulting in a lack of discernment. The Israelites' arrogance in their own strength is tragic (Deut 32:15–18), since they are in reality helpless without God's power. Deut 32:30 demonstrates this fact plainly, since through God's help one man is said to pursue a thousand, and two men can scatter ten thousands.[189] Similarly, the Corinthians' confidence in their "surge of spiritual energy" is manifest in their slogan, πάντα ἔξεστιν (1 Cor 6:12–13; 10:23).[190] In contrast to confidence in human power, it is only when God "sees that their power is gone" that the Lord will vindicate his people

---

[187] Deut 32:4 MT: הַצּוּר; LXX: θεός. See also Deut 32:13, 15, 18, 30, 31, 37. 1 Corinthians 10 is also the only place in the NT that uses πέτρα as an explicit descriptor for Christ. Michael P. Knowles, "'The Rock, His Work is Perfect': Unusual Imagery for God in Deuteronomy XXXII," *VT* 39.3 (1989): 307–322; Joong Ho Chong, "The Song of Moses (Deuteronomy 32:1–43) and the Hoshea-Pekah conflict" (Ph.D. diss., Emory University, 1990), 227–232.
[188] Wayne Meeks anticipated some of these connections in his "Midrash and Paraenesis," passim.
[189] Deut 32:30: "How will one pursue thousands and two remove myriads (LXX: πῶς διώξεται εἷς χιλίους καὶ δύο μετακινήσουσιν μυριάδας) unless God sold them and the Lord delivered them up?" This rhetorical question lies in juxtaposition with the account in 1 Sam 18:7 when God's power energizes his chosen ones: "Saul has killed his thousands, and David his myriads" (LXX: Ἐπάταξεν Σαουλ ἐν χιλιάσιν αὐτοῦ καὶ Δαυιδ ἐν μυριάσιν αὐτοῦ).
[190] John M.G. Barclay, "Thessalonica and Corinth: Social Contrasts in Pauline Christianity," *JSNT* 47 (1992): 62.

and have compassion upon them.¹⁹¹ Craigie notes that the rhetorical questions found in Deut 32:37–38 are "designed to create awareness that other possible sources of strength were also useless," and so too, the rhetorical questions in 1 Cor 10:22.¹⁹²

The various allusions to Deuteronomy 32 build up to Paul's statement that the Corinthians cannot take part in the table of the Lord and of demons simultaneously (1 Cor 10:21). When Paul is made aware of their dual participation in temple meals and the God's temple meal (= Lord's supper), he summarizes the Corinthians' activity as a provocation of the Lord's jealousy and as a testing of God's power (10:22). The theme of God's power in the context of idolatry and unfaithfulness was not unfamiliar in Jewish contexts during this time, as any reader of Deuteronomy would have been aware. A similar motif can also be found in Wisdom 12:17–18, "For you show your strength when people doubt the completeness of your power (ἰσχὺν γὰρ ἐνδείκνυσαι ἀπιστούμενος ἐπὶ δυνάμεως τελειότητι) ... for you have the power to prevail whenever you choose."¹⁹³ Therefore, the rhetorical question concerning God's power in 1 Cor 10:22 is, as Rosner argues, "a frightening threat of judgment" posed to the Corinthians that their undiscerning involvement in temple meals will not go unpunished by the jealous Lord.

Correlative to the Corinthians' disregard for God's power is their flirtation with demonic powers, particularly as they are localized in such sacrificial meals. Paul struggles somewhat in articulating the hazard posed by demons, since on one hand he fully appreciates the assertion of Ps 23:1 LXX in 1 Cor 10:26 ("The earth is the Lord's and everything in it"¹⁹⁴), while on the other hand he recognizes the danger inherent in the eating of sacrificial foods. The issue, however, is not one-sided, as if the Corinthians were merely participating in powerless pagan meals and worship.¹⁹⁵ That is, the dispute is not primarily

---

191 Deut 32:36 MT. Deut 32:36 LXX states their powerless condition more directly: "he saw them paralyzed."
192 Peter C. Craigie, *The Book of Deuteronomy*, NICOT (Grand Rapids: Eerdmans, 1976), 387. Also Rosner, "'Stronger than He?,'" 175.
193 Rosner, "'Stronger than He?,'" 177.
194 Paul's appeal to Psalm 23:1 LXX implies that since all food and drink is technically part of God's creation, it cannot be inimical in the ontological sense. Ambrosiaster (*In Epistulas ad Corinthios I* 10:26) simply claims: "*ut omnia munda ostenderet*."
195 For example, in his monograph *Götter, "Götzen," Götterbilder: Aspekte einer paulinischen "Theologie der Religionen"* (Berlin: De Gruyter, 2005), 447–448, Johannes Woyke asserts that pagan gods are meaningless and powerless ("bedeutungs- und machtlos") and the consideration of their existence is in the end meaningless ("ob sie darüber hinaus überhaupt existieren, ist bedeutungslos").

over the maintenance of *social* boundaries, but rather over the breach of *cultic* prohibitions. In 1 Cor 10:14–22, Paul portrays powers present within different meals: in the Lord's supper commemorating the death of Jesus with the expectation of his coming and in the pagan meals offered to demons.[196] There is also evidence from other ancient sources that observed powers—often inimical—held by such δαιμόνιον, and therefore, there is no reason to doubt that a similar understanding informed Paul's view of demons in 1 Cor 10.[197]

Paul highlights the strictures placed upon the Corinthians by juxtaposing "the Lord" to "demons," each connected to a "table" that was either a source of life or of pollution and harm (1 Cor 10:16–17, 21–22).[198] Since Paul does not elaborate upon what the table of the Lord or of demons entails, it is likely that the Corinthians were fully aware of what these were referring to, namely the participation in their respective cults or rituals. The example of the Israelites that Paul briefly mentions in 1 Cor 10:18 provides a helpful connection between consumption and cultic activity. Unfortunately, this verse is often interpreted in isolation from Paul's earlier exposition on the Israelites' consumption of prohibited meals.[199] The qualification, Israel "according to the flesh" (κατὰ σάρκα), is not simply an idiomatic reference to historical Israel, but in light of the broader context, it also serves as a subtle cri-

---

196 See the secondary literature on 1 Cor 8:1–13 vs. 10:1–22 (e.g., Weiss, Smithals, Héring, Works, Fotopoulos). See also Vahrenhorst, *Kultische Sprache*, 191–192.
197 E.g., Homer, *Il.* 8.166; Hesiod, *Op.* 314; Aeschylus, *Cho.* 566; *Pers.* 354; *Sept.* 812; Sophocles, *Oed. tyr.* 828; *Trach.* 1023–30; Euripides, *Iph. aul.* 1514; Hippocrates, *De morbo sacro* 15; Plato, *Apol.* 40a; Herodotus, *Hist.* 5.87.2; Isocrates, *Areop.* 73 (κακοδαίμονες); Epictetus, *Diatr.* 1.14.11–17; 3.22.53; Plutarch, *Def. orac.* 10; *Is. Os.* 25; *Sept. sap. conv.* 8; Ps 90:6 LXX (see also 90:13); Ps 95:5 LXX; Isa 13:21–22; 34:14; Tob 3:8, 17; 6:8, 14–17; 8:3; 1 En 69:12; Pss. Sol. 5:1–13; 11Q11; Tg. Ps. 91:5–6; Midr. Ps. 91. See Dale B. Martin, "When Did Angels Become Demons?," *JBL* 129.4 (2010): 657–77; Rohintan Keki Mody, "The Relationship Between Powers of Evil and Idols in 1 Corinthians 8:4–5 and 10:18–22 in the Context of the Pauline Corpus and Early Judaism" (Ph.D. diss., University of Aberdeen, 2008), 39–57, 235–287.
198 Earlier in the chapter, Paul strictly refers to "the Christ" (ὁ Χριστός; 1 Cor 10:4, 9, and 16). It is possible that early Christian tradition has established the technical designations, "cup of the Lord" (ποτήριον κυρίου) and "table of the Lord" (τραπέζης κυρίου), that required the use of the title "Lord" rather than "the Christ" in 1 Cor 10:21–22. This is somewhat unlikely, however, since no other NT writing contains such language and even in early Christianity, it is not found until Origen. Prior to Paul, there is some evidence of this language in Jewish sources: Ezek 44:16; Mal 1:7–12; likely post-dating Paul: T. Levi 8:16.
199 E.g., Hollander, "Idea of Fellowship," 460: "According to Paul the case of the people of Israel is somewhat similar: people who together eat food offered to the God of Israel are 'partners in the altar' (v.18)." See also Conzelmann, *1 Corinthians*, 172; Fitzmyer, *First Corinthians*, 392; Hays, *First Corinthians*, 168. This theme of eating that occurs in each of the episodes described in 1 Cor 10:6–10 is explored in 2.5.2 below.

tique of Israel's eating of foods that lie beyond permitted boundaries.²⁰⁰ Carla Works concludes, "there is nothing inherent in the word itself that connotes a sacrifice to the God of Israel,"²⁰¹ and indeed, the analogy best makes sense if it is Israel's participation in sacrifices *other than* those of YHWH that is correlated to the Corinthians' involvement in pagan sacrifices.

The argument of 1 Cor 10:18–22 is now given greater clarity. The Israelites put themselves at great risk in consuming prohibited sacrifices that made them "participants of the altar" (1 Cor 10:18), i.e. an altar not belonging to YHWH.²⁰² Their identification as such implied that they would become indistinguishable from other participants in these cults, a crime that violated the strict boundaries placed upon God's people that were later codified in the Shema (e.g. Deut 6). Such transgressions, however, were more than just breaking of a law: Paul points out in 1 Cor 10:20 that these cultic activities had the power to turn one into a participant of demons. Fellowship meant partaking of the body and blood, either of the Lord or of demons. The problem was therefore twofold. At the horizontal level, the Corinthian assembly was becoming too lax about maintaining its status as the "temple of God," their permissive κοινωνία in various sacrifices rendering them indistinguishable from other inhabitants of Corinth who most certainly dabbled in multiple cultic associations.²⁰³ At the vertical level, these activities opened them up to dangerous powers beyond the human. These powers lay outside the community, bringing death and destruction on members who ventured beyond the safety of God's temple. Like the many Israelites who fell in the wilderness by pursuing prohibited foods, so also the Corinthians if they continue to partake of other sacrificial foods. Günther Röhser concludes thus: "Die Fragen von v. 22 machen zusätzlich deutlich, dass es um die Konkurrenz zweier Vertikalbeziehungen geht: Christus oder die Dämonen."²⁰⁴

---

200 It is not necessary, however, to follow Fee (*First Epistle to the Corinthians*, 470n38) in positing the existence of "another Israel κατὰ πνεῦμα." See also Zeller, *Der erste Brief*, 339.
201 Works, *Church in the Wilderness*, 100.
202 This also makes the best sense chronologically; the story of Israel in 1 Corinthians 10 has been exclusively about their wilderness experience, and therefore, the priestly consumption of the offerings (e.g., Lev 7:6–36; 10:12–15; Deut 18:1–4) would postdate this period in Israel's history.
203 On the social dimension of κοινωνία, see footnote #183. Also Wayne A. Meeks, *First Urban Christians: The Social World of the Apostle Paul*, 2ⁿᵈ ed. (New Haven: Yale University Press, 2003), 160.
204 Günther Röhser, "Vorstellungen von der Präsenz Christi im Ritual nach 1Kor 11,17–34," in *Mahl und religiöse Identität im frühen Christentum*, ed. Matthias Klinghardt and Hal Taussig (Tübingen: Francke, 2012), 140.

2.4.5 Power in 1 Corinthians 11:17–34

1 Corinthians 11:17–34 is both the most interesting and the most enigmatic passage regarding the presence of power in the Corinthian assembly because it provides the most explicit account of the consequences of transgression, yet remains basically silent concerning the mechanism underlying these repercussions. Despite the elusive nature of the evidence, some insights about power in the Corinthian assembly can be teased out of these verses.

Paul's discussion of the Lord's supper in this passage suggests that eating the bread and drinking the cup of the Lord are more than the consumption of products made up of wheat flour and grapes (1 Cor 11:27). This much is clear when just a few verses later, Paul links the eating and drinking to the manifestation of weakness, illness, and even death among many members of the Corinthian assembly (11:30). What is significant is that Paul at least assumes that the ritual of sharing in the "body and blood of the Lord" (1 Cor 11:27) is not just a Christianized version of a routine Hellenistic meal, but part of a powerful religious experience that held life and death in fine balance.

Unfortunately, just at this juncture when we encounter what Origen later called ἡ τοῦ ἄρτου δύναμις,[205] modern interpreters demythologize the content of Paul's message and pursue other—one could argue, rather parochial—questions related to dining spaces, economic conditions, and historical parallels.[206] Reading 1 Cor 11:17–34 in the context of the earlier chapters on eating provides important clues that must inform how this latest account is to be read and interpreted. In 1 Cor 5 and 10, Paul has been drawing tighter limits on who can partake of the "spiritual food and drink" (e.g. 10:3–4), requiring careful discernment of current members of the assembly. Furthermore, the space marked by the assembly of God (=temple) is clearly separate from the space without, both in how they behave with respect to insiders/outsiders and in how they participate in their sacred meal. The Lord's supper of 1 Cor 11 is also part of this meal eating event, occurring in a distinct time and place, and therefore, marked off as a ritual that involves power: power not just in their commemoration of the death of their Lord, but in their common participation of his body and blood (see 1 Cor 10).

Günther Röhser has argued convincingly that 1 Cor 10 needs to be considered in the discussion of 1 Cor 11:17–34, particularly as the former helps illumi-

---

[205] Origen, *Comm. Matt.* 10.25. A later contemporary of Paul, Ignatius of Antioch (ca. 35–107 CE), calls the "one bread" (εἷς ἄρτος) the "medicine of immortality, the antidote we take in order not to die but to live forever in Jesus Christ" (ὅ ἐστιν φάρμακον ἀθανασίας, ἀντίδοτος τοῦ μὴ ἀποθανεῖν ἀλλὰ ζῆν ἐν Ἰησοῦ Χριστῷ διὰ παντός) in *Eph.* 20.2.
[206] See the review of literature in chapter 1.

nate the vertical dimension of the latter text, which he calls "der besonderen Präsenz Christi."[207] He observes further:

> Denn da alle entsprechenden Begriffe und Aussagen in Kap. 11 umstritten sind, müssen inhaltliche Zusammenhänge aus Kap. 10 herangezogen werden, um die Berechtigung der christologisch-theologischen Perspektive gegenüber der sozialtheologischen zu erweisen. Anders gesagt: Zur horizontalen muss die vertikale Dimension hinzukommen, wenn der Ansatz beim "Realsymbol" tragfähig sein soll (die Annahme einer "gewöhnlichen" Präsenz ist hingegen weniger strittig, weil sie "rein geistig" vorzustellen und nicht an ein materielles Symbol gebunden ist).[208]

Through conversation with 1 Cor 10, important analogies can be made about the presence of Christ and divine power available through the meal in 1 Cor 11. Just as the Israelites consumed divine food in the form of manna in the wilderness, so also the Corinthians now participate in the Lord's supper—a divine meal—in the form of bread. Just as Israel consumed divine drink in the form of water from the rock (= Christ in 1 Cor 10:4), so now the Corinthians consume divine drink (= blood of Christ in 1 Cor 10:16).[209] Additionally, 1 Cor 10 recounts two types of temple meals, one temple meal associated with other deities in the Corinthian pantheon, and one temple meal associated with Jesus Christ.

This experiential aspect of the meal often goes unnoticed in studies focused on the social and historical dimensions of 1 Corinthians 11:17–34. In contrast, Johnson suggests, "Whether we ourselves want to declare in favor of transcendence, we can entertain the notion that participants at such meals considered themselves engaged by a power that was truly Other."[210] Paul and his readers both assumed that contact with power in the meal was just as real as the physical substance of the bread and drink, and their symbolic world within which these relationships exist must be accepted prior to any appeal to modern sensibilities.

---

[207] Röhser, "Vorstellungen," 136.
[208] Röhser, "Vorstellungen," 136.
[209] 1 Cor 10:16 and 11:17–34 have a long history of interpretation. The history of theology on the relationship between wine/drink and the blood of Christ is long and complex. It is not the place here to discuss the issue of "real presence," but it should nevertheless be recognized that Paul understood this meal as participation in the divine. See Fee, *First Epistle to the Corinthians*, 465–469 for discussion and secondary literature.
[210] See "Meals are Where the Magic Is," in Luke Timothy Johnson, *Religious Experience in Earliest Christianity: A Missing Dimension in New Testament Studies* (Minneapolis: Fortress Press, 1998), 137–179. Vahrenhorst incorrectly argues that 1 Cor 11:17–34 contains no cultic terminology (*Kultische Sprache*, 193).

In 1 Cor 5, Paul urged the Corinthians to celebrate the feast only after the contaminating element was expelled from the assembly and in 1 Cor 10, he tells them that their participation in the Lord's table is exclusive of the table meals of other cults, or as Paul states more negatively, "of demons" (10:20–21).[211] Both sections assume that these meals bring the participants into contact with power, and that such a ritual signified more than just an identity marker for yet another voluntary association in the ancient world. The same train of thought continues in 1 Cor 11 with Paul's description of the Lord's meal. 1 Cor 10:16 describes the "cup" and "bread" that mediated the Corinthians' becoming participants of the "blood" and "body" of Christ, and so also the same language is used in 1 Cor 11:27. How is a person to have "fellowship" (κοινωνία) with or be "guilty" (ἔνοχος) of the blood and body of one who died decades prior? Modern readers might interpret such language as Paul's wishful thinking, though there is no indication given by him or by his auditors that they doubted the reality of such powerful encounters with the Lord. Their meal signified not just fellowship with one who remained dead irrevocably — as it would have been for any other human being—but an experience of their risen Lord who is coming (1:7–9), an echo of the pre-Pauline Aramaic prayer, מרן אתה that Paul proclaims in the closing of his letter (16:22).[212]

The level of discernment required in partaking of the Lord's meal increases with each episode in 1 Cor 5, 10, and 11. In the first section (1 Cor 5:1–13), the incestuous man is basically treated as an outsider, to be put outside of the assembly, into the space in which there is no provision of the Lord's supper. In the second section (10:1–22), the Corinthians are warned not to cross back and forth across boundary lines of the assembly and the outside space: the former consists of the table of the Lord and the Spirit and power of God and the latter consists of other sacrificial foods and demonic powers. Finally, in the third episode (11:17–34), even those inside are cautioned to take care, lest they too incur the penalty of their unworthiness, i.e. in physical illnesses and death.

---

211 The problem is not relegated simply to the act of sacrifice, as if Paul criticized the Corinthians' participation in other rituals of sacrifice and remained agnostic about the ensuing consumption of foods. As 1 Cor 10:18 emphasized, it is the act of consumption that created the opportunity for inimical powers to lay hold of the assembly. Zeller, *Der erste Brief*, 342.
212 Zeller, *Der erste Brief*, 376. Similar language found in Rev 22:20 and Did 10:6. Some have suggested that the curse in 1 Cor 16:22 included a ban from the Lord's meal. I find this suggestion to be highly intriguing in light of my reading of 1 Cor 5:1–13, 10:1–22, and 11:17–34, but it is beyond the scope of this project to discuss this verse further. See discussion in Fee, *First Epistle to the Corinthians*, 834 and 834n6.

2.4.6 Power in 1 Corinthians 5:1–13, 10:1–22, and 11:17–34

In these three chapters of 1 Corinthians, one finds the presence of power that not only energizes the Corinthian assembly, but the proximity of inimical powers that brings death and destruction upon errant members. Power functions variously to: (1) authorize the judgment upon the incestuous individual in 1 Cor 5; (2) bring harsh judgment upon those who test God in 1 Cor 10; and (3) harm those who participate in the Lord's supper in an unworthy manner in 1 Cor 11. What is more, in all three places, meal eating is inscribed within the Corinthian assembly as an event involving power beyond the merely human—be it harmful or beneficial. Furthermore, the space *outside* the assembly is portrayed as that which is inhabited by inimical powers, whether Satan or other demons. In contrast, the Spirit of God resides *within* the temple of God where the members of the community can safely partake of the Lord's supper, provided they act in accordance with the ethics befitting God's people.[213] One cannot come to the table of the Lord having ignored the blatant offense of another so-called brother (1 Cor 5), consumed substances from the table of demons (1 Cor 10), or disregarded other members of the community (1 Cor 11).

It is not by accident that Paul emphasizes the fact that the Corinthian assembly is an entity *that belongs to God* in his Corinthian correspondence (ἐκκλησία τοῦ θεοῦ), something he does not do in any of his other letters.[214] The Corinthians' inability to see their assembly as a divinely energized temple has led to questionable behaviors that put the entire community at risk, and these sections highlight the need for the Corinthians to recognize the boundaries of the ναὸς θεοῦ and behave in accordance with God's call upon them.

2.5 Peril in 1 Corinthians

The two prior sections alluded to several occasions when Paul anticipated the Corinthian assembly to be at peril, due to the transgressions of some of its members. These details are evaluated more fully, particularly with respect to the pos-

---

[213] Johnson, *Religious Experience*, 176. See also Valeriy Alikin, "Eating the Bread and Drinking the Cup in Corinth: Defining and Expressing the Identity of the Earliest Christians," in *Mahl und religiöse Identät im frühen Christentum*, ed. Matthias Klinghardt and Hal Taussig (Tübingen: Francke, 2012), 119–130.

[214] 1 Cor 1:2; 10:32; 11:22; 2 Cor 1:1. The usual address is either to "the saints and/or the church that is in x" (x = location) or to a specific person. See Rom 1:7; Gal 1:2; Eph 1:1; Phil 1:1; Col 1:2; 1 Thess 1:1; 2 Thess 1:1 ("the church of the Thessalonians"); 1 Tim 1:2; 2 Tim 1:2; Titus 1:4; Phlm 1.

sibility of death and destruction that Paul illustrates in 1 Corinthians 5:1–13, 10:1–22, and 11:17–34. Related to the prospect of peril are the inimical forces that lie in wait to destroy God's people. Temples and other sanctuaries were not simply spaces within which one experienced divine beneficence. These places also maintained the potential to encounter malevolent forces or to receive punishment for transgressions.

2.5.1 Peril in 1 Corinthians 5:1–13

The incestuous figure of 1 Corinthians 5 posed such a threat to the assembly that he must be, without equivocation, "cast out from among you" (1 Cor 5:13). Paul's accusation in 1 Cor 5:2 that the Corinthians did not yet remove this offender "from your midst" (ἐκ μέσου ὑμῶν) is a possible allusion to Num 19:20 that refers to the desecration of God's sanctuary.[215] Thus, Paul appropriates the words of Deut 17:7 LXX in 5:13 as the final authorization of the community's act to expel the individual as a cleansing act. Paul has already judged this infectious individual, and the Corinthians are to follow suit by "handing over such a one to Satan" (5:3–5).[216] To what end? Paul qualifies this activity with two purpose clauses: (1) εἰς ὄλεθρον τῆς σαρκός and (2) ἵνα τὸ πνεῦμα σωθῇ.

The earlier analysis of τὸ πνεῦμα in 1 Cor 5:5 established the possibility that it is not the individual's spirit being referred to, and indeed, the fate of the individual is patently not the subject of Paul's discussion throughout the entire chapter. The implication of this interpretation is that the first clause in 5:5, εἰς ὄλεθρον τῆς σαρκός, cannot function simply as shorthand for the "excommuni-

---

215 Vahrenhorst, *Kultische Sprache*, 158–159. Num 19:20, καὶ ἄνθρωπος, ὃς ἐὰν μιανθῇ καὶ μὴ ἀφαγνισθῇ, ἐξολεθρευθήσεται ἡ ψυχὴ ἐκείνη ἐκ μέσου τῆς συναγωγῆς, ὅτι τὰ ἅγια κυρίου ἐμίανεν, = "And a person who is defiled and not purified, that soul will be completely destroyed from the midst the congregation, because he defiled the sanctuary of the Lord."
216 Paul's metaphor of the yeast/leaven in this chapter indicates that one person's transgression can potentially contaminate the whole community and make the entire assembly liable. The Hebrew Bible narrates various examples of this. For example, Exod 16:27–28 where "certain people" (τινες ἐκ τοῦ λαοῦ) broke the Sabbath and the Lord accuses the entire nation ("how long are you ["Εως τίνος οὐ] unwilling to listen"); Num 16:24–27 where the Israelites are to separate from Kore, Dathan, and Abiron, "so that you do not perish together in all their sin" (μὴ συναπόλησθε ἐν πάσῃ τῇ ἁμαρτίᾳ αὐτῶν). From the broader Mediterranean, see, for example, Plutarch, *Quaest. rom.* 109 (ἡ δὲ ζύμη καὶ γέγονεν ἐκ φθορᾶς αὐτὴ καὶ φθείρει τὸ φύραμα μειγνυμένη = "Yeast is itself also the product of corruption, and corrupts the dough with which it is mixed."). DeMaris, "Elimination," 45–6; Rosner, "Corporate Responsibility," 470–473; Vahrenhorst, *Kultische Sprache*, 157–158.

cation" of the sinful man with the aim that he is eventually accepted back into the Christian community following a period of personal mortification.[217] In a recent publication, David Smith interpreted the entire verse (παραδοῦναι τὸν τοιοῦτον τῷ σατανᾷ κ. τ. λ.) in light of curses and magical incantations from antiquity to show the finality of destruction.[218] Given Paul's use of curse-language elsewhere (1 Cor 12:3; 16:22; Gal 1:8–9), others have argued that it is highly unlikely that ὄλεθρον τῆς σαρκός signified a temporary condition.[219]

If not pedagogical and if not temporary, then what did this "destruction" in 1 Cor 5:5 refer to? Simply, it must mean physical harm or possibly, even death.[220] Since "handing over x" (παραδίδωμι x) usually meant entrusting a person to an agent who would inflict harm,[221] it is highly probable that Paul envisions a similar outcome.[222] This interpretation makes even better sense in light of Paul's closing remark in 5:13 that is taken directly from Deuteronomy. Some have minimized this link to Deuteronomy in 1 Cor 5 and even more broadly in the entire Corinthian correspondence,[223] though others have established the role that Deuteronomy plays throughout 1 Corinthians.[224]

---

217 John Calvin's interpretation of 1 Cor 5:5 in this manner remains influential among modern exegetes where he asserts that the person is not given over to Satan in "perpetual bondage, but it is a temporary condemnation and not only so, but that which is likely to be for his salvation" (*in perpetuam servitutem dedatur, sed esse damnationem temporariam: neque id modo, sed quae future sit salutari*). Also Calvin, *Commentary on First Corinthians* 5:1–5; Smith, *Curse*, 116–117.
218 See Smith, *Curse*, esp. 57–113.
219 John Fotopoulos, "Paul's Curse," 275–309; C.F.D. Moule, "A Reconsideration of the Context of *Maranatha*," *NTS* 8 (1960): 307–310. Cursing is also extant in the Jewish tradition, particularly in connection to sexual immorality. See, for example, Gen 9:25–27; Deut 27:20 ("Cursed [MT: ארר/LXX: ἐπικατάρατος] be anyone who lies with his father's wife (MT: אשת אביו /LXX: γυνὴ τοῦ πατρὸς αὐτοῦ), because he has violated his father's rights. All the people will say 'Amen!'"; 28:45.
220 Conzelmann (*1 Corinthians*, 97) unequivocally states that it "can hardly mean anything else but death (cf. 11:30)." I agree with him in principle, but the statement need not mean death to the exclusion of other physical infirmities. See Smith, *Curse*, 158.
221 E.g. 1 Cor 11:23 is a simple example of such use of παραδίδωμι. See also, Deut 1:27; Judg 2:14; 1 Sam 30:15; Ezra 9:7; Ps (LXX) 77:48; 117:18; Ezek 23:28; Tob 3:4 (δίδωμι); Matt 4:12; 5:25; 10:4, 17, 21; 17:22; 18:34; 20:18, 19; 24:9; 26:2, 15, 45; 27:26; Mark 9:31; 10:33; 13:9, 12; 14:41; 15:15; Luke 9:44; 12:58; 18:32; 20:20; 21:12, 16; 24:7, 20; John 13:2; 19:16; Acts 8:3; 12:4; 22:4.
222 For this use of παραδίδωμι and other similar terminology (e.g., καταγράφω, κατατίθημι, ἀνατίθημι, ἀνιερόω, *dono, mando*, and *trado*), see Smith, *Curse*, 88–98.
223 For example, see Stanley, *Paul and the Language of Scripture*, 194–197, where, in his analysis of scriptural interpretation in 1–2 Cor and Gal, he skips over 1 Cor 5:13 and 10:22. See also, E. Earle Ellis, *Paul's Use of the Old Testament* (Grand Rapids: Eerdmans, 1957); Dietrich-Alex Koch, *Die Schrift als Zeuge des Evangeliums. Untersuchungen zur Verwendung und zum Verständnis der Schrift bei Paulus*, BHT 69 (Tübingen: Mohr Siebeck, 1986); Christopher M. Tuckett, "Paul, Scrip-

2.5 Peril in 1 Corinthians — 91

The sentence in question reads: ἐξάρατε τὸν πονηρὸν ἐξ ὑμῶν αὐτῶν (1 Cor 5:13b). This citation lacks any introductory formula, but Paul's use of ἐξαίρω ("purge") is suggestive of his awareness of the Deuteronomic context of such language.[225] This is apparent when comparing 1 Cor 5:13b to similar forms of this sentence found only in Deuteronomy:[226]

1 Cor 5:13	ἐξάρατε τὸν πονηρὸν ἐξ ὑμῶν αὐτῶν.
Deut 13:6	ἀφανιεῖς τὸν πονηρὸν ἐξ ὑμῶν αὐτῶν.
Deut 17:7; 19:19; 21:21; 22:21, 24; 24:7	ἐξαρεῖς τὸν πονηρὸν ἐξ ὑμῶν αὐτῶν.
Deut 17:12; 22:22	ἐξαρεῖς τὸν πονηρὸν ἐξ Ισραηλ.

Deuteronomy contains instructions about Israel's proper response toward God's grace and consequently, the people are given strict commands to avoid idolatry (e.g., Deut 5; 12:1–7) and sexual immorality (e.g., Deut 17–18; 22). There are also strong resonances between the various figures meriting dissociation in 1 Cor 5:11 (πλεονέκτης ἢ εἰδωλολάτρης ἢ λοίδορος ἢ μέθυσος ἢ ἅρπαξ) and the corresponding activities forbidden in Deuteronomy: greed/robbery (Deut 24:7); idola-

---

ture and Ethics: Some Reflections," *NTS* 46.3 (2000): 403–424; Allen D. Verhey, "Ethics, New Testament Ethics," *ISBE* 2:179; Peter S. Zaas, "'Cast Out the Evil Man from Your Midst' (1 Cor 5:13b)," *JBL* 103.2 (1984): 259–261. To be fair, Stanley asserts at the outset that he will focus on what he calls "explicit citation," and according to his "strict guidelines," a text such as 1 Cor 5:13 can rightly be excluded because an uninformed reader would not be aware of the fact that a citation is being offered. This is somewhat disingenuous since Stanley's own study shows that the presence of an introductory formula has no bearing on how the source text(s) were handled by Paul or any of the other authors cited for that matter, which makes his reception-oriented guidelines more tenuous than it may first appear. Furthermore, even Stanley is aware of other secondary literature (e.g. Hays, *Echoes*) that established the rationale for a more nuanced understanding of Paul's engagement with the Jewish scriptures than the dichotomy he proposes between "explicit citation" and everything else. It is also not necessary, however, to adopt a maximalist position that seeks to find scriptural allusions behind nearly everything Paul wrote. On the maximalist/minimalist distinction, see Francis Watson, "Scripture in Pauline Theology: How Far Down Does It Go?," *Journal of Theological Interpretation* 2.2 (2008): 181–192.

224 Sean M. McDonough, "Competent to Judge: The Old Testament Connection Between 1 Corinthians 5 and 6," *JTS* 56.1 (2005): 99–102; Brian S. Rosner, *Paul, Scripture, and Ethics: A Study of 1 Corinthians 5–7* (Grand Rapids: Baker, 1999); idem, "Deuteronomy in 1 and 2 Corinthians."

225 The verb, ἐξαίρω, occurs only here in the NT, and the phrase, ἐξαίρω τὸν πονηρόν, occurs only in Deuteronomy and 1 Corinthians.

226 The chapter:verse references from Deuteronomy are from the LXX. Philo also makes reference to Deuteronomy in *De ebrietate* 14 (ἐξαρεῖς τὸν πονηρὸν ἐξ ὑμῶν αὐτῶν), likewise without indication that he is citing from the Hebrew Bible. Just as in 1 Cor 5, the context of his citation makes the connection more certain.

try (Deut 13:1–5; 17:2–7); slander (Deut 19:16–19); and drunkenness (Deut 21:18–21). Each prohibition is then followed by the exhortation to "purge the evil from your midst" (ἐξαίρω [or ἀφανίζω] τόν πονηρόν ἐξ ὑμῶν).²²⁷ Furthermore, Deut 17:2–7 outlines a clear description of a five-step process of getting rid of the polluting individual from the community,²²⁸ and just as in 1 Corinthians 5, the concern lies with persons already assumed to be a member of the community and not with those belonging to the outside (Deut 17:2a, Ἐὰν δὲ εὑρεθῇ ἐν σοί; also Deut 19:15–21; 1 Cor 5:12).

The various occurrences of "purge" (ἐξαίρω/ἀφανίζω) in Deuteronomy all point to the death penalty as the means to remove guilt from Israel, and Paul's statement to similarly purge the evil in 1 Cor 5:13 accords with the understanding that ὄλεθρος τῆς σαρκός in 5:5 meant physical harm or death.²²⁹ Neither in Deuteronomy nor in 1 Corinthians 5 does one find any indication that re-

---

227 The marginal note from the NA²⁸ mark Deut 17:7 LXX as the text cited by Paul in 1 Cor 5:13 (see Fee, *First Epistle to the Corinthians*, 227; McDonough, "Competent to Judge," 101), but it is not necessary to strictly limit Paul's citation to one specific verse from Deuteronomy to the exclusion of others. It may also be possible that this is precisely why Paul's citation lacks an introductory formula; he is not appealing to one specific verse or passage from Deut, but rather bringing into conversation the various places such language occurs.

228 Step #1: The person is found who has done evil and transgressed a boundary (Deut 17:2–3). #2: The misconduct is known to the community (17:4a). #3: An investigation is to take place to discern whether a transgression has in fact taken place (17:4b). #4: The requirement of multiple witnesses (17:6). #5: The placement of sentencing upon the offender to occur outside of the community (17:5a, 7). Smith (*Curse*, 140–1) argues that it is not clear that 1 Cor 5:13 is a citation of Deut 17:7 LXX since there are other places in Deuteronomy that repeats the same language (see the chart above). Even if 1 Cor 5:13 is not a direct reference to Deut 17:7, my overall thesis stands, namely that Paul was aware of the broader context in Deuteronomy when he drew upon this book in crafting the closing remark of 1 Cor 5.

Furthermore, Paul was likely aware of the Deuteronomic due process since elsewhere in the Corinthian correspondence he makes direct reference to it with regard to a member who has sinned (2 Cor 13:1–2). Therefore, it is not difficult to suggest that here too in 1 Cor 5:1–13, the same process informs Paul's exhortation to the Corinthian assembly regarding the incestuous individual. In 1 Cor 5:1–2, Paul begins with the fact that not only has the transgression been found, but that it is well-known to the rest of the community (Steps #1–2). A need for an investigation and the collection of witnesses (Steps #3–4) are rendered superfluous since the incest is occurring in plain sight to all the members in Corinth. What Paul urges is the completion of this process through judgment (Step #5). On Paul's use of Deut 19:15 in 2 Cor 13:1, see Laurence L. Welborn, "'By the Mouth of Two or Three Witnesses': Paul's Invocation of a Deuteronomic Statute," *NovT* 52 (2010): 207–220.

229 Every use of ἐξαίρω or ἀφανίζω translates the Hebrew verb בָּעַר (= "utterly remove, partic. of evil and guilt." BDB, s.v.). See 1 En. 10:8; 12:4; 16:1; T. Levi 18:4; T. Sol. 18:40; Pss. Sol. 4:22, 24; 17:36.

habilitation of an errant member was the goal of such ordinances. There is also other evidence from antiquity that this language was used in the context of curses and magic. For example, in the pseudonymous Testament of Solomon, there is an intriguing conversation that takes place between Solomon and the thirty-six elements (18:1), in which one of the demons claims that he has the ability to purge flesh (18:40, σάρκας ἀφανίζω), which certainly meant physical suffering.[230]

Under the auspices of divine power, Paul explicitly identifies "Satan" as the agent to whom the transgressor should be entrusted (παραδοῦναι τὸν τοιοῦτον τῷ σατανᾷ; see 1 Cor 5:4–5). This language is reminiscent of what happened to Job (Job 2:6 LXX, εἶπεν δὲ ὁ κύριος τῷ διαβόλῳ Ἰδοὺ παραδίδωμί σοι αὐτόν), though the situation is not exactly parallel since Job is recognized as a righteous man of God in contrast to the incestuous man of 1 Cor 5. The similarity is nevertheless significant because it indicates that Satan or a devil figure is able to inflict great physical pain upon those who enter into its domain. In both 1 Cor 5 and Job, it is indeed divinely sanctioned harm, but Paul never attributes Satan's activity to God. Despite God's presence in the midst of the assembly through the Holy Spirit, Paul acknowledges throughout his letters that the power of Satan is able to tempt, and even harm, God's people.[231]

What is the process by which the incestuous figure will suffer physically under malevolent forces? This will only become clearer when the other two sections (10:1–22 and 11:17–34) are analyzed, but for now, it is important to recognize that both the Hebrew Bible and the New Testament consistently associate Satan and demons with physical—and not simply spiritual—suffering and death.[232] Also, such physical torments are not interpreted as having a redeeming quality, i.e. that they generate "repentance" in the ailing person. As already

---

[230] The manuscripts behind the modern editions of the Testament of Solomon are quite late, though recent scholarship now accepts that various pieces of the Solomonic tradition are attested much earlier and possibly even originates as early as the first century BCE. For other attestations of this tradition, see Josephus, *Ant.* 8.42–46; 11Q11; Orig. World 107; Testim. Truth 70; Apoc. Adam 7.13. Sarah L. Schwarz, "Demons and Douglas: Applying Grid and Group to the Demonologies of the Testament of Solomon," *JAAR* 80.4 (2012): 909–931.

[231] In the Pauline corpus: 1 Cor 7:5; 2 Cor 2:11; 11:14; 12:7; 1 Thess 2:18; 2 Thess 2:9; 1 Tim 1:20; 5:15. In the NT: Mark 1:13; Luke 13:16; 22:3; John 13:27; Acts 5:3; 26:18; Rev 12:9; 20:2.

[232] The following will be a brief analysis of NT passages dealing with "Satan." For the Hebrew Bible and Second Temple Judaism more broadly, see the relevant evidence and secondary literature in Derek R. Brown, "The God of This Age: Satan in the Churches and Letters of the Apostle Paul" (PhD diss., University of Edinburgh, 2011). I disagree, however, with Brown when he follows the traditional understanding of "handing over" as leading to the salvation of the individual. To his credit, Brown accepts the possibility that the individual could in fact suffer harm by Satan.

noted, Job is an important example, whose experience clearly shows Satan inflicting much harm on him and his family. This includes the loss of his possessions, his children, his health, and even his life would have likely been taken had not God set specific limits to Satan's power (Job 1:13–19; 2:1–8).

In the New Testament, there are various references to Satan and demons to similar effect. Matthew describes the healing of a mute man who was possessed by a demon (Matt 9:32, ἄνθρωπον κωφὸν δαιμονιζόμενον).[233] Mark recounts the story of the Gerasene man who "cut himself with stones" (Mark 5:5, κατακόπτων ἑαυτὸν λίθοις).[234] Luke tells the story of a crippled woman who had suffered for 18 years because of Satan (Luke 13:16, ἣν ἔδησεν ὁ σατανᾶς).[235] John names the "devil" as "a murderer from the beginning" (John 8:44, ἐκεῖνος ἀνθρωποκτόνος ἦν ἀπ' ἀρχῆς), and the same figure is named as "the one who has the power of death" in Hebrews (2:14, τὸν τὸ κράτος ἔχοντα τοῦ θανάτου, τοῦτ' ἔστιν τὸν διάβολον).[236] Acts 10:38 describes Jesus's activity as "healing all who were oppressed by the devil," implying physical ailments. There is also the episode of Ananias and Sapphira in Acts 5:1–11 where the two behaved in a way that Peter attributes to Satan's activity (5:3, διὰ τί ἐπλήρωσεν ὁ σατανᾶς τὴν καρδίαν σου). Their greed is viewed as "lying" and "testing" God's Spirit (5:3, 9) and consequently, both receive death as the penalty. Finally, Paul himself mentions a thorn given to him "in the flesh, a messenger of Satan to torment" him in 2 Cor 12:7.[237]

Besides Satan's power to destroy, there is one other consequence of the man's expulsion that makes him vulnerable to destruction or death. There is a logical link between "celebrating the feast" (ἑορτάζω) that Paul mentions in 1 Cor 5:8 and the need to purge the evil before such meals can be shared among the members of the assembly. Paul desires that the Corinthians exist in harmony and share the meal together, but the latter is prohibited to the so-called brother or sister who does not act as his or her identification should suggest

---

233 See also the man who was mute and blind because of a demon in Matt 12:22 (δαιμονιζόμενος τυφλὸς καὶ κωφός).
234 Mark describes this man as one "with an unclean spirit" (Mark 5:2, ἐν πνεύματι ἀκαθάρτῳ). Matthew names in this story "two demoniacs" (Matt 8:28, δύο δαιμονιζόμενοι) and Luke tells his readers that it was a man "who had demons" (Luke 8:27, ἔχων δαιμόνια).
235 See also the physical suffering of a boy in Luke 9:39: "Suddenly a spirit sizes him (καὶ ἰδοὺ πνεῦμα λαμβάνει αὐτόν) and all at once he shrieks. It convulses him until he foams at the mouth; it mauls him and will scarcely leave him." Mark identifies it as a "mute spirit" (Mark 9:17, πνεῦμα ἄλαλον) while Matthew, upon Jesus's rebuke, calls it a "demon" (Matt 17:18).
236 See also the reference to "the devil" in Rev 2:10.
237 This may be part of the reason behind the Corinthians' description of Paul that he relays in 2 Cor 10:10 (ἡ δὲ παρουσία τοῦ σώματος ἀσθενής) .

(5:11). In this symbolic world, the space *within* the Corinthian assembly is one of wholeness and health, inhabited and energized by the Spirit and the power of the meal, while the space *without* is one devoid of the Spirit and the meal, the place where Satan has power ("Zugriffsbereich des Satans"[238]) to cause suffering and destruction. In other words, the participation in the feast and of the paschal lamb is not extended to the incestuous man, not simply because of what it signifies, but also because of what it imparts to faithful members of the assembly, that is quite literally, *life* in community. Otherwise, why does Paul follow the "purging" of the man in 1 Cor 5:1–5 with the discussion of feasting, Passover, and then the prohibition of meal with infectious individuals in 5:6–11? Unfortunately, one is not helped here by English translations of the particle μηδέ in 5:11 as "not even" which minimizes the force of Paul's stricture.[239]

The way this particle is translated presents meal-eating as if it was the least important activity the Corinthians should desist from in relation to the incestuous man, but that is precisely the opposite of Paul's argument in 1 Cor 5:1–13. Paul does not mean that the Corinthians should stop associating with the immoral man in every arena of life, including that unimportant detail of sharing a meal with him as a community. Instead, it should be understood that the prohibition of association (ἔγραψα ὑμῖν μὴ συναναμίγνυσθαι) is coordinate with the prohibition of meal-sharing (τῷ τοιούτῳ μηδὲ συνεσθίειν) in the corporate context.[240] Wayne Meeks hinted at this understanding: "he no longer had access to that special fellowship [i.e. the Lord's supper] indicated by use of the term brother."[241] Since the Corinthian assembly is the ναὸς τοῦ θεοῦ energized by the Spirit of

---

[238] Karl-Heinrich Ostmeyer, "Satan und Passa in 1. Korinther 5," *ZNW* 5.9 (2002): 44. See also Vahrenhorst, *Kultische Sprache*, 161: "Der Raum außerhalb der Gemeinde ist für Paulus keineswegs neutrales Gebiet." I disagree, however, with Vahrenhorst's comments (typical of many interpreters) that 1 Cor 5 envisages a rehabilitation of the offender.

[239] E. g., Conzelmann, Fee, Fitzmyer, Hays; CEB; ESV; NASB; NIV; NLT; NRSV. It is true that BDF §445 translates μηδὲ as "not even" in the case when it "stands at the beginning of the whole sentence or follows an οὐ (μή) within the same clause." But, the same construction is used elsewhere (e. g., Rom 6:12–13; 1 Cor 10:7–10; 2 Cor 4:2; Eph 4:27; Col 2:21; 2 Thess 3:10) and this type of emphasis is usually not added to translations of those verses. Against BDF see Smyth (§2163 A, "*and not, nor*") and BAGD, "s.v." ("*and not, but not, nor*" [*not even* only applies to certain situations]). For an overview of the "not even" versus "not" translations, see Jonathan Schwiebert, "Table Fellowship and the Translation of 1 Corinthians 5:11," *JBL* 127.1 (2008): 159–164.

[240] Fee, *First Epistle to the Corinthians*, 226; Hays, *First Corinthians*, 87; Smith, *Curse*, 139; Schwiebert, "Table Fellowship." *Contra* Zeller, *Der erste Brief*, 208.

[241] Meeks, *First Urban Christians*, 130; Schwiebert, "Table Fellowship," 164.

God, to be excluded from the sharing in the body and blood of the Lord meant that the person was as good as dead.

This interpretation accords best with the death-curse structure of 1 Cor 5:5, that anticipated physical harm to be inflicted upon the man, as someone who was no longer a participant in the life-giving Spirit and meal of the Corinthian assembly and is now one given over to Satan's power. Therefore, in 1 Cor 5, there are two facets of this mechanism of harm to be exacted upon the incestuous man: first, the person is given over to the domain of "Satan" who is now able to inflict significant physical harm upon any who have been removed from protection provided within God's assembly, and second, the person is simultaneously excluded from the communal feast of this temple of God, the meal that continues to provide life and fellowship with the risen Lord. Vahrenhorst rightly concludes, "Die in 1 Kor 5 konkret geforderte Trennung von einem Gemeindeglied wird also unter der in 3,16 explizit gemachten Voraussetzung verständlich, 'dass die Gemeinde und ihre einzelnen Glieder Tempel des heiligen Geistes sind.'"[242]

2.5.2 Peril in 1 Corinthians 10:1–22

In 1 Corinthians 10, there are various references to destruction, both as the recollection of Israelite history and as the current situation of the Corinthians. The remembrance of the wilderness experience is apropos since Paul tells the Corinthians that what happened to the Israelites will likely happen to them if they do not behave properly. Paul highlights this possibility first of all by illustrating with startling imagery that many of their forefathers were "strewn about in the wilderness" (κατεστρώθησαν[243] ἐν τῇ ἐρήμῳ) despite their status as baptized participants of God's spiritual food and drink (1 Cor 10:2–5).[244] If such calamity

---

[242] Vahrenhorst, *Kultische Sprache*, 164 citing Friedrich Wilhelm Horn, *Das Angeld des Geistes: Studien zur paulinischen Pneumatologie*, FRLANT 154 (Göttingen: Vandenhoeck & Ruprecht, 1992), 240.

[243] Καταστρώννυμι: Herodotus, *Hist.* 8.53.14; 9.69.13, 76.1; Xenophon, *Cyr.* 3.3.64; Num 14:16; Jdt 7:14, 25; 14:4 LXX; 2 Macc 5:26; 11:11; 12:28; 15:27; Diodorus Siculus, *Bib. hist.* 14.114.6; 15.80.5; 19.108.6; Josephus, *J.W.* 5.404; Philo (καταστορέννυμι), *Abr.* 234; *Legat.* 222; *Mos.* 2.255; *Virt.* 43.

[244] 1 Cor 10:1–4 highlights the privileged position of Israel, rendering God's subsequent judgment upon them even more striking with the emphatic Ἀλλ' οὐκ ἐν τοῖς πλείοσιν that begins 10:5.

can strike God's people in the past, then it is certainly possible for the Corinthians now. The wilderness tradition serves as a stern warning to the Corinthians.[245]

Paul asserts that the experience of the Israelites should serve as an admonition "to not be cravers of evil, as they craved" (1 Cor 10:6). This phrase is noted in NA[28] as a reference to Numbers 11:4–34, and many scholars agree with this assessment.[246] What they have failed to recognize, however, is how this connection demonstrates that food and drink continued to be objects of stumbling for the Israelites. Furthermore, Paul's comment about "not craving evil" should not be spiritually interpreted or generalized, but understood in this same context vis-à-vis the consequences of desiring and consuming prohibited substances.[247] Paul's words are relayed not simply as the preference for a particular diet, but as the account of misdeeds arising from neglecting God and the meal associated with godself.[248]

The examples from the Israelites describe the dangers associated with meals. First, 1 Cor 10:6 (see Num 11:4–34) illustrates how this "craving" for meat manifested itself among God's people to their own destruction.[249] Second, 1 Cor 10:7 cites Exod 32:6 which is located in the context of the Israelites consuming sacrificial foods offered to a deity other than YHWH God (Exod 32:5–6a). Third, 1 Cor 10:8 is an allusion to Num 25:1–9, where they polluted themselves

---

245 Zeller, *Der erste Brief*, 330.
246 In the commentary tradition: Calvin; Ciampa and Rosner; Collins; Fitzmyer; Hays; Horsley; Weiss; Zeller, and in other published works such as Gary D. Collier, "'That We Might Not Crave Evil': The Structure and Argument of 1 Corinthians 10.1–13," *JSNT* 55 (1994): 55–75; Meeks, "Midrash and Paraenesis," 68; Mitchell, *Paul and the Rhetoric of Reconciliation*, 138–9; Works, *Church in the Wilderness*, 70–71. On the insignificance of Numbers: Fee. With no reference to Numbers: Conzelmann; Robertson-Plummer.
247 E.g. Conzelmann asserts that Paul's warning about ἐπιθυμία is "umfassend" (*Der erste Brief*, 205).
248 For example, Francis Watson (*Paul and the Hermeneutics of Faith* [London: T&T Clark, 2004], 364) argues that "desire" is the root issue and Carla Works (*Church in the Wilderness*, 71) builds upon Watson and states that "distrust of God and forgetfulness of God's care" lie at the heart of Israel's problems. Both scholars are certainly correct in their assessment, but do not go far enough to discuss why Israel's misdeeds are continually associated with consumptions of prohibited substances.
249 The relevant verses are as follows: "³The rabble among them craved with desire (ἐπεθύμησαν ἐπιθυμίαν); and after they sat down, they wept—also the sons of Israel—and said, "Who will feed us with meat? ... ⁶But now our soul is parched; our eyes see nothing but manna ... ³³ The meat was still between their teeth before it was consumed and the Lord became angry against the people and the Lord struck the people with a very great plague. ³⁴And the name of that place was called Tombs of Craving (Μνήματα τῆς ἐπιθυμίας), because they buried the people that craved (τὸν ἐπιθυμητήν)." See also Philo, *Spec.* 4.126–130.

with the daughters of Moab and consumed sacrifices of Moabite idols (Num 25:2). Fourth, 1 Cor 10:9 commands the Corinthians to not test Christ, lest they experience the same manner of destruction as the Israelites in the wilderness. The details of this verse point to Num 21:4–7 as the event being described, when the Israelites complained against God and Moses due to their lack of bread and water, along with their overall discontent with the foods currently available.[250] The verb ἐκπειράζω from 1 Cor 10:9 does not occur in Num 21, but the Israelites' speaking out against God (lit.: "to speak evil against") is more than sufficient to encompass such an act.[251] The Israelites' craving for sustenance beyond what God provided led to their death. Fifth and finally, 1 Cor 10:10 exhorts them "to not grumble" (μὴ γογγύζετε) as the Israelites did, since it would bring destruction upon themselves. Such complaining is noted throughout the wilderness tradition, and more importantly, usually found in accounts of Israelite cravings for food and drink (see LXX Exod 15:24; 16:2–12; 17:3; Num 14:2, 27–29, 36; Ps 105:25).

These five episodes that Paul illustrates from the wilderness tradition all explain with certainty how the Israelites "craved for evil" through their participation in and consumption of food and drink that were expressly forbidden. Thus, the threat of destruction for the Corinthians exists because of their participation in what Paul calls the cup and table of demons (1 Cor 10:21, ποτήριον/τράπεζα δαιμονίων). The accounts from Israelite history are further proof that even those who took part in "spiritual food and drink" were unable to avoid their cravings for other objects of consumption, and consequently, were struck down in the wilderness (1 Cor 10:2–5). This inability to control "cravings" (ἐπιθυμία) in the wilderness remained an important *topos* for other Jewish writers, seen in the Wisdom of Solomon, for example, where the author turns the story of Israelite craving on its head.[252] Similarly in Corinth, what may be perceived as a harm-

---

[250] Num 21:5 MT: לחם הקלקל, "bread of misery"/ LXX: ὁ ἄρτος ὁ διάκενος, "empty bread."
[251] Num 21:5 LXX: καὶ κατελάλει ὁ λαὸς πρὸς τὸν θεὸν καὶ κατὰ Μωυσῆ. The psalter later understood the complaint to be a form of testing. See Ps 77:18–19a LXX: καὶ ἐξεπείρασαν τὸν θεὸν ἐν ταῖς καρδίαις αὐτῶν τοῦ αἰτῆσαι βρώματα ταῖς ψυχαῖς αὐτῶν καὶ κατελάλησαν τοῦ θεοῦ. Notice also two other linguistic parallels: the first concerns "soul" (ψυχή) in Numbers 21:5 and Ps 77:18 LXX, and the second concerns testing God and provoking him to jealousy ([ἐκ]πειράζω/ παραζηλόω) in Ps. 77:56–58 LXX and 1 Cor 10:9, 22. Note that Ps 105 LXX also contains many of the same elements.
[252] Wis 16:1–14 conveys that God provided quails to the Israelites as food "for the craving of appetite" (16:2, εἰς ἐπιθυμίαν ὀρέξεως) and the Egyptians, "while craving for food" (16:3, ἐπιθυμοῦντες τροφήν), could not be satisfied. The Egyptians turned away from their appetite while the Israelites "partook of the delicacies" (16:3, ξένης μετάσχωσι γεύσεως). The Egyptians were eventually destroyed by snakes (16:5, διεφθείροντο ὄφεων). On the negative relationship be-

less feast in the temple is, in reality, a misapprehension of the nature of the Lord's table and sacrificial foods.²⁵³ Their partaking of the Lord's table does not make them automatically invincible to hostile forces, just as spiritual food did not for the Israelites. The Corinthians' participation in the table of demons is the same "idolatry" displayed by the Israelites and liable to the same kinds of punishments that God meted out in the wilderness.

The tension remains: is it God who destroys or is it demons? Just as in the wilderness accounts, there is a sense that God allows the hostile forces to harm by withdrawing his protection over the people. In 1 Cor 10:10, Paul mentions the mysterious agent of destruction (ὁ ὀλοθρευτής). Given the prominence of the Exodus material in this chapter, it most likely recalls "the destroyer" of Exod 12:23 (ὁ ὀλεθρεύων) where the ambiguity concerning God's agency remains.²⁵⁴ What Paul does make explicit is the reality of death that has been overlooked by the Corinthians.²⁵⁵Despite Paul's repeated insistence that the destruction of the Israelites are to serve as "examples" (1 Cor 10:6, 11), modern scholars seldom address the role that the earlier group's destruction plays for the Corinthians' present situation.²⁵⁶ The various OT parallels throughout this chapter are correctly identified and analyzed, but the notion that Paul views the same punishments to be just as real and possible for the Corinthians are rarely, if at all, discussed.²⁵⁷ The Corinthian assembly at peril is not a moment that lies at a distant future but is regarded by Paul as a possibility in the present.

---

tween ὄρεξις ("appetite" or "craving") and foods, see 4 Macc 1:33, 35; Sir 18:30; 23:6; Philo, *Det.* 113; *Ebr.* 222; *Leg.* 3.138; *Virt.* 136; Josephus, *J.W.* 5.549. On later rabbinic interpretation of the destruction via serpents, see Tg. Ps.-J. Num 21:6; Tg. Neof. Num 21:6.
253 Zeller, *Der erste Brief*, 337. If the sustenance provided to the Israelites were understood as life-giving "spiritual food and drink," then more so would be the current sustenance provided to the Corinthians within the temple of God. Johnson, *Religious Experience*, 175n138.
254 Another Jewish text, Wisdom of Solomon, makes the relationship between "the destroyer" (Wis 18:25, ὁ ὀλεθρεύων) and God closer than either Exodus or 1 Corinthians. See Wis 18:20–25.
255 Francis Watson, *Paul and the Hermeneutics of Faith* (London: T&T Clark, 2004), 336–37.
256 In the NT, νουθεσία is strictly Pauline in usage (1 Cor 10:11; Eph 6:4; Titus 3:10) and occurs only once in the LXX, in a similar context of portraying another group's destruction in the wilderness (Wis 16:6).
257 For example, Fee, *First Epistle to the Corinthians*, 459 (also Conzelmann, *1 Corinthians*, 168n43; Robertson-Plummer, *First Epistle*, 207–208) interprets this entire subsection (1 Cor 10:1–13) as operating at the level of eschatological discourse, asserting: "This can only mean that the Corinthians, too, as Israel, may fail of the eschatological prize, in this case eternal salvation." This is strange since the Israelite experience of the wilderness is not conveyed in 1 Corinthians 10 as the forefathers' inability to obtain an "eschatological prize," but as immediate punishments meted out through physical suffering and death. It is true that Paul makes direct reference to "the ends of the ages" (NT/LXX hapax, τὰ τέλη τῶν αἰώνων), but he pulls this re-

2.5.3 Peril in 1 Corinthians 11:17–34

In these verses, one encounters a more thorough account of what Dieter Zeller calls the "kausalen Zusammenhang Zwischen Sünde und leiblichem Verderben," hinted at by Paul in 1 Cor 5:5.[258] The details, however, remain slim: Paul merely affirms that due to the Corinthians' unworthy participation in the Lord's supper, many of them have become weak and sick (11:30). Indeed, not a few deaths (κοιμῶνται ἱκανοί) attest to the gravity of the situation. Such physical sufferings should not be interpreted simply as a divine judgment of individual faults, but as the sign of a diseased communal body. When a certain branch of a tree falls or a limb of a person is diseased, it can mean not only that the lesser parts are weaker or weakened, but also that the main trunk or body is under attack from a dangerous agent.

One important point of debate lies in how the clause, ἐν ὑμῖν πολλοὶ ἀσθενεῖς καὶ ἄρρωστοι καὶ κοιμῶνται ἱκανοί, in 1 Cor 11:30 is understood. According to Ilaria Ramelli, "practically all contemporary commentators agree" that the phrase is interpreted in "a physical sense, as bodily sickness and death." She proceeds through her history of research to show that the disease and death should be interpreted in a "spiritual sense."[259] Unfortunately, there are significant deficiencies with Ramelli's study that should be discussed, which will, in turn, provide clarity with respect to important questions surrounding 1 Cor 11:17–34.

First, she overstates her case by asserting that "all other commentators ... claim that 1 Cor 11:30 must be understood in a physical and literal way."[260] If anything, there is a tendency among scholars to overlook this verse and its immediate literary context, with Joseph Fitzmyer rightly observing that 11:30 has received scant attention in the history of interpretation.[261] To be sure, scholars have commented upon the verse, but the discussion is almost always highly abbreviated and lacks substantive discussion of what is actually taking place in

---

ality forward and views life and death hanging in the balance in the present. Other commentators note the seriousness of what happened in the wilderness but do not elaborate much beyond stating that the Corinthians may face a similar fate as the Israelites: e.g., Fitzmyer, Hays, Zeller. Exception: Collins, *Works*.

258 Zeller, *Der erste Brief*, 378.
259 Ilaria L. E. Ramelli, "Spiritual Weakness, Illness, and Death in 1 Corinthians 11:30," *JBL* 130.1 (2011): 146. The only exception to this rule is, according to Ramelli, Sebastian Schneider, "Glaubensmängel in Korinth: Eine neue Deutung der 'Schwachen, Kranken, Schlafenden,' in 1 Kor 11,30," *Filologia Neotestamentaria* 9 (1996): 3–19.
260 Ramelli, "Spiritual Weakness," 146.
261 Fitzmyer, *First Corinthians*, 447.

Corinth.²⁶² This is not surprising since Paul's view of the relationship between the assembly and the Lord's supper does not comport easily with modern, Western understandings of causes underlying illnesses and deaths. The discomfort is such that some have tried to consider other social or economic conditions that contributed to the ailments. Ramelli's analysis does not take this modern bias into account, which is a significant obstacle to properly understanding Paul's view of the assembly.

Second, she claims silence among early interpreters vis-à-vis 1 Cor 11:30, though she equivocates by asserting that, "many more fathers, such as Origen and authors related to him, offer a decidedly spiritual interpretation."²⁶³ It is a weak argument to assert that there are "very few and sparse patristic comments on this verse," and subsequently lean heavily upon Origen and a few others for their "spiritual" interpretation.²⁶⁴ In addition, her assertion that John Chrysostom "[did] not spend a single word on v. 30" is plainly wrong.²⁶⁵

Finally, how the terms ἀσθενής, ἄρρωστος, and κοιμάω would have been understood within their ancient context is not discussed. Since both patristic and modern exegesis lack any serious interest in defining the disease and death described in 1 Cor 11:30, it is important to examine the use of similar language in antiquity. The verb (κοιμάω) most certainly means "to die" or "to be dead," as a

---

262 Some scholars believe that there may have been a famine during time in Corinth that caused the physical infirmities described by Paul. This is certainly a possibility, but it is remarkable that Paul makes no mention of it and frames the entire discussion not in terms of sustenance, but in their behavior. For this hypothesis, see Bradley B. Blue, "The House Church at Corinth and the Lord's Supper: Famine, Food Supply, and the *Present Distress*," CTR 5 (1991): 221–239; Bruce W. Winter, "Secular and Christian Responses to Corinthian Famines," TynBul 40.1 (1989): 86–106.
263 Ramelli, "Spiritual Weakness," 150.
264 Ramelli also notes a passage from Clement of Alexandria (*Strom*. 1.1.10.5), a passage from John Cassian (*Conl*. 22.5), and fragments from Didymus the Blind (*Fragm. in Ps*. 416; 417). This list hardly can be understood as "many more fathers" in support of a spiritual interpretation ("Spiritual Weakness," 150). The evidence from Clement is not decisive, and Origen heavily influenced John Cassian and Didymus, as Ramelli herself admits. For further evidence of Origen's influence, see Dominic Keech, "John Cassian and the Christology of Romans 8,3," VC 64 (2010): 280–299; Grand D. Bayliss, *The Vision of Didymus the Blind: A Fourth-Century Virtue-Origenism* (Oxford: Oxford University Press, 2015); Richard A. Layton, *Didymus the Blind and His Circle in Late-Antique Alexandria: Virtue and Narrative in Biblical Scholarship* (Urbana: University of Illinois Press, 2004).
265 Ramelli, "Spiritual Weakness," 150. In a number of writings, John Chrysostom makes direct reference to 1 Cor 11:30 (+ surrounding verses), and often in a manner that cannot be interpreted as "spiritual" exegesis. See, for example, *Stag*. 1.3; *Hom. Matt*. 18:23 5; *Diab*. 1.8; *Laz*. 3; *Mart*. 3; *Stat*. 5.4; *Exp. Ps*. 142; *Hom. Heb*. 5; *Hom. Phil*. 9; *Hom. 2 Cor. 4:13* 3.

commonly used Greek euphemism since Homer.²⁶⁶ The other two words (ἀσθενής and ἄρρωστος), however, receive very little attention in Ramelli's article since she develops the notion of the "death of the soul" as the main—or sole—point of 1 Cor 11:30. Because the evidence from the time between Paul and Origen is sparse, as Ramelli herself admits, her decision to map an interpreter's framework from the fourth century directly onto that of Paul from the first is questionable, especially because she fails to consider the synchronic use of these important terms.

In the first five centuries of the Common Era, the dual use of the terms ἀσθενής and ἄρρωστος is limited to Greek medical literature, *always* in reference to physical, and not spiritual, maladies.²⁶⁷ Also, the individual occurrences of ἀσθενής and ἄρρωστος in Greek literature of all genres clearly demonstrate that these words did not maintain the semantic range that Ramelli posits.²⁶⁸ The terms are also used constantly and consistently throughout the Hippocratic (ca. 5th BCE) and Galenic (ca. 2nd CE) corpora to describe physical conditions, likely indicating established uses of ἀσθενής and ἄρρωστος when Paul also wrote his letter to the Corinthians. In other words, without good *contextual* and *contemporary* evidence

---

266 See BDAG, s.v. Even Ramelli is well aware of this common usage of κοιμάω ("Spiritual Weakness," 154–155), though she pushes the idea of this "death" even further to what she calls the "death of the soul."
267 Hippocrates, *Acut.* 9.29; Galen, *Thras.* (Kühn 5.823.12); *De usu partium* (Kühn 3.75.3); *Temp.* 3 (Kühn 1.630.1); *MM* 8.544K; *HVA* (Kühn 15.559.2); *Cons.* (Dietz 111.12). Early Christian texts citing Paul are the only exception to this rule. The abbreviations of the Galenic corpus follows R. J. Hankinson, ed., *The Cambridge Companion to Galen* (Cambridge: Cambridge University Press, 2008).
268 For ἀσθενής: E.g., Pindar, *Pyth.* 55; Aeschylus, *Prom.* 517; Thucydides, 4.126.4; 7.48.1, 75.3; Euripides, *Med.* 807; *Hec.* 798; *Heracl.* 23; Herodotus, *Hist.* 6.111; 9.31; Isocrates, *Plat.* 20; Aristophanes, *Eccl.* 539; Xenophon, *Mem.* 1.4.6; 2.6.12; *Cyr.* 5.2.22; Num 13:18; Judg 16:13; 1 Sam 2:10; Prov 22:22; 31:5, 9; Job 36:15; Dan 1:10; Matt 25:43, 44; Luke 10:9; Acts 4:9; 5:15, 16; 2 Cor 10:10; 1 Thess 5:14; 1 Clem. 38:2; Pol, *Phil.* 6.1; Diogn. 10:5; Josephus, *Ant.* 3.45; 5.308; 6.181; *J.W.* 3.62, 110, 523; 4.62, 489; 6.415; Dio Chrysostom, *Aegr.* 11.3; *3 Regn.* 137; *4 Regn.* 29. Inscriptional evidence in: *IG* II² 1365.27–29 (Attica, 2nd CE).

For ἄρρωστος: E.g., Isocrates, *Panath.* 9; *Big.* 33; *Aeginet.* 20; Hippocrates, *Acut.* 9.13; *Epid.* 2.3.11; Aristotle, *Hist. an.* 634b; Mal 1:8; Sir 7:35; Matt 14:14; Mark 6:5, 13; 16:18; Josephus, *J.W.* 5.526; Plutarch, *Ages.* 27.2; *Quaest. conv.* 635C; Diodorus Siculus, *Bib. hist.* 3.13.3; 4.71.1; 13.18.6; Appian, *Bell. civ.* 4.6.44; Epictetus, *Diatr.* 3.13.21, 26.23; *Ench.* 48.2; Dionysius of Halicarnassus, *Ant. rom.* 7.12.3, 68.3; Strabo, *Geogr.* 3.3.7; 16.1.20; Galen *De usu partium* (Kühn 3.262.5); *MM* 2.91K, 103K; 9.621K, 626K; 12.824K; *Nat.Fac.* 3.4.153. See TLG for the frequent use of both terms in the Hippocratic and Galenic corpora.

for a "spiritual" reading, the more straightforward interpretation is that Paul was thinking about physical bodies and physical ailments.[269]

1 Cor 11:30 reflects Paul's view that transgressions in the Corinthians' participation of the meal carry current and physical consequences, witnessed by the many illnesses and even deaths of many members *within* the assembly. This is an important point that proves that certain behaviors can bring death-dealing forces of the outside world *into* the group itself.[270] In 1 Cor 5 and 10, Paul illustrated the dangers existing in the space beyond the boundary of the assembly and at the liminal space between the assembly and the world, where some members were flirting with hostile forces. Here, Paul points to the internal dangers when those who act "unworthily" pervert the preeminent meal of God's temple, i.e. the Lord's supper. When members violate the principle of selfless giving and fail to properly discern the body of Christ (1 Cor 11:17–29)—which is part of the significance underlying their commemoration of the Lord's supper in the first place—the meal stands as an agent of their judgment rather than of their solidarity with Christ.

In this light, Paul's statement in 1 Cor 11:22 can be understood as an indictment against those in Corinth who have not properly "discerned the body of Christ" (11:29). It is not that they have despised God's assembly by shaming the have-nots, but that they have already violated the Lord's supper by turning the meal into something else altogether (11:20, 22).[271] Paul is not saying that *the*

---

[269] Also problematic is Ramelli's dismissal of Dale Martin's *The Corinthian Body* that argues against a dualism between spirit/body. My interpretation does not depend on such a bifurcation, but only shows that something harmful and real is occurring upon real human bodies. Also Schrage, *Korinther*, 3:53.

[270] Troy Martin brings to bear ancient medical discussions of *pneuma* on the reading of 1 Cor 11:17–34 and suggests that Paul's description of death and disease in this section "assume the health-giving and life-giving role of the Spirit." See Troy W. Martin, "Paul's Pneumatological Statements and Ancient Medical Texts," in *The New Testament and Early Christian Literature in Greco-Roman Context: Studies in Honor of Davie E. Aune*, ed. John Fotopoulos (Leiden: Brill, 2006), 105–126, esp. 124–25. Also Barrett, *First Epistle to the Corinthians*, 275; Johnson, "Life-Giving Spirit." Schrage (*Korinther*, 3:52–53) is less convinced though he observes the possibility of reading this text alongside 1 Cor 10:4–20: "Zwar wird man angesichts von 10,4.20 substanzhafte und machthaltige Vorstellungen nicht ausschließen, und die Kritik an einem magischen Verständnis darf nichts vom Realismus des Paulus und seiner nachdrücklichen Warnung vor aller Spiritualisierung abbrechen, als ob das Sakrament nur das sogenannte Innenleben berühre und nicht den Menschen als ganzen bis in seine Leiblichkeit und das Essen und Trinken hinein von seiner Herrsachaft beansprucht werde."

[271] For a contextualization of Paul's indictment that the Corinthians are "despising the assembly of God" (ἢ τῆς ἐκκλησίας τοῦ θεοῦ καταφρονεῖτε), see the relevant discussion of this language in chapter 3.

Lord's supper somehow becomes toxic as Dale Martin suggests.[272] Martin is partially right that the meal is now indeed deadly, but he misses the import of Paul's assertion at the beginning that "it is not the Lord's supper" (11:20). Their inability to understand and maintain the sanctity of God's temple is demonstrated by their lack of care for other members and by their ritual failure in proper participation of *the* meal associated with this temple.[273] The result? The perverted meal brings about physical illnesses and deaths.

2.6 Meals within the Temple of God

The close readings of 1 Corinthians 5:1–13, 10:1–22, and 11:17–34 in the context of power and peril reveal the importance of meals within the temple of God. The Corinthians' meals serve to tie these sections of Paul's letter together as well as to bring greater clarity to what it means for the Corinthians to be ὁ ναὸς τοῦ θεοῦ. These sections describe in various ways how meals within the temple of God should be understood: first, in relation to an offender within their midst; second, in relation to other temple meals in Corinth; and third, in relation to the substance of the meal itself. Mary Douglas has shown that there is a clear connection between table (consumed foods) and altar (temple), and such is also the case in 1 Corinthians.[274] Moreover, the anxiety surrounding meals can be seen in each situation, reflecting the idea that "the otherwise perhaps diffused dangers to the system are here brought to specific and concrete focus through the medium of food and drink."[275]

In 1 Corinthians 5:7–8, the use of imagery from Exodus informs the Corinthians' present experience. Paul refers to the Passover, unleavened bread, and the Paschal lamb, with good indication that such thoroughly Jewish ideas would be readily comprehensible to the Corinthians.[276] Paul brings these details together

---

[272] Dale B. Martin, *The Corinthian Body* (New Haven: Yale University Press, 1995), 191. This is somewhat reminiscent of an older proposal by Lietzmann that what was originally the φάρμακον ἀθανασίας (Ignatius, *Eph.* 20.2) through unworthy use became the φάρμακον θανάτου (Lietzmann, *Korinther*, 59).
[273] Peter-Ben Smit, "Ritual Failure, Ritual Negotiation, and Paul's Argument in 1 Corinthians 11:17–34," *JSPL* 3.2 (2013): 165–193; Peter Dijkhuizen, "The Lord's Supper and Ritual Theory: Interpreting 1 Corinthians 11:30 in Terms of Risk, Failure, and Efficacy," *Neot* 50.2 (2016): 446–476.
[274] Mary Douglas, "Deciphering a Meal," *Daedalus* 101.1 (1972): 61–81.
[275] Johnson, *Religious Experience*, 165; See the chapters "Powers and Dangers" and "External Boundaries" in Mary Douglas, *Purity and Danger: An Analysis of Concepts of Pollution and Taboo* (London: Routledge, 1966), 95–129.
[276] Fee, *First Epistle to the Corinthians*, 218.

in 1 Cor 5:8 with ὥστε ἑορτάζωμεν, a likely reference to the Corinthians' participation in the table of the Lord.[277] The importance of this meal can be seen further in Paul's exclusion of the offender (1 Cor 5:11; see discussion in 2.5.1). The meal offered within the temple of God must be guarded: it is not to be shared with those who will pollute the sanctuary.[278]

In 1 Cor 10:1–22, one can see the competitive nature of temple meals at work. Andrew McGowan detects this tension: "To participate in the Christian meal is, for Paul, to renounce the table of demons, but it is also to create another table whose logic is actually quite similar to that which he attacks."[279] There is potential for harm when Corinthians participated in the table of demons, and Paul regards the consumption of those foods to be incompatible with participation in the meal provided within the temple of God, i.e. the table of the Lord. Paul's use of the Exodus material proved how the craving of forbidden substances of consumption, particularly as they were connected to other deities, became a stumbling block for the Israelites. Likewise, Paul recognizes the temptations present in the meals of other gods and temples in Corinth, and he warns the Corinthians to watch out, lest they too fall into the same pitfall as their forebears in the wilderness.[280]

Finally, in 1 Cor 11:17–34, the perversion of the Lord's supper turns it into a moment of condemnation against the Corinthians.[281] The substances that were to provide fellowship with Christ and life to the assembly now wreak havoc upon the consumers (1 Cor 11:30). Paul chastises the Corinthians for not recognizing the solemn nature of this ritual: "When you come together, it is not really to eat the Lord's supper" (11:20). The Corinthians have neglected to acknowledge the sacred nature of foods offered within God's temple. Just as during the exodus with the Israelites, the Corinthians' participation in meals in the assembly not only united the members with one another, but it also gave expression to the relationship between human beings and God.[282] The Lord's meal was accessible to

---

277 Gordon P. Wiles, *Paul's Intercessory Prayers: The Significance of the Intercessory Prayer Passages in the Letters of St Paul* (Cambridge: Cambridge University Press, 1974), 142–43; 146–47.
278 Vahrenhorst, *Kultische Sprache*, 163.
279 Andrew McGowan, *Ascetic Eucharists: Food and Drink in Early Christian Ritual Meals* (Oxford: Clarendon Press, 1999), 273.
280 The destructive nature of foreign meals is seen also in 1 Cor 8.
281 It is beyond the scope of this study to discuss the question of historical development with regard to early Christian liturgy. The classic study along this vein is Hans Lietzmann's 1926 monograph, *Mass and Lord's Supper: A Study in the History of Liturgy*, trans. D. H. G. Reave (Leiden: Brill, 1953).
282 Philo likewise brings in temple imagery in his description of the Passover meal in *Spec.* 2.148 (Colson, LCL): "On this day every dwelling-house (ἑκάστη …οἰκία) is invested with the out-

all within the temple of God, but they must approach this table having abstained from other prohibited meals. They can only participate in this meal within the ritually constructed space (= the Corinthian assembly) and can only do so after they have properly tested oneself to ensure purity and allegiance to Jesus Christ.

2.7 A Synthetic Summary of Temple Discourse

The assembly of God exists as the temple *within* which God provides life-giving sustenance through the indwelling Spirit and through participation in the Lord's supper. The space *without* is envisioned as the place dominated by inimical forces that can destroy those that venture beyond the safety of God's temple, and the place where there is no mutual fellowship and participation in the Lord's meal. Both the Spirit and the meal are understood as sacred subjects that could be imperiled or perverted (1 Cor 5:5 and 11:20, respectively) when members of the community do not behave in a manner worthy of those that belong to God. At the periphery of the assembly, where the people can come in closer contact with foreign practices and entities, they are liable to be affected and assailed by powers that can harm. An example is found in 1 Cor 10, when the Corinthians did not properly distinguish between the table of the Lord and the table of demons. This is traversing the boundary that sets the temple of God apart from the space without, and Paul warns the Corinthians that such acts make them liable to harm by demonic agents. The other two sections also contain a similar view of the nature of the assembly. In 1 Cor 5, Paul exhorts the Corinthians to expel the incestuous man into the domain of Satan, and in 1 Cor 11, Paul tells them that improper behavior toward one another turns the meal into something else (1 Cor 11:20), perverting the Lord's supper into elements that can harm and kill.

Close readings of 1 Corinthians 5:1–13; 10:1–22; and 11:17–34 demonstrate how each of these sections of Paul's letter can be read in conversation due to the convergence of various themes therein. They expound what it means for the Corinthians to be the temple of God. Three important topics (Exodus tradition, power, and peril) were used as a way to draw out the subtle picture that

---

ward semblance and dignity of a temple (ἱερείου)." In post-70 CE Judaism, the meal became central to Jewish piety, though in a different turn than that of Paul with respect to the Temple. See discussion and primary sources from rabbinic material in Lanuwabang Jamir, *Exclusion and Judgment in Fellowship Meals: The Socio-historical Background of 1 Corinthians 11:17–34* (Eugene: OR: Pickwick Publications, 2016), 48–52.

Paul presents about nature of the Corinthian assembly. The traditions about the tabernacle, participation in meals, experience of divine power, and potential for destruction all explicate the experience of the Corinthians as God's temple. The following graphic illustrates how these three chapters contribute to a more nuanced understanding of the Corinthian assembly:

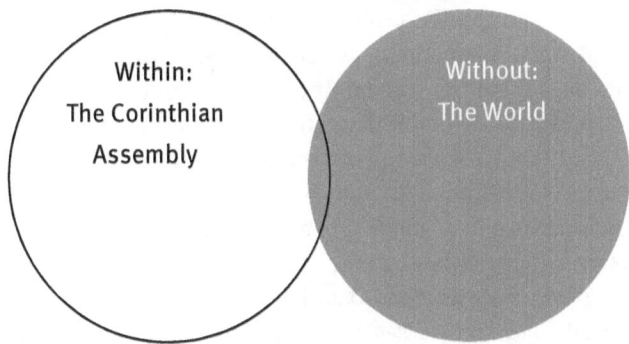

Paul portrays the space "within" as the Corinthian assembly, the temple of God in which the Spirit of God dwells. The space "without" is seen as the world, the domain of Satan and demons. Furthermore, within the assembly are holiness, life, and participation in the Lord's table, and outside the assembly are impurity, death, and participation in the table of demons. The liminal space at the periphery of the assembly is where some—who are supposed members of God's ἐκκλησία—fail to distinguish the boundary and engage in acts that are befitting of those that belong to "the world." As the overlapping space indicates, Paul is aware of the danger that the world presents to the assembly of God. If the Corinthians continue down the path of least resistance—that is, remain callous towards πορνεία among their own, do not cease participation in various cultic meals, and behave improperly during the Lord's meal—then the temple of God will remain susceptible to corruption and even to destruction, a threat that was explicitly noted as possible in 1 Cor 3:16–17. The most serious indication of this possibility is seen in 1 Cor 11:17–34, when the Corinthians' improper behavior turns the Lord's meal into something else altogether and opens up the assembly to dangerous forces that usually remained at the periphery or outside the community.

The presence of Exodus material in these three places in 1 Corinthians demonstrates the importance of the construction of new identity for the Corinthians as it was for the Israelites during the exodus. Paul highlights the danger of transgressing boundaries, which was an offense that Israel repeated time and again. The exodus tradition also becomes an important basis for Paul to make connections to the risen Lord, placing the Lord on a level par with that of God in the Hebrew Bible. Above all, the tabernacle that was so pivotal during the exodus parallels the importance of temple in the construction of Christian identity and community in Corinth.

In 1 Corinthians 5:1–13, 10:1–22, and 11:17–34, there is also power that can either provide life to the community or bring disease and death to those that venture beyond its limits. While the specific problem that Paul addresses in each chapter may be different, one common thread in all three chapters is that there exist powers that can imperil the community. Paul's exhortations aim to avert such disaster by adjusting the Corinthians' understanding of communal meals, ethical conduct, and their fellowship with one another and with Christ.

One important outcome of this analysis is to highlight the central place of meals for the life of the Corinthian assembly.[283] There is certainly an analogue to the Roman *convivium* as many scholars have shown, both in form and space within which these meals took place. Such comparisons, however, do not come close enough to describing what Paul emphasizes regarding the significance of the meal for the life of the assembly. The connection to the Roman meals cannot explain why Paul unequivocally denies the meal to the incestuous man (1 Cor 5), why he so adamantly refuses the Corinthians' dual participation in the meals from local cults *and* the Lord's meal (1 Cor 10), and why he could view the meal as somehow effecting physical maladies to those who do not come worthily to the Lord's table (1 Cor 11). More relevant are temple sacrifices and their concomitant meals that hold influence upon religious adherents to the cult. But unlike those sacrifices that remained simply as physical sustenance, Paul implies this meal provided within the temple of God can bring both health and harm to its participants.

The start of this study posed two initial questions with which to interrogate the three passages from 1 Corinthians. These questions concern the form and the function of Paul's language dealing with the Exodus, power, and peril in relation to God's temple. In order to gain further insight into Paul's perceptions, his lan-

---

[283] See Markus Bockmuehl, "The personal presence of Jesus in the writings of Paul," *SJT* 70.1 (2017): 39–60: "there are … tantalising remarks about the eucharist in 1 Corinthians, which remain without parallel in the other letters. Here we need to consider the idea that Christ is the Passover lamb that believers must prepare to eat with the unleavened bread of truth and sincerity (5:7–8); that the bread and wine are participation in the body and blood of Christ (10:16); that to eat them means eating the body and drinking the blood of 'the Lord Jesus' (11:27) in the same way as when he said 'this is my body' (11:23–7); and finally that a crucial requirement is to discern and respect that body (11:29). Taken individually, none of these passages is self-interpreting as a sacramental account. But it seems to me difficult to resist a cumulative interpretation resembling what was later called 'real presence' in the eucharist" (57).

guage must be located within the context of the ancient Mediterranean world, both Greco-Roman as well as Jewish. Are the discussions found in 1 Corinthians (i.e., pollution, powers that can benefit or harm within sacred spaces, and participation in ritual) found elsewhere? Is there evidence from the ancient Mediterranean context that speaks of gathered assemblies and sacred spaces in similar fashion? Are Paul's perceptions and presuppositions commonplace? Are they genuinely unique or are they a distinctive twist on shared views? These are the questions that lead to the comparative analyses that follow.

2.8 Chart I: Components of the Lord's Supper Tradition in the Synoptic Gospels and 1 Corinthians 11

	Matt 26:26–28	Mark 14:22–24	Luke 22:19–20	1 Cor 11:23b–25
#1	²⁶Ἐσθιόντων δὲ αὐτῶν λαβὼν ὁ Ἰησοῦς ἄρτον καὶ εὐλογήσας ἔκλασεν καὶ δοὺς τοῖς μαθηταῖς εἶπεν·	²²Καὶ ἐσθιόντων αὐτῶν λαβὼν ἄρτον εὐλογήσας ἔκλασεν καὶ ἔδωκεν αὐτοῖς καὶ εἶπεν·	¹⁹καὶ λαβὼν ἄρτον εὐχαριστήσας ἔκλασεν καὶ ἔδωκεν αὐτοῖς λέγων·	²³ᵇἔλαβεν ἄρτον ²⁴καὶ εὐχαριστήσας ἔκλασεν καὶ εἶπεν·
#2	λάβετε φάγετε, τοῦτό ἐστιν τὸ σῶμά μου.	λάβετε, τοῦτό ἐστιν τὸ σῶμά μου.	τοῦτό ἐστιν τὸ σῶμά μου τὸ ὑπὲρ ὑμῶν διδόμενον· τοῦτο ποιεῖτε εἰς τὴν ἐμὴν ἀνάμνησιν.	τοῦτό μού ἐστιν τὸ σῶμα τὸ ὑπὲρ ὑμῶν· τοῦτο ποιεῖτε εἰς τὴν ἐμὴν ἀνάμνησιν.
#3	²⁷καὶ λαβὼν ποτήριον καὶ εὐχαριστήσας ἔδωκεν αὐτοῖς λέγων· πίετε ἐξ αὐτοῦ πάντες,	²³καὶ λαβὼν ποτήριον εὐχαριστήσας ἔδωκεν αὐτοῖς, καὶ ἔπιον ἐξ αὐτοῦ πάντες. ²⁴καὶ εἶπεν αὐτοῖς·	²⁰καὶ τὸ ποτήριον ὡσαύτως μετὰ τὸ δειπνῆσαι, λέγων·	²⁵ὡσαύτως καὶ τὸ ποτήριον μετὰ τὸ δειπνῆσαι λέγων·
#4	²⁸τοῦτο γάρ ἐστιν τὸ αἷμά μου τῆς διαθήκης τὸ περὶ πολλῶν ἐκχυννόμενον εἰς ἄφεσιν ἁμαρτιῶν.	τοῦτό ἐστιν τὸ αἷμά μου τῆς διαθήκης τὸ ἐκχυννόμενον ὑπὲρ πολλῶν.	τοῦτο τὸ ποτήριον ἡ καινὴ διαθήκη ἐν τῷ αἵματί μου τὸ ὑπὲρ ὑμῶν ἐκχυννόμενον.	τοῦτο τὸ ποτήριον ἡ καινὴ διαθήκη ἐστὶν ἐν τῷ ἐμῷ αἵματι· τοῦτο ποιεῖτε, ὁσάκις ἐὰν πίνητε, εἰς τὴν ἐμὴν ἀνάμνησιν.

3 Accessing Sacred Spaces in Greek and Roman Contexts

3.1 Introduction

The previous chapter showed the importance of 1 Corinthians 3:16–17 for Paul's exhortations throughout his letter. On Paul's discussions of boundaries, power, and punishments, the best framework with which to understand Paul's language is temple discourse. This chapter discusses the experiences of Greeks and Romans in relation to sacred spaces, including discourse on prescriptions regarding the sacred, benevolent and malevolent powers, participation in rituals, and penalties for transgressions.[1] The investigation sifts through ancient Greek and Roman sources, both epigraphic and literary, in order to establish a broader database within which to situate Paul's language found in 1 Corinthians. One obvious location for such investigation is "sacred space" broadly defined (i.e. *temenos*), containing within it important monumental temples. Part of the inquiry involves an analysis of inscriptional evidence for permitted behaviors within temples. There are also literary accounts of cult gatherings that supplement the currently available material evidence. Various examples of sanctuary trans-

---

[1] On ancient Greek perceptions of pollution, see the classic work by Robert Parker, *Miasma: Pollution and Purification in Early Greek Religion* (Oxford: Oxford University Press, 1983); Andreas Bendlin, "Purity and Pollution," in *A Companion to Greek Religion*, ed. D. Ogden (Oxford: Wiley-Blackwell, 2007), 178–89. Whether or not the Romans perpetuated the same ideas about pollution will be discussed in 3.3 below. All translations are mine unless otherwise noted.

The categories of "Greek" and "Roman" are not mutually exclusive. For example, there are many "Greek" inscriptions cited whose provenance is of the Roman imperial period. I use the categories here primarily for heuristic purposes and there will be times when I will point to a "Greek" evidence in the subsection dealing with "Roman" materials because of its later dating. On the enduring use of the Greek language in inscriptions from the Roman imperial period, see Mika Kajava, "Religion in Rome and Italy," in *The Oxford Handbook of Roman Epigraphy*, ed. C. Bruun and J. Edmondson (Oxford: Oxford University Press, 2015), 397–419. In a survey of ancient sacred spaces, one could potentially add other religious architecture such as Egyptian, Mesopotamian, and Hittite temples. Chronology and geography place these structures further out from Paul's purview, but they may form yet another layer of background information useful for interrogating Paul's ideas. For introduction to these structures, see Michael B. Hundley, *Gods in Dwellings: Temples and Divine Presence in the Ancient Near East* (Atlanta: Society of Biblical Literature, 2013).

gression show how Greeks and Romans interpreted such events in light of their respective perceptions of sacred space.²

3.2 Transgressions in the Greek Context

As early as the Bronze Age, there is evidence that Greeks maintained a distinct category of 'sacred space,' recognizing its qualitative difference from all other inhabited spaces.³ Within the general area designated as sacred space, Greeks built temples from the pre-Archaic period on. These monumental structures were viewed as houses of the gods, both in the figurative and the literal senses, since the physical cult statue of the respective gods were housed within them.⁴ Temples also played an important stabilizing role in the early *poleis*, and the cult statues of these temples demanded careful attention as the main

---

2 It is important not to confuse the larger sacred space—usually called the *temenos*—with the monumental structure (temple) housed within it—usually named as the *hieron* or *naos*. It is not my intention to conflate the two, but for the purposes of my investigation, any acts that violate an accepted boundary or law of the sacred space (whether the *temenos*, *naos*, or otherwise) are analyzed in this chapter. The following interpretation will show that no matter where exactly the transgression took place, there are formal similarities for how such acts are received and recompensed in the Greek/Roman traditions. For overviews of Greek and Roman sanctuaries, see Michael V. Fox, ed., *Temple in Society* (Winona Lake, IN: Eisenbrauns, 1988); Susan E. Alcock and Robin Osborne, eds., *Placing the Gods: Sanctuaries and Sacred Space in Ancient Greece* (New York: Oxford University Press, 1994); Gottfried Gruben, *Griechische Tempel und Heiligtümer* (München: Hirmer, 2001); Susan G. Cole, *Landscapes, Gender, and Ritual Space: The Ancient Greek Experience* (Berkeley: University of California Press, 2004); Jas Elsner and Ian Rutherford, eds., *Pilgrimage in Graeco-Roman and Early Christian Antiquity: Seeing the Gods* (Oxford: Oxford University Press, 2005); John W. Stamper, *The Architecture of Roman Temples: The Republic to the Middle Empire* (Cambridge: Cambridge University Press, 2005); Verity J. Platt, *Facing the Gods: Epiphany and Representation in Graeco-Roman Art, Literature, and Religion* (Cambridge: Cambridge University Press, 2011); David L. Balch and Annette Weissenrieder, eds., *Contested Spaces: Houses and Temples in Roman Antiquity and the New Testament* (Tübingen: Mohr Siebeck, 2012).
3 Cole, *Landscapes*, 15–16. Also Walter Burkert, "The Meaning and Function of the Temple in Classical Greece," in *Temple in Society*, ed. M. V. Fox (Winona Lake, IN: Eisenbrauns, 1988), 29–31.
4 It is well known that the concept of the "cult statue" was far more fluid in Greek thought, as even their terms for what fall under the modern category of cult statue were many and this included their form and material: *agalma, xoanon, hedos, bretas, andrias, eikon,* and *hidryma*. For a helpful review of this problem, see Joannis Mylonopoulos, "Divine Images *Versus* Cult Images. An Endless Story about Theories, Methods, and Terminologies," in *Divine Images and Human Imaginations in Ancient Greece and Rome*, ed. Joannis Mylonopoulos (Leiden: Brill, 2010), 1–20.

focus of cult rituals.⁵ The rituals performed within the circumscribed boundaries of such spaces also functioned as a way to clearly distinguish what took place "inside" as opposed to all other activities that occurred "outside."⁶ Access to these grounds and the implements that were contained within them became defining markers of membership for a particular community.

3.2.1 Prescriptions Regarding the Sacred

Belonging to a cult community did not mean that an individual could do whatever she or he pleased with the equipment used for rituals performed within sacred areas. An early inscription from Argos distinguishes the legitimate use of ritual tools by the collective (δαμόσιον) in contrast to their unauthorized use by a private individual (ἰδιώτας), the latter act incurring a monetary penalty (ἀφακεσάσθο) determined by the local official (δαμιοργός).⁷ Another famous marble stele from the Amphiareum at Oropus delineates guidelines for taking

---

5 On the stabilizing influence of the temples upon early Greek *poleis*, see Burkhard Fehr, "The Greek Temple in Early Archaic Period: Meaning, Use and Social Context," *Hephaistos* 14 (1996): 165–91. On the function of cult images in rituals, see Irene Bald Romano, "Early Greek Cult Images and Cult Practices," in *Early Greek Cult Practice: Proceedings of the Fifth International Symposium at the Swedish Institute at Athens, 26–29 June, 1986*, ed. R. Hägg, N. Marinatos, and G. C. Nordquist (Stockholm: Svenska Institutet i Athen, 1988), 127–34.
6 Jonathan Z. Smith, *To Take Place: Toward Theory in Ritual* (Chicago: University of Chicago Press, 1987), 104 (emphasis added), observes that when one enters a temple, one enters marked off space "in which, at least in principle, *nothing* is accidental; *everything*, at least potentially, demands attention." To be sure, the space itself should not be understood as the thing that makes a place "holy" or "sacred," over against another. The defining factor was the Greeks' belief that the god manifested him or herself within a particular space, and such places became locales where monumental structures were built within which divine images were housed. The inside/outside dynamic is complicated somewhat by the fact that in Greek temples, the sacrifices were consumed technically "outside" the temple structure. Nevertheless, the participants remained within a specific space and therefore the distinction between what is considered inside or outside *spatially* should not be pressed too far.
7 *SEG* 11.314 (ca. 6th BCE). Also *SEG* 11.336 (Argos, 7th BCE). In order to show the prevalence of the Greek and Roman views on transgressions in sanctuary space both geographically and chronologically, I have provided the locations and dating of the evidence when appropriate and available. For all inscriptional evidence, I follow the current best reconstructions and therefore, I will refrain from using brackets. To remain within the safe limits of the available data, I tried to avoid any texts that are highly fragmentary. Most inscriptions contain partial reconstructions of one or two letters, and a few with only two or three reconstructed words. The reconstructions are taken from the most recent publications that exist concerning the various inscriptions (e.g., *LSCG*, *LSS*, etc.)

care of the ἱερέα τοῦ Ἀμφιαράου.[8] First, the νεωκόρος (sacred officer) is given the solemn task "to take care of the sanctuary and of the visitors to the sanctuary according to the law" (ἐπαναγκάζειν … τοῦ τε ἱεροῦ ἐπιμελεῖσθαι κατὰ τὸν νόμον καὶ τῶν ἀφικνεμένων εἰς τὸ ἱερόν, lines 6–8). Second, there are descriptions of various possible offenses and their concomitant fines (lines 9–20), followed by the fee for seeking divine healing (θεραπεύεσθαι ὑπὸ τοῦ θεοῦ, lines 21–24).[9]

These accounts assume that those engaging in cult rituals had the right of entry to a sacred space, but were there any restrictions concerning access to various sanctuaries? Certainly not everyone was allowed to enter a holy precinct, and some sanctuaries even forbade any one to ever enter a particular area of the *temenos*. For example, an inscription from the Athenian Acropolis simply reads:[10]

Διὸς Καται- βάτο ἄβατον ἱερόν.	A sacred place of Zeus Kataibates, not to be entered.

What is so striking about this inscription and others like it,[11] is that no rationale is ever given for why access is completely restricted. It suggests that no reasons had to be given because the level of sanctity required such unqualified protection: these spaces remained inaccessible and that was all that needed to be said.[12]

---

8 *LSCG* 69 (Oropos, 4th BCE).
9 Lines 38–40. Unfortunately, the inscription does not specify further what these transgressions were, only using the verb ἀδικέω: (1) Lines 9–10, ἂν δέ τις ἀδικεῖ ἐν τοῖ ἱεροῖ ἢ ξένος ἢ δημότης and (2) Lines 14–15, ἄν τις ἰδίει ἀδικηθεῖ ἢ τῶν ξένων ἢ τῶν δημοτέων ἐν τοῖ ἱεροῖ. A few lines later, however, the inscription mentions that the sacrificial meat should not be carried out of the temple, a boundary line that should not be crossed (τῶν δὲ κρεῶν μὴ εἶναι ἐκφορὴν ἔξω τοῦ τεμένεος, lines 31–32). Another anecdote concerning Menedemus's exile, due to his suspected thievery from the temple of Amphiaraus at Oropus, provides a literary—though chronologically late—parallel to boundaries seen here and in *SEG* 11.314 (Diogenes Laertius, 2.142). The Oropus stele also stipulates that those seeking dream incubation in the shrine are to be separated according to gender (lines 43–45, ἐν δὲ τοῖ κοιμητηρίοι καθεύδειν χωρὶς μὲν τὸς ἄνδρας χωρὶς δὲ τὰς γυναῖκας), implying yet another boundary that should not be crossed when dealing with the gods.
10 *IG* II² 4964 (ca. 400–350 BCE). Translation from Eran Lupu, *Greek Sacred Law: A Collection of New Documents (NGSL)*, 2nd ed. (Leiden: Brill, 2009), 20.
11 *LSS* 49 (Delos, 5th BCE); 128 (Kallion in Aetolia, 5th BCE); *LSCG* 121 (Chios, undated). Pausanias also discusses sacred areas that perpetually remained off-limits: *Descr.* 8.30.2, 31.5, 36.3, 38.6.
12 The brevity of the language is notable: *LSS* 49: Ξένωι οὐχ ὁσίη ἐσιέναι; *LSCG* 121: Ἱρόν. οὐκ ἔσοδος.

The boundary stone of a temple in Corinth from the fifth-century BCE reads:[13]

Ὅρος ἱερὸς ἄσυλος.	A holy boundary stone, inviolable.
μὲ καταβιβασσκέτο.	Let no one transgress.
ζαμία.	Lest he suffer loss.

A small shrine in Priene contains the following mandate on one doorpost:[14]

Εἰσίναι εἰς τὸ	Enter into the sanctuary
ἱερὸν ἁγνὸν ἐν	pure in white clothing.
ἐσθῆτι λευκῆι.	

There were various other offenses that disqualified one from gaining entry, ranging from carrying certain animals,[15] to contacting bodily pollutants,[16] or bringing forbidden items.[17] Sometimes, an entire class of people—even royalty—was denied entry no matter the circumstances of their visit.[18]

Thucydides provides a helpful literary parallel to what happens when a sacred space is intentionally violated. He describes the Boeotians' accusation that the Athenians were "doing unjustly by transgressing the laws of the Greeks" (οὐ

---

13 *LSS* 34 (Corinth, 5th BCE).
14 *LSAM* 35 (Priene, 3rd BCE).
15 *LSCG* 136 (Ialysos, ca. 300 BCE). This list includes beasts of burden (lines 21–3), swine (lines 26–7), and sheep (lines 30–33).
16 Such pollutants include certain foods, menstruation, childbirth, miscarriage, sexual intercourse, and contact with a corpse. See *LSCG* 55.3–7 (Attica, 2nd CE); 95 (Delos, after 166 BCE); 124 (Eresos, 2nd BCE); 139 (Lindos, 2nd CE); 171 (Isthmus, 2nd BCE); *LSAM* 12 I (Pergamon, after 133 BCE); 18 (Maeonia, 147 BCE); 20 (Philadelphia, 1st BCE); 29 (Metropolis in Ionia, 4th BCE); 51 (Miletus, end 1st BCE); *IG* II² 1365.8–11 (Attica, ca. 2nd CE); *LSS* 54 (Delos, 2nd BCE); 59 (Delos, Roman period); 91 (Lindos, 3rd CE); 106 (Camiros, undated); 108 (Rhodes, 1st CE); 118 (Cyrene, 2nd CE); 119 (Ptolemais, 1st CE).
17 *LSCG* 124 (Eresos, 2nd CE); *LSS* 59; 60 (Minoa, 5–4th BCE); 91; *LSAM* 68 (ca. 150 BCE?); *SEG* 36.1221 (Xanthos, late 3rd–early 2nd BCE).
18 *LSS* 49 on foreigners; 56 on women and men wearing certain articles of clothing (Delos, 2nd BCE); 75 on uninitiated (Samothrace, 1st BCE ~ *LSCG* 65.36); *LSCG* 82.5–6 on women (Elateia, end 5th BCE); 109 on the uninitiated and women (Paros, 5th BCE); 110 on Dorians (Paros, 5th BCE); 124.10–11, 18–20 on traitors and women, except priestesses and prophetesses; Herodotus, *Hist.* 5.61 on all other Athenians excluded from the Gephyraians' temple in Athens; 6.81 on King Cleomenes of Sparta being denied entry to the temple of Hera at Argos; Plutarch, *Mor.* 267D on the *neokoros* of the temple barring entry to any slaves or Aetolians; Pausanias, *Descr.* 6.20.3 excluding everyone but the woman tending the god.

δικαίως δράσειαν παραβαίνοντες τὰ νόμιμα τῶν Ἑλλήνων).¹⁹ Such law required invaders "to abstain from the holy places" (ἱερῶν ... ἀπέχεσθαι) of their opponents, but the Athenians had applied normal practices of profane space (ἐν βεβήλῳ) by drawing sacred water for common use (πρὸς τὰ ἱερὰ χέρνιβι χρῆσθαι).²⁰ The response of the Boeotians to the Athenian offense is notable: (1) they call upon the affected spirits and Apollo (ἐπικαλουμένους τοὺς ὁμωχέτας δαίμονας καὶ τὸν Ἀπόλλω); (2) they warn the Athenians to withdraw from the sacred space (προαγορεύειν αὐτοὺς ἐκ τοῦ ἱεροῦ ἀπιόντας); and (3) they tell the Athenians to remove their own things from the temple (ἀποφέρεσθαι τὰ σφέτερα αὐτῶν)—that is, to expel pollutants from the sacred space. And according to Thucydides, all of this was done, presumably in the interests of the god and of the Boeotians (ὑπέρ τε τοῦ θεοῦ καὶ ἑαυτῶν Βοιωτούς).

There are also laws concerning the state of the visitor. Some required proper ritual preparation prior to entry into the sanctuary. Others evaluated the inner condition of the visitant. The regulation of the Andanian mysteries contains lengthy descriptions about how one should be prepared in order to access the sacred space, including a public record of how one can continue to maintain the required level of purity.²¹ By the fourth century BCE, the interior state of the entrant also became a subject of discussion. The temple of Asclepius at Epidaurus, on the Argolid Peninsula, maintained a famous elegiac above the portal:²²

---

19 The following citations come from Thucydides, 4.97.
20 Walter Burkert, *Greek Religion: Archaic and Classical*, trans. J. Raffan (Malden, MA: Blackwell Publishing, 1985), 269, notes that if ἱερός signified that which belonged to the god or the sanctuary, then βέβηλος was the opposite.
21 *LSCG* 65 (92 BCE). Line 37: ἀναγραψάντω δὲ καὶ ἀφ' ὧν δεῖ καθαρίζειν καὶ ἃ μὴ δεῖ ἔχοντας εἰσπορεύεσθαι ("They also shall record publicly from what one must be pure and what one not have in order to enter.") See also *LSCG* 136. See also *SEG* 19.427 (Dodona, 3rd BCE) that attributes divinely sent bad weather due to the "impurity" (ἀκαθαρτία) of an individual.
22 From 4th BCE. See Edelstein, *Asclepius*, 1:163–4 (T 318). Also *LSS* 82 (Mytilene, undated); 108.4–6 (Rhodes, ca. 1st CE): ναοῖο θυώδεος ἐντὸς ἰόντα ἔνμεναι. Plato, *Hipparch.* 229a also describes an inscription on a Hermes memorial: στεῖχε δίκαια φρονῶν ("go with just intentions"). See also how Socrates relates the mind to one's behavior toward the gods in *Gorgias* 507a–b (Lamb, LCL): "And further, the sensible man (ὁ σώφρων) will do what is fitting as regards both gods and men; for he could not be sensible if he did what was unfitting ... as regards men, his actions will be just, and as regards the gods, pious (ὅσια)." Concerning this passage in *Gorgias*, W. R. Connor observes:

"Here *to dikaion* and *to hosion* are presented as two distinct aspects of *sophrosyne*. Their coordination in passages such as this alerts us to a pattern in classical Athenian speech in which the two words are closely linked, and indeed to the further possibility that the same action might be described as *dikaion* when viewed from a human perspective and *hosion* when the reactions

> Ἁγνὸν χρή ναοῖο θυωδέος ἐντὸς ἰόντα
> ἔμμεναι· ἁγνεία δ'ἐστὶ
> φρονεῖν ὅσια.

> Pure must be the person
> entering the fragrant temple;
> And purity is to think holy thoughts.

Literary evidence as early as Homer also shows a keen interest in the purification of worshippers as they approached the altars to make sacrifices to the gods. Both the *Odyssey* and *Iliad* depict scenes of meticulous attention that participants in sacred ritual paid to cleanliness.[23] Other Greek writers also highlighted the importance of proper washing prior to sacrifices.[24] The endurance of this view regarding the sacred can be seen in various Greek authors through the centuries.[25]

In *Frogs*, the playwright Aristophanes gives further nuance on how one must position her or himself in the presence of the gods. The Chorus asserts that one "must remain silent and recuse oneself from the rites if he or she has not purified the mind" (lines 354–55, εὐφημεῖν χρὴ κἀξίστασθαι ... γνώμῃ μὴ καθαρεύει).[26] Two monuments from the sanctuary of Mēn both mention divine favors that may be given to those who serve with a simple soul or mind.[27] An inscription

---

of the gods are conjectured. Thus among the writers of this society *hosios* may occur in close parallel to *dikaios*, but often with a hint of divine involvement or concern. When *hosios* is combined with *hiera*, it provides a way of referring to two types of activities of importance to human society but also of special interest to the gods—the ritual observances of sacrifice, offering and festival, and the social normal of justice, fair treatment etc."

In "'Sacred' and 'Secular': Ἱερὰ καὶ ὅσια and the Classical Athenian Concept of the State," *Ancient Society* 19 (1988): 163–64. In other words, the classic bifurcation of sacred and secular is problematized, though it need not mean that the two are blurred without distinction.

23 Homer, *Od.* 3.440–441; *Il.* 6.297–310.
24 Aristophanes, *Lys.* 1129–1131; *Pax* 948–62; *Av.* 850, 958–59; Menander, *Dysk.* 440; Euripides, *Iph. aul.* 1568–69. See also the scholia in Aeschylus, *Sept.* 700. Improper behavior could also risk rejection of said sacrifices: Homer, *Od.* 1.60–69; 3.273–75; 13.184–87 (see 13.174); Herodotus, *Hist.* 1.19.2–3 (also inflicted by sickness); 6.81–82; Sophocles, *Ant.* 999–1022; *El.* 637–59 (killing Agamemnon); *Phil.* 8–11; Euripides, *Alc.* 119–120 (see 12–14); Xenophon, *Mem.* 2.2.13; Demosthenes, *Andr.* 78; Isocrates, *Archid.* 31; Antiphon, *On the Murder of Herodes*, 82; Plutarch, *Sera* 560E; Xenophon of Ephesus, 1.5.6–8; Pausanias, *Descr.* 5.21.5; 10.13.8; Aelian, *Var. hist.* 3.43; Philostratus, *Vit. Apoll.* 1.10 (the horror surrounding the openly incestuous relationship is strikingly similar to that of Paul in 1 Cor 5).
25 E. g., Clement of Alexandria, *Strom.* 5.1.13; Porphyry, *Abst.* 2.19; Cyril of Alexandria, *Jul.* 9.310. Also Hippocrates, *Morb. sacr.* 4.54–60; *SEG* 28.421 (Megalopolis, ca. 200 BCE); 60.891 (Astypalaia, ca. 300 BCE).
26 Aristophanes, *Ran.* 327–35, 385, 404–12. Also *LSS* 108 (line 7, νόῳ καθαρόν).
27 *IG* II² 1365.25–26, 1366.11–12 (Attica, 2nd CE): εὐείλατος γένοιτο ὁ θεὸς τοῖς θεραπεύουσιν ἁπλῇ τῇ ψυχῇ. While both these inscriptions are fairly late, the cult of Mēn was imported into Attica as early as 3rd BCE. John S. Kloppenborg and Richard S. Ascough, *Greco-Roman Associations: Texts, Translations, and Commentary. I. Attica, Central Greece, Macedonia, Thrace* (Berlin:

at Euromos, likely from the doorpost of the temple, instructs any potential entrant to consider the following:[28]

εἰ καθαράν, ᾧ ξεῖνε φέρεις φρενα, καὶ τὸ δίκαιον ἤσκηκες ψυχῇ, βαῖνε κατ'εὐίερον· εἰ δ'ἀδίκων ψαύεις, καί σοι νόος οὐ καθαρεύει, πώρρω ἀπ' ἀθανάτων ἔργεο καὶ τεμένους.	If you, friend, have a pure heart and practice righteousness in your soul, then you can enter this holy place; but if you touch unjust things and your mind is not pure, take yourself far from this sanctuary of the immortals.

Such focus on the mental condition of the worshipper was an important development within Greek notion of gathering within sacred spaces, and the subsequent discussion will show how Romans adopted and modified this perspective.[29]

3.2.2 Divine Power

The sanctuary of Asclepius housed within it powers beneficial to suppliants. The most famous temple of Asclepius was located at Epidaurus of the northern Peloponnese since the 5th century BCE. There were several other Asclepieia spread throughout the Greek world, such as those at Aegina, Athens, Corinth, Delphi, Kos, Pergamon, and Tricca (Thessaly). Such widespread popularity clearly indicates that suppliants expected an encounter with power that could provide some sort of benefit, one that even the Greek medical tradition accepted as valid.[30]

Walter de Gruyter, 2011), 270–78. See also *SEG* 50.1352bis (Oenoanda, late-Hellenistic) which mentions the need to have a pure conscience (line 8, γνώμᾳ καθαρᾷ).
28 *SEG* 43.710 (Euromos, either 2nd BCE or 1st CE). Also *LSCG* 53.31–32 (Attica, 2nd CE): "It is unlawful for anyone to enter this most holy assembly of eranistai without being first examined if he is pure and pious and good" (δοκιμασθῇ εἴ ἐστι ἁγνὸς καὶ εὐσεβὴς καὶ ἀγαθός).
29 Angelos Chaniotis, "Greek Ritual Purity: From Automatisms to Moral Distinctions," in *How Purity Is Made*, ed. P. Rösch and U. Simon (Wiesbaden: Harrassowitz Verlag, 2012), 123–39, argues that such distinction made between purities of the mind and body is a new development in Greek thought. For example, he observes that the earliest instance of this is found during the late 5th century BCE in Euripides' works. First in *Hippolytus*, when Phaedra responds to the nurse (lines 316–7): "My hands are clean, but my mind has pollution" (μίασμά) and second in *Orestes* (line 1604): *Menalaus*, "Yes my hands are clean" (ἁγνός), *Orestes*, "But not your heart."
30 The Greek medical tradition, at least during this early period, also allowed for such experiences. Hippocrates, *Morb. sacr.*, 4.40–50, suggests that if the gods were responsible for the ill-

Given this expectation, the encounters with power in the Asclepieia affected individuals rather than gathered groups.

Records of various healings from Asclepian sanctuaries show how divine power manifested itself in the mending of human bodies. A certain cripple named Kephisias, for example, was carried into the temple at Epidaurus upon a stretcher. Following his earnest entreaty of the divine, the god healed him.[31] According to Angelos Chaniotis, such stories would have been read aloud by the priests and pilgrims, reinforcing the notion among the thousands of visitors that power resided within the sanctuary irrespective of the eventual result of their particular pilgrimage.[32] Literary evidence supports the popularity of the Asclepian sanctuary: in Aristophanes' *Wasps*, for example, Bdelycleon travels with his father Philocleon to be healed by Asclepius at the island of Aegina.[33] Around the fourth and third centuries BCE, the Asclepius cult was in full bloom. Scholars estimate that over 200 sanctuaries of Asclepius were built during this period,[34] and other preexisting sanctuaries, such as those in Athens and Corinth, underwent significant renovations.[35]

---

ness in the first place, then it stands to reason that the sick should be carried to the sanctuaries (ἐς τὰ ἱερὰ φέροντας) with sacrifices and prayers to the gods. Also *Aer*. 22.8–13. Bronwen L. Wickkiser, *Asklepios, Medicine, and the Politics of Healing in Fifth-Century Greece: Between Craft and Cult* (Baltimore: The Johns Hopkins University Press, 2008), 33, rightly observes that the medical writers were not all agreed upon the intersection between the gods and healing, but also admits that "it is significant that no evidence whatever has survived from the classical period to prove" that there were medical practitioners who rejected the role of gods in healing.

It is also the case that ancient Greek physicians claimed Asclepius as a patron, though the fact that technical medicine and the Asclepius cult were intertwined does not negate the reality that many of the events occurring in the sanctuaries involved "power" unexplained by roots, drugs, or other local anatomical procedures. On Asclepius' patronage of ancient physicians, see also Plutarch, *Quaest. conv.* 745 A; Galen, *San. tuend.* 1.8.20; Pliny the Elder, *Nat.* 29.1.4. This does not mean, however, that Asclepius held monopoly over all healing associated with sanctuaries. See, e.g., Pausanias, *Descr.* 2.7.7–8 (Artemis and Apollo), 32.6 (Pan Lyterios); 8.41.8–9 (Apollo); 9.22.1–2 (Hermes); *LSS* 115 A.4–7 (Cyrene, 4th BCE; the Troizenian festival honoring Apollo). The fact that many of these other healing accounts are associated with Apollo is not surprising since he is accepted as Asclepius's father (Hippocrates, *Ep.* 15.32).

31 See Edelstein, *Asclepius*, 1:236 no. 36 (T 423). Also in Lynn R. LiDonnici, *The Epidaurian Miracle Inscriptions: Text, Translation and Commentary* (Atlanta: Scholars Press, 1995), 113 (B 16).
32 Chaniotis, "Greek Ritual Purity," 129–30. Also *IG* IV² 1.121 (Epidaurus, 4th BCE); 1.122 (Epidaurus, ca. 4th BCE); 1.258 (Epidaurus, ca. 4th BCE); *IvP* III.161 A (Pergamon, 2nd CE).
33 Aristophanes, *Vesp.* 121–23. Also Aristophanes, *Plut.* 633–747; Menander, *P.Didot* 1.9–11; Pausanias, *Descr.* 5.26.2.
34 PECS, s.v. "Epidauros." An inscription from the Asklepieion at Epidaurus contains a long list of θεαροδόκοι (recipients of cult-envoys) of various cities throughout the Greek world contributing to the building program at Epidaurus = *IG* IV² 1.94–95 (Epidaurus, ca. 365 BCE).

Other stories of power include the reattachment of a severed head following a healing procedure,[36] suspension from the feet while fluid is drained (with the head temporarily removed!),[37] pregnancy brought on by the touch of the god,[38] restoration of speech to a mute boy during a cult ritual,[39] rehabilitation of a paralyzed hand,[40] cure from blindness,[41] and removal of an ulcer on the head.[42]

3.2.3 Participation in Rituals

It is certain that much of what took place in the sanctuaries was sacred: people came to provide votive offerings, engage in cultic activity, and in the "mysteries" which in extant sources remain mostly as shadowy descriptions. Whatever the reason, ancients did not enter into a sanctuary with the same attitude as we

---

35 For Athens see John Travlos, *Pictorial Dictionary of Ancient Athens* (London: Thames and Hudson, 1971), on "Asklepieion" and for Corinth, see Carl Roebuck, *Corinth XIV: The Asklepieion and Lerna* (Princeton: The American School of Classical Studies at Athens, 1951).
36 Aelian, *Nat. an.* 9.33; also *IG* IV² 1.122.10–19.
37 *IG* IV² 1.122.1–6 (trans. LiDonnici): "Arata of Lacedaemon, dropsy. For her sake, her mother slept here, while she remained in Lacedaemon, and she saw a dream. It seemed to her the god cut off the head of her daughter and hung the body neck downwards (τὸν θεὸν ἀποταμόντα τὰν κεφαλὰν τὸ σῶμα κραμάσαι κάτω τὸν τράχαλον ἔχον). After much fluid had run out, he untied the body and put the head back on the neck. Having seen this dream she returned to Lacedaemon and found on her arrival that her daughter was well (ὑγιαίνουσαν) and that she had seen the same dream." While dreams were often the vehicle of Asclepius's activity, it is not the case that he *only* operated within dreams. For instance, in Pausanias, *Descr.* 10.38.13, there occurred at a sanctuary of Asclepius something which "the woman thought ... was a dream, but was at once proved to be a waking vision" (τοῦτο ... τῇ γυναικὶ ὄψις ὀνείρατος, ὕπαρ μέντοι ἦν αὐτίκα).
38 *IG* IV² 1.122.60–63.
39 *IG* IV² 1.121.41–48.
40 LiDonnici, *Epidaurian Miracle Inscriptions*, 87 (A3).
41 LiDonnici, *Epidaurian Miracle Inscriptions*, 89 (A4), 93 (A9). The latter account emphasizes that while he had eyelids, in one eye "there was nothing within them and they were completely empty" (ἐνεῖμεν δ᾽ἐν αὐτοῖς μηθέν, ἀλλὰ κενεὰ εἶμεν ὅλως). Such disability notwithstanding, the miracle ends with him departing "seeing with both eyes" (βλέπων ἀμφοῖν ἐξῆλθε).
42 Aeschines, *Anth. Gr.* 6.330. In this epigram, Aeschines contrasts the "human arts" (θνητῶν τέκνας) with "the divine" (τὸ θεῖον). The most extravagant testimony of these healing accounts is found in Aelius Aristides (117–180 CE) who will be treated in detail in the next section dealing with Roman tradition. While his primary language was Greek, Aelius was an active participant in what is now called the Second Sophistic, a cultural phenomenon that came to fruition in the Roman imperial context. See, G. W. Bowersock, *Greek Sophists and the Roman Empire* (Oxford: Clarendon, 1969) and other relevant literature cited in Luke Timothy Johnson, *Among the Gentiles: Greco-Roman Religion and Christianity* (New Haven: Yale University Press, 2009), 312n1.

might bring to visiting a museum today, as passive observers of something benign and inactive housed within. Rather, ancient visitors of sanctuaries were active participants in the events that took place within, and they expected to encounter an active power. Such entrants included distant travelers seeking healing, those hoping to find divine guidance—often through an incubation ritual in dreams—and local priests performing important duties in the sanctuaries.

One of the most important rituals for engagement with the gods was participation in various meals, which above all included the act of sacrifices to the gods and the subsequent partaking of sacred portions.[43] These sacrifices would have entailed a host of sounds and smells, the latter often understood as signaling the presence and pleasure of the gods.[44] In the recorded regulations of the Andanian Mysteries, there are strict guidelines περὶ ἱεροῦ δείπνου that took place in conjunction with sacrifices.[45] Dio Chrysostom describes the close connection between sacrifice and meals as follows: "What sacrifice is acceptable to the gods without the participants in the feast?"[46] In *That Epicurus Actually Makes a Pleasant Life Impossible*, Plutarch also makes an important observation that is worth quoting at length:

> No visit delights us more than a visit to a temple, no occasion than a holy day; no act or spectacle than what we see and what we do ourselves that involve the gods, whether we celebrate a ritual or take part in a choral dance or attend a sacrifice or ceremony of initiation. For on these occasions our mind is not plunged in anxiety or cowed and depressed ... No, wherever it believes and conceives most firmly that the god is present (ἀλλ'ὅπου μάλιστα δοξάζει καὶ διανοεῖται παρεῖναι τὸν θεόν), there more than anywhere else it puts away all feelings of pain, of fear and of worry ... but in processions and at sacrifices (ἐν δὲ πομπαῖς καὶ θυσίαις) not only crone and gaffer, not only men without wealth or station, but even ... the servants of household and farm feel the life of high spirits and a merry heart.[47]

---

43 See Dennis E. Smith, *From Symposium to Eucharist: The Banquet in the Early Christian World* (Minneapolis: Fortress Press, 2003), esp. his introductory chapter (1–12) where he helpfully lays out his view of meals as participating in what many historians of religion discussed separately as "secular" versus "sacred." The scope of the present study does not permit parsing out the details of various meals in antiquity vis-à-vis Paul's discussion of meals in 1 Corinthians. It is important, however, to attend to the *religious* and *experiential* dimension of meals, especially when gods are invoked, since these are the moments that specifically have as their goal the suppliants' encounter with divine power and/or presence.

44 E.g., Homer, *Il.* 1.317; *Hym. Hom. Herm.* 4.322; Exod 30:34–38; Lev 1:13; Pliny the Elder, *Nat.* 24.102 (a plant, presumably with its smells: *deos evocare*). For discussion and relevant primary and secondary literature, see Candace Cherie Weddle, "Making Sense of Sacrifice: Sensory Experience in Greco-Roman Cult" (Ph.D. diss., University of Southern California, 2011), 43–71.

45 *LSCG* 65.95–99.

46 Dio Chrysostom, *3 Regn.* 3.97 (Cohoon, LCL).

47 Plutarch, *Suav. viv.* 1101E–F (Einarson and de Lacy, LCL).

Plutarch continues to describe the "feast held on occasion of some sacred rite or sacrifice" (ἐφ'ἱεροῖς καὶ θυηπολίαις):

> When they believe that their thoughts come closest to god as they do him honor and reverence, it brings pleasure and favor (ἡδονὴν καὶ χάριν) of a far superior kind. Of this a man gets nothing if he has given up faith in providence. For it is not the abundance of wine or the roast meats that cheer the heart at festivals, but good hope and the belief in the favorable presence of the god (δόξα τοῦ παρεῖναι τὸν θεὸν εὐμενῆ) and his gracious acceptance of what is done. For while we leave the flutes and the crowns out of certain festivals, if the god is not present at the sacrifice (θεοῦ δὲ θυσίᾳ μὴ παρόντος) ... what is left bears no mark of sanctity or holy day and leaves the spirit untouched by the divine influence (ἄθεόν ἐστι); rather let us say for such a man the occasion is joyless and even distressing (ἀτερπὲς αὐτῷ καὶ λυπηρόν).[48]

What is noteworthy about Plutarch's description of the feast is how the same event and indeed, the same substances, can be experienced differently by the attendant based on two factors: (1) the posture of the worshiper him/herself; and (2) the presence of the gods themselves. He contrasts the experience of "pleasure and favor" over against that of "joylessness and distress" and some of this depends on whether or not the god is present at the particular meal.[49]

Another feature of these feasts is how they were often reimagined as events led by the gods themselves. Human agents chose the animals for sacrifice, performed the necessary rites, and killed and parceled out the animal for the following meals, and yet there is evidence that the gods were often portrayed as the ones who invited guests to participate in these feasts. Various inscriptions found at Panamara, near Stratonikeia on the southwestern part of modern Turkey, attest to the lively cult of Zeus Panamaros including his feasts. Read the following excerpts from the extant material evidence:

---

48 Plutarch, *Suav. viv.* 1102 A–B (Einarson and de Lacy, LCL slightly modified).
49 Images were an important part of this process since the worshipers could not be assured of the gods' presence without an image. This did not mean, however, that the image automatically meant the god was present as seen in the following ancient examples: Diodorus Siculus, *Bib. hist.* 17.41.7–8; Quintus Curtius Rufus (in Latin), *Hist. Alex. Mag.* 4.3.19–22; Plutarch, *Alex.* 24.3–4; Pausanias, *Descr.* 3.15.7, 11; 9.38.5. F. S. Naiden, *Smoke Signals for the Gods: Ancient Greek Sacrifice from the Archaic through Roman Periods* (Oxford: Oxford University Press, 2013), 40–47.

Εἰ καὶ πάντας ἀνθρώπους ὁ θεὸς ἐπὶ τὴν ἑστίασιν καλεῖ καὶ κοινὴν καὶ ἰσότιμον παρέχι τράπεζαν τοῖς ὁποθενοῦν ἀφικνουμένοις ... καλῶ πρὸς τὸν θεὸν ὑμᾶς καὶ παρακαλῶ ... τῆς παρ'αὐτῷ μετέχιν εὐφροσύνης.	Since the god calls all people to the feast, allowing them to share a common table where all have equal rights, to those who come from wherever ... I call you to the god and I urge you ... to share in god and I urge you ... to share in the good cheer in his presence.[50]
Καὶ ὁ θεὸς ὑμᾶς ἐπὶ τὴν ἱερὰν ἑστίασιν καλῖ, πᾶσιν μὲν ἀνθρώποις αἰεὶ τοῦτο παρέχων, μάλιστα δὲ οἷς ἐστίν κοινωνία τῶν ἱερῶν.	And the god calls you to his sacred feast, as he always supplies this to all humankind, but especially to those who have participation in the sacrifices.[51]

The above inscriptions are striking not only for their linguistic similarity to Paul's language in 1 Corinthians, but also for their interpretation of the meal. The participants draw near to god who stands alone as the host who "furnishes" the feast—note the verb παρέχειν—and so the presence of the god and the sanctity of this place and time are assumed in these meals.[52] In one of the inscriptions above, it also asserts that during the partaking of the meal, the god bestows equal honors (ἰσότιμος) upon all who come regardless of her or his origin (ὁποθενοῦν).

Greeks often employed technical terms that referred to the careful examination prior to meal-eating: κρίνειν, διακρίνειν, and δοκιμάζειν (with the noun, δοκιμασία and the opposite verb form, ἀποδοκιμάζειν, for rejection). If the to-be-eaten substance did not pass muster, then it would be disqualified from consumption. Such language was also used to refer to the "the approved" within the roll of membership groups or to designate certain individuals who could handle sacred objects.[53] One Athenian law concerning the Delphic amphictyony called

---

[50] *IStratonikeia* 22.2–4, 7–9 (Caria, 2nd BCE–2nd CE).
[51] *IStratonikeia* 25.2–3 (Caria, 2nd BCE–2nd CE). See also from the same provenance *IStratonikeia* 29; 33; 35; and 255. Additionally, P. Coll. Youtie 1.51–52 (Oxyrhynchus, 100–299 CE); P. Köln 1.57 (Oxyrhynchus, 200–299 CE). For full citations of the various inscriptions, see Jean Hatzfeld, "Inscriptions de Panamara," *BCH* 51 (1927): 57–122.
[52] On the importance of the "table of the god," see Polybius, 4.35.4; and Diodorus Siculus, *Bib. hist.* 5.46.7. Also *IG* II² 1322 (Rhamnous, after 229 BCE); and 1933 (Athens, 330–320 BCE). See also P. Oxy. 1485 (Oxyrhynchus, 100–225 CE): ἐρωτᾷ σαι(*) διπνῆσαι(*) ὁ ἐξηγητὴς ἐν τῷ Δημητρίῳ σήμερον ἥτις ἐστίν θ ἀπὸ ὥρας ζ = "The exegetes ask you to dine in the (temple of) Demeter today, which is the 9th, starting at the 7th hour."
[53] E.g., *IG* II² 1361 (Piraeus, 330–23 BCE); *IG* II² 1369 (Liopesi, 2nd CE); XII⁶ 1:172 (Samos, ca. 250 BCE). The concept of "examination" (δοκιμασία) has a long history beyond the religious/sacred which I do not address here. For this discussion, see Christophe Feyel, *Dokimasia: La place et le role de l'examen préliminaire dans les institutions des cités grecques* (Nancy: ADRA, 2009).

for the "approval" of individuals who were then qualified to control the sacrifices,[54] and a different regulation from Ceos designated the testing of the sacrifices by certain committee members.[55] One fragmentary inscription concerning the Eleusinian Mysteries commands the examination of the sacred portions prior to sacrifice.[56] In an inscription from Sicily, there are striking resemblances to the language found in 1 Corinthians:

> ὁμοίως δὲ καὶ αἱ κατὰ πόδας ἀρχαὶ πᾶσαι θυόντω καθ'ἕκαστον ἐνιαυτὸν ταύται τᾶι ἁμέραι τοῖς γενετόρεσσι καὶ τᾶι Ὁμονοίαι ἱερεῖον ἑκατέροις, ὅ κα δοκιμάζωντι, καὶ οἱ πολῖται πάντες ἑορταζόντω παρ'ἀλλάλοις κατὰ τὰς ἀδελφοθετίας.

> And likewise, all subsequent magistrates sacrifice every year on this day, to the ancestors and to *Homonoia*, an animal for sacrifice examined by both parties, and all the citizens will celebrate a feast with one another according to the rites of brotherhood.[57]

There is both a concern for proper examination of the to-be-consumed substance,[58] and for a united celebration of the feast with other members of the community.

---

54 *CID* 1.10 lines 14–15 (Delphi, 380–79 BCE): καὶ τὰ ἱερήϊα ἀθρόα συναγόντων τὸ ἔθνος τον δοκιμ[α ... ἐκ] στόμβαν ὅ[ρ]κον ὀμόσας εἴπερ τοὶ ἱερομνάμονες δοκιμαζέτω = "And they will gather together the slaughter victims, having indeed taken the oath, let the *hieromnamones* conduct the examination."
55 *IG* XII[5] 647.14 (Ceos, early 3rd BCE): δοκιμάζειν δὲ τὰ ἱερεῖα τοὺς προβούλους. See also *ISmyrna* 603; *LSCG* 65; *SEG* 55.931 (Cos, 150–100 BCE); Pausanias, *Descr.* 9.19.7; Plutarch, *Def. orac.* 437B.
56 *Agora XVI* 56.4–7 (Eleusis, 4th BCE): [...]ται παραλαβόν[τ...] [..εἰ δὲ] μή, ὅταμ πρῶτον ο[ἷόν τε ἧι ...] [...] δοκιμας<θ>ῶσι θύεν τ[...] [ὃν δ]ὲ ἱεροφάντην τὴν με[...]. For details on the interpretation and reconstruction of this inscription, see Kevin Clinton, "A Law in the City Eleusinion Concerning the Mysteries," *Hesperia* 49.3 (1980): 258–88. The following inscriptions not available in English are important parallels: *Bargylia* 1 lines 3–5 (Caria, 120 BCE): καὶ παραγέτωσαν τὰ θ[ρέμματ]α εἰς τὴν ἐκκλησί[αν τοῦ] μηνὸς τοῦ Ἑρμαιῶνος τῆι εἰκάδι· δ[οκιμ]ασθέντων δὲ αὐτῶν καὶ ἀχθέντων εἰς τὸ ἱερὸν τῆς Ἀρτέμιδος τῆς Κινδυάδος = "And let them lead the animals to the assembly of the people on the 20th month of the Hermanion. And after they have been approved and brought into the sanctuary of Artemis Kindyas"; *Bargylia* 2 line 15 (Caria): περὶ δὲ τ[ῆ]ς δοκιμασίας καὶ περὶ τῆς κρίσεως = "And concerning the approval and concerning judgment"; *Bargylia* 3 lines 21–24 (Caria, after 133 BCE): δὲ καὶ το[ύ]των τῶν θρεμμάτων τὴν τε παραγωγὴν καὶ τὴν δοκιμασίαν ἐν τῆι αὐτῆι ἐκλησίαι ... δοκιμασθέντω[ν] δὲ τούτων = "And the furnishing and examination of these animals occur during the same meeting ... and after these animals are examined."
57 *Decreti di Entella Nak. A* (Nakone, ca. 250 BCE).
58 Literary evidence echoes the same sentiments: Herodotus, 2.38–39; Diodorus Siculus, *Bib. hist.* 1.88.4; Plutarch, *Is. Os.* 363B–C; Achilles Tatius, *Leuc. Clit.* 3.25.6–7; *Scholia* of Demosthenes, *Mid.* 21.171 names the ἱεροποιόν as one who ensures that the sacrifices are "not unacceptable or

While technically not about meals per se, some inscriptions employed δοκιμάζειν and διακρίνειν to refer to "approvals" and "arbitrations" that involved sacred spaces.[59] One building contract inscription from Delos provides explicit instructions for making known the "examination" (δοκιμασία) of the sanctuary construction through proper "judgment" (διακρίνειν). The relevant lines read:[60]

> When the work is completed, let the contractor announce to the commissioners and to the architect; let the commissioners and the architect make known the results of their examination (τὴν δοκιμασίαν) within ten days from the time they received the announcement ... [on disputes:] let the commissioners pronounce their judgment (διακρινέτωσαν) while serving in the sanctuary.

Another sanctuary building contract from Lebadeia stipulates that the workers' noncompliance will be fined by the *naopoioi* and could be subject to expulsion from working on the building (ζημιωθήσεται ὑπὸ τῶν ναοποιῶν ... ἐξελαυνέσθω ἐκ τοῦ ἔργου),[61] and then provides various scenarios concerning proper "approval" for the work.[62] This process of vetting both the consumed and the consumer is one that Paul himself employs (see chapter 5).

---

mutilated" (μὶ ἀδόκιμα καὶ πηρά). See also *BGU* 1.250 (Papyrus from Fayoum, ca. 100–130 CE); *P. Gen.* 1.32 (Fayoum, 148 CE).

59 E.g., *IG* II² 244 (Piraeus, 338/7 BCE); *IG* II² 1670 (Eleusis, 330 BCE); *IG* II² 1678 (Delos, 350 BCE); *IDelos* 500 (Delos, 297 BCE); *IDelos* 504 B (Delos, 280 BCE); *IDelos* 505 (Delos, early-3rd BCE); *Halikarnassos* 6 (Halicarnassus, early-3rd BCE); *IG* VII 3073 (Lebadeia, end-3rd BCE); *F. Delphes* III,3 383 (Delphi, 180/79 BCE).

60 *ID* 502 A.19–20, 22–23 (Delos, 297 BCE): ἐπειδὰν δὲ συντελεσθῆι τὸ ἔργον, ἐπαγγειλάτω ὁ ἐργώνης τοῖς ἐπιστάταις καὶ τῶι ἀρχιτέκτονι· ἀφ' ἧς δ'ἂν ἡμέρας ἐπαγγείλει, ἀποφαινέσθωσαν ἐπίσταται καὶ ἀρχιτέκτων τὴν δοκιμασίαν ἐν δέκα ἡμέραις ... διακρινέτωσαν οἱ ἐπιστάται ἐν τῶι ἱερῶι καθίσαντες. See also A.5–7 on the "rejection" (ἀποδοκιμάζειν) of the sanctuary work if it is not built to standard.

61 *IG* VII 3073 i.17, 20 (Lebadeia, early-2nd BCE).

62 *IG* VII 3073 i.27–29: περὶ δὲ τῶν προπεποιημένων οἱ ἐξ ἀρχῆς ἔγγυοι ἔστωσαν ἕως τῆς ἐσχάτης δοκιμασίας = "And concerning the works that have been completed, let the first guarantors stand until the final approval" / i.57–58: καὶ συντελέσας ὅλον τὸ ἔργον, ὅταν δοκιμασθῇ, κομισάσθω τὸ ἐπιδέκατον τὸ ὑπολειφθὲν κτλ. = "And after completing the entire job, whenever it is approved, let him receive the tenth which remains etc." / i.62–64: ἐὰν δέ τι πρόσεργον δῇ γενέσθαι συμφέρον τῷ ἔργῳ, ποιήσει ἐκ τοῦ ἴσου λόγου καὶ προσκομιεῖται τὸ γινόμενον αὐτῷ, ἀποδείξας δόκιμον = "And if it be necessary for additional work for the job, he will do it from equal account and he will be paid extra what is due to him, after demonstrating its approval." See also the approval of various materials/techniques for the sanctuary project in i.83–87; ii.99–101, 120–25, 149–50, 154–59, 184–86; *IG* VII 3074.10–13 (Lebadeia, 2nd BCE). There is also a fragmentary contract inscription, fully published in 1896 by A. de Ridder and A. Choisy, "Devis de Livadie," *BCH* 20 (1896): 318–35 that has not been published in any recent English literature (for citation, I use *Livadie* 1 to refer to this inscription). *Livadie* 1 (Lebadeia, end-3rd

3.2.4 Penalties for Transgressions

In the Greek sacred laws, there are varying degrees of penalty for transgressions, the simplest being financial restitution for one's error. For example, the law of the Andanian mysteries stipulates that if a man steals during the days when the mysteries and sacrifices are taking place, he is to repay double the amount (ἀποτινέτω διπλοῦν).[63] Similarly, if one is found to err in the management of the temple treasury (τι εὑρίσκωνται ἀδικοῦντες), the fine was double the amount (διπλασίου) plus an extra one thousand drachma.[64] The sanctuary of Apollo Erithaseus was to remain protected, and any who broke the boundary of this sacred space by cutting wood in the sanctuary or carrying any forbidden items out of the sanctuary would be fined fifty drachmas along with his name being handed over to the proper authorities.[65] One inscription even demanded an uncommonly high penalty of one thousand drachmas for cutting or removing trees within the sanctuary.[66] Two other Greek inscriptions mention a fine for those who transgressed the sanctuary by bringing into it forbidden animals.[67] Finally, there are various legislations of money penalties exacted upon those that misbehaved within a sanctuary.[68]

BCE) lines 3–5: [ὅταν αὐ]τῶ ἀποδείξῃ παρα ... [τοὺς λίθους τοὺς] κειμένους, καθὼς γέγραπται, [δ]οκίμο[υς ... ὄντας], ἐνιτελείτω τὰ κατάλοιπα τῶν ἔ[ργ]ω[ν] = "when he will show him ... the blocks laid, just as it has been written, being <u>approved</u>, let him complete the remainder of the job." Also *Livadie* 1.17–18, 37–40, 45–47.

63 *LSCG* 65.76. While this rule does not actually identify whether or not the crime took place within the sanctuary, the entire list of laws are singularly focused on the inner workings of the sacred space, and therefore, it is likely that stealing *in* the precinct of the sanctuary is what is in view here.

64 *LSCG* 65.51–52. An addendum to this rule commands that the judges do not reduce this fine under any circumstance (καὶ οἱ δικασταὶ μὴ ἀφαιρούντω μηθέν).

65 *LSCG* 37.5–9, 14–17 (Attica, end 4th BCE). See *IG* II² 1328 (Piraeus, 183/2 BCE). See also *LSCG* 91 (Euboea, 4th BCE) and *LSS* 81 (Samos, 1st CE) for a fine of one hundred drachmas. These fines only applied to the freeman; see below for the penalty for slaves.

66 *LSCG* 150 A.1–5 (Kos, 4th BCE). The protection of trees in sacred spaces was a common trope in the Greek world: *IG* II² 2499 (Athens, 306/5 BCE); *LSCG* 36.17–21 (Piraeus, 4th BCE); 37; 91; 111 (Paros, 5th BCE); 148 (Gortyne, 3rd BCE); 150B (Kos, 4th BCE); *LSS* 36 (Akraiphia, 5th BCE); 53 (Delos, 3rd BCE); 81; 91; *IG* XIV 645 (Herakleia, 4th BCE). The Latin evidence is also similar: *CIL* I² 366 (Spoletium [Umbria], ca. 241 BCE); 2872 (Trevi); Cato, *Agr.* 139–40.

67 *LSCG* 84.14–18 (Korope, 100 BCE): either fifty drachmas for a freeman or one obol per animal for the slave; *LSCG* 116.9–20 (Chios, 4th BCE): half a hektos (possibly of grain) for animals, five staters to the god for spreading manure, and five staters for the witness who fails to report the crime; *LSCG* 136.30–3: one obol per animal brought into the sanctuary.

68 *LSS* 128.4–6: "But if any creeps secretly into the shrine, he is fined four staters." (εἰ δὲ τίς κα παρέρπῃ, ζαμία τέτορες στατῆρες); *SEG* 31.122 (Liopesi, early 2nd CE): fighting, ten drachma for

Beyond the fines levied, the extreme measure of exclusion can be exercised upon transgressors. A famous incident in Athenian history resulted in the exile of the Athenian commander Alcibiades in 415 BCE. He was charged with defacing the Hermae that stood at the entrance of many temples and with performing certain sacred rites in his own home, which was understood as "profaning the mysteries" (καταλύσει τὰ μυστικά).[69] In a law of the *eranistai* (νόμος ἐρανιστῶν), if any are caught fighting or causing a disturbance within the most holy assembly of *eranistai*, such persons will be cast out from the *eranos*.[70] Another law commands the priests to "exclude from the mysteries" (ἀποκωλυόντω τῶν μυστηρίων) certain disobedient individuals.[71] A law quoted by Demosthenes bars any "woman taken in adultery" (ἐφ' ᾗ ... ἂν μοιχὸς ἁλῷ γυναικί) from attending the public sacrifices (τῶν ἱερῶν τῶν δημοτελῶν), even when foreigners and slaves were afforded this right by law.[72] The rationale given is so "that our sanctuaries may be kept free from all pollution and profanation" (μὴ μιάσματα μηδ' ἀσεβήματα γίγνηται ἐν τοῖς ἱεροῖς) and if any woman is found guilty, she is to be cast out from the home of her husband and from the sanctuaries of the city.[73] In some exceptional cases, the transgressor could pass through the boun-

---

the "one who initiated" (ὁ ἀρξάμενος) and five drachma for "whoever joined in" (ὁ ἐξακολουθήσας); *LSCG* 53.40–44 (Attica, end of 2nd CE): for "fighting or disturbances ... twenty-five Attic drachmas" (μάχας ἢ θορύβους ... Ἀττικαῖς κε). Related to this are inscriptions found on sarcophagi that exact monetary penalties for any acts that disturb its integrity: *IK* 57.167 (Pisidia, undated); 57.168 (Pisidia, before 212 CE); 57.169 (Pisidia, after 212 CE); 57.170 (Pisidia, 2–3rd CE); 57.172 (Pisidia, after 212 CE).

69 Thucydides, 6.28–29. Alcibiades's opponents voted to send him away temporarily while they mounted a case against him. See Andocides, *On the Mysteries*; Plutarch, *Alc.* 19–22. Andocides in his defense speech notes that under the ancient law, the penalty for this transgression is death (*On the Mysteries* 110: νόμος δ' εἴη πάτριος, ὃς ἂν θῇ ἱκετηρίαν μυστηρίοις, τεθνάναι). Hermae were also located at the entrances of houses and public spaces, not just temples.

70 *LSCG* 53.31–32, 40–43: τὴν σεμνοτάτην σύνοδον τῶν ἐρανιστῶν ... εἰ δὲ τις μάχας ἢ θορύβους κεινῶν φαίνοιτο ... ἐκβαλλέσθω τοῦ ἐράνου. See Herodotus, 5.72; *SEG* 31.122 (line 9); *IG* II[2] 1368 (Athens, 164–5 CE), temporary expulsion (lines 82–4, 99–106).

71 *LSCG* 65.41. See Andocides, *On His Return*, 2.15. In Euripides, *Ion* 1314–19, Ion suggests: τοὺς μὲν γὰρ ἀδίκους βωμὸν οὐχ ἵζειν ἐχρῆν, ἀλλ' ἐξελαύνειν· οὐδὲ γὰρ ψαύειν καλὸν θεῶν πονηρὰν χεῖρα· τοῖσι δ' ἐνδίκοις—ἱερὰ καθίζειν, ὅστις ἠδικεῖτ', ἐχρῆν· καὶ μὴ 'πὶ ταὐτὸ τοῦτ' ἰόντ' ἔχειν ἴσον τόν τ' ἐσθλὸν ὄντα τόν τε μὴ θεῶν πάρα.

72 Demosthenes, *Neaer.* 85–86. The law even stipulates that if a woman "transgresses the law" (παρανομεῖν), anyone may inflict upon them any kind of punishment save only death.

73 Demosthenes, *Neaer.* 86: τι ἁμάρτῃ τοιοῦτον, ἅμα ἔκ τε τῆς οἰκίας τοῦ ἀνδρὸς ἐκβεβλημένη ἔσται καὶ ἐκ τῶν ἱερῶν τῶν τῆς πόλεως.

daries of the sanctuary, but the gods would not accept his or her sacrifice. Therefore they remain, for all intents and purposes, excluded from the temple.⁷⁴

Besides financial penalties and exclusions, there were sometimes penalties that one had to pay with his or her body. In one account of "the disobedient or the improperly behaved towards what is holy," the priests were exhorted to whip such individuals.⁷⁵ Another decree states that in cases when the person could not pay the necessary fine, he or she must pay with physical punishments.⁷⁶ The removal of any items from the sanctuary of Apollo in Attica led to flogging with fifty lashes if the perpetrator was a slave.⁷⁷ The failure to exercise punishments could also hold dire consequences for bystanders, as evident in Aeschines. In *Against Ctesiphon*, he warns the Athenians that if they leave "unpunished ... the ones guilty of the ban of the curse" (ἀτιμωρήτους ... ταῖς ἀραῖς ἐνόχους) the curse warns: "May they who fail to punish them never offer pure sacrifice unto Apollo, nor to Artemis, nor to Leto, nor to Athena Pronaea, and may the gods refuse to accept their sacrifices."⁷⁸

The above examples show instances when human agents meted out the punishments, but there is also evidence that the gods or other divine agents directly acted upon transgressors. The specifics of the penalty are often left vague, but this may have been an intentional method to strengthen the threat: the unpredictability or ambiguity of the language encourages compliance. One such threat is found in the regulations for the Cult of Mēn in Attica where if "anyone meddles in the things of the god or is a busybody, he or she incurs sin (ἁμαρτίαν) against Mēn Tyrannos which is not able to be expiated (ἣν οὐ δύνηται ἐξειλάσασθαι)."⁷⁹ What does it mean that one's sins cannot be expiated before the god? The text does not elaborate further, but in a society where participation in cult was inti-

---

74 ἀπόδεκτος ἡ θυσία παρὰ τοῦ θεοῦ. See *IG* II² 1365.11–15; and 1366.7–9. See also the curses and/or the ineffectiveness of sacrifices in Herodotus, *Hist.* 6.91; 7.133–134; Sophocles, *Ant.* 999–1022; Isocrates, *Archid.* 31; Plutarch, *Them.* 13; *IG* II² 13200 (Attica, ca. 161 CE).
75 *LSCG* 65.40: τὸν δὲ ἀπειθοῦντα ἢ ἀπρεπῶς ἀναστρεφόμενον εἰς τὸ θεῖον μαστιγούντω ... καὶ ἀποκωλυόντω τῶν μυστηρίων. This command is repeated in this law: lines 43, 76, 79, 101–2, 105, 110, and 165. See *LSCG* 37.9–10. See also: *Iscr. di Cos* 178.26–31 (Cos, 195 BCE); *LSCG* 122.7–8 (Samos, 3rd BCE); 137B.13–15 (Lindos, 1st CE); *LSAM* 52B.11–13 (Milet, 1st CE).
76 *IG* II² 1369.42–44 (= *LSCG* 53). See also *IG* II² 1635 (Delos, 374 BCE).
77 *LSCG* 37.7–12. See also *LSCG* 84.16–18.
78 Aeschines, *Ctes.* 121 (Adams, LCL slightly modified). See Aeschylus, *Sept.* 181–202.
79 *LSCG* 55.14–16: ὃς ἂν δὲ πολυπραγμονήσῃ τὰ τοῦ θεοῦ ἢ περιεργάσηται, ἁμαρτίαν ὀφιλέτω Μηνὶ Τυράννωι, ἣν οὐ δύνηται ἐξειλάσασθαι. On the language of expiating the gods, see Herodotus, *Hist.* 7.141 (also Clement of Alexandria, *Strom.* 5.14.132; Eusebius, *Praep. ev.* 13.13); Menander, *Frg.* 544K; Plutarch, *Sept. sap. conv.* 149D. See chapter 4 for this language in Jewish sources.

mately tied to the fabric of society, receiving such a punishment would have been extremely undesirable.[80]

One inscription notes, "if anyone disobeys one of these things [i.e. the regulations], he will learn the powers of Zeus (τὰς δυνάμις τοῦ Διός),"[81] while another stele records an act of thievery from the bathhouse of Mēn Axiottenos. It was only after the thief knew that the god was indignant (ὁ θεὸς ἐνεμέσησε τὸν κλέπτην)—presumably a reference to divine punishment[82]—that the thief returned the stolen robe and admitted his guilt.[83] The god then commanded that his powers be recorded upon a stele (ἐκέλευσε ... στηλλογραφῆσαι τὰς δυνάμεις) as a public reminder of what took place. A similar incident is found on a marble stele from Kula that describes the consequences of stealing a precious stone from the god.[84] At a certain point in time, the god showed himself, destroying the one who committed this act (ἐπιφανεὶς ὁ θεός ... καὶ τοῦτο πυήσασαν ... διέρηξε).[85] The god was also angry because they failed to acknowledge his power (περισυρούσης αὐτῆς τὴν δύναμιν τοῦ θεοῦ ... ὁ θεὸς τοῦτο ἐνεμέσησε).[86]

---

[80] See also *LSAM* 29 (Metropolis in Ionia, 4th BCE), lines 12–14: "Whoever may do wrong, let Meter Gallesia not be gracious to him" (ὃς δ'ἂν ἀδικήσηι, μὴ εἴλως αὐτῶι ἡ Μήτηρ ἡ Γαλλησία) and Xenophon, *Anab.* 5.3.13 (~ *LSCG* 86 [Ithaca, 2nd CE]), noting an inscription on the temple of Artemis he had built: "If any one does not do these things (i.e. the proper cult requirements), the goddess will deal with him" (ἂν δέ τις μὴ ποιῇ ταῦτα τῇ θεῷ μελήσει).

[81] *LSAM* 19 (Maionia, 173 CE), lines 6–9: εἴ τις δὲ τούτων ἀπειθήσι ἀναγνώσεται τὰς δυνάμις τοῦ Διός.

[82] According to TLG, there are less than a handful of instances of θεός/θεοί as subjects of νεμεσάω, but they are significant for how to interpret the same phrase on the stele. See Hesiod, *Op.* 740–1: "Whoever crosses a river with hands unwashed of wickedness, the gods are angry with him and bring trouble upon him afterwards (τῷ δὲ θεοὶ νεμεσῶσι καὶ ἄλγεα δῶκαν ὀπίσσω)."; Dionysius Halicarnassus, *Ant. rom.* 8.50.3: "I observe also that those who act arrogantly and treat with insolence the prayers of suppliants all incur the indignation of the gods and in the end come to a miserable state (ἅπαντας νεμεσωμένους ὑπὸ θεῶν καὶ εἰς συμφορὰς καταστρέφοντας οὐκ εὐτυχεῖς)." Also Plutarch, *Mar.* 39.6. The only other inscriptional occurrence of this language is found in the next evidence noted.

[83] *TAM* V.1 159 (Lydia, 164–5 CE).

[84] *SEG* 37.1001 (Kula, 2nd CE).

[85] *SEG* 37.1001, lines 12–14. The verb διαρρήγνυμι means literally "to burst," "to smash," or "to split." See Dio Chrysostom, *Virt.* 32. See LSJ, s.v.; BDAG, s.v. Divine epiphany and the punishment of "the one who did x" resulting in his or her destruction is formally very similar to Paul's exhortation in 1 Cor 5. See also a Greek inscription from the Roman period, *IC* II xvi 28 lines 10–12 (Crete, Roman period) that threatens destruction upon anyone who might remove an object from the shrine: πυρὶ καὶ ὅσα κακὰ καὶ ὀλέθρια γίνεται, ταῦτα γενέσθω τῷ τολμήσαντι ἐκ τούτου τοῦ ἡρῴου μετακινῆσαί τι.

[86] *SEG* 37.1001, lines 15–16, 17–18.

Such warnings about proper recognition of the gods and their powers within sacred spaces also occur in contexts that elaborate more explicitly what happened to transgressors. According to Pausanias, unlawful entry into a temple at Thebes led to the transgressors being "destroyed" (ἐφθάρησαν) by heavenly thunder and lightning.[87] A certain Stratonikos cut a tree belonging to Zeus Didymites and was punished for disbelieving the god's power, and was put into a death-like state (τὴν ἰδίαν δύναμις διὰ τὸ ἀπιστῖν ... κατέθηκεν ἰσοθανάτους).[88] The stele was erected in gratitude after his recovery from this great danger (σωθεὶς ἐγ μεγάλου κινδύνου), concluding with a stern caution: "Let no one ever disparage his powers (αὐτοῦ τὰς δυνάμις μή τίς ποτε κατευτελήσι)."[89] In another record, Menophilus is said to have erred by purchasing sacred wood. He was punished by the god and suffered much for this deed (διὰ τοῦτο ἐκολάσθη ὑπὸ τοῦ θεοῦ ... πολλὰ παθόντος αὐτοῦ),[90] and in order to make proper amends, Menophilus proclaims to everyone, "one must not despise the god" (παραγγέλλει πᾶσιν ἀνθρώποις, ὅτι οὐ δεῖ καταφρονεῖν τοῦ θεοῦ).[91]

The negative connotation associated with despising gods or the things belonging to the gods is a common theme that stretches all the way back to Euripides and is one that Paul himself repeats in 1 Cor 11:22 (ἢ τῆς ἐκκλησίας τοῦ θεοῦ καταφρονεῖτε).[92] A few examples show the endurance of this perspective. In the tragedian Euripides' *Bacchae*, Cadmus, the former king of Thebes tries to convince his grandson Pentheus to respect the gods. Cadmus sets himself up as the example: "I do not scorn the gods, mortal that I am" (οὐ καταφρονῶ 'γὼ τῶν θεῶν θνητὸς γεγώς).[93] Centuries later, Dio Chrysostom makes a similar entreaty, to "trust in a great power and source of aid, that which proceeds from

---

[87] Pausanias, *Descr.* 9.25.10.
[88] *TAM* V.1 179b (Lydia, 2nd CE), lines 5–8. The only other occurrence of ἰσοθάνατος in the inscriptional evidence is in *SEG* 38.1236 (Lydia, 2nd CE) where it is also the penalty for transgression within sacred space.
[89] *TAM* V.1 179b, lines 8–9, 11–12. On witnessing to the gods' "powers," see also *TAM* V.1 317 (Lydia, 114–5 CE); 318 (Lydia, 156–7 CE); 319 (Lydia, 196–7 CE); 464 (Lydia, undated); *SEG* 28.1568 (unknown, 1st BCE–2nd CE); *BIWK* 35 (N. Lydia, 210 CE); 47 (Kula, 146–7 CE); 65 (N. Lydia, 2–3rd CE); *ILydiaHM* 85 (Saittai, 205–6 CE).
[90] *TAM* V.1 179a (Saittai, 2nd CE), lines 5–7.
[91] *TAM* V.1 179a, lines 10–13. Also *BIWK* 106 (Phrygia, 2–3rd CE).
[92] Euripides, *Bacch.* 199; Lysias, *Andoc.* 11.1; Aeschines, *Tim.* 67; Ps.-Aristotle, *Oec.* 1352a; Diodorus Siculus, *Bib. hist.* 3.47.2; 4.22.3; 23.13.1; Dionysius of Halicarnassus, *Ant. rom.* 2.20.2; Plutarch, *Cat. Min.* 35.7; *Lys.* 8.4; *Ages.* 9.3; Dio Chrysostom, *Def.* 1–2; Athenaeus, *Deipn.* 13.67; Josephus, *Ant.* 1.43; 4.181, 217; 6.150; 8.251; 9.173; 12.357; Clement of Alexandria, *Strom.* 3.3.12; Justin, *1 Apol.* 25. See also, 2 Macc 4:14; 4 Macc 4:9; Wis 14:30; Hos 6:7; Matt 6:24; Rom 2:4; 1 Cor 11:22.
[93] Euripides, *Bacch.* 199 (Kovacs, LCL).

the gods, though most men scorn it and deem it useless" (κρείττονι πεποιθὼς δυνάμει καὶ βοηθείᾳ τῇ παρὰ τῶν θεῶν, ἧς καταφρονοῦσιν οἱ πολλοὶ καὶ ἀνωφελῆ νομίζουσιν).⁹⁴ These discussions about the gods and their δύναμις are significant since they bear close similarity to language that is replete in Paul's Corinthian correspondence, particularly in 1 Cor 5 (see chapter 2).

There are also extant texts that modern scholars have categorized as "confessional inscriptions" (*Beichtinschriften*) so termed because they tend to follow a formal pattern: transgression–punishment–confession–divine response.⁹⁵ The inscriptions do not always contain all four components, but regardless of ultimate form, they are important for what they reveal about sacred boundaries and the gods' actions toward transgressions. The following confession is found on one marble stele from the village of Kula (Lydia):⁹⁶

| Ἀντωνία ... Ἀπόλλωνι Θεῷ Βοζηνῷ διὰ τὸ ἀναβεβηκένε με ἐπὶ τὸν χορὸν ἐν ῥυπαρῷ ἐπενδύτῃ, κολασθῖσα δὲ ἐξωμολογησάμην κὲ ἀνέθηκα εὐλογίαν, ὅτι ἐγενόμην ὁλόκληρος. | Antonia ... to Apollo, God Bozenos because I entered the area in a filthy garment, and being punished I confessed and dedicated a eulogy because I became whole. |

Another confessional inscription is highly relevant for how it describes in clearer detail the divine punishment for transgression:⁹⁷

| Ἀριστονείκου ἐλεηθεὶς καὶ ἁμαρτήσας καταπίπτω εἰς ἀσθένειαν καὶ ὁμολογῶ τὸ ἁμάρτημα Μηνὶ Ἀξιωτηνῷ καὶ στηλογραφῶ. | I, NN son of Aristoneikos, who was shown mercy and who sinned, fell ill. And I confess the sin to Mēn Axiottenos and inscribed this stele. |

The language about falling into illness (καταπίπτω εἰς ἀσθένειαν) is notable, since it is a clear association between the experience of physical maladies and a transgression against the divine ("sin" = ἁμάρτημα; see 1 Cor 11:17–34).⁹⁸

---

94 Dio Chrysostom, *Or.* 45.1–2 (Crosby, LCL).
95 Georg Petzl, "Die Beichtinschriften Westkleinasiens," *EA* 22 (1994): article occupies entire volume; and Philip A. Harland, *Greco-Roman Associations: Texts, Translations, and Commentary. II. North Coast of the Black Sea, Asia Minor* (Berlin: Walter de Gruyter, 2014), 198–9 (erroneously called "*Beichinschrift*").
96 *TAM* V.1 238 (Kula [Lydia], undated).
97 *CMRDM* 77 (= *ILydiaKP* 1.25; Sardis, undated).
98 On the need to amend for "sins," see *CMRDM* 42 (Ayazviran, 143–4 CE). See also *TAM* V.1 460 (Lydia, 118–9 CE) on Trophime being punished by the gods and made insane (lines 5–7, προσελθεῖν ἐκολάσετο αὐτὴν καὶ μανῆναι ἐποίησεν) because she failed the call to service.

Other inscriptions show even harsher punishments for sanctuary transgressions or for failing to properly acknowledge the gods. A regulation about the "inviolability" (ἄσυλος) of a sanctuary of Dionysus Bachius warns that anyone who does wrong to a suppliant or to the enclosed area is "to be utterly destroyed" (ἐξώλη εἶναι), including his family.[99] Another inscription vividly portrays the penalty for anyone who violates the sacred fish or mistreats the vessel of the god: "any who does these things is evil and may he perish in an evil destruction (κακῇ ἐξωλείᾳ ἀπόλοιτο), having become fish food."[100] One list of prescriptions for participation in a private cult warns—following a long list of commands—that the gods will remain gracious to those who obey, giving them all good things, but they will hate the transgressors, bringing upon them "great retributions" (μεγάλας τιμωρίας).[101] An inscription from Smyrna advises that proper care for purity is required lest the failure to do so warrant the "cause of wrath" (μήνειμα) from the god Dionysus Bromios.[102] Diodorus Siculus also describes a sacred precinct of the Palici near Sicily—so ancient and sacred[103] and so energized by a divine force[104]—where the greatest oaths are made (11.89.5, οἱ μέγιστοι τῶν ὅρκων ἐνταῦθα συντελοῦνται) strictly to ensure its trustworthiness. Those who falsely swear are quickly overtaken by a divine punishment, with some losing their sight when they leave the sanctuary.[105]

Also *CMRDM* 80 (Sardis, 160–1 CE); *BIWK* 1 (Mysia, 1–2nd CE); 12 (Saittai, 253–4 CE); 69 (Kula, 156–7 CE); 71 (Kula, 156–7 CE).
99 *LSAM* 75, lines 7–12: ἱκέτην μὴ ἀδικεῖν. Ὅρος ἱερὸς ἄσυλος Διονύσου Βάκχου· τὸν ἱκέτην μὴ ἀδικεῖν μηδὲ ἀδικούμενον περιορᾶν, εἰ δὲ μή, ἐξώλη εἶναι καὶ αὐτὸν καὶ τὸ γένος αὐτοῦ. Such language is also found in various other cursing contexts involving the gods: *IG* XI⁴ 1296 (Delos, mid-3rd BCE); Aristophanes, *Thesm.* 331–51; Sophocles, *Phil.* 1326–28; Demosthenes, *Fals. leg.* 19.71; Aeschines, *Fals. leg.* 87. Somewhat more generally, see Hesiod, *Op.* 238–45; *TAM* V.1 509 (Lydia, 2nd CE[?]).
100 *LSAM* 17 (Smyrna, 1st BCE): Ἰχθῦς ἱεροὺς μὴ ἀδικεῖν, μηδὲ σκεύος τῶν τῆς θεοῦ λυμαίνεσθαι, μηδὲ ἐκφέρειν ἐκ τοῦ ἱεροῦ ἐπὶ κλοπήν· ὁ τούτων τι ποιῶν κακὸς κακῇ ἐξωλείᾳ ἀπόλοιτο, ἰχθυόβρωτος γενόμενος.
101 *LSAM* 20 (lines 46–50): οἱ θεοὶ τοῖς μὲν ἀκολουθοῦσιν ἔσονται ἵλεως καὶ δώσουσιν αὐτοῖς ἀεὶ πάντα τἀγαθά ... ἐὰν δέ τινες παραβαίνωσιν, τοὺς τοιούτους μισήσουσι καὶ μεγάλας αὐτοῖς τιμωρίας περιθήσουσιν. Earler lines 32–35 provide further warnings regarding this space: θεοὶ γὰρ ἐν αὐτῶι ἵδρυνται μεγάλοι καὶ ταῦτα ἐπισκοποῦσιν καὶ τοὺς παραβαίνοντας τὰ παραγγέλματα οὐκ ἀνέξονται.
102 *LSAM* 84 (Smyrna, 2nd CE).
103 Diodorus Siculus, *Bib. hist.* 11.89.1: γὰρ τὸ τέμενος τοῦτο διαφέρειν τῶν ἄλλων ἀρχαιότητι καὶ σεβασμῷ.
104 Diodorus Siculus, *Bib. hist.* 11.89.3: δοκεῖν ὑπὸ θείας τινὸς ἀνάγκης γίνεσθαι τὸ συμβαῖνον.
105 Diodorus Siculus, *Bib. hist.* 11.89.5: καὶ τοῖς ἐπιορκήσασι συντόμως ἡ τοῦ δαιμονίου κόλασις ἀκολουθεῖ· τινὲς γὰρ τῆς ὁράσεως στερηθέντες τὴν ἐκ τοῦ τεμένους ἄφοδον ποιοῦνται. On

Similarly, instructions for the household association of Dionysius assert that the gods "watch over these things … not tolerating the ones who transgress the commands … but if any transgress, they will hate them and inflict great punishments (μεγάλας τιμωρίας) upon them."[106] The commands remind adherents that an adulterous woman is a pollutant and "should not be present" (μηδὲ … παρατυγχάνειν), otherwise "she will receive evil curses from the gods" (κακὰς ἀρὰς παρὰ τῶν θεῶν ἕξει).[107] The lengthy regulations conclude with the assurance that "it will become evident" (φανεροὶ γίνωνται) who have remained true to the god.[108]

More rarely, death was meted out upon transgressors, as proof that one's life could be forfeit if he or she did not deal properly with the gods. One man's disobedience (ἠπίθησεν) led to the god killing (ἀπεστελέσετο) his son and grandchild,[109] while perjury before the god in another case resulted in death (ἀπέκτεινεν ὁ θεός).[110] In Ephesus, some 45 people were condemned to death for their mistreatment of the sanctuary and their affront to the *theoroi* (κατεδικάσαντο θάνατου … τὰ ἱερὰ ἠσέβησαν καὶ τοὺς θεωροὺς ὕβρισαν).[111] Ajax the Lesser is killed because he polluted the temple of Athena.[112]

3.3 Transgressions in the Roman Context

This section investigates how the Romans—from the early period of the Republic into the Imperial era—understood transgressions within sacred spaces. There is certainly much overlap with Greek ideas, though there are also subtle differences that are important to note. One initial point of divergence between the Greek and Roman conceptualities is linguistic: Latin does not use a singular term like the

---

blindness as divine punishment, see also *Bib. hist.* 4.84.4. In *Bib. hist.* 15.49, Diodorus narrates the violation of a *temenos* in Helice (identified as ἠσέβησάν … εἰς τὸ θεῖον), leading to Poseidon's wrath and the destruction of the "offending cities" (τὰς ἀσεβούσας πόλεις λυμήνασθαι).
106 *TAM* V 1539 (Lydia, 100 BCE), lines 33–5, 48–50.
107 *TAM* V 1539, lines 37–44.
108 *TAM* V 1539, lines 56–60. Interestingly, the use of this phrase to distinguish the approved and rejected is found in the NT only in the Pauline corpus and only in 1 Corinthians: 3:13; 11:19; and 14:25. Luke 8:17 is only obliquely related to this theme.
109 *SEG* 35.1158 (Katakekaumene, undated).
110 *NewDocLyd* 51 (Lydia, 102–3 CE).
111 *IEph* 1a.2 (Ephesus, 4th BCE).
112 Homer, *Od.* 4.499–511; Apollodorus, *Epit.* 6.6; Hyginus, *Fabulae* 116; Proclus, *Chrestomathia* II; Quintus Smyrnaeus, *Fall of Troy* 14.530–640; Tryphiodorus, *The Taking of Ilios* 647–48. See also Pausanias, *Descr.* 1.20.7.

Greek word, μίασμα, to define pollution,[113] though Jack Lennon observes that attending to the broader context of various accounts reveal much conceptual overlap between the Greeks and Romans.[114] The evidence in the following section is organized as follows: (1) inscriptions that are public representations of boundaries and punishments; (2) literary evidence from writers such as Cicero that spell out an ideal with regard to sacred spaces and the gods; (3) accounts from historians that serve as a historical representation of what happened in various situations; and (4) Aelius Aristides who serves as a unique firsthand account of an individual's religious experience with respect to sanctuaries. The diversity of the available evidence illustrates how transgressions were seen and understood in the Roman context.

3.3.1 Divine Power

A Pisidian monumental inscription carved on a pillar begins with a dedicatory Latin inscription to Mercury, with the lines thereafter written in Greek. It lists various responses that correspond to combinations of throwing of dice. A few responses are worth noting:

τόν τε νοσοῦντα θεοὶ σώσουσ' ἀπὸ κλείνης.	And the gods will save the sick man from his bed.[115]
καὶ τὸν κάμνοντ'ἐν νούσῳ σώσειν θεὸς αὐδᾷ.	And the god proclaims that he will save the man who is struggling with a disease.[116]

---

113 Mark Bradley, "Approaches to pollution and propriety," in *Rome, Pollution and Propriety: Dirt, Disease and Hygiene in the Eternal City from Antiquity to Modernity*, ed. M. Bradley (Cambridge: Cambridge University Press, 2012), 21.
114 According to Jack Lennon, there are various terms that correspond to the Greek idea of pollution and it is necessary to contextualize their use in ancient sources "when drawing conclusions about what was considered 'impure' or dangerous in Roman ritual and society." Such terms—which feature in various sources below—are: *polluere, inquinare, foedare, funestare, scelerare, masculare,* and *contaminare* to name a few. See Jack Lennon, "Pollution, religion and society in the Roman World," in *Rome, Pollution and Propriety*, 43–59 (43) with the phrase quoted from Gabriele Thome, "Crime and Punishment, Guilt and Expiation: Roman Thought and Vocabulary," *Acta Classica* 35 (1992): 77.
115 *IK* 57.5 Side A, VIII (Pisidia, 117–38 CE).
116 *IK* 57.5 Side A, IX.

There are various other inscriptions in this monument that contain the same theme, pointing to the gods as agents of healing or as protectors from illnesses.[117] A Latin inscription from Rome reads:[118]

> *Felix publicus Asinianus pontificum Bonae Deae agrestic Feliculae votum solvit iunicem albam libens animo ob luminibus restitutis derelictus a medicis post menses decem bineficio dominaes medicinis sanatus per eam restituta omnia ministerio Canniae Fortunatae.*
>
> Felix Asinianus, public slave of the *pontifices*, discharged his vow to rustic Bona Dea Felicula by sacrificing a white heifer willingly in mind on account of the restoration of his eyesight after he had been abandoned by doctors after ten months thanks to the good service of the goddess, cured by the remedies administered by her. Everything was restored during Cannia Fortunata's term as *ministra*.

The line between the actions of physicians and that of the goddess is an important one that was often blurred by Asclepius cult rituals (see discussion of Aelius Aristides below).[119] In contrast to attestations of divine healings, the Mercury monument also contains oracles that list various warnings:

μηδὲ βιάζου θνητὸς ἐὼν θεόν, ὅς σέ τι βλάψει.	Since you are a mortal, do not force the god, who will do you some harm.[120]
πάλι μηδ'ἄλλοθι βαῖνε, μή σοι θὴρ ὀλοὸς καὶ ἀλάστωρ ἐγγύθεν ἔλθῃ.	Go back and not somewhere else, lest a deadly beast and tormentor come near.[121]

---

117 See also Side B, XX: "The gods will readily save the one who is ill" (ἐν νούσῳ δέ τ'ἐόντα θεοὶ σώσουσιν ἑτοίμως); Side C, XXXIV: "The oracle ... reveals that the sick man has been saved" (μανύει καὶ τὸν νοσέοντα σεσῶσθαι); Side C, XXXVIII: "God proclaims that he saves the stranger who is ill" (τὸν ξεῖνον νοσοέοντα σῴζειν θεὸς αὐδᾷ); Side C, XLIII: "You will escape a dangerous disease" (ἐκφεύξῃ γὰρ νούσου χαλεπῆς); Side D, XLVII: "An she will free the sick person from his bonds (and save him)" (λύσει δὲ ἐκ δεσμῶν); and Side D, LIV: "You will escape from disease" (ἐκφεύξῃ ... νόσου). See letters from 2–3rd CE for supplications to the divine for health: *BGU* 523 (Arthur S. Hunt and Campbell C. Edgar, *Select Papyri*, LCL [Cambridge: Harvard University Press, 1932], 1:304–5); Hunt and Edgar §120–121; 125; 133–134; and 136–137.
118 *CIL* VI 68 (Via Ostiense [Rome], ca. 1st BCE–1st CE; trans. Kajava).
119 See, for example, *ILS* 3846 (W. Dacis, 100–150 CE): "To Asclepius and Hygieia, for the well-being (*pro salute*) of Iunia Cyrilla, because they restored her from a long illness by the virtue of the divine power of these waters (*quod a longa infirmitate virtute aquarum numinis sui revocaverunt*), her husband Titus B.A. dedicated this in fulfillment of a vow freely and deservedly." Translation from Gil H. Renberg, "Public and Private Places of Worship in the Cult of Asclepius at Rome," MAAR 51/52 (2006/2007): 87–172 (129 n. 200). Also *ILS* 3847 (Rome, ca. late-2nd CE); *IKibyra* 1.82, 83 (Kibyra, Roman imperial period).
120 *IK* 57.5 Side C, XLV. Also *BIWK* 33 (Lydia, Roman Imperial period).
121 *IK* 57.5 Side D, L.

The reference to the "tormenter" (ἀλάστωρ) in a context of transgression is not without significance, since this figure was often an unidentified executor of vengeance, much like the reference to the ambiguous "destroyer" (ὁ ὀλοθρευτής) in 1 Cor 10:10 that has eluded clear identification.[122] Furthermore, two related concepts are found in these monumental inscriptions: the gods as sources of benefit—usually healing from sickness—or as agents of harm.

The language of warning is also quite similar to that of "despising the gods" noted earlier in Greek sources, and it includes the notion that the awareness of one's mortality—in contrast to the immortality of the gods—should be sufficient reason to prevent one from engaging in forbidden acts. Roman writers also cautioned against contempt for the gods, demonstrating the persistence of the concern for proper posture towards the gods.[123]

One of the oldest extant Latin inscriptions maintains similar religious reservations as those seen in Greek sources. Known as *lapis niger*, named for the black stone pavement of this site, the inscription was discovered in Rome between the Forum and the Comitium in 1898, and underneath the black pavement was found a rectangular stele, likely of late sixth-century BCE.[124] Other ancient sources took note of this special site that served as a possible place of burial of Ro-

---

[122] For other references to ἀλάστωρ see: Aeschylus, *Pers.* 354; *Agam.* 1501, 1508; Euripides, *Herc. fur.* 1234; *Tro.* 941; *El.* 979; *Hel.* 1337; *Phoen.* 1556; Sophocles, *Oed. col.* 788; *IGUR* III.1155 (Rome, 161 CE); *IG* XIV 1389 Side B.91–95 (Rome, 161 CE); Athanasius, *Apol. Const.* 7.14; Evagrius, *Eulog.* 7; Socrates Scholasticus, *Hist. eccl.* 4.19.3; 7.38.28; Theodoret of Cyrus, *Inc. dom.* 6; *Interpretatio in Ezechielem* 13:16; *Interpretatio in xii prophetas minores* Zach 3:1–2; *Interpretatio 2 Cor.* 2:11; *Interpretatio 2 Thess.* 2:3; *Interpretatio 2 Tim.* 3:13; *Haer.* 1.Prologue; 2.11; 4.6; 5.23. Within later Christian discourse, ἀλάστωρ is also used synonymously with "demons" or "Satan."

[123] Livy, *Ab urbe cond.* 3.57.2 ("despising gods and humankind" [*deorum hominumque contemptor*]); 21.63.6 ("waging war with the immortal gods" [*sed iam cum dis immortalibus ... bellum gerere*]), 7 ("despising" them [*spretorum*]); Suetonius, *Nero* 56 ("holding all religious rites in contempt" [*religionum usque quaque contemptor*]); Vergil, *Aen.* 7.648 ("contemptuous of the gods" [*contemptor divom*]); Ovid, *Metam.* 3.512 ("contemptuous of the gods" [*contemptor superum*]); 8.742–3 ("he scorned the power of the gods" [*qui numina divum sperneret*]); 13.761 ("contemptuous of Olympus and the gods" [*dis contemptor Olympi*]). Though written in Greek, see also the following evidence from the Roman context: Dionysius of Halicarnassus, *Ant. rom.* 2.20 ("despising the gods" [καταφρονεῖ τῶν θεῶν]); Eunapius, *Vit. phil.* 472 ("despising the divine things" [τὸ καταφρονεῖν τοῦ θείου]); *BIWK* 107 (Phrygia, 2–3rd CE), lines 11–13 ("no one should despise the gods" [μηδίνα καταφρονεῖ τῶν θεῶν]); *NewDocLyd* 85 (Lydia, 205–6 CE), lines 16–17 ("nobody at any time should disparage the gods" [μή τίς ποτε παρευτελίσι τοὺς θεούς]); and *SEG* 35.1157 (Katakekaumene, 191–2 CE). See also the following inscriptions from the sanctuary of Apollo Lairbenos: *BIWK* 109 (Phrygia, 2–3rd CE); 111 (Phrygia, 3rd CE); 112 (Phrygia, 3rd CE); 117 (Phrygia, undated); 120 (Phrygia, undated); and 121 (Phrygia, undated).

[124] Tenney Frank, "On the Stele of the Forum," *CP* 14.1 (1919): 87–88.

mulus (or his foster-father Faustulus) and as a sanctuary dedicated to the god Vulcan.[125] Festus Pompeius named this location as a *"locum funestum significat."*[126] The inscription is fragmentary, but reads as follows:[127]

> *quoi hoi ... | ... sakros es|ed sor ...*
> *... ia.ias | recei | ic ... | ... evam | quos | re ...*
> *... m | kalato|rem | hai ... | iod | iouxmen|ta | kapia | dotau ...*
> *m | ite | rit ... | ... m | quoi ha|velod | nequ ... | od | iouvestod*
> *loiuquiod ...*
>
> He who ... [does something] ... shall be forfeited to Soranus [or He who dirties this place ... shall be cursed.] Whomever the king finds passing along the road, let him order the herald to seize the reins of their draught animals and force them to detour. Whoever does not take the proper detour but traverses this spot, let him be sold at auction according to the law.

Some of the reconstructed translation is debated given the incomplete nature of the inscription, but the phrase *sakros esed* is most certainly parallel to the standard Latin phrase, *sacer erit*, which usually means "he or she shall be (or must be) cursed."[128] The implication is that the offender be given over to a particular god, to receive the due penalty for her or his offense, which the rest of the sentence likely filled out in greater detail.[129] To be *sacer* meant that the penalty would be of a religious or divine character, regardless of whether the original offense was directly against the gods. The vulnerability of such a state can be seen in Dionysius of Halicarnassus, for example, who observes the custom of Romans

---

125 Jörg Rüpke, *Religion in Republican Rome: Rationalization and Ritual Change* (Philadelphia: University of Pennsylvania Press, 2012), 9.
126 In Festus, *De verborum significatu* 184 L: *Niger lapis in comitio locum funestum significat, ut ali, Romuli morti destinarum, sed non usu ob in [...] Faustulum nutr[...]*. See also Dionysius of Halicarnassus, *Ant. rom.* 1.87.2; 3.1.2; Livy, *Ab urbe cond.* 24.20; Tacitus, *Ann.* 13.58; Scholia on Horace, *Epod.* 16.13–14.
127 *ILS* 4913 (Rome, ca. 6th BCE). Translation adapted from Gregory S. Aldrete, *Daily Life in the Roman City: Rome, Pompeii and Ostia* (Westport, CT: Greenwood Press, 2004), 52–53 and supplemented by other secondary literature cited below.
128 Louise Adams Holland, "Qui Terminum Exarasset," *AJA* 37.4 (1933): 549–553; Leon ter Beek, "Divine Law and the Penalty of *Sacer Esto* in Early Rome," in *Law and Religion in the Roman Republic*, ed. Olga Tellegen-Couperus (Leiden: Brill, 2012), 11–29.
129 The letters following *sakros esed, sor ...,* have prompted scholars to suggest either a name, *Sor[anoi]* (= "to Soranus," a god of the underworld) or a qualifier for the transgression, *sor[des]* (= "dirt," a prohibition of some physical state). See also Festus, *De verborum significatu* 260 L; 505 L. See ter Beek, "Divine Law," 20.

wherein a person may be lawfully put to death when she or he is declared ὅσιος[130] or ἱερός,[131] both Greek analogues to the Latin term *sacer*.[132]

There are also cases in which transgressions committed in sacred spaces incurred a fine, similar to Greek sacred laws. An inscription from Luceria (Apulia) concerning a sacred grave reads:[133]

> *In hoce loucarid stircus ne quis fundatid neve cadaver proiecitad neve parentatid. Sei quis arvorsum hac faxit, ceivium quis volet pro ioudicatod numum L manum iniectio estod. Seive magisteratus volet moltare, licetod.*
>
> In this grove let no one pour out manure or cast away a corpse or perform sacrifices for dead ancestors. If anyone acts contrary to this, let there be a laying of hands upon him for judgment rendered, by whoever wishes, in the amount of fifty sesterces. Or if a magistrate wishes to fine him, let this be allowed.

In some cases, the offense required an "atoning sacrifice" (*piaculum*) to the gods in addition to the fine:[134]

> *Honce loucom ne quis violatod neque exvehito neque exferto quod louci siet neque cedito nesei quo die res deina anua fiet; eod die quod rei dinai causa fiat sine dolo cedre licetod. Sei quis violasit, Iove bovid piaclum datod; seiquis scies violasit dolo malo, Iovei bovid piaclum datod et asses ccc moltai suntod. Eius piacli moltaique dicatorei exactio estod.*
>
> Let no one damage this grove. No one shall cart or carry away anything belonging to the grove, or cut wood in it, except on the day when holy worship takes place every year. On that day it shall be permitted without prejudice to cut wood for the purpose of sacred worship. If anyone does damage, he shall make an atoning sacrifice (*piaclum*) to Jupiter with an ox; if anyone does damage knowingly (*scies*) and with malicious intent (*dolo*

---

130 Dionysius of Halicarnassus, *Ant. rom.* 2.10.3 (Cary, LCL slightly modified), "And whoever was convicted of doing any of these things was guilty of treason by virtue of the law (ἔνοχος ἦν τῷ νόμῳ τῆς προδοσίας) sanctioned by Romulus, and might lawfully be put to death by any one who so wished as a victim devoted to Jupiter of the infernal regions (τὸν δὲ ἁλόντα τῷ βουλομένῳ κτείνειν ὅσιον ἦν ὡς θῦμα τοῦ καταχθονίου Διός). Ter Beek, "Divine Law," 26 suggests that the Greek phrase τοῦ καταχθονίου Διός corresponds to the Latin *sacer Ditis*.
131 *Ant. rom.* 2.74.3 (Cary, LCL slightly modified), "If any person destroyed or changed the boundary stones, the offender should be considered forfeit to the god (ἱερὸν ἐνομοθέτησεν εἶναι τοῦ θεοῦ), so that anyone who wished may kill him as a sacrilegious person (κτείνειν αὐτὸν ὡς ἱερόσυλον) with impunity and clean from pollution (τὸ καθαρῷ μιάσματος).
132 Festus, *De verborum significatu* 5 L, a citation from the laws of Numa Pompilius: "If a person acts otherwise, he himself shall be forfeit (*sacer esto*) to Jupiter." See also 260 L; 422 L; 423 L. Cited in ter Beek, "Divine Law," 27–28.
133 *ILS* 4912 (Luceria [N. Apulia], late-3rd BCE).
134 *CIL* I² 366 (Spoletium [Umbria], ca. 241 BCE). On *piaculum*, see Rüpke, *Religion in Republican Rome*, 108.

malo), he shall make an atoning sacrifice to Jupiter with an ox, and moreover let there be a fine of 300 aspieces. The duty of exacting the sacrifice and fine shall rest with the *dicator*.

The literary evidence is no less explicit when it came to how one must approach the gods in daily life and during special rituals. Even a highly educated elite figure such as Marcus Tullius Cicero recognized the importance of proper behavior toward the gods.[135] In *De Legibus*, Cicero argues before his auditors, Quintus and Atticus, that "the gods are lords and managers of all things" (*dominos esse omnium rerum ac moderatores deos*) and that they always maintain an account of each person's thoughts and actions.[136] He then narrates an impressive list of laws concerning religion (Quintus asks for the *leges de religione*) which is then followed by a sustained argument concerning these laws.

A few points are worth investigating further. Cicero's list of laws begins thus: "They must approach the gods in purity (*caste*), they must display piety (*pietatem*)."[137] The concern for the inner state of the human being—similar to that found in the Greek tradition—is demonstrated here, made certain when Cicero further explains that this purity is about the "purity of mind, of course (*animo videlicet*), in which everything else resides."[138] According to Cicero, there is a stratification of pollution: the physical impurity, he notes, can be removed by water or the passing of time, but "a stain on the mind (*animi labes*) does not fade with time, nor can it be washed out by any river."[139] Vigilance in maintain-

---

135 The Roman claim that part of their success lay with their unsurpassed piety toward the gods stretches back to the Mid-Republic: *Syll.*³ 601 (letter to the Teans, 193 BCE), esp. lines 13–16; *Syll.*³ 611 (letter to Delphi, 189 BCE), esp. lines 23–25; Cicero, *Nat. d.* 2.3; 3.2; *Har. resp.* 19; Sallust, *Bell. Cat.* 12; Livy, *Ab urbe cond.* 44.1; 45.39; Posidonius *ap.* Athenaeus, *Deipn.* 6.274; Dionysius of Halicarnassus, *Ant. rom.* 2.18.1–3; Pliny the Elder, *Nat.* 28.5; Polybius 3.112.6. On taking Roman "religion" seriously, see Denis Feeney, *Literature and Religion at Rome: Cultures, Contexts, and Beliefs* (Cambridge: Cambridge University Press, 1998).
136 Cicero, *Leg.* 2.15 (Ziegler trans. adapted in James E. G. Zetzel ed., *Cicero: On the Commonwealth and On the Laws* [Cambridge: Cambridge University Press, 1999]; all translations of Cicero's *De legibus* come from this volume unless otherwise noted.)
137 Cicero, *Leg.* 2.19 (Ziegler trans., slightly modified). Also Aulus Gellius, *Noct att.* 4.9.9 (Rolfe, LCL slightly modified): "Temples indeed and shrines (*templa quidem ac delubra*) ... are to be approached, not unceremoniously and thoughtlessly, but with purity and in due form (*non volgo ac temere, sed cum castitate caerimoniaque adeundum*), must be both revered and feared, rather than profaned."
138 Cicero, *Leg.* 2.24. Cicero qualifies this statement, however, by acknowledging that "it doesn't exclude physical purity, but it should be understood how much the mind is superior to the body: purity of body should be respected in approaching the gods, but *it is all the more important* to preserve that of the mind" (emphasis added).
139 Cicero, *Leg.* 2.24. He repeats a similar sentiment in *Nat. d.* 2.71.

ing one's inner purity also allows one to better receive and interpret divine signs.[140]

Cicero then explains the notion of equal access to the gods when he rehearses the law that "they must leave behind luxuries."[141] He interprets this statement to mean that "expense should be rejected" and that its aim is for "poverty and wealth to be treated equally among men."[142] Cicero asks pointedly, "then why should we bar poverty from approaching the gods by adding expense to rituals?" He asserts that "nothing will be less appealing to the god himself" than preventing anyone from enjoying "equal access" to the divine.[143] Though it is possible that Cicero is merely using rhetorical flourish to paint an idealized picture, it is still noteworthy that one belonging to the Roman equestrian order can entertain the idea of equal access to the gods irrespective of her or his economic status.[144] It should be noted, however, that not all Romans conceived of the gods similarly. In *De natura deorum*, Cicero also recounts the argument between Cotta the Academic and Velleius the Epicurean that shows that Romans did not all subscribe to the same perspective of gods, sanctuaries, and transgressions.[145]

The next provision in Cicero's writing asserts that "god himself will enforce the law" if anyone acts contrary to the law.[146] Pliny the Elder remarks that "it agrees with life's experience to believe that the gods exercise an interest in human affairs, and that punishment for wickedness (*poenasque maleficiis*),

---

140 Plautus, *Curc.* 260–69; *Poen.* 449–56.
141 Cicero, *Leg.* 2.19.
142 Cicero, *Leg.* 2.25.
143 Cicero did not mean, however, that all rituals and all sanctuaries were accessible to all people at all times. Just as many Greek temples and cults barred access to certain individuals or to an entire class of people, Romans did likewise. For example, the sanctuary of Ceres did not permit access to men and even to women if they were in a period of mourning. See Cicero, *Verr.* 2.4.99–101 (Cicero accuses Verres of plundering the temple and calls his act a kind of covetousness that the "power of the gods" [*deorum vis*] could not even restrain.); Livy, *Ab urbe cond.* 22.56; 34.6.15; Juvenal, *Sat.* 6.50–51. See also the evidence concerning Bona Dea, commonly called "the Women's Goddess" (Γυναικεία Θεός, Θεὸς Γυναικεία, or *Feminarum Dea*), whose worship was limited to females. For the archaeological and literary sources, see H. H. J. Brouwer, *Bona Dea: The Sources and a Description of the Cult* (Leiden: Brill, 1989). See below for a detailed account of the violation of the rites of Bona Dea and its significance for understanding Roman perspectives on the sacred.
144 See Cicero's account of Romulus's successor, Numa Pompilius, and the establishment of a simple and democratic form of Roman religious institution, in Cicero, *Rep.* 2.25–27.
145 Cicero, *Nat. d.* 1.81. See also Artemidorus, *Onir.* 2.34.
146 Cicero, *Leg.* 2.19.

though sometimes slow in coming ... is never frustrated."[147] Cicero also explains that establishing "god himself" (*deus ipse*) as judge and enforcer of the law acts to "reinforce religion by the fear of imminent punishment" (*praesentis poenae metu religio confirmari videtur*).[148] The mention of such punishment here is noteworthy, since it is repeated multiple times throughout the list. A later command exhorts that the augurs must "foresee the anger of the gods (*divorumque iras*) and take heed of it," a reference to some form of divine punishment.[149] All must refrain from what the augur has declared "unjust, unholy, criminal, or ill-omened" (*iniusta nefasta, vitiosa dira defixerit*) because the penalty of disobedience is death (*capital*).[150] There are also cases when some "offense against religion is committed that cannot be expiated" (*sacrum commissum, quod neque expiari poterit*), a highly vulnerable situation for any Roman worshiper.[151] The removal of objects belonging to sacred spaces is considered as murder,[152] and the violation of a solemn pledge incurs some penalty (*iuris esto*).[153] Also, perjury demands the "divine penalty [of] destruction" (*periurii poena divina exitium*).[154]

One significant development in the Roman conception of the divine is the concern for maintaining the *pax deorum*, a stability that first originated with the individual's right standing before the gods that extended to include the

---

147 Pliny the Elder, *Nat.* 2.26 (Rackham, LCL slightly modified). Also Seneca, *Ep.* 95.50: "The first way to worship the gods is to believe in the gods; the next to acknowledge their majesty, to acknowledge their goodness without which there is no majesty ... controlling all things by their power ... they do chasten and restrain certain persons, and impose penalties, and sometimes punish by bestowing that which seems good outwardly."
148 Cicero, *Leg.* 2.25.
149 Cicero subsequently (*Leg.* 2.22) refers to a law that requires that "no impious person dare to appease the anger of the gods (*iram deoram*) with gifts" and appeals to Plato, *Leg.* 4.716b–717a in his interpretation of this law (*Leg.* 2.41). He does not explain the nature of this punishment from the gods, but he briefly mentions in his subsequent exegesis of the laws (*Leg.* 2.44) that there is a "twofold punishment from the gods" (*duplicem poenam esse divinam*). The first is "the ravaging of their minds when alive" (*vexandis vivorum animis*) and the second is "a reputation that causes their destruction to be greeted by the approval and pleasure of the living" (*ea fama mortuorum, ut eorum exitium et iudicio vivorum et gaudio conprobetur*).
150 Cicero, *Leg.* 2.21 (Ziegler trans., slightly modified).
151 See the discussion of relevant terminology in Jack J. Lennon, *Pollution and Religion in Ancient Rome* (Cambridge: Cambridge University Press, 2014), 35–44.
152 Cicero, *Leg.* 2.22: *Sacrum sacrove commendatum qui clepsit rapsitve parricida esto*. See also the account of King Masinissa and the stolen item from the temple of Juno in Cicero, *Verr.* 2.4.103.
153 Cicero (*Leg.* 2.22) mentions the *vota*, referring to something promised to the gods. The penalty in view, therefore, is likely of divine origin.
154 Cicero, *Leg.* 2.22.

well-being of the Roman state.¹⁵⁵ In other words, an *individual*'s transgressions could potentially place the entire *community* (or state) at risk from divine wrath. For example, during the consulship of Marcus Claudius Marcellus, the Syracusans were able to make a successful complaint in the senate against Marcellus because of the latter's disregard for sanctuaries (ca. 212 BCE):

> Apart from the city-walls and the emptied houses and the sanctuaries of the gods (*deum delubra*), broken open and despoiled (*spoliata*) by removal of the statues of the gods themselves and their adornments, nothing had been left at Syracuse.¹⁵⁶

Marcellus tries to defend himself by naming Syracuse as enemies that deserved what happened (see Livy, *Ab. urbe cond.* 26.31), and though Marcellus did not face any real legal consequences, this incident marked an important turning point in how Romans thereafter treated sacred objects and personnel.¹⁵⁷

How did the Romans know when or if the *pax deorum* was disrupted? The occurrence of prodigies signaled (when frequent in number) to the Romans that a transgression might have or will take place and they thereafter performed the necessary expiatory rites in order to curtail divine wrath. Only a few years after the Marcellus incident there were reports of a large number of prodigies that did not go unnoticed.¹⁵⁸ This all occurred around the time of Roman siege of Locri that was approved under a similar pretext as that of Syracuse and Tar-

---

155 See, for example, Livy's reference to sacrifices being made to the gods in order to secure the *pax deorum* in *Ab urbe cond.* 7.2.2 (ca. 364 BCE). *Ira deorum* is often noted as the complementary response to the disruption of *pax deorum*. Also Livy, *Ab urbe cond.* 40.37. See also Cicero, *Leg.* 2.26 (Keyes, LCL slightly modified): "The Greeks and Romans have done a better thing: for our wish, in order to promote piety towards the gods, has been for the gods to inhabit the same cities as us (*qui ut augerent pietatem in deos, easdem illos urbis quas nos incolere voluerunt*). For this idea encourages a religious attitude that is useful to the states (*civitatibus*).
156 Livy, *Ab urbe cond.* 26.30 (Moore, LCL).
157 For example, Livy notes specifically that Fabius Maximus "showed more magnanimity in refraining from plunder of that kind than did Marcellus" in the former's siege of Tarentum (*Ab urbe cond.* 27.16; Moore, LCL). Concerning various statue images, Fabius ordered that "their angry be left to the Tarentines" (*deos iratos Tarentinis relinqui iussit*) likely in reference to their cooperation with Carthage. Also Plutarch, *Fab.* 22.5 (Perrin, LCL): "While everything else was carried off as plunder, it is said that the accountant asked Fabius what his orders were concerning the gods, for so he called their images and statues (περὶ τῶν θεῶν τί κελεύει, τὰς γραφὰς οὕτω προσαγορεύσαντα καὶ τοὺς ἀνδριάντας); and that Fabius answered: 'Let us leave their angered gods (τοὺς θεοὺς ... κεχολωμένους) for the Tarentines.'"
158 Unusual number of showers of stones (Livy, *Ab urbe cond.* 29.10); two suns, daylight during nighttime, meteor shooting from east to west, lightning striking walls and gates in Tarracina and Anagnia, and a loud sound and "dreadful rumble" (*horrendo fragore*) heard in the temple of Juno Sospita in Lanuvium (Livy, *Ab urbe cond.* 29.14). Also Appian, *Hann.* 56.

entum. Locri had broken alliance with Rome and defected to the Carthaginian side, so one could reasonably expect that Roman treatment of this enemy territory would follow the *ius belli*.

According to Livy, however, the Romans not only raped and pillaged the city and its inhabitants, but worse, they did not hold back from sacrilege in their violation of temples (*spoliatione abstinuit ... alia modo templa violata*), including the treasury of the temple of Persephone.[159] A delegate from Locri was sent to ask the Roman senate to make restitution in order to "free your state from impiety" (*exsolvere rem publicam vestram religione*). He also described an earlier event—among a thousand others[160]—when Pyrrhus also robbed the sanctuary of Persephone to a disastrous end.[161] The delegate warned that the goddess would not rest from exacting penalties upon those who desecrated her temple until the treasury was restored. In response, the Romans put to death Plemius, the Roman in charge at Locri, repaid double amount stolen to the temple of Persephone, and performed proper expiatory rites (*sacrum piaculare*).[162] It is noteworthy that unlike in Syracuse and Tarentum, the Romans made eventual restitution for what happened at Locri. They acknowledged that impious acts by the few endangered the entire community and acknowledged that the thievery could be seen as "wicked deeds against gods and men" (*nefarie in deos hominesque*).[163]

---

159 Livy, *Ab urbe cond.* 29.8.
160 The delegate argues that "this and a thousand other occurrences which were repeated to them [i.e. Romans], not merely to increase religious feeling but as facts repeatedly confirmed for us and our ancestors by the evident power of the goddess (*deae numinae*), they nevertheless dared to lay sacrilegious hands upon those treasure-chambers that were not to be touched, and by that unspeakable plunder to bring pollution (*contaminare*) upon themselves and their homes and upon your soldiers" (Livy, *Ab urbe cond.* 29.18; LCL, Moore slightly modified).
161 Livy, *Ab urbe cond.* 29.18 (Moore, LCL). The delegate continues on to note that from this great disaster, the impious ones learned that gods do exist (*Qua tanta clade edoctus tandem deos esse*).
162 Livy, *Ab urbe cond.* 29.19.
163 Livy, *Ab urbe cond.* 29.21 (Moore, LCL): "The praetor and legati went to Locri and, as they had been instructed, made religion their first concern (*religionis curam habuere*). For they sought out and restored to the treasure-chambers all the sacred money ... and they performed the rite of expiation (*piaculare sacrum*)." Less than five years later, money was reported to have again disappeared from the treasury of Persephone along with reports of various prodigies throughout the country. The senators quickly responded with an investigation and ordered a rite of expiation for the impiety (Livy, *Ab urbe cond.* 31.12). See also the senatorial response to Flaccus removing marble tiles from the roof of the temple of Hera Lacinia in Livy, *Ab urbe cond.* 42.3. For expanded discussion, see Jack Wells, "Impiety in the Middle Republic: The Roman Response to Temple Plundering in Southern Italy," *CJ* 105.3 (2010): 229–243.

Another prescription concerned a transgression that often occurred beyond circumscribed sacred boundaries, namely *incestum* (sometimes *stuprum*). As Philippe Moreau has shown in his recent study, however, these acts were highly polluting regardless of where they took place. They were not only contrary to the natural order that Romans held in high regard, but more importantly, they endangered the *pax deorum*.[164] For instance, Catullus closes one poem with the following lines:

> The unnatural mother (*ignaro mater* = stepmother) impiously coupling with her unconscious son
> Did not fear to pollute her family gods (*non veritast divos scelerare Penates*).
> Then all right and wrong, confounded in impious madness (*omnia fanda nefanda malo permixta furore*),
> Turned from us the righteous will of the gods (*iustificam ... mentem ... deorum*).
> Wherefore they deign not to visit such companies,
> Nor endure the touch of clear daylight.[165]

Cicero also remarks that incest must receive the "ultimate penalty" (*incestum ... supremo supplicio*).[166] This manner of interpreting incest, i.e. as pollution and violation of the sacred—acts that warrant divine punishment—also accords well with the rationale behind Paul's adamant command to eject the incestuous man from the community (1 Cor 5 and relevant analysis in chapter 2).

One famous historical account of the polluting of sacred space in the Roman world concerned the Emperor Nero. Around 60 CE, Nero's love of self-gratification put him in "disgrace and danger" (*infamiam et periculum*) when he swam in the waters of *Aqua Marcia* of Rome, and thereby polluted (*polluere*) the "sacred waters" and the "sanctity of the place" (*potus sacros et caerimoniam loci*).[167] Tacitus regards Nero's transgression as both precipitating a public downfall ("dis-

---

[164] Philippe Moreau, *Incestus et Prohibitae Nuptiae: Conception romaine de l'inceste et histoire des prohibitions matrimoniales pour cause de parenté dans la Rome antique* (Paris: Les Belles Lettres, 2002); Lennon, *Pollution*, 72–4. Accusations of incest were often leveled against "enemies" of the Roman state, such as foreigners or former emperors who were viewed as unfit rulers. See, e.g., Tacitus, *Ann.* 14.2; Suetonius, *Cal.* 24; *Nero* 28; *Dom.* 22. Modern readers should be aware that despite the etymological similarity, the Latin term, *incestum*, was somewhat broader than what is considered "incest" today since the former included unchaste acts by the Vestal and sacrilegious acts of Clodius during the Bona Dea.
[165] Catullus, 64.403–8 (Cornish, LCL).
[166] Cicero, *Leg.* 2.22.
[167] Tacitus, *Ann.* 14.22. Concerning the purity of *Aqua Marcia*, see Pliny the Elder, *Nat.* 31.24; Statius Papinius, *Silv.* 1.5.23–26; Strabo, *Geogr.* 5.3.13. See also *NewDocLyd* 83 (Kollyda, Roman imperial period) that describes a punishment for entering unsuitably into a sacred space (line 6: εἰσῆθεν ἄθετος).

grace") but more than that, a physical condition ("danger"). The operation of divine wrath is confirmed (*iram deum ... adfirmavit*) before the eyes of the public by what happened next to Nero's body: he falls gravely ill (*anceps valetudo*).[168] His status as the most powerful man in the Roman Empire did not exempt Nero from observing certain rules regarding the sacred.[169] Tacitus also recounts the burning of Rome's Capitoleum that occurred during the civil war leading up to the Flavian dynasty. He called its burning "the saddest and most shameful crime (*luctuosissimum foedissimumque*) that the Roman state had suffered since its foundation."[170] In the *Civil Wars*, Appian recounts the expulsion of Petronius and Quintus from shrines due to their involvement in the murder of others, and Pausanias likewise describes the ineffectiveness of seeking asylum at sanctuaries for certain criminals.[171]

According to Livy, harming a tribune of the plebs who was deemed sacrosanct would receive its due penalty:

> They rendered those magistrates inviolate, not only by religion, but also by law (*et cum religione inviolatos eos tum lege etiam fecerunt*), solemnly enacting that he who should hurt the tribunes of the plebs, his head would be devoted to Jupiter (*eius caput Iovi sacrum esset*) by the aediles and the decemviral judges, and that his possessions should be sold at the temple of Ceres, Liber, and Libera.[172]

In typical fashion, Livy does not elaborate upon what 'devotion' to the gods exactly entailed, but it is clear that the loss of possessions and public disgrace would have been devastating to any individual, and the inscriptional evidence earlier filled-out in more detail the status of being *sacer*. The persistence of the religious dimension of *sacer* can be seen, for example, in Macrobius who remarks: "Anything marked out for the gods is said to be 'consecrated' (*sacer*)."[173]

---

[168] Tacitus, *Ann.* 14.22. Posthumously, Nero quickly became the prototypical tyrant, the first Roman emperor to be officially named as a public enemy (*hostis*) by the Senate. Many of his images (portraiture, monuments, inscriptions, and coinage) were systematically destroyed under emperors Galba and Vespasian. See Suetonius, *Galb.* 15.1; *Nero* 49.2; Tacitus, *Hist.* 1.20, 78; Plutarch, *Galb.* 16.1–2; *Otho* 3.1. A Roman play from the first century CE names Nero has a hater of gods and men (*Octavia* 89 (*spernit superos hominesque simul*); 240–41 (*hostis deum hominumque*); also Suetonius, *Nero* 28 (on his violation of a Vestal Virgin).
[169] See also the concern for purity before the gods in Vergil, *Aen.* 2.717–20; Livy, *Ab urbe cond.* 1.45.
[170] Tacitus, *Hist.* 3.72.
[171] Appian, *Bell. civ.* 5.1.4, 7; Pausanias, *Descr.* 4.25.5–6.
[172] Livy, *Ab urbe cond.* 3.55 (Foster, LCL slightly modified).
[173] Macrobius, *Sat.* 3.7.3 (Kaster, LCL: *Nam quicquid destinatum est dis sacrum vocatur.* Earlier in 3.3.2, Macrobius asserts, "The 'sacred' (*sacrum*), as Trebatius says in his first book *On Reli-*

From the foregoing survey of the material, literary, and historical evidence, it is not difficult to see that Romans espoused a robust understanding of sacred boundaries. Like the Greeks, Romans fully accepted the reality that gods could intervene in the lives of human beings, and particularly so in sacred spaces and in sacred rituals.

3.3.2 Participations in Rituals

Like the Greeks, Romans believed in the place of meals and sacrifices *with* the gods as an important part of their religious experience. In one of Aelius Aristides's orations, Εἰς τὸν Σάραπιν (*Or.* 45: "Regarding Sarapis"), he writes the following about the place of the gods in these rituals:

> And humans have true fellowship in sacrifices with this god alone above all others (θυσιῶν μόνῳ τούτῳ θεῷ διαφερόντως κοινωνοῦσιν ἄνθρωποι τὴν ἀκριβῆ κοινωνίαν), summoning him to the feast (καλοῦντές ... ἐφ' ἑστίαν) and making him both their chief guest and host, so that while different gods contribute to different banquets, he is the universal contributor to all banquets and is the *symposiarch* for those who assemble together for his sake (τοῖς ... κατὰ ταυτὸν συλλεγομένοις) ... so he is both a participant in the libations and the receiver of libations (ὁμόσπονδός τε καὶ ὁ τὰς σπονδὰς δεχόμενος).[174]

The dual position of the god as both the recipient of libations and the actual host is noteworthy: in the minds of these worshipers, the god joins them in the feast when they gather together and becomes the energizing force behind this event.[175] Visual representations of the gods joining in such feasts were provided by images, or more provocatively, the presence of empty dining couches.[176] A statuette

---

gious Scruples is 'whatever is considered to belong to the gods' (*quicquid est quod deorum habetur*)."

174 Aelius Aristides, *Or.* 45.26–27 (Behr trans. slightly modified). See also P. Oxy. 1484 (ca. 2nd-early 3rd CE): Ἔρωτα σε Ἀπολλώνιος δειπνῆσαι εἰς κλείνην τοῦ κυρίου Σαράπιδος ὑπὲρ μελλοκουρίων τῶν [ἀδελφῶν ?] ἐν τῷ Θοηρίῳ = "Apollonius asks you to dine at the table of the lord Sarapis for the coming-of-age celebration of his brothers at the temple of Thoeris." See also P. Oxy. 110; 523; 1485; and Pindar, *Paean.* Frg. 52P.
175 Ovid, *Fast.* 4.353–60; 6.249–68; Statius Papinius, *Silv.* 3.1.138.
176 Often referred to as the rite of the *lectisternium* (pl. *lectisternia*): Livy, *Ab urbe cond.* 5.13.4–8; 40.59; Valerius Maximus, *Fact. dict. mem.* 2.1.2; Dionysius of Halicarnassus, *Ant. rom.* 12.9; *Hist. Aug.* on Marcus Aurelius 13; *CIL* VI 32323 (Rome, 17 BCE). Georg Wissowa, *Religion und Kultus der Römer*, 2nd ed. (München, C.H. Beck, 1912), 422–423.

of Fortunae at Praeneste (ca. first century BCE) points to the importance of goddesses on litters that rest on a couch.[177]

A silver Roman denarius, dated to the later decades of the same century demonstrate similar iconography, showing the torsos of twin Fortunae resting on a couch:[178]

During these meals, libations were often accompanied by prayers along the lines of *dii propitii* ("may the gods be gracious") as a direct appeal to the gods to continue in their patronage of and divine favors upon the participants,[179] representing what John Scheid calls "reciprocal gift-giving between men and gods."[180]

Unlike the Greeks, however, who extended invitation to the meals—and "equal-honors" as noted earlier—to all citizens, the Romans maintained a strict hierarchical system with respect to the meals. Jörg Rüpke argues: "Das kostenlose Speisen von Opfern, die vom Gemeinwesen ausgerichtet und finanziert werden, kann damit nicht – ein dritter Unterschied zu Griechenland – Sache der Vollbürger sein, sondern ist ein (gehütetes) Privileg. Dieses *ius publice epulandi* ist auf (Ex-) Magistrate und öffentliche Priester beschränkt."[181] This right was either extended only to those holding certain positions, such as magistrates and

---

177 See Macrobius, *Sat.* 1.23.13. See image in Otto J. Brendel, "Two Fortunae, Antium and Praeneste," *AJA* 64.1 (1960): 41–47 (Plate 7).
178 Image from Brendel, "Two Fortunae" (Plate 8, Figs. 2–3). Permission received from American Numismatic Society.
179 E.g., Petronius, *Sat.* 60; Vergil, *Aen.* 1.723–56; Cato, *Agr.* 132, 134; Plutarch, *Quaest. conv.* 614D–615C.
180 John Scheid, "Sacrifices for Gods and Ancestors," in *A Companion to Roman Religion*, ed. J. Rüpke (Oxford: Blackwell, 2007), 267.
181 Jörg Rüpke, *Die Religion der Römer: Eine Einführung* (München: Verlag C. H. Beck, 2001), 146.

priests,¹⁸² or the portions were unevenly divided based on one's position in the *collegia*.¹⁸³

3.3.3 *Excursus:* Aelius Aristides and Divine Power

Perhaps no single person better recounts divine powers that can intervene in the lives of suppliants than Aelius Aristides (117–180 CE), a famous orator hailing from Asia Minor.¹⁸⁴ His father Eudaemon was possibly a friend of Emperor Hadrian and he was fabulously wealthy,¹⁸⁵ to the degree that Aristides could later boast that he never accepted fees for his declamations.¹⁸⁶ Unfortunately, he was not dealt a similar hand in physical health: Aristides would struggle with various ailments throughout most of his adult life. This is fortuitous for modern readers, however, since he left behind many recorded interactions with the divine that serve as an important firsthand account of ancient religious experience.

During one of his earliest bouts in April 142 CE, Aristides sought healing from the god Sarapis in Smyrna, and his speech, *To Sarapis*, is an account of this event (*Oration* 45). In 144 CE, Aristides fell ill again during his journey home from Rome, and back in Smyrna, he initially turned to the doctors for medical attention to no avail.¹⁸⁷ Around December of the same year, he received his

---

182 E.g. Suetonius, *Aug.* 35.2–3 (*epulandique publice ius*).
183 *CIL* XIV 2112, II.18–20 (Lanuvium, 136 CE).
184 Aristides is a good example of the difficulty in defining what exactly is "Greek" versus "Roman" in our ancient sources. I have used such nomenclature as a heuristic device, but Aristides defies facile identification with one or the other. Though his time period is fairly late—almost near the third century CE—he is highly indebted to the Second Sophistic movement that was interested in being "Greek" above all else. Furthermore, Aristides's persistent rejection of public office (despite his intellectual, economic, and political strengths) would have been unthinkable to a "Roman" figure such as Cicero. Also, the *Sacred Tales* reveal Aelius Aristides to be a valetudinarian, setting him apart from any other figure during this time period. Finally, much, if not all, of the evidence adduced below are his firsthand accounts of "good" things that happened to him due to the gods rather than punishments or transgressions. These facts notwithstanding, his writings are still an important source of ancient religious experience.
185 C. A. Behr, *Aelius Aristides and the Sacred Tales* (Amsterdam: Adolf M. Hakkert, 1968), 4. See Philostratus, *Vit. soph.* 2.9.
186 Aelius Aristides, *Or.* 28.127; 33.19.
187 Aristides notes the doctors' helplessness in *Hier. log.* 2.5, 69. See also Aelian, *Nat. an.* 9.33 for the efficacy of the "irresistible power of a god" (ἀμάχῳ ... θείᾳ δυνάμει) in comparison to the impotence of even "the cleverest of doctors" (οἱ τῶν ἰατρῶν δεινοί). Brook Holmes observes that the limit of contemporary medicine is a Leitmotif in *Hieroi Logoi* ("Aelius Aristides' Illegible

first revelation from Asclepius that was "the momentous change ... which was for ever after to govern Aristides' life."[188] The god Asclepius then called Aristides to his famous Temple at Pergamum where the orator stayed for two years as an incubant at the Temple.[189] From this point forward, Aristides would remain devoted to the god Asclepius and his writings are fascinating testimonies to the powers of the divine.

It is striking to find that scholars overwhelmingly display a "profound dislike" of Aelius Aristides,[190] and such a negative bias often predetermined how his discourse about gods, divine power, and healing was read and interpreted. As the editor and translator of the most recent editions of Aristides's corpus, Charles Behr played no small part in this trajectory of Aristides scholarship.[191] Behr accused Aristides of being "neurotic" while others also psychoanalyzed him to various—and often ignoble—ends.[192] Some even accused Aristides of being a hypochondriac, though even the unrivaled physician, Galen, is noted to have observed that Aristides actually suffered from an illness.[193] Recent schol-

---

Body," in *Aelius Aristides between Greece, Rom, and the Gods*, ed. W.V. Harris and Brooke Holmes [Leiden: Brill, 2008], 81–113 [84]). Charles Behr lists the *Sacred Tales* as Orations 47–52 in his *Complete Works* (vol. 2), but for the sake of clarity and style (following SBLHS2), the work is referred in the footnotes as *Hieroi Logoi* (*Hier. log.*) 1–6, with paragraph markers corresponding to those of Behr.

188 Behr, *Aelius Aristides*, 25. See Aelius Aristides, *Hier. log.* 2.7.

189 Aelius Aristides, *Hier. log.* 2.7, 70; 4.14.

190 Alexia Petsalis-Diomidis, *Truly Beyond Wonders: Aelius Aristides and the Cult of Asklepios* (Oxford: Oxford University Press, 2010), 124. She is one of the few recent exceptions to this unfortunate rule (and bias).

191 Behr, *Aelius Aristides* and *The Complete Works*, 2 vols. (Leiden: Brill, 1981–86).

192 Behr, *Complete Works*, 1:1–4. See also Campbell Bonner, "Some Phases of Religious Feeling in Later Paganism," *HTR* 30.3 (1937): 119–40 who calls Aristides "an outstanding example of the neurasthenic with an absorbing religious complex" (125), who was "credulous to the point of silliness" (129). Also M. and D. Gourevitch, "Le cas Aelius Aristide ou mémoire d'un hystérique au 2e siècle," *Information psychiatrique* 44 (1968): 897–902; G. Michenaud and J. Dierkens, *Les rêves dans les "Discours sacrés" d'Aelius Aristide: Essai d;'analyse psychologique* (Brussels: Université de Mons, 1972); Peter Brown, *The Making of Late Antiquity* (Cambridge: Harvard University Press, 1978), 41–5 (though he also sympathizes with Aristides, "The poor man as had to bear far too heavy a weight of *odium psychologicum* from modern scholars" [41]); P. Andersson and B.-A. Roos, "On the psychology of Aelius Aristides," *Eranos* 95 (1997): 26–38; Adolf Hoffmann, "The Roman Remodeling of the Asklepieion," in *Pergamon: Citadel of the Gods*, ed. Helmut Koester (Harrisburg, PA: Trinity Press International, 1997), 41–49.

193 See, for instance, the preserved Arabic translation of Galen's *Commentary on Plato's Timaeus* in Heinrich O. Schröder, *Galeni in Platonis Timaeum commentarii fragmenta*, CMG 1 (Leipzig: B. G. Teubner, 1934), 33. Satyrus, Galen's teacher, also personally diagnosed Aristides (*Or.* 49.8).

ars of Aelius Aristides have, however, engaged in more nuanced and charitable readings of his *oeuvre* that provide a better framework with which to situate what Aelius Aristides wrote within the broader Roman imperial context.

Luke Timothy Johnson rightly suggests that our concern should not lie with determining the "authenticity" of Aristides's religion or with the false dichotomy between his private religious attitudes and his public persona.[194] Others agree with this assessment and conclude that Aristides's public orations operate with the same religious-intellectual consciousness as his *Sacred Tales*.[195] The upshot of these conclusions is that Aristides's writings, whether the *Sacred Tales* or *Orations*, all contribute to a general picture of how a Roman citizen during the second-century perceived of sacred spaces and the powers of gods that manifested itself in human lives.[196] Unlike earlier judgments of Aristides as an eccentric figure of his time, it is rather the case that Aristides and his works fit right into the center of the religious/cultural frame of the time.[197]

Throughout his *Orations*, Aristides provides ample evidence of the central place that religion held in his life.[198] He talks about elaborate annual sacrifices that still take place in various cities at their respective temples (*Or.* 1.341; 29.4). His home city, Smyrna, is described as "an embroidered gown" with its network of temples that a visitor encounters as he or she walked from east to west (*Or.* 17.10–11; 18.6; also 1.341, 364; 3.218, 252, 285). The ubiquitous presence of the temples throughout Aristides's known world is matched equally by the presence of the gods themselves (*Or.* 43.18), who continue to receive prayers, honors, and thanksgiving from humankind (*Or.* 1.191–193, 330, 338; 2.52, 411; 3.245, 270, 392; 24.16–17; 7.1; 9.46; 16.11; 26.108–109; 30.1; 30.28). He also notes various oracles from the gods, as one kind of evidence of their intervention in human history (*Or.* 1.37, 87, 167; 3.97, 218, 310).[199] Aristides mentions the Great Mysteries, particularly those of Eleusis and Samothrace (*Or.* 1.330, 363, 373; 22) and he does not discriminate in giving honors to a host of well-known gods and heroes (*Or.* 1.404;

---

[194] Johnson, *Among the Gentiles*, 54–5.
[195] See Ido Israelowich, *Society, Medicine and Religion in the* Sacred Tales *of Aelius Aristides* (Leiden: Brill, 2012), 137; Petsalis-Diomidis, *Truly Beyond Wonders*, 124–125.
[196] In other words, it is unnecessary—and ultimately unhelpful—to pit Aristides's ostensibly "private" *Sacred Tales* against his "public" *Orations*.
[197] Petsalis-Diomidis, *Truly Beyond Wonders*, 276; Israelowich, *Society*, 144.
[198] Several of the primary source noted are found in Johnson, *Among the Gentiles*, 55–58, supplemented by my own findings from Aristides's corpus.
[199] For instance, Aristides asserts in *Or.* 40.12, "Why should one speak of ancient history. For the activity of the god is still now manifest (ἔτι γὰρ καὶ νῦν ἐναργὴς ἡ κίνησις τοῦ θεοῦ)."

3.276, 290, 327; 17.5–6, 16; 24.52; 26.104–105; 28.2; 29.4; 33.20; 34.59–60; 35.1–2; 37; 40; 41; 46.1–4).

Among these divine figures, Asclepius stands as *the* god par excellence in Aristides's life. He figures prominently in both the *Sacred Tales* and *Orations*, and is referred to as a "savior god" in conjunction with Sarapis (e. g. Or 27.39, δύο τῶν σωτήρων θεῶν) who engages in "saving/healing" (σῴζειν) acts on behalf of humankind.[200] In his "Oration Regarding Asclepius" (*Or.* 42), Aristides ascribes to Asclepius "great and many powers ... [that are] beyond the scope of human life" (42.4, δυνάμεις μεγάλαι τε καὶ πολλαί ... οὐχ ὅσον ὁ τῶν ἀνθρώπων βίος χωρεῖ).[201] His *Orations* are replete with declarations about Asclepius, including the god's power.[202] While these writings are certainly illuminating, it is Aristides's *Sacred Tales* that serve, above all, as a unique window into his religious experience.[203] In Aristides's oeuvre there is explicit recognition that divine power (which Aristides almost always refers to as δύναμις) was accessible to humans, and not always as a direct result of human action or intervention.[204]

Aristides is important not so much for any explanations of *negative* effects or consequences of misbehavior as for accounts of the *positive* outcomes of proper behavior within sacred spaces. Aelius Aristides is highly motivated by obedience to the gods, as he time and again ignores the advice of friends and doctors while consistently obeying the various divine instructions he receives throughout his

---

200 Note also the importance of Zeus and Sarapis in Aristides's religious discourse: *Or.* 1.1. Also 1.190, 322; 2.379; 3.100, 265–266; 4.19; 18.1; 23.57; 24.42; 26.2, 104–105; 27.39; 28.45–50; 28.109; 36.104; 43.7–15, 17, 256; 45.16–17, 19, 33.
201 See also *Or.* 42.5 (Behr trans.), "the god possesses all power" (πάσας ἔχων ὁ θεὸς τὰς δυνάμεις) and 42.6, "some say they have been resurrected when they were dead ... to some he has given added years of life from his predictions" (εἰσὶν οἵ φασιν ἀναστῆναι κείμενοι ... ἔτι καὶ χρόνους ἔστιν οἷς ἐπέδωκεν ἐκ προρρήσεως).
202 *Or.* 28.156; 33.2, 17; 38.2, 42; 39.5; 42.2, 5, 12, 14.
203 See Johnson, *Among the Gentiles*, 58–63 for an analysis of Aristides's *Sacred Tales*.
204 James B. Rives, *Religion in the Roman Empire* (Malden, MA: Blackwell Publishing, 2007), 98: "[The Romans] did not ... conceive of divine power solely in passive terms, as something that impinged on their lives only when they sought it out ... there was a widespread tendency to perceive divine power as an inherent part of the natural world, which one might encounter at any time." That Romans did not merely view their relationship with the gods as tit-for-tat may be seen in one example, among others, in Livy, *Ab urbe cond.* 40.40 when Fulvius Flaccus vowed a temple to Fortuna Equestris and celebrated games to Jupiter Optimus Maximus *after* his enemies were routed. Jason P. Davies, *Rome's Religious History: Livy, Tacitus and Ammianus on their Gods* (Cambridge: Cambridge University Press, 2004), 87–88.

lifetime. He expresses profound indebtedness to the gods,²⁰⁵ and his writings are replete with pilgrimages to numerous sacred spaces around the Mediterranean. His accounts serve as an illuminating counterpoint to many accounts of punishments illustrated in the Greek and Roman evidence: his oeuvre testifies to the 'salvation' that is extended to faithful suppliants in sacred spaces.

3.4 Summary of Evidence from Greek and Roman Contexts

The evidence from the Greek and Roman contexts yield important conclusions about sanctuaries and the power and punishment related to these spaces. First, there are various similarities as well as differences that are found within the Greek and Roman sources.²⁰⁶ Both traditions demonstrate plenty of evidence within temple discourse, where lines are drawn concerning permitted and forbidden actions and personnel. Both acknowledge temples as a prime location for one's encounter with the gods and their powers, and the evidence clearly shows that salvation and punishments are tied to one's behavior within these sacred spaces. In the Roman sources, however, accounts of punishments or destruction for transgressions are far more scarce than those found in the Greek material. Aelius Aristides is a perfect example of this positive valence around divine *dynamis* in the Roman context: one may have expected to find that his impeccable education and immense wealth would temper his zealous religiosity, but his *Sacred Tales* and *Orations* reveal a man who, throughout his lifetime, sought and experienced salvation from the gods in the sanctuaries dedicated to them.

---

205 Aelius Aristides, *Hier. log.* 4.53: ἄρα πᾶν τοὐμὸν εἴη τοῦ θεοῦ δωρεά ("since everything of mine is a gift of the god"). Also 4.29: ἔσωζεν οὖν διὰ πλείονος ἀξιῶν ἢ ὅσου περ ἦν τὸ σωθῆναι ("therefore, he saved through means worth more than the act of being saved.")

206 A word should be said here about the variety of genres represented in the evidence collected. It is certainly true that accounts of Epidaurean miracles is not the same thing as temple epigraphy which again is not the same thing as Cicero's reflections about religious pollution. What I have aimed to show, however, is that certain generic constraints not withstanding, there appears to be a fairly consistent assumption underlying the Greeks' and Romans' views about one's participation in sacred rituals and encounters with divine powers. The sheer amount of evidence marshaled in this chapter shows that while Romans might differ from the Greeks and that while each maintained somewhat different qualities, they are far more akin to one another than, as I will show in the next chapter, to Jewish religious sentiments. Their shared ideas about pollution, transgression, maintenance of sacred spaces, and concern for sacrificial meals are attested in a variety of sources from numerous contexts.

Second, the analysis shows that Paul's premise that offending the god can lead to punishments (especially in the framework of sacred space) is a shared premise found in other Greeks and Romans. The divine *dynamis* in sanctuaries can work for good or for harm depending on how one behaved, and Paul's discourse about the Corinthian assembly (particularly in 1 Cor 5:1–13, 10:1–22, and 11:17–34) offers a similar vision about how one must regard ὁ ναὸς τοῦ θεοῦ.

There are, however, several differences between Paul and the foregoing evidence that must be noted. In the Greek and Roman sources, *correct* behavior is not synonymous with *moral* behavior.[207] On one hand, the necessary precautions were to be made, such as wearing proper clothing, examining the to-be-consumed substances, and so on, but it need not necessarily include upholding a moral code. For Paul on the other hand, the concern was entirely moral from the start: the πορνεία of 1 Cor 5, the εἰδωλολατρία of 1 Cor 10, and the σχίσμα of 1 Cor 11.

Moreover, nearly all the evidence found from the Greek and Roman contexts deal with *individuals*. That is, if a person committed transgression within a sacred space, then the punishment will be meted out to that specific offender. Such punishments could be monetary, corporal, or even symbolic (e.g. the concept of being 'devoted' to the gods), but regardless of exact form, the recipient of the punishment was almost always restricted to a particular person. In 1 Corinthians, however, Paul reveals a more fluid connection between the transgressions of an individual and the well-being of the community. A good example of this found in his communal consciousness in 1 Corinthians 5, as shown in chapter 2. Perhaps this difference can be attributed to the polytheistic nature of Greek and Roman religions that was far more forgiving than a strictly monotheistic one. The transgression against the temple of one deity need not pose a threat to the entire system, and the offense against one god did not immediately imply that one offended all the gods.[208] In fact, since the time of Homer and beyond, there were instances when the gods were at odds against one another,

---

[207] There are, however, a few minor references to moral behavior in Aelius Aristides: *Or.* 2.201; 16.31; 24.48–50; 29.7, 14; *Hier. log.* 5.37. See also Johnson, *Among the Gentiles*, 63n25.

[208] An important exception to this Greek and Roman way of religiosity may be Plutarch, who straddled the fence between the two poles of *atheotēs* and *deisidaimonia* ("atheism" and "superstition," respectively). He placed great value on the cult for its essential stabilizing influence for the city-state, though his religion was tied so closely to the civic order that Plutarch was certainly not in the same vein of seekers of divine benefits such as Aelius Aristides. Also *De superstitione* 1–14; *Is. Os.* passim (see especially his hermeneutic regarding myths/rituals in 11 and 68); *Mor.* 1128B–1130E; *E Delph.* passim. For a discussion of Plutarch's religion, see Johnson, *Among the Gentiles*, 93–110.

3.4 Summary of Evidence from Greek and Roman Contexts — 153

using human agents for their own competitive aims. On-the-ground reputations of various sanctuaries were also at stake, as certain well-known temples and oracles competed with one another around the Mediterranean world.

Perhaps the most striking difference between Paul and the foregoing prescriptions about sacred spaces, rituals, and transgressions is the complete absence of a prior authoritative figure or text to justify the current religious order. There are countless inscriptions and literary accounts that contain illustrations or exhortations of what must be done within sacred spaces, but not once do they cite an earlier source such as Homer to reinforce the obedience of certain rules. To put this phenomenon in Pauline terms, the use of term such as γέγραπται would have been incomprehensible to the Greeks and Romans.[209] Chapter 2 showed how the exodus tradition is woven in throughout 1 Corinthians 5:1–13, 10:1–22, and 11:17–34, which creates the foundational justification for why the Corinthians are to behave in a certain way. In order to truly understand Paul in these passages, one cannot ignore the scriptural underpinnings, but the same cannot be said for any sources found in the Greek and Roman milieux.

In summary, there are various premises underlying sacred space that Paul shares with other Greeks and Romans of the ancient Mediterranean. But it is also apparent that Paul departed from these shared premises in significant ways. One might attribute these differences to his Jewish heritage. Did Paul draw from traditions within ancient Judaism for the tighter connection between individual and community along with his employment of an earlier authority? Was Paul innovative in his idea that a single pollutant can infect and endanger the whole? How did other Jews in the Mediterranean world circumscribe sacred spaces and what were their views concerning divine powers accessible within them? The following chapter will consider these questions with respect to the ancient Jewish context.

---

209 The frequency of Paul's employment of γέγραπται in 1 Corinthians is second only to his letter to the Romans within the Pauline corpus: Rom 1:17; 2:24; 3:4, 10; 4:17; 8:36; 9:13, 33; 10:15; 11:8, 26; 12:19; 14:11; 15:3, 9, 21; 1 Cor 1:19, 31; 2:9; 3:19; 4:6; 9:9; 10:7; 14:21; 15:45; 2 Cor 8:15; 9:9; Gal 3:10, 13; 4:22, 27. On Greek religion, see the following astute comment by Michael H. Jameson: "For the organization of religious thought and practice the Greeks lacked formulated doctrines and sacred texts and an authoritative, exegetical clergy, although there were sources of exegesis on detailed ritual matters, and some sectarian groups possessed esoteric texts." In "Religion in the Athenian Democracy," in *Cults and Rites in Ancient Greece: Essays on Religion and Society*, ed. Allaire B. Stallsmith (Cambridge: Cambridge University Press, 2014), 232–233.

4 Accessing Sacred Spaces in Jewish Contexts

4.1 Introduction

The available Jewish evidence is plentiful and diverse, allowing for a thick description of how others within the Jewish tradition interacted with the concept of temples and sacred spaces. The data analyzed include textual authorities such as the Hebrew Bible, pseudepigraphic writings, literary documents from Jewish figures such as Philo and Josephus, and the extant texts from Qumran.[1] It also includes non-literary texts from material culture that function as on-the-ground illustrations of how temples functioned within the Jewish tradition, analogous to the inscriptional evidence analyzed in chapter 3. The nature of the evidence differs somewhat from those of the previous chapter, however, since the object of worship was not as diverse as the pantheon of gods found in Greek and Roman religions. Moreover, the role played by a set of writings (i.e. the Hebrew Bible) in the formation of Jewish consciousness vis-à-vis "the temple"—whether in Jerusalem or otherwise—offers a stark contrast to the way that other Greeks and Romans formed ideas and boundaries around the concept of sacred space.

4.2 The Hebrew Bible and Other Related Writings

No text has so shaped and influenced Jewish thinkers, Paul included, on the issue of transgressions in sacred spaces as the Hebrew Bible. The Pentateuch, above all, speaks directly to the question of behavior in sacred spaces. Other writings hint at similar strictures placed upon the Israelites with respect to

---

[1] The texts analyzed in the following subsections do not exhaust all discussions of temples in Jewish writings, but have been selected for their concerns with boundaries and power vis-à-vis sacred spaces. For example, the reader might question why Josephus did not merit his own subsection given the importance of the Jerusalem temple in his oeuvre. There are, however, not many references to encounters with divine power and punishment for transgressions with respect to temples in the Josephan corpus. On the one hand, it is not necessary or advisable for the purposes of the present study to engage in a close reading of all of Josephus's writings. But on the other hand, Josephus is used judiciously when necessary (for example, see 4.4 below on material culture). For a helpful index of references to "temple" in Jewish pseudepigraphic texts, see James H. Charlesworth, ed., *The Old Testament Pseudepigrapha*, 2 vols. (Peabody, MA: Hendrickson Publishers, 1983), 2:999. I would like to thank Carl R. Holladay for making me aware of this reference.

God, sacred spaces, holy objects, and meals. The Hebrew Bible also provides several elaborate instructions concerning the creation and maintenance of sacred spaces. Attending to these details will show the level of gravity with which the Israelites—and subsequently, Jews—protected the sanctity and purity of their sacred spaces.

Genesis 1–3 contains one of the earliest examples of temple discourse. The Garden of Eden serves as an archetype of later sanctuaries.[2] Later Jewish interpreters recognized it to be so. Scholars such as Martin Buber argued that subtle connections between the creation of the world and the subsequent building of the tabernacle encouraged this interpretation of the Hebrew Bible.[3] Genesis Rabbah, for example, understood the command to "work" in Genesis 2:15 as an allusion to sacrifices, and interpreted the expulsion of humankind in Gen 3:24 in the following way: "So he (God) drove out the human; ויגרש, which intimates that He showed him the destruction of the Temple (חרבן בית המקדש)."[4] This conceptualization of Eden as sacred space can be seen in several verbal and conceptual parallels between the garden and later Israelite/Jewish sanctuaries.

First, the most fundamental characteristic that marks the garden as sacred space is the presence of God within it as he "walked" among humankind (e.g. Gen 3:8).[5] We have already seen how divine presence was a clear marker of sacred spaces in other sanctuaries. Second, God's command in Gen 2:15 for human "work" (עבד) in the garden is echoed in later texts that pertain to tabernacle

---

[2] Some of the following analysis draws from Gordon J. Wenham's brief but convincing reading in his "Sanctuary Symbolism in the Garden of Eden Story," in *I Studied Inscriptions from Before the Flood: Ancient Near Eastern, Literary, and Linguistic Approaches to Genesis 1–11*, ed. Richard S. Hess and David Toshio Tsumura (Winona Lake, IN: Eisenbrauns, 1994), 399–404. See also Richard Davidson, "Earth's First Sanctuary: Genesis 1–3 and Parallel Creation Accounts," *AUSS* 53.1 (2015): 65–89.

[3] Martin Buber and Franz Rosenzweig, *Die Schrift und ihre Verdeutschung* (Berlin: Im Shocken Verlag, 1936), 36. For the inner-biblical connection between creation and temple-building, see Michael Fishbane, *Text and Texture: A literary reading of selected texts* (Oxford: Oneworld, 1998 [1979]), 12–13.

[4] Gen 3:24: "God drove out (ויגרש) the human (from Eden)." = Gen. Rab. 21.8 (quoted above). See also Gen 2:15: "The Lord God took the human and put him in the Garden of Eden to till and keep it (לעבדה ולשמרה)." = Gen. Rab. 16.5: "לעבדה ולשמרה ('to till it and to keep it') is an allusion to sacrifices." This interpretation uses verbal connections to Exod 3:12 ("You will serve [תעבדון] God upon this mountain") and to Num 28:2 ("You will take care [תשמרו] to offer to me") to make this argument.

[5] The *hitpael* form of הלך is later used to refer to God's divine presence in sanctuaries: Lev 26:12; Deut 23:15; and 2 Sam 7:6–7.

"service" (עבדה).⁶ Third, the placement of cherubim as a guard before the tree of life at Eden's eastern point (Gen 3:24) parallels other sanctuaries.⁷ The wilderness tabernacle was to be entered from the east (Exod 27:13–16; also Ezek 44:1), and the temple of Solomon housed cherubim in its innermost part (1 Kgs 6:23–28). Fourth, the planting of trees in the Garden, greatest among them the trees of life and of the knowledge of good and evil (Gen 2:9), is significant because trees and holy groves often distinguished divine precincts in various ancient Mediterranean cultures.⁸ Finally, the violation of God's rule concerning trees incurred divine punishment, including physical ramifications (Gen 3:16–19), permanent expulsion from the sacred grounds (Gen 3:24), and most pertinent to this study, death (Gen 2:17; also Sir 25:24; Rom 5:12–17; 1 Cor 15:21).

The story of Moses, in turn, begins with an encounter with God on sacred grounds. In Exodus 3, Moses finds himself at Horeb, where many of the hallmarks of sacred space are noted: (1) the topography; (2) a supernatural light; (3) an angelic figure; and most importantly, (4) a divine epiphany that specifically tells Moses that the place is קדש or ἅγιος (Exod 3:5 MT and LXX).⁹ What would

---

6 E.g., Exod 7:16; 36:24; 39:42; Num 3:8; 4:28, 33; 8:19, 26; 18:6, 21; Ezek 44:14; 1 Chr 6:32; 23:24; 28:13.

7 This is the case especially in evidence from other Near Eastern contexts. See the discussion in Peter Thacher Lanfer, *Remembering Eden: The Reception History of Genesis 3:22–24* (Oxford: Oxford University Press, 2012), 128–29.

8 E.g., Homer, *Od.* 6.162–69, 293–94; Sappho, *Frg.* 2. See chapter 3 for the literary and epigraphic evidence that show trees as markers of sacred spaces in both Greek and Roman contexts. I. Kottsieper, "Bäume als Kultort," in *Das Kleid der Erde: Pflanzen in der Lebenswelt des alten Israel*, ed. U. Neumann-Gorsolke and P. Riede (Stuttgart: Calwer, 2002), 169–187; Izak Cornelius, "Paradise Motifs in the 'Eschatology' of the Minor Prophets and the Iconography of the Ancient Near East," *JNSL* 14 (1988): 41–83; and Michaela Bauks, "Sacred Trees in the Garden of Eden and Their Ancient Near Eastern Precursors," *JAJ* 3.3 (2012): 267–301.

Lanfer (*Remembering Eden*, 136–37) also observes that later interpreters likened the garden as a kind of holy of holies in a temple. Genesis 2:9 locates the tree of life "in the midst" (בתוך) of the garden which is intensified in the Targumic tradition and the Syriac Peshitta. Targum Neofiti reads, "in the midst of the midst of the garden" (בגו מציעות גנתה) and the Syriac Peshitta reads, "in the middle of paradise." (bmṣ'th dprdys'). See also Ephrem the Syrian, *Hymns on Paradise* 3.16: "God did not permit Adam to enter that innermost tabernacle; this was withheld, so that first he might prove pleasing in his service of that outer tabernacle."

9 In Genesis 28:11–19, Moses's ancestor, Jacob, also encountered a transformative divine epiphany within a sacred space, an area that was renamed fittingly as Bethel ("house of God") by Jacob. Commentators have noted that the threefold mention of המקום ("the place") to begin this story in Gen 28:11—repeated again in verses 16, 17, and 19—hints at the significance of this particular geographical location. See. Gordon J. Wenham, *Genesis 16–50* (Dallas, TX: Word Books, 1994), 221. In Gen 28:18, Jacob marks this place with an anointed stone pillar that was not unlike the Greek boundary stones (*horoi*) used throughout the Mediterranean to in-

then set the Israelites on a long journey to the Promised Land begins because God gave Moses a charge from within a sacred space, much in the way that divine inspiration was given to visitors of sanctuaries in the Greek and Roman world.¹⁰ The wilderness tradition also forms a significant part of Paul's understanding of the Corinthian assembly, as demonstrated in chapter 2.

In Exodus 25–40, the readers encounter what is usually called the "tabernacle texts," an elaborate set of descriptions and instructions concerning the tabernacle that occupies about one third of the entire book.¹¹ The level of specificity is remarkable. The narrative first begins with details about the ark, the table for the bread of the presence, other important furnishings, and about the construction of the tent itself (Exod 25–26). The next chapters provide instructions about the altar and the courtyard, with minute details about priestly garments (Exod 27–28 + Exod 30).¹² Like other ANE temples, this tabernacle is built with surrounding walls that clearly demarcate the space within from the space without (Exod 27:9–15).¹³ Exodus 29 describes the ritual performance necessary to designate certain individuals "holy" (29:1, להם לקדש / LXX: ἁγιάσαι αὐτούς) and therefore, worthy to serve as God's priests. The final list of instructions for the tabernacle (Exod 31:1–11) notes that "the spirit of God" energizes the construction of the sacred space (31:1). The reference to רוח אלהים in 31:3 (LXX: πνεῦμα θεῖον) is noteworthy, symbolizing the presence of the deity at the very inception of the

---

dicate the limits of the *temenos* or sacred area. See Merle K. Langdon, "Mountains in Greek Religion," *CW* 93.5 (2000): 461–470; Marietta Horster, "Religious Landscape and Sacred Grounds: Relationships between Space and Cult in the Greek World," *RHR* 227.4 (2010): 435–458.

10 See chapter 3 for various Greek and Roman visitations to sacred spaces. It is notable that Moses prefaces all that he sees and hears on the mountain by identifying it as המראה הגדל / τὸ ὅραμα τὸ μέγα ("a great vision") in Exod 3:3 since this terminology for vision is often used in the Hebrew Bible to signal imminent epiphanies from divine figures. The LXX is fairly consistent in its use of ὅραμα, while the MT makes use of various synonyms. See, for example, Gen 15:1; 46:2; Num 12:6; Isa 20:2; Dan 1:17.

11 Carol Meyers, *Exodus*, NCBC (Cambridge: Cambridge University Press, 2005), 219. It is generally understood that the tabernacle was equivalent to other ancient Near Eastern temples, though its one distinguishing feature was its portability. See Pekka Pitkänen, "Temple Building and Exodus 25–40," in *From the Foundations to the Crenellations: Essays on Temple Building in the Ancient Near East and Hebrew Bible*, ed. Mark J. Boda and Jamie Novotny (Münster: Ugarit-Verlag, 2010), 255–280.

12 This echoes the concern for proper attire before entry in sanctuaries, observed at Priene, for example in *LSAM* 35. See chapter 3 for relevant citations and analyses.

13 Michael B. Hundley, "Before YHWH at the Entrance of the Tent of Meeting: A Study of Spatial and Conceptual Geography in the Priestly Texts," *ZAW* 123.1 (2011): 21.

tabernacle.¹⁴ The significance and function of the tabernacle are clear when the Lord tells the Israelites that it is a sanctified place where the Lord will dwell among his people (Exod 29:42–46).

Just as one would now expect the Israelites to complete God's plan for the tabernacle, Exodus 32–34 interrupts the narrative flow with the incident of the golden calf. Hurowitz has shown that this is not unusual in light of other Mesopotamian stories of the creation of sacred spaces that also recount similar incidents of misbehavior or rebellion.¹⁵ Paul also recalls this same story in his admonition to the Corinthians, warning them about the proper maintenance of communal integrity and practice (1 Cor 10:7). Israel's perversion of the sacred space is evident in their creation of a cult image and sacrificial altar, and the accompanying celebration of the "feast of the Lord" (חג ליהוה / LXX: ἑορτὴ τοῦ κυρίου) in Exod 32:1–5. Moses executes the punishment for this transgression by commanding those who remained loyal to God to purify the group by killing the transgressors, who number about 3,000 people (32:26–28). The divine punishment on the rest of the survivors manifests itself as disease upon the people (32:35), and as a possible withdrawal of God's presence from their midst.¹⁶ The retribution here is therefore twofold: (a) a horizontal (i.e. human agent) capital punishment for the offenders and (b) a vertical (i.e. divine agent) residual punishment for those that remained. The narrative arc concludes with the covenant renewal episode of Exod 34, and the tabernacle text resumes with more descrip-

---

14 This presence of the "spirit of God" is repeated again in Exod 35:31. See chapter 2.2 for discussion of this text as it concerns 1 Corinthians. See Pekka Pitkänen, *Central Sanctuary and Centralization of Worship in Ancient Israel: From the Settlement to the Building of Solomon's Temple* (Piscataway, NJ: Gorgias Press, 2003), 46.

15 Victor (Avigdor) Hurowitz, *I Have Built You an Exalted House: Temple Building in the Bible in Light of Mesopotamian and Northwest Semitic Writings*, JSOTSS 115 (Sheffield: Sheffield Academic Press, 1992), 111. Scholars have argued for the composite nature of Exod 25–40 (i.e., 25–31, 32–34, then 35–40) due to this interruption, but these arguments are not germane to my discussion. Whatever their origins, these chapters have been included in their current order and this form is the one that Paul knew and read as it became incorporated into his vision for the Corinthian assembly.

16 See also Exod 32:10; Num 11:33; Deut 28:58–61; and 1 Sam 6:19. Exod 33 emphasizes the tenuous nature of God's divine presence (especially in light of their recent transgression), as God signals God's withdrawal from the Israelites (33:3). The rest of the chapter then addresses the anxiety concerning God's presence among the Israelites, and culminates with Moses's assertion that divine presence is necessary because it is what makes them unique among all other groups (33:16). The psalter contains many references to the importance of God's presence in the temple: Ps 11:4; 18:6; 27:4; 48:9; 65:4.

For examples of ANE deities abandoning their sanctuaries due to violations, see Pitkänen, "Temple Building," 262–266.

tion and completion of the tabernacle, when the promise of God dwelling among the people is finally realized (Exod 35–40).

The narrative account concerning the building of the tabernacle could transition directly from Exodus 40:34–38 to Numbers 9:15–17.[17] The intervening section, Leviticus 1:1–Numbers 9:14, forms the entirety of God's laws recited to Moses on Sinai, constituting what Jacob Milgrom calls "the center of the Pentateuch … [and] the foundation of Israel's life."[18] It is not the place here to provide an in-depth exegesis of this section of the Pentateuch, but I highlight a few points germane to the foregoing discussion.

First, Leviticus 1–7 in particular expounds upon the importance of tabernacle sacrifices and meals that were adumbrated in Exodus.[19] A notable aspect of Israel's sacrificial meals was the exclusion of individuals that were deemed to be polluting agents. Exodus 12 clearly bars foreigners, uncircumcised individuals, and certain slaves from partaking in the Passover meal, and Leviticus extends this prohibition to other meals, in stratified fashion depending on the level of one's purity.[20] For example, an unclean person could not eat of the sacred meal until he washes himself, and a priest's daughter could or could not partake of the sacred meal depending on her level of purity.[21] Second, improper behavior towards the "sacred place/things" incurred guilt before God. In Leviticus 5:15, the

---

17 Exod 40:34 (NRSV): "Then the cloud covered the tent of meeting, and the glory of the Lord filled the tabernacle." / Num 9:15 (NRSV): "On the day the tabernacle was set up, the cloud covered the tabernacle, the tend of the covenant; and from evening until morning it was over the tabernacle, having the appearance of fire."
18 Jacob Milgrom, *Leviticus 1–16: A New Translation with Introduction and Commentary* (New York: Doubleday, 1991), 61.
19 E.g., Exod 20:24; 23:14–17; 24:3–8; and 29. See Ronald S. Hendel, "Sacrifice as a Cultural System: The Ritual Symbolism of Exodus 24,3–8," *ZAW* 101.3 (1989): 366–390. See chapter 3 for secondary literary on the sensory aspects of the killing, cooking or burning, and eating of sacrifices in the Greek and Roman contexts. For the anthropological discussion of "holiness" in meals and bodies, see Mary Douglas, "Deciphering a Meal," *Daedalus* 101.1 (1972): 61–81; idem, *Purity and Danger: An Analysis of the Concepts of Pollution and Taboo* (London: Routledge, 2001 [1966]).
20 In other words, the categories "pure" and "impure" should not be understood as two mutually exclusive categories, but should be understood as two ends of a single spectrum. In the study of ancient Judaism, scholars have also debated at length about varieties of "impurity" (e.g., ritual vs. moral). To enter this debate is not the aim of this chapter. This chapter shows that in whatever form they may come, both ancient Israel and early Judaism demonstrated anxieties and answers for "impurity" of various kinds, particularly as it relates to sacred space. For a helpful overview of the aforementioned debate, see Jonathan Klawans, *Impurity and Sin in Ancient Judaism* (Oxford: Oxford University Press, 2000), esp. 3–20.
21 See also Exod 12:43–45, 48; Lev 22:4, 6, 10, 12–13.

Lord tells Moses that even if someone may unintentionally transgress in the "sacred things of the Lord," she or he must make restitution for that error.[22] Leviticus is the only biblical book to contain the exhortation, "You will revere my sanctuary," stated twice in 19:30 and 26:2.[23]

Third, transgressions of an *individual* can be commuted to *others* (people or other inanimate objects) in various ways. Lev 4:3 states that the sin of one priest can endanger "the people" (העם / LXX: τὸν λαόν), and 10:6 further specifies the consequences as wrath upon "the entire congregation" (כל העדה / LXX: πᾶσαν τὴν συναγωγήν).[24] In other cases, a transgression can defile the sanctuary or the land.[25] Some offenses required the offender be "cut off from his people" (נכרתה מעמיה), lest she/he endanger or pollute others.[26] The most serious version of this penalty is noted in Lev 22:3, when an impure person might approach "the sacred donations" (הקדשים / LXX: τὰ ἅγια): "he will be cut off from *my presence*."[27] To be barred from proximity to God's presence would have been recognized as a terrible punishment, and later Greek translators provide the following gloss of the Hebrew text: "he will be destroyed from God's presence."[28]

---

[22] The phrase קדשי יהוה (LXX: τῶν ἁγίων κυρίου) is ambiguous. Milgrom translates it rather vaguely as "the Lord's sancta" (*Leviticus 1–16*, 320). Despite the difficulty in its exact translation, it is clear that the phrase refers to the tabernacle itself, its holy ornaments or objects within, and/or the sacrifices tied to the sacred space. The economic restitution observed in Lev 5:15b is not without parallels in Greek sanctuaries (see chapter 3). See also *Leviticus 1–16*, 354 for various penalties meted out by man and by gods for sacrilegious acts in Hittite laws.

[23] The syntax is identical in both verses: "You will keep my sabbaths and revere my sanctuary (ומקדשי תיראו / LXX: ἀπὸ τῶν ἁγίων μου φοβηθήσεσθε). I am the Lord." Later rabbinic interpreters elaborated upon what this "fear" of the sanctuary may entail, with prohibitions against carrying a staff, traveling bag, shoes, and/or money-belt, and also prohibiting dust on one's feet, the use of the sanctuary as a shortcut, and spitting (m. Ber. 9.5; *Sifra* Qedoshim 7.9; b. Yebam. 6b). See Jacob Milgrom, *Leviticus 17–22: A New Translation with Introduction and Commentary* (New York: Doubleday, 2000), 1700. See the subsequent section for analysis of texts from Qumran.

[24] This individual-communal relationship is mentioned once in Genesis 20:9, though not in the context of sacred space as it is here in Leviticus.

[25] Lev 15:31; 18:24–28; and 22:9. There are also cases when the name of God can be profaned: Lev 18:21; 19:12; 20:3; 21:6; 22:2, 32.

[26] Lev 7:20, 21, 25, 27; 17:4, 9, 10, 14; 18:29; 19:8; 20:3, 5, 6, 17, 18. See also Gen 17:14; Exod 12:15, 19; 30:33, 38; and 31:14.

[27] Emphasis added. Milgrom (*Leviticus 17–22*, 1850) argues that the verb "approach/encroach" in Lev 22:3 (יקרב) "implies the illegitimate use of a sacred object."

[28] LXX: ἐξολεθρευθήσεται ἡ ψυχὴ ἐκείνη ἀπ' ἐμοῦ. See Paul's reference to destruction and "the destroyer" in 1 Cor 10:1–22. According to TLG, the language of the destruction of the soul occurs in Greek literature for the first time in the LXX: Gen 17:14; Exod 12:15, 19; 31:14; Lev 17:4; 18:29; 19:8; Num 9:13; 15:30; 19:20. The same language is found again only in later Christian texts.

Fourth, activities in sacred space entailed more than the proper performance of sacrifices or other rituals: one's life was at stake when she or he entered into the sanctuary of God. Moses charges Aaron and his sons to remain within the sanctuary precincts to guard against violations, "so that you might not die" (Lev 8:35).[29] In an ironic turn of events, Aaron's eldest sons, Nadab and Abihu, do the exact opposite by bringing "unauthorized fire" into the sanctuary (10:1, אש זרה / LXX: πῦρ ἀλλότριον).[30] The punishment is swift and certain: the Lord kills them by fire (10:2). Further instructions are then given to Aaron and his other sons: to maintain proper behavior in the sanctuary with the warning of death if they leave the sanctuary or become intoxicated on sacred grounds (10:6–9). Throughout Leviticus, there are threats of death for polluting the sacred place or things of God.[31]

The book of Numbers also portrays the importance of purity with respect to sacred space. Numbers begins with a strict warning that any outsider who approaches the tabernacle will face the death penalty (1:51). The Levites are commanded to surround the tabernacle in hierarchical fashion, as a boundary that must be maintained lest "wrath" fall upon the entire community (1:52–53, קצף / LXX: ἁμάρτημα).[32] The Lord then chooses a certain group, the Kohathites, and only those between ages 30–50, whose service concerned the most sacred of the sacred space (4:3–4). Very specific instructions are given (4:5–15a, 16–17), and the Lord cautions multiple times that mishandling holy objects or misbehav-

---

E. g., Justin Martyr, *Dial.* 10.3; 23.4; Eusebius, *Dem. ev.* 1.3.10; and *SEG* 27.30 (Laureion, 4th CE; this inscription, however, does not mention "soul").

29 Milgrom, *Leviticus 1–16*, 541: "during their consecratory week they are not to leave the sanctuary premises at all—not even to relieve themselves." Milgrom concludes, "death here is by divine agency" (542). See also Lev 16:2, 13.
30 See Num 3:4; 26:61. Targum Onqelos later interpreted this phrase as "alien/profane fire" (ישתאא נוכריתא) in Tg. Onq. on Leviticus 16:1.
31 Lev 15:31; 20:2–3; 22:9; and 27:29. The status of חרם ("devoted") given to transgressors for their destruction or death occurs first in Exod 22:19 ("Whoever sacrifices to any god other than the LORD alone will be devoted to destruction [יחרם].) This parallels the language of *sacer* used in Hellenistic contexts (see chapter 3). Leviticus 20 is striking for the way it connects the defiling of sanctuary (v. 3) to sexual ethics (vv. 10–21). It also expounds for the first time the fact that Israel is not holy in and of itself (20:8). For discussion of the *piel* causative form, מקדשכם, see Milgrom, *Leviticus 17–22*, 1740–2. The piel form, "the one who makes holy," occurs elsewhere in: Exod 31:13; Lev 21:8, 15, 23; 22:9, 16, 32.
32 Num 2:1–34 gives greater detail on the order and organization of this strict hierarchy and Num 8:19 identifies the result of wrath as a "plague among the Israelites." Num 16–17 contains a lengthy account of the consequences of breaking the hierarchy around the tabernacle (e. g., fire, opening of the earth, plague). See also the discussion of Lev 10:6 above and the connection between קצף and מות. See Num 3:4, 10, 38; 11:1; 18:5; 25.

ior within the sacred space will result in death (4:15, 19–20; also 17:13; 18:1, 3, 7, 22, 32). Numbers 5:3, 19:13, and 19:20 relay the possibility that individual transgression can bring pollution to the camp or the sanctuary (טמא / LXX: μιαίνω).³³

Other texts in the Hebrew Bible show the durability of the conviction that polluting sacred space or objects tied to that space can yield disastrous results. In 1 Samuel 4–5, the relationship between the ark and divine presence is clear when the Israelite elders wished to bring out the ark before battle "so that he [God] may come among us and save us" (1 Sam 4:3). Israel's opponents, the Philistines, also appear to accept the notion that God remained in close proximity to the ark when they conclude that "gods have come into the camp" at hearing of the ark (4:7). As the story unfolds, the Israelites lose the battle, the Philistines capture the ark, and the wife of Phinehas bears a child named Ichabod to signify the departure of God's presence (4:10–11, 21–22). Subsequently, the ark is placed within another deity's sanctuary that lead to severe consequences not only for the cult statue of Dagon, but also for the people of Ashdod, Gath, and Ekron (5:2–12).³⁴

Another episode describes the transfer of the ark from Kiriath-Jearim to Jerusalem (2 Sam 6:2; 1 Chr 13:5). The oxen shook the cart upon which the ark of God lay, presumably putting it at risk of falling off the cart and causing damage or pollution. At this moment, Uzzah reached out with his hands and took hold of the ark (2 Sam 6:6; also 1 Chr 13:9).³⁵ The text does not specify the nature of

---

33 In Numbers, the camp is akin to the tabernacle, since the former is noted as the place where God dwells among humanity (Num 5:3). This is confirmed by the several times that pollutants are ordered "outside" the encampment: Num 12:14, 15; 15:35, 36; 31:19; Deut 23:10–14. Relevant to this spatial imagery is God's response to the Israelite's complaint: he burns the outer edges of the camp (Num 11:1, בקצה המחנה). Mark K. George observes: "This divine action is interesting because it is spatial in nature. Rather than kill members of the congregation, as is typical for the deity, the fire burns a spatial zone. The significance of this zone is explained by tabernacle spatial logic. The edge of camp space marks the divine line between Israel and the rest of the world." In "Socio-Spatial Logic and the Structure of the Book of Numbers," in *Constructions of Space IV: Further Developments in Examining Ancient Israel's Social Space*, ed. Mark K. George (London: Bloomsbury, 2013), 35.

34 The call for a guilt offering so as to not return the ark of the God of Israel "empty-handed" (1 Sam 6:3, ריקם / LXX: κενός) confirms that a transgression has taken place. This term is sometimes used to describe the proper way to approach God, presumably within the sanctuary: Exod 23:15; 34:20; Deut 16:16.

35 2 Sam 6:7 contains the phrase, על השל, that commentators puzzle over because the translation of של is uncertain and/or the phrase is viewed as a corrupt derivation of a similar phrase, על הארון על האשר שלח ידו ("on account of the fact that he put his hand upon the ark"), from 1 Chr 13:10. Major translations also diverge on how to interpret this phrase: "error" or "mistake" (KJV, NKJV, RV, CEB, ASV, ESV), "irreverence" (NIV, GNT, NASB), "put his hand" (RSV, NRSV),

the transgression, but does recount the Lord's anger against Uzzah, who was struck down immediately (2 Sam 6:7; also 1 Chr 13:10).[36]

Israelite and Jewish concerns about the maintenance of sacred spaces and the power encountered therein are also noted in later texts.[37] 2 Maccabees begins with the rebellion of Jason against "the kingdom (of God)," further explained as burning the gate of the temple and spilling the blood of innocents (2 Macc 1:7, 8).[38] The author then exhorts his readers, "now, you will celebrate the festival of Tabernacles (1:9, σκηνοπηγίας)," which is later linked to the purity of the temple (1:18). This temple's "sanctity and inviolability" (σεμνότης καὶ ἀσυλία) was ostensibly known and honored throughout the entire world.[39] Regardless of this status, King Seleucus IV sent a senior official named Heliodorus to enter the Jerusalem temple in order to take from its treasury (3:7, 13). At the moment of his entry—that is, the transgression of a sacred boundary—the ruler of the spirits presented himself with such a great manifestation that Heliodorus and his companions were "stricken by the power of God" (καταπλαγέντας τὴν τοῦ

---

and omitted or ambiguous (NAB, NLT). See A. A. Anderson, *2 Samuel*, WBC (Dallas: Word Books, 1989), 103–104 A. Graeme Auld, *I & II Samuel: A Commentary* (Louisville: Westminster John Knox Press, 2011), 408 and 412.

36 The ambiguity of the text gave rise to various interpretations. The Chronicler believed that because the Levites did not carry the ark initially, God burst out in anger (1 Chr 15:13). Josephus later held Uzzah responsible for his own death because Uzzah had touched the ark while not being a priest (*Ant*. 7.81).

37 The distinction between the Hebrew Bible and non-HB texts should not be pressed too heavily since many of the texts mentioned in the following paragraphs are found in some variations of the HB canon.

38 See 2 Macc 5:6, 8. See also 1 Macc 7:17 (referring to Alcimus, not Jason) citing Ps 79:3 ("they spilled their blood like water all around Jerusalem"). Verse 1 of this Psalm reads: "O God, the Gentiles have come into Your inheritance; they have defiled Your holy temple." Cited in Daniel R. Schwartz, *2 Maccabees* (Berlin: Walter de Gruyter, 2008), 142. See also the accounts concerning the Temple in 1 Macc 1:44–59; 4:41–54.

39 2 Macc 3:12 (NRSV): "And he said that it was utterly impossible that wrong should be done to those people who had trusted in the holiness of the place and in the sanctity and inviolability of the temple that is honored throughout the whole world." The respect afforded to sanctuaries around the Mediterranean was not uncommon among rulers, including the Seleucids (See *OGIS* 228 [Smyrna, 242 BCE]; *ISmyrna* 573 [Smyrna, 242 BCE]; the Heliodorus stele [178 BCE]). *Asylia* is a well-documented technical term—among other related terms—in the ancient Mediterranean world. It is related to, though should not be conflated with, the modern idea of *asylum*. See Ulrich Sinn, "Greek sanctuaries as places of refuge," in *Greek Sanctuaries: New approaches*, ed. Nanno Marinatos and Robin Hägg (London: Routledge, 1993), 70–87; Kent J. Rigsby, *Asylia: Territorial Inviolability in the Hellenistic World* (Berkeley: University of California Press, 1996).

θεοῦ δύναμιν), becoming weak and afraid.⁴⁰ Heliodorus is then given corporal punishment by two angelic figures for his sacrilege and is eventually carried out on a stretcher. The reader is told that these transgressors "clearly recognized the sovereign power of God" (3:28, φανερῶς τὴν τοῦ θεοῦ δυναστείαν ἐπεγνωκότες).⁴¹

1 Enoch 24–27 envisions the temple as a garden, nestled among great mountains, with a tree that surpassed all others in its fragrance and fruit (1 En. 24:2–5). The archangel Michael tells Enoch that this mountain is like "the throne of God" (25:3, θρόνου θεοῦ) and that its fruit will only be given to the righteous and holy in "the holy place … the house of the Lord" (25:5, ἐν τόπῳ ἁγίῳ … τὸν οἶκον τοῦ θεοῦ). The sanctuary is noted as a place of healing and life where their lifespans will be extended with threat from plagues, torments, or calamities (25:6).⁴²

---

40 2 Macc 3:24: "But when he (Heliodorus) arrived at the treasury with his bodyguards, then the ruler of the spirits and of all authority while present made such a great manifestation (παρόντος ὁ τῶν πνευμάτων καὶ πάσης ἐξουσίας δυνάστης ἐπιφάνειαν μεγάλην ἐποίησεν) that all who had been so bold as to accompany Heliodorus were stricken by the power of God, and became faint and afraid (καταπλαγέντας τὴν τοῦ θεοῦ δύναμιν εἰς ἔκλυσιν καὶ δειλίαν τραπῆναι)." An account from Lindos also describes a foreigner being "stricken" or "shocked" by divine epiphany: καταπλαγεὶς ὁ βάρβαρος τὰν τᾶς θεοῦ ἐπιφάνειαν (*Syll.*³ 725 D.33–34 [Lindos, 99 BCE]). This barbarian general even declared that the Lindians were protected: τοὺς ἀνθρώπους τούτους θεοὶ φυλάσσουσι (D.46–47).

41 This episode with Heliodorus concludes in dramatic fashion. Heliodorus's associates beg the high priest Onias to make amends before God so that "he may gift life" (τὸ ζῆν χαρίσασθαι) back to Heliodorus as he lay on his deathbed (2 Macc 3:31). Onias then offers sacrifice on behalf of Heliodorus and the angelic figures appear again to Heliodorus, telling him that he will live again because of Onias (3:32–33). He is commanded to "report to everyone the mighty power of God" (διάγγελλε πᾶσι τὸ μεγαλεῖον τοῦ θεοῦ κράτος) and Heliodorus subsequently bears witness to the deeds of the great God (3:34–36). The conclusion ends as follows in 3:37–39: "When the king asked Heliodorus what person would be suitable to send on another mission to Jerusalem, he replied: 'If you have an enemy or plotter against your government, send him there, for you will get him back flogged, if he survives at all; because there is truly some power of God about the place (διὰ τὸ περὶ τὸν τόπον ἀληθῶς εἶναί τινα θεοῦ δύναμιν). For he who has his dwelling in heaven watches over that place himself and brings it aid, and he strikes and destroys the ones who come to do it harm (τοὺς παραγινομένους ἐπὶ κακώσει τύπτων ἀπολλύει)." See also my discussion in chapter 3 concerning Livy, *Ab urbe cond.* 29.18, where transgressors of a sacred space eventually acknowledge the "power" of the gods after experiencing a crisis.

42 See also the Jewish inscription associated with the remains of a synagogue at Delos in *IJO* 1: Ach62 (1ˢᵗ BCE): Λαωδίκη Θεῶι Ὑψίστωι σωθεῖσα ταῖς ὑφ'αὑτοῦ θαραπήαις εὐχήν = "Laodice, to the God Most High, having been saved by his therapies, (fulfilling) a vow." For evidence of Jews living on Delos at least since the 1ˢᵗ BCE, see Josephus, *Ant.* 14.213–216, 231–232; 1 Macc 15:22–23.

In several places, the Book of Jubilees relays the dangers posed by Gentile activity, both to the community and to the sanctuary. The author warns of impending calamities such as disease, famine, and death:[43]

> [13] Blow upon blow, wound upon wound, distress upon distress, bad news upon bad news, disease upon disease, and every (kind of) bad punishment like this, one with the other: disease and stomach pains ... fever, cold, and numbness; famine, death ... [14] All of this will happen to the evil generation that makes the earth commit sin through pollution, [44]sexual impurity, contamination, and their detestable actions (23:13–14).

To note that the earth is marked by sin (*mədr ta'ebbəsa*) is odd since it was the evil generation that was responsible in the first place; the polluting actions of the few can make the entire world liable before God. Also, the distresses named by the author emphasize the *physical* consequences for transgressions.[45] In another section of the book, the author describes more explicitly the pollution of the sanctuary:

> [22:16]Separate from the nations, and do not eat with them, do not act as they do ... for their actions are something that is impure ... all their ways are defiled and something abominable and detestable ... [17]they worship demons ... [18]They have no mind to think ... how they err in saying to a piece of wood, "You are my god" or to a stone, "You are my Lord, you are my deliverer" ... [19]May he [God] remove you from their impurity and from all their error ... [22]There is no hope in the land of the living for all who worship idols ... For they will descend to sheol and will go to the place of judgment (22:16–19, 22) ... [23:17]Everything that they do is impure and something detestable; all their ways are characterized by contamination and corruption. [18]The earth will indeed be destroyed because of all that they do ... [21]They will defile the holy of holies with the impure corruption of their contamination. [22]There will be a great punishment from the Lord for the actions of that generation (23:17–18, 21–22).

Other texts, such as Judith and Tobit emphasize the need to maintain purity as not to contaminate sacred spaces and also describe the dangers posed by impure deeds.[46]

---

43 Following translations are adapted from James C. VanderKam, *The Book of Jubilees* (Louvain: Peeters, 1989). I will note below when I diverge from his translation.
44 VanderKam, *Jubilees*, 143 here translates three named transgressions (*rək"s, zəmmut*, and *gəmmane*) into two ("sexual impurity" and "contamination"). The first word, however, should not be subsumed under the second—as referring simply to sexual sin—since it refers to a broader category of pollution and impurity.
45 See the notes on VanderKam, *Jubilees*, 142–43 for a good discussion of these physical conditions.
46 See Jdt 9:7–13; Tob 1:4; 13:10, 12; Jub 1:10, 16–17; 3:10–13; 8:19 (names the Garden of Eden as "the holy of holies and the dwelling of the Lord"); 23:21; 30:13–15; T. Benj. 9:1–5; T. Levi 5:1;

4.3 Philo

As a near contemporary of Paul, Philo of Alexandria echoes some of the sentiments of Paul vis-à-vis temple, but with his own distinctive traits. In his *Life of Moses*, Philo discusses the tabernacle (informed by Exodus 25) and the Jerusalem temple in light of their respective environments:

> ⁷¹While he [Moses] was still staying on the mount, he was being instructed in all the mysteries of his priestly duties: and first in those which stood first in order, namely the building and furnishing of the sanctuary (τὰ περὶ τὴν τοῦ ἱεροῦ καὶ τῶν ἐν αὐτῷ κατασκευήν). ⁷²Now, if they had already occupied the land into which they were migrating, they would necessarily have had to erect a magnificent temple in the purest place (περισημότατον νεὼν ἐν τῷ καθαρωτάτῳ), with costly stones for its material, and build great walls around it, with plenty of houses for the attendants, and call the place the holy city. ⁷³But, as they were still wandering in the desert and had as yet no settled habitation, it suited them to have a portable sanctuary (ἥρμοττε φορητὸν ἔχειν ἱερόν).⁴⁷

What is noteworthy about Philo's statement here—and elsewhere, as shown below—is his conviction that locating a sacred space within an area marked as "pure" (notice the superlative of the adjective, καθαρός) was not optional. Indeed, Philo implies that purity and divine presence/power were intimately tied together such that without the former, access to the latter could be threatened.

Similarly, in his account concerning the formation of the Septuagint, Philo observes that the translators "looked for the purest place (ἐσκόπουν τὸ καθαρώτατον) of all the spots outside the city."⁴⁸ According to Philo, this task was divinely inspired, and given the magnitude of such a work, it is not surprising to him that the translators deliberately searched for a "pure" location to complete their duty.⁴⁹ To be sure, "purity" does not always equal "sacred," but it

---

9:9–10; 14:5–15:2; 16:1–5; Pr Azar 1:16, 31; Sir 24:1–4; 1 Esd 1:47–55; Pss. Sol. 1:8; 2:3, 12–13; 8:9–13; T. Mos. 5:3; 4 Ezra 10:21–22; Apoc. Ab. 25.1–6; 27.3–7.

47 Philo, *Mos.* 2.71–73 (slightly modified Colson, LCL). On translation of the term, καθαρός, which diverges from that of Colson, see Daniel R. Schwartz, "Humbly Second-Rate in the Diaspora? Philo and Stephen on the Tabernacle and the Temple," in *Envisioning Judaism: Studies in Honor of Peter Schäfer on the Occasion of his Seventieth Birthday*, ed. R. S. Boustan et al. (Tübingen: Mohr Siebeck, 2013), 81–89.

48 Philo, *Mos.* 2.34.

49 In *Mos.* 2.34, Philo explicitly notes that the translators were suspicious of any areas within the city due to the presence of various animals with their accompanying diseases and deaths, as well as the "impure practices" (οὐκ εὐαγεῖς πράξει) of the city inhabitants. To be sure "purity" does not always equal "sacred" in these accounts, but it is nevertheless significant that Philo did not find the practices of the translators to be extraordinary. Given that Philo regards the product of their work to be basically supernatural in nature, this example is relevant for my overall conis nevertheless significant that Philo did not find this practice of the translators to be extraordinary. Since Philo regards the product of their work to be supernatural in nature, the foregoing example is relevant for my discussions about how one could obtain access to divine benefits or powers, particularly in the context of a sacred—or in this particular instance, pure—space. To put it differently, not every pure location afforded access to God, but certainly any place where one could access God *had* to be pure. In *Flaccum*, Philo recounts the story of Alexandrian Jews purposefully seeking out the "purest place" (τῷ καθαρωτάτῳ) where they might pray to God.[50] If God was able to hear their prayers at every place, why the need to discriminate where they prayed? Philo is not implying that God could not hear the prayers of his people if they prayed elsewhere, but his statement nevertheless suggests that access to God can be affected by the location.

These accounts reveal one striking difference between Paul and Philo vis-à-vis encountering the divine, that is the role of "the city." In the latter, one finds suggestions that the city, its inhabitants, and the activities found therein present risks to a person's purity, which in turn would affect how she or he might engage God. Paul certainly understood the temptations that existed within a city such as Corinth, but he does not follow the same train of thought as that of Philo (see my discussion in chapter 5). Philo's comments on one of *the* defining moments of Judaism, namely, Moses's reception of the Torah, demonstrate this difference clearly:

> To the question why he [God] promulgated his laws not in cities but in the depths of the desert (οὐκ ἐν πόλεσιν ἀλλ' ἐν ἐρήμῳ βαθείᾳ), we may answer in the first place that most cities are full of countless evils, both acts of impiety towards God and wrongdoing between persons ... Pride also brings divine things (τὰ θεῖα) into utter contempt ... For men have employed sculpture and painting to fashion innumerable forms which they have enclosed in shrines and temples and after building altars have assigned celestial and divine honors to idols of stone and wood and suchlike images, all of them lifeless things ... so too throughout the cities those who do not know the true, the really existent God have deified hosts of others who are falsely so called ... He [God] had also a second object in mind. He who is about to receive the holy laws must first cleanse his soul and purge away the deep-set stains which it has contracted through contact with the motley promiscuous horde of men in cities.[51]

---

cern about how one could obtain access to divine benefits or powers, particularly in the context of a "sacred"—or in this particular instance, "pure"—space.
50 Philo, *Flacc.* 122. Also *Mos.* 2.214.
51 Philo, *Decal.* 2–10 (slightly modified Colson, LCL). In *Ebr.* 101–3, Philo expands upon Exod 9:29 ("Moses said to him [Pharaoh], 'As soon as I have gone out of the city, I will stretch out my hands to the Lord'") by claiming that Moses had to escape the city because the mind "while con-

It is clear that Philo views the city to be of a polluting nature, to the degree that it required one to escape in order to encounter God properly.⁵²

How does Philo's perspective connect to sacred spaces? It is instructive to return back to the earlier cited contrast between the tabernacle and the Jerusalem temple in Philo's *Life of Moses*. It was shown earlier that Philo considers "the city" to be dangerous since it contains polluting agents and worship of other non-real deities. In *On the Migration of Abraham*, Philo refers to the law that calls for the people to "expel from the sacred assembly" (ἐκκλησίας ἱερᾶς ἀπελήλακε) any polluting individuals.⁵³ According to Daniel Schwartz, Philo's comments in *Life of Moses* "seems to imply some disparagement of the Temple insofar as it is located in a city … [it] puts the Temple a priori at a disadvantage."⁵⁴ Just following the above quotation, Philo calls the construction of the tabernacle a ἔργον ἱερώτατον (*Mos.* 2.74), with the overall preference for a movable sanctuary that was patently not located within or limited to a specific locale.⁵⁵

4.4 Material Culture

Material evidence concerning the Jerusalem Temple also reflects a vision of purity that the Hebrew Bible and other writings displayed. Unfortunately, due to the twofold destruction of the Jerusalem Temple and the many centuries of building and rebuilding, the relevant material evidence concerning the Jewish temple space is sparse. There is, however, an important inscription from Herod's temple mount that provides good evidence for how that sacred space was protected

---

tained in the city of the body and of mortal life is cramped and confined, and like a man who is bound in prison confesses plainly that he is unable to relish the free air." But once escaping from the city, it is able to pour out "its energies" (ταῖς ἐνεργείαις).

52 See also *Contempl.* 19–20 where Philo makes a similar observation concerning the Therapeutae and the city. On Philo's criticism of "cities" see David T. Runia, "The Idea and the Reality of the City in the Thought of Philo of Alexandria," *JHI* 61.3 (2000): 361–379, esp. 370–372.
53 Philo, *Migr.* 69. See also *Spec.* 1.315–16 that metes out execution for those who lead the community into foreign religious practices.
54 Schwartz, "Humbly Second-Rate," 84.
55 Schwartz, "Humbly-Second Rate," 88–89 also discusses Stephen and his attack against the Jerusalem temple in Acts 7, with the suggestion that Stephen's perspective echoes that of Philo. The conclusion is that as Diaspora Jews, they were apt to consider the house of God to not be confined to a specific space. If true, it also could have contributed to Paul's view of the Corinthians as the temple of God. Paul does not suggest the temple be constructed beyond the city walls as Philo does, but the notion that the assembly *is* the temple of God frees the sacred space from being tied to a specific location. It also means that such a temple could be mobile in the same vein as the tabernacle as seen in both Philo and Stephen.

from unqualified visitors. There are two limestone inscriptions that read as follows:

> Μηθένα ἀλλογενῆ εἰσπορεύεσθαι ἐντὸς τοῦ περὶ τὸ ἱερὸν τρυφάκτου καὶ περιβόλου. Ὅς δ'ἂν ληφθῇ, ἑαυτῶι αἴτιος ἔσται διὰ τὸ ἐξακολουθεῖν θάνατον.
>
> No foreigner shall enter within the balustrade around the sanctuary or within the precinct. Whoever is caught doing so, will himself be the cause for the resulting death.[56]

Chapter 3 presented various inscriptional warnings concerning transgressions in other sacred spaces. In light of this evidence, the above Jerusalem inscription is not particularly exceptional; to transgress the boundaries of sacred space meant a variety of punishments could be meted out, death included.[57]

The presence of this inscription is corroborated by evidence in Josephus and Philo. For example, in his description of the Jerusalem temple grounds, Josephus observes:

> Proceeding across this towards the second court of the temple, one found it surrounded by a stone balustrade, three cubits high and of exquisite workmanship; in this at regular intervals stood slabs giving warnings, some in Greek, others in Latin characters, of the law of purity (τὸν τῆς ἁγνείας ... νόμον), to wit that no foreigner was permitted to enter the holy place (μηδένα ἀλλόφυλον ἐντὸς τοῦ ἁγίου παριέναι).[58]

Both Josephus and Philo also attest to the death penalty for transgressors:

> *Josephus:* Such, then, was the first court. Within it and not far distant was a second one, accessible by a few steps and surrounded by a stone balustrade with an inscription prohibiting entrance of foreigner under threat of the penalty of death (θανατικῆς ἀπειλουμένης τῆς ζημίας).[59]

---

56 *OGIS* 598 (complete) and *SEG* 8.169 (fragmentary). For later rabbinic sources, see: m. Kelim 1.8–9; b. ʿErub. 104b; b. Pesaḥ. 3b.
57 *Contra* Stephen R. Llewelyn and Dionysia van Beek, "Reading the Temple Warning as a Greek Visitor," *JSJ* 42 (2011): 1–22, esp. 7. Llewelyn and van Beek assert that the death penalty is unusual here in light of other Hellenistic evidence, but see the varieties of divine punishment in Greek/Roman contexts in chapter 3. One slight distinction here is that what is left ambiguous in other Greek/Roman sacred space inscriptions is explicit in the Jerusalem warning.
58 Josephus, *J.W.* 5.193–194 (adapted from Thackeray, LCL). See also *J.W.* 6.122–5; *Ag. Ap.* 2.102–7.
59 Josephus, *Ant.* 15.417 (Marcus and Wikgren, LCL). Other successive boundaries/limitations are noted in 15.418–420. See also Josephus's comments in *Against Apion* 2.102: "All those who saw the design of our temple (*constructionem templi nostri*) know what it was like and how its sanctity was kept intact and impenetrable (*intransgressibilem eius purificationis integritatem*)." Translation from John M.G. Barclay, *Flavius Josephus: Translation and Commentary, Volume 10. Against Apion*, ed. Steve Mason (Leiden: Brill, 2007), 222.

Philo: Still more abounding and peculiar is the zeal of them all for the temple (ἡ περὶ τὸ ἱερὸν σπουδή), and the strongest proof of this is that death without appeal is the sentence against those of other races who penetrate into its inner confines (θάνατος ἀπαραίτητος ὥρισται κατὰ τῶν εἰς τοὺς ἐντὸς περιβόλους παρελθόντων).[60]

Philo is horribly disturbed by Gaius's plan to defile the temple; this was not interpreted as an isolated incident for Jews of a particular city, but as something that "brought danger not on one part of the Jews only, but on the entire nation" (*Legat.* 184, οὐχ ἑνὶ μέρει τοῦ Ἰουδαϊκοῦ τὸν κίνδυνον ἐπάγον ἀλλὰ συλλήβδην ἅπαντι τῷ ἔθνει).[61]

Several scholars since Elias Bickerman have proposed various ideas about the identity of the authority underlying the inscription (who had the right or the power to execute the death penalty?) and the identity of the prohibited 'foreigners' (who was the intended target of the inscription?).[62] There is no clear consensus on either question, but what is undeniable from the literary and material evidence is that such inscriptions existed within the temple precincts of Jerusalem, and that some authority would exact the death penalty upon the transgressors. It is inconceivable that these inscriptions would be so attested in contexts about the sanctity of the temple—whose purity was of highest regard in Judaisms of various forms as seen in the Hebrew Bible, early Jewish literature, and even in Qumran—and then for the penalty of transgression to remain unenforced.[63]

---

60 Philo, *Legat.* 212 (Colson, LCL).
61 See also *Legat.* 198 where there is no greater harm done to the Jews than defiling the temple. Elsewhere, Philo upholds the sanctity of the temple *literally* and not just figuratively or allegorically as he is often interpreted (*Migr.* 92). See John M.G. Barclay, *Jews in the Mediterranean Diaspora: From Alexander to Trajan (323 BCE–117 CE)* (Edinburgh: T&T Clark, 1996), 418–421.
62 Elias J. Bickerman, "The Warning Inscription of Herod's Temple," *JQR* 37.4 (1947): 387–405; S. Zeitlin, "The Warning Inscription of the Temple," *JQR* 38.1 (1947): 111–116; A. M. Rabello, "The 'Lex de Templo Hierosolymitano', Prohibiting Gentiles from Entering Jerusalem's Sanctuary," *CNFI* 21 (1970–71): 3.28–32 and 4.28–32; Joseph M. Baumgarten, "Exclusions from the Temple: Proselytes and Agrippa I," *JJS* 33 (1982): 215–225; Peretz Segal, "The Penalty of the Warning Inscription from the Temple of Jerusalem," *IEJ* 39 (1989): 79–84; Daniel R. Schwartz, *Agrippa I: The Last King of Judaea* (Tübingen: Mohr Siebeck, 1990), 127–130; Llewelyn and van Beek, "Reading the Temple Warning."
63 In modern terms, this would be akin for a sovereign nation to secure its borders using the threat of prosecution for trespassers then never prosecuting the wrongdoer. The implication of this policy would be to effectively render the 'sanctity' of the borders, so to speak, completely useless. That others recognized Jewish sacred places as 'inviolable' is noted in a papyrus in *CPJ* 3.1449 (Lower Egypt, late 2nd BCE[?]): βασιλίσσης καὶ βασιλέως προσταξάντων ἀντὶ τῆς προανακει μένης περὶ τῆς ἀναθέσε ως τῆς προσευχῆς πλάκος ἡ ὑπογεγραμμένη ἐπιγραφήτω· βασιλεὺς Πτολεμαῖος Εὐεργέτης τὴν προσευχὴν ἄσυλον. REGINA ET REX IUSSERUNT = "By the orders of the queen and king, in place of the previous plaque concerning the dedication of the

4.5 Qumran

Perhaps apart from Paul's peculiar statement to the Corinthian assembly, "You are the temple of God" (1 Cor 3:16, ναὸς θεοῦ ἐστε), no other group in the ancient Mediterranean so imagined itself as a temple as the community at Qumran.[64] This concept of community as temple signaled a significant paradigm shift within temple discourses in antiquity.[65] Other Greek, Roman, and Israelite/Jewish sources show concern with behavior and boundaries around a *physical* sacred space or temple, but the Qumran community conceptualizes a *metaphorical* sacred space that is constituted by members of the group.[66] The former perspective recognizes supplicants and sacred spaces as discrete entities. People may enter or exit a temple, and though the corruption or purity of a person could affect the purity of a temple, they were never understood to be the same thing. The latter perspective observed in Qumran and in Paul, however, is quite different since the corruption and purity of individual members and of the sacred space to which they belonged are intimately tied together, and at times, nearly indistinguishable.

---

proseuche [synagogue?] let what is written below be written. King Ptolemy Euergetes (proclaimed) the *proseuche* (is) inviolable. The queen and king gave the order." See also another papyrus *CPJ* 1.129 (Fayum – Middle Egypt, 218 BCE) that confirmed the protected status of the προσευχή τῶν Ἰουδαίων.

64 See Bertil Gärtner, *The Temple and the Community in Qumran and the New Testament*, SNTSMS 1 (Cambridge: Cambridge University Press, 1965). In the following citations of primary sources, I follow the common practice of using the names of well-known scrolls rather than their manuscript numbers.

65 Carol Newsom names the metaphor of community as temple as a "quite unprecedented transference of meaning" (*The Self as Symbolic Space: Constructing Identity and Community at Qumran* [Leiden: Brill, 2004], 156). Gärtner argues that this is an innovation in Qumran because no such parallel for this symbolism exists in other Jewish evidence (*The Temple and the Community*, 47). See also OT Peshitta on Jeremiah 7:4b which originally read, "This (MT: המה / LXX: ἐστίν) is the temple of the Lord, the temple of the Lord, the temple of the Lord" = "The temple of the Lord, the temple of the Lord, you (pl. = *'ntwn*) are the temple of the Lord."

66 There are also texts that speak of a future temple in eschatological terms, but in these accounts, the people of God remain separate from the temple structure. E.g.: Ezek 37:26–28; 40:1–43:12; Hag 2:9; Tob 14:5; 1 En. 90:28–29; Jub. 1:28; 2 Bar. 4:2–6; 4 Ezra 10:51–56; Sib. Or. 5.422–427. On Jewish expectations of the restoration of the temple, see E. P. Sanders, *Jesus and Judaism* (Philadelphia: Fortress Press, 1985), 77–90. For the significance of the image and symbol of the "temple," see Gregory Stevenson, *Power and Place: Temple and Identity in the Book of Revelation* (Berlin: Walter de Gruyter, 2001), passim.

Some have questioned whether the interpretation of Qumran as temple is borne out by the evidence, but they represent the minority position.[67] One caveat that must be stated at the outset, however, is that the Scrolls do not present a monolithic view vis-à-vis temple, anthropology, pneumatology, and so on. Scholars of the Dead Sea Scrolls have argued at length about the complexities of the textual history as well as the development of the community itself.[68] The follow-

---

[67] The majority position is represented by the following (and cited in relevant notes below): Matthew Black, *The Scrolls and Christian Origins: Studies in the Jewish Background of the New Testament* (London: Nelson, 1961), 42; Georg Klinzing, *Umdeutung des Kultus in der Qumrangemeinde und im Neuen Testament* (Göttingen: Vandenhoeck & Ruprecht, 1971), 50–93; Lawrence H Schiffman, "Community Without Temple: The Qumran Community's Withdrawal from the Jerusalem Temple," in *Gemeinde ohne Tempel = Community Without Temple: zur Substituierung und Transformation des Jerusalemer Tempels und seines Kults im Alten Testament, antiken Judentum und frühen Christentum*, ed. Beate Ego et al. (Tübingen: Mohr Siebeck, 1999), 267–284; Colleen M. Conway, "Toward a Well-Formed Subject: The Function of Purity Language in the Serek Ha-Yahad," *JSP* 21 (2000): 103–120; Robert A. Kugler, "Rewriting Rubrics: Sacrifice and the Religion of Qumran," in *Religion in the Dead Sea Srolls*, ed. J. J. Collins and R. A. Kugler (Grand Rapids: Eerdmans, 2000), 91; Florentino García Martínez, "Priestly Functions in a Community without Temple," in *Gemeinde ohne Tempel*, 303–319; Jodi Magness, *The Archaeology of Qumran and the Dead Sea Scrolls* (Grand Rapids: Eerdmans, 2002), 32–38, 119; Hannah K. Harrington, "Purity and the Dead Sea Scrolls—Current Issues," *CBR* 4.3 (2006): 397–428; Albert L.A. Hogeterp, *Paul and God's Temple: A Historical Interpretation of Cultic Imagery in the Corinthian Correspondence* (Leuven: Peeters, 2006), 75–114; Cecilia Wassen, "Visions of the Temple: Conflicting Images of the Eschaton," *Svensk exegetisk årsbok* 76 (2011): 41–59. The opposing arguments are found in: Philip R. Davies, "The Ideology of the Temple in the Damascus Document," *JJS* 33.1–2 (1982): 287–301; John R. Lanci, *A New Temple for Corinth: Rhetorical and Archaeological Approaches to Pauline Imagery* (New York: Peter Lang, 1997), 7–23. Davies was published before 4QMMT was made available in 1994, and as far as I can tell, Lanci does not cite 4QMMT or CD at all. His focus lies exclusively in three passages from 1QS (5:5–6; 8:4–10; 9:3–6) and a fragment from 4QFlorilegium. Lanci is also wrong to read the community-as-temple motif as temple-replacement. Finally, he commits a logical fallacy when he concludes: "Qumranic temple theology is not easily clarified ... harmonization of the different theologies is itself problematic. The differences may be the result of assorted authors, or perhaps because the texts come from diverse periods, in the development of the Qumran community" (17). I fully accept his conclusion that Qumran texts should not be forced into *one* theology, but his argument cuts both ways: just because one passage adduced from the scrolls does not mean *x*, that does not mean other passages from the same text or other texts could not mean *x*.

[68] In current Qumran scholarship, it is well known that there were stratifications of various texts and developments of the community itself, but it is not the place here to discuss these issues. I fully acknowledge that the Qumran community was not a static entity with a consistent and codified self-understanding from one scroll to another, but I use the evidence to show that in whatever iteration of this Jewish community during a given time period, ideas of the community as temple existed. Whether the view espoused by one text disagrees with that of another text is ultimately of no consequence to the overall aim of this chapter. For the sake of argument, how-

ing discussion does not claim to present "*the* view of x" in Qumran. But the extant evidence, even with sometimes conflicting voices, are marshaled to show how other Jewish groups in the Mediterranean world roughly contemporaneous with Paul understood and discussed concepts such as temple, purity, spirit, and transgression.

The Scrolls appeal to a host of architectural metaphors to describe the Qumran community, reinforcing the notion that this group understood itself as a kind of building: "wall" (הומה), "foundation" (סוד or יסוד), "[precious] cornerstone" (פנה [יקר]), "dwelling" (מעון), and "house" (בית).[69] The authors of the Scrolls frequently identify members of their community as priests, using titles such as "sons of Zadok" or "sons of Aaron" to refer to certain members of the group.[70] It would be strange indeed to say one is a priest without the accompanying sanctuary within which to perform one's priestly duties. An exemplary use of such language is found in 1QS 8:4–10 that parallels Paul's words in 1 Corinthians:

> [4]When such men as these come to be in Israel, [5]then the council of the community being established in truth, an eternal planting, house of holiness for Israel, and holy [6]of holies for Aaron; true witnesses to justice, chosen by God's will to atone for the land and to repay [7]the wicked their reward. It will be the tested wall, the precious cornerstone. [8]Its foundations will neither be shaken nor swayed, (*vacat*) a dwelling, a holy of holies [9]for Aaron, all of them knowing the covenant of justice, offering a sweet odor. They will be a house of perfection and truth in Israel, [10]upholding the covenant of eternal statutes. They will be an ac-

---

ever, I will use phrases such as "the Qumran community" or "the sectarians," but readers need not take this to mean that all scrolls agree on the various concepts discussed below. On the various debates over the chronology of Qumran and textual developments, see the discussions and literature cited in: Alison Schofield, *From Qumran to the Yaḥad: A New Paradigm of Textual Development for* The Community Rule, STDJ 77 (Leiden: Brill, 2009), esp. 21–67; Dennis Mizzi and Jodi Magness, "Was Qumran Abandoned at the End of the First Century BCE?" *JBL* 135.2 (2016): 301–320.

69 See 1QS (Rule of the Community or Serek Hayaḥad) 3:25; 8:5, 7, 8, 9; 11:8; 1QSa 1:12; 1QH[a] (Hodayot) 10:12; 15:11–12; 16; 1QM 12:2; 4Q174 (4QFlorilegium) f1–2i:6 ("sanctuary of humankind"); 4Q249e f1 i–3:8; 4Q258 6:2, 4; 7:4; 4Q259 2:16; 4Q403 f1 i:41. For expanded discussion of these metaphors and their intertextual connection to Isa 28:16 ("See, I am laying in Zion a foundation stone, a tested stone, a precious cornerstone, a sure foundation. The one who trusts will not be alarmed."), see Carol A. Newsom, *Self as Symbolic Space*, 156–160. See also 1 Cor 3:9 ("You are God's field, God's building") that links agricultural and architectural imagery in reference to sacred space, and of course, 1 Cor 3:16 ("Do you not know that you are the temple of God?").

70 E.g., CD (Cairo Genizah copy of the Damascus Document) 3.21–4.1; 1QS 5:2, 9, 21; 9:7; 1QSa 1:2, 23, 24; 2:3, 13; 1QM (War Scroll) 7:10; 17:2; 1QSb 3:22; 4Q174 f1–2ii:4; 4Q249c 1:5; 4Q249f f1–3:2; 4Q249 g f1–2:1; f3 7:13; 4Q258 2:1; 7:7; 4Q266 2:3, 19; 4Q267 f5 3:8; 4Q279 f5 4; 4Q390 f1–3; 4Q397 f6 13:14; 11Q19 (Temple Scroll) 22:5; 34:13; 11Q20 5:25.

ceptable sacrifice; to atone for the land and to decide judgment of wickedness, so that there will be no more iniquity.

The reference above to "an eternal planting" in 1QS 8:5 (מטעת עולם) harks back to Genesis, where the garden was envisioned as a prototype of the later temple.[71] Two other descriptors for the sect, "a holy house for Israel" (בית קודש לישראל) and "a holy of holies for Aaron" (קודש קודשים לאהרון), state in no uncertain terms that this sectarian community indeed viewed itself as not just a building, but a type of temple.[72] No Jewish community would have referred to itself as קודש קודשים (1QS 8:5–6, 8) without recognizing what such a statement would have implied about *the* holy of holies located in Jerusalem (see further discussion below).[73]

Another text, 4QFlorilegium, contains language about the sectarians viewing themselves as a temple: "And he [God] said to build him a sanctuary of humankind (מקדש אדם), in which they shall offer sacrifices before him, the works of the Law." Obedience to law as a form of liturgical duty is a common trope in the Dead Sea Scrolls, but more important is the expression, מקדש אדם, that has been interpreted in various ways.[74] Some interpreters read the phrase to mean

---

[71] See 1QS 11:8; 4Q418 f81 10–14; 4Q500; 1 Enoch 10:16; 24–26; 84:6; 93:2–5; Jub 3:12; 8:19; 1QapGen (Genesis Apocryphon) 14:13–17. For discussion of this imagery in Second Temple literature, see Patrick A. Tiller, "The 'Eternal Planting' in the Dead Sea Scrolls," *DSD* 4.3 (1997): 312–335. See also Julie Hughes, *Scriptural Allusions and Exegesis in the Hodayot* (Leiden: Brill, 2006), 150–55; Paul Swarup, *The Self-Understanding of the Dead Sea Scrolls Community: An Eternal Planting, A House of Holiness* (London: T&T Clark, 2006). Wassen ("Visions of the Temple," 55) argues: "One would think that the garden metaphor would be particularly appropriate at Qumran since the garden made for an ideal sanctuary without an altar."

[72] See also: 3Q15 (Copper Scroll) 11:7; 4Q320 f4 iii; 11Q19 46–47.

[73] Similar language occurs in: 1QS 9:6; 1QSb 4:28; 4Q258 6:2; 4Q259 2:14, 17; 4Q403 f1 i:41, 44; 4Q418 f81 4. The implied criticism of the Jerusalem temple goes beyond just the use of one particular phrase. The Community Rule also maps unto the community the atoning activities that occurred at the temple. It asserts that the community "shall atone for the land and shall return to the wicked their reward ... [the community] shall be an acceptable sacrifice, in order to atone for the land and to determine the judgment of wickedness" (1QS 8:6–7, 10; also 9:4–5). The creation of a "rival temple" is not unique to Qumran, though it is unique in constructing such an idea in symbolic terms. Various other Jewish communities during the Second Temple created physical rivals to the Temple of Jerusalem: (1) Elephantine; (2) Mt. Gerizim; and (3) Leontopolis. For discussion, see Jörg Frey, "Temple and Rival Temple—The Cases of Elephantine, Mt. Gerizim and Leontopolis," in *Gemeinde ohne Tempel*, 171–203.

[74] For various interpretations of this phrase and its context in 4QFlor, see: Gärtner, *The Temple and the Community*, 34–35; Allan J. McNicol, "The Eschatological Temple in the Qumran Pesher 4QFlorilegium 1:1–7," *OJRS* 5.2 (1977): 133–141; Daniel R. Schwartz, "The Three Temples of 4QFlorilegium," *RevQ* 10 (1979): 83–91; Devorah Dimant, "4QFlorilegium and the Idea of the

something like "a sanctuary among humankind" or "a manmade sanctuary," but the lack of the preposition ב and other contextual clues militate against such free interpretations.[75] Other texts have clearly shown how the Qumran sectarians referred to themselves using temple-related terms, and 4QFlorilegium only makes explicit that which was implied by the use of architectural terms elsewhere. 4Q164, for example, illustrates a similar interpretative strategy when it exegetes the architectural metaphors from Isaiah 54:11–12.[76]

Besides the architectural elements already noted, the above quotation from 1QS also shows the personnel dimension of sacred space. Every temple retains within its precincts a select class of people who served as priests or priestesses, and the same is true at Qumran. The reference to "Aaron" already makes such a connection to priesthood, but other factors also emphasize the priestly self-understanding of this community. They identify themselves as a special group "chosen" by God, to complete various duties that are akin to what the priests would have performed at the Jerusalem temple: making atonement, performing sacrifices, and upholding the covenant (1QS 8:6, 9–10; also 4QFlor f1 2i:6).[77]

Community as Temple," in *Hellenica et Judaica: Hommage à Valentin Nikiprowetzky*, ed. André Caquot et al. (Leuven: Peeters, 1986), 165–189; Michael O. Wise, "4QFlorilegium and the Temple of Adam," *RevQ* 15.1–2 (1991–92): 103–132; George J. Brooke, "Miqdash Adam, Eden and the Qumran Community," in *Gemeinde ohne Tempel*, 285–301; Timothy Wardle, *The Jerusalem Temple and Early Christian Identity* (Tübingen: Mohr Siebeck, 2010), 157–162. Wise ("Temple of Adam," 108) contains a very useful table of previous scholarship regarding how the "temples" in 4QFlor have been interpreted. On the relationship between temple sacrifices and Torah observance, see Lawrence H. Schiffman, "Qumran Temple? The Literary Evidence," *JAJ* 7.1 (2016): 71–85.

75 E.g.: John M. Allegro, "Fragments of a Qumran Scroll of Eschatological *Midrashim*," *JBL* 77.4 (1958): 350–354 (352: "a man-made sanctuary"); Y. Yadin, "A Midrash on 2 Sam. Vii and Ps. I–ii (4Q Florilegium)," *IEJ* 9.2 (1959): 95–98 (96: "a Sanctuary amongst men"); Friedrich Nötscher, "Heiligkeit in den Qumranschriften," *RevQ* 2 (1959–60): 163–181 (173: "Er ist ein von Menschenhand ... Heiligtum"). Gärtner, *The Temple and the Community*, 35: "To interpret the sentence as meaning that God commanded that a temple should be built 'among men' is too vague in this context."

76 Isa 54:11b–12a: "I will lay your foundations with sapphires, I will make your battlements with rubies." = 4Q164 f1:1–5: "'I will make sapphires your foundation.' This passage means that they founded the congregation of the Yahad on the priests, and the company of his chosen, like the sapphire among the stones ... 'I will make of rubies all your battlements.' This refers to the twelve priests who make the Urim and the Thummim shine in judgment."

77 1QS 8:9, for example, describes the community's offering of "sweet fragrance" which refers to the fragrant odor that emanates from the altar of sacred space (see Exod 29:18, 25, 41; Lev 1:9, 13; 2:12; Num 15:3, 24; 18:17). On the liturgical function of Levites at the temple, see, for examples: 1 Chr 23:2–5; 2 Chr 19:11; Ezra 6:16–18; Sir 50:1–20; Josephus, *Ant.* 11.59–63; 20.216–218; m. Sukkah 5:4; m. Tamid 7.3; m. Bikkurim 3.3; m. Pesahim 5.7; m. Arakhin 2.6. See other primary and

Around this complex network of ideas between temple and priests, there are three other details that require further elaboration: (1) distinction between the pure and impure; (2) maintenance of membership; and (3) punishment for transgressions.

4.5.1 (Im)purity of the Temple

The maintenance of purity in sacred spaces was paramount since sanctuaries were understood to house the presence of the gods. This was true not only in the context of Greek and Roman religions, but also in Israelite/Jewish contexts.[78] Accounts in the Hebrew Bible show the threat that human sin and impurity posed for God's immanent presence among the Israelites. Baruch A. Levine describes the dangerous nature of impurity:

> One becoming impure as the result of an offense against the deity introduced a kind of demonic contagion into the community. The more horrendous the offense, the greater the threat to the purity of the sanctuary and the surrounding community by the presence of the offender, who was a carrier of impurity … The deity had made a vital concession to the Israelites by consenting to dwell amidst the impurities endemic to the human situation (Leviticus 16:16). If his continued residence was to be realized, Yahweh required an extreme degree of purity (Exodus 25:8).[79]

---

secondary literature cited in Torleif Elgvin, "Temple Mysticism and the Temple of Men," in *The Dead Sea Scrolls: Texts and Context*, ed. C. Hempel (Leiden: Brill, 2010), 229 n. 5. For material evidence that corroborates Qumranic cultic activity, see Jodi Magness, "Were Sacrifices Offered at Qumran? The Animal Bone Deposits Reconsidered," *JAJ* 7 (2016): 5–34. While she is less optimistic about the idea of Qumran as temple, she concludes that Qumran "apparently functioned … as a sacred precinct in which animal sacrifices were offered" (34).

78 See Walter Burkert, "The Meaning and Function of the Temple in Classical Greece," in *Temple in Society*, ed. Michael V. Fox (Winona Lake, IN: Eisenbrauns, 1988), 27–47; idem, *Greek Religion*, trans. John Raffan (Malden, MA: Blackwell Publishing, 1985), 84–98; Stevenson, *Power and Place*, 42–54; 121–134.

For sanctuaries as the locus of divine presence or power, see: Silius Italicus, *Punica* 10.432–33; Livy, *Ab urbe cond.* 6.33.4–6; Herodotus, *Hist.* 1.159; Dio Cassius, *Rom. hist.* 41.61.1–4; 42.26.1–4; Diodorus Siculus, *Bib. hist.* 16.27.1–2; and discussion in chapter 3. There is, however, the perpetual tension of transcendence versus immanence, but to discuss this question is beyond the scope of this present chapter. For discussion, see Stevenson, *Power and Place*, 122–28.

79 Baruch A. Levine, *In the Presence of the Lord: A Study of Cult and Some Cultic Terms in Ancient Israel* (Leiden: Brill, 1974), 75. See also Jacob Milgrom, "Israel's Sanctuary: The Priestly 'Picture of Dorian Gray'," *RB* 83 (1976): 392: "Impurity was feared because it was considered demonic. It was an unending threat to the gods themselves and especially to their temples, as

Since the Qumran community envisioned itself as a kind of temple, the sectarians carefully distinguished between the pure and impure in order to guarantee the continued presence of God.⁸⁰

The Scrolls speak frequently about the workings of the "spirit of holiness" and "God's spirit" in their own community as validation that God now dwelt within their group.⁸¹ The Temple Scroll highlights this availability of divine presence to sectarian worshipers.⁸² It also notes that an impure person may not enter into the sanctuary because that would "defile" the sacred space.⁸³ In his study of purity at Qumran, Michael Newton asserts: "the rules of purity must be kept because God is present and he will only remain present as long as his dwelling place is kept pure."⁸⁴ 1QSa 2:3–9 outlines the following demands for purity that are relevant for the present discussion:

> ³No man afflicted with any human uncleanness ⁴shall enter the assembly of God (קהל אל). No man afflicted with these ⁵shall receive his office from the congregation. No man afflicted physically ... ⁷or a tottering old man who cannot do his part in the congregation ⁸shall enter to take their place in the congregation among the men of reputation, ⁹for the angels of holiness are among their congregation (כיא מלאכי קודש בעד[תם]).

---

exemplified by the images of protector gods set before temple entrances (e.g., the *šēdu* and *lamassu* in Mesopotamia and the lion-gargoyles in Egypt) and, above all, by the elaborate cathartic and apotropaic rites to rid buildings of demons and prevent their return."

80 For a helpful overview of recent research, see Harrington, "Purity and the Dead Sea Scrolls."
81 E.g., 1QS 3:7; 4:21; 8:16; 1QSb 2:22–24; 1QHᵃ 8:30; 15:10; 16:13; 20:15; 23:33; CD 2:12. For biblical use of God's spirit in reference to divine presence, see: Gen 6:3; Ps 51:11; Ezek 36:25–27; 39:29; Isa 44:3; Hag 2:4–5. Also 11Q19 (Temple Scroll) 51:7–9.
82 11Q19 29:2–10: "These (are) [...] for burnt-offerings ... [...] In the house upon which I [shall make] my name [to dwell ...] burnt-offerings, [day] after day, according to the ruling of this regulation, continually, from the children of Israel together with their vow offerings. And all the gifts that they are to bring to find favor with Me. And they will find favor. They will be My people and I will be theirs, forever. I shall dwell with them for all eternity. I shall sanctify My [te]mple with My glory, for I will make My glory to dwell upon it until the day of creation, when I Myself will create My temple; I will establish it for Myself forever, in fulfillment of the covenant that I made with Jacob at Bethel." Translation adapted from Florentino García Martínez and Eibert J.C. Tigchelaar, eds., *The Dead Sea Scrolls Study Edition* (Leiden: Brill, 1999), 1228–1289. See also: 11Q19 45:12–14; 46:9–12; 47:3–6, 11; 52:15–16; 53:9–10; 56:5.
83 11Q19 45:10: "They shall not enter my sanctuary (מקדשי) while unclean, for that would defile it (וטמאו)."
84 Michael Newton, *The Concept of Purity at Qumran and in the Letters of Paul* (Cambridge: Cambridge University Press, 1985), 51.

These demands are grounded by the final clause of this list: "for the angels of holiness are among their congregation." The communion with heavenly beings hints at the vision of this congregation as a sacred space.[85]

Qumran's high regard for purity followed the accepted notion that divine presence was incompatible with a polluted sanctuary, and because the state of the Jerusalem Temple had fallen to an unacceptable level of impurity, the sectarians believed that God had abandoned that sacred space, or at the very least that the divine presence in that specific place had become tenuous.[86] Moreover, the Qumran community asserted that *their* temple was now the locus of divine presence, which in turn implied that the *other* temple—the one located in Jerusalem— was not.[87] The halakhic section of 4QMMT (Miqṣat Ma'ase ha-Torah) contains

---

[85] See 1QH[a] 14:16; 4Q400–407 (known as *Songs of the Sabbath Sacrifice*). See also: Ps 24:3–6; Isa 6:1–3. In her study that investigates the relationship between impurity and demonic power, Cecilia Wassen concludes: "As a pure sanctuary where humans and angels could meet, the community had to be vigilant about the threat posed by the forces of evil" ("What Do Angels Have against the Blind and the Dead? Rules of Exclusion in the Dead Sea Scrolls," in *Common Judaism: Explorations in Second Temple Judaism*, ed. Wayne O. McCready and Adele Reinhartz [Minneapolis: Fortress Press, 2008], 129).

[86] Schwartz, "Three Temples," 83–91; Eyal Regev, "Temple and Righteousness in Qumran and Early Christianity: Tracing the Social Difference Between the Two Movements," in *Text, Thought, and Practice in Qumran and Early Christianity: Proceedings of the Ninth International Symposium of the Orion Center for the Study of the Dead Sea Scrolls and Associated Literature, Jointly Sponsored by the Hebrew University Center for the Study of Christianity, 11–13 January, 2004*, ed. Ruth A. Clements and Daniel R. Schwartz (Leiden: Brill, 2009), 63–87; Wassen, "Visions of the Temple." The fragile nature of God's presence is already presaged in the Hebrew Bible. See, for examples, 2 Chr 23:19; Ezek 11:22; Lam 2:7. Cited in Milgrom, *Leviticus 1–16*, 258–9. For other Jewish parallels for the fragile nature of divine presence in the temple, see the account of the siege of Jerusalem in Josephus, *J.W.* 6.299–300 ("the priests went by night into the inner temple, as their custom, to perform their service, they said that, at first, they felt a shaking, and heard a great noise, and after that they heard a sound of a great multitude saying, 'let us leave this place' [μεταβαίνομεν ἐντεῦθεν]"). This story is repeated in Tacitus, *Hist.* 5.13: "Suddenly the doors of the shrine opened and a voice of more than a mortal tone cried: 'The gods are departing.'"

[87] Lawrence Schiffman calls it "community as a substitute Temple" in "Qumran Temple?," 72. Dimant is more measured in her opinion that the sectarians may have considered the Second Temple to be "temporarily polluted" ("4QFlorilegium," 187). See also Martin Goodman, "The Qumran Sectarians and the Temple in Jerusalem," in Hempel, *Dead Sea Scrolls: Texts and Context*, 263–73; Hilary Evans Kapfer, "The Relationship between the Damascus Document and the Community Rule: Attitudes toward the Temple as a Test Case," *DSD* 14 (2007): 152–77. The cited literature here indicates that the Qumran community's attitude toward the Temple is multi-faceted and could be construed in a variety of ways along the spectrum between positive and negative attitude toward the Second Temple. The primary sources cited above show, however, that *some* at Qumran did hold negative views about the Jerusalem Temple. Whether the Qumran com-

strong rhetoric against what "they" of Jerusalem practice as opposed to what "we" of Qumran practice, particularly as these activities relate to temple service.⁸⁸

Another text, the pesher on Habakkuk, castigates the actions of the Jerusalem high priest: "The city refers to Jerusalem, where the Wicked Priest committed his abhorrent deeds (מעשי תועבות), defiling the Temple of God (ויטמא את מקדש אל)."⁸⁹ The author then explains that the "abhorrent deeds" was the priest's greed in the form of exploitation of the poor.⁹⁰ Also, the Damascus Document (CD 4:15–18) identifies "three traps of Belial" as fornication (זנות), wealth (הון), and defiling the sanctuary (טמא המקדש). All of these anxieties concerning the purity of the temple parallel Paul's framework for preserving the holiness of God's temple in 1 Corinthians 5:1–13, 10:1–22, and 11:17–34 (also 1 Cor 3:17).⁹¹

4.5.2 Maintenance of Membership

If the community must remain pure in order to guarantee the continued presence of God's spirit among them, then how did it go about maintaining the necessary levels of purity among its members? The Community Rule, Damascus Document, and various other scrolls from Qumran evince elaborate processes of vetting those who desired to be a part of this community and of scrutinizing already confirmed members. These texts also reveal the ideology of this community as one with strict distinctions made between insiders and outsiders.

First, there is a strict vetting process by which a person is allowed to enter this community. 1QS 6:14 declares: "Every person of Israel who volunteers to join the Council of the Community shall be examined by the leader of the congrega-

---

munity did in fact withdraw from participating in the Jerusalem cult ultimately has no bearing on my overall analysis.

88 Eyal Regev, "Abominated Temple and a Holy Community: The Formation of the Notions of Purity and Impurity in Qumran," *DSD* 10.2 (2003): 243–278. For examples, see 4QMMT C:7–8: "But you know that we have separated from the majority of the people and from all their uncleanness" and CD 5:6–7: "They also defile the sanctuary, for they do not separate clean from unclean according to the Law." See 1QpHab 8:8–13 (reference to "the Wicked Priest"); CD 6:16–17 (= Lev 10:10; 11:47; 20:25); 20:22–23. Hanne von Weissenberg argues that 4QMMT is more positive toward its concern for the Jerusalem Temple ("The Centrality of the Temple in 4QMMT," in Hempel, *Dead Sea Scrolls: Texts and Contexts*, 293–305).
89 1QpHab 12:7–9. See also 1QpHab 9:4–12; CD 1:3–5; 1Q14 f8; 4QFlor.
90 1QpHab 12:9–10. See also, CD 6:11–17; 1QpHab 8:8–13; 12:6–10; 4Q366 f3 ii:20–22. See Regev, "Abominated Temple," 257–58; Klawans, *Impurity and Sin*, 69–71.
91 Brian S. Rosner, "Temple and Holiness in 1 Corinthians 5," *TynBul* 42.1 (1991): 137–145.

tion concerning his understanding and his deeds (ולמעשיו לשכלו).''[92] Once the person is approved for entry (1QS 6:16a), the process of his full acceptance would take place over a period of two years. The candidate is forbidden from partaking of the טהרת הרבים ("pure meal of the congregation") during the first year and is forbidden from partaking of the משקה הרבים ("drink of the congregation") until the end of his second year (1QS 6:16 and 20, respectively). These meals are distinct markers of the understanding of the Qumran community as a type of sacred space.[93] The candidate's property also enters a similar probationary period, initially kept separate from the community, then put under the authority of the "overseer" (מבקר), and eventually fully incorporated into the rest (1QS 6:17, 19–20, and 22).

Second—and related to the extensive process of acceptance as outlined above—the community draws a clear boundary between those who belong within and those who remain without. No one is allowed to keep his feet in two worlds. In other words, the community required complete adherence among its members: one could not enter or exit as one might wish. The Community Rule pronounces abundant blessings upon their own and severe curses upon others (יברככה versus ארור אתה in 1QS 2:2 and 5, respectively). The author calls one group, "all the men of the membership of God" (2:1–2, כול אנשי גורל אל) and another group, "all the men of the membership of Belial" (2:4–5, כול אנשי גורל בליעל).[94] Moreover, the reference to blessings from Numbers 6:24–26 for the insiders are matched equally by imprecations invoked against the outsiders:[95]

---

92 See also 1QS 5:21, 23; 6:18; CD 13:11; Josephus, *J.W.* 2.138–140; *Life* 10–12. On "the Essene hypothesis" involving the evidence from Josephus, see Kenneth Atkinson and Jodi Magness, "Josephus's Essenes and the Qumran Community," *JBL* 129.2 (2010): 317–42; Jonathan Klawans, "The Essene Hypothesis: Insights from Religion 101," *DSD* 23 (2016): 51–78.
93 Michael Newton suggests (*Concept of Purity*, 34):

Although they [i.e. the meals] were not considered to be 'cultic' in the sense of 'mediating salvation' ... they were no less expiatory than the praise and perfection of way and indeed the whole of life as it was lived in the community. Furthermore, the way in which they were eaten sought to recreate the conditions under which the priests ate the offerings in the Temple.

See also *Concept of Purity*, 35–36 for discussion of what Newton calls the "temple-like character that is attached to the meal."
94 The incompatibility of one deity with the other is noted also by Paul in 1 Cor 10:1–22 and 2 Cor 6:15.
95 Numbers 6:24–26: "May the Lord bless you and keep you. May the Lord make his face to shine upon you and be gracious to you. May the Lord lift up his countenance upon you and give you peace."

Blessings (1QS 2:2–4):
²May He bless you (יברככה) with all ³good thing and may He preserve you from all evil (וישמורכה מכול רע).
May He enlighten (ויאיר) your mind with wisdom for life and may He show you favor (ויחונכה) with the knowledge of eternal things (בדעת עולמים).
⁴And may He lift up His gracious countenance (וישא פני חסדיו) upon you for eternal peace (לשלום עולמים).

Curses (1QS 2:5–9):
⁵May you be cursed (ארור) for all your wicked, guilty deeds (בכול מעשי רשע אשמתכה)[96].
⁶May God hand you over to terror by the hand of implacable avengers (נוקמי נקם)[97]. May He bring destruction (כלה) after you by the hands of those who repay ⁷evil with evil
May you be cursed (ארור) without mercy (לאין רחמים), according to the darkness of your deeds. And cursed (וזעום) are you in the darkness of ⁸eternal fire (אש עולמים). May God have no mercy when you call on him, may He not forgive by atoning for your sins (לכפר עווניך).
⁹May He lift up His angry countenance (ישא פני אפו) upon you for vengeance (לנקמתכה), and may there be no peace (ולוא שלום...) for you by the mouth of an intercessor.

The curses are noticeably longer, which some scholars have understood as an intentional way to highlight the dangers of apostasy before new members.[98] Both sets contain a threefold structure with parallel terminology, where positive

---

96 אשמה occurs throughout the Hebrew Bible to refer to incurring "guilt" before God or to a "guilt" offering that must be made. E.g., Lev 4:13, 22; 5:3, 4, 19; Num 5:6; 18:9; 1 Sam 6:3, 4, 17; Isa 24:6; Jer 2:3; 50:7; 51:5; Ezek 22:4; 44:29; Hos 4:15; 10:2; 13:16; Hab 1:11; Ps 5:10; 68:21; Prov 14:9. In the Septuagint, אשמה is most often translated using the πλημμελ- word group. In Greek material culture, πλημμελ- words are rare, but two occurrences are relevant for the present discussion: *LSAM* 28 (Teos, 14–37 CE) and *IIasos* 247 (Iasos, imperial period). The first inscription, a *lex sacra* concerning the temple of Dionysos and its regulations, concludes: "if any person incurs guilt, that person is *asebē* (lines 17–18, τὸν δὲ εἴς τι τούτων πλημμελήσαντα εἶν[αι ἀσε]βῆ)." The second fragmentary inscription describes guilt regarding certain funds (lines 5–6, τὸν ἰς τὰ καθωσιωμένα τοῖς Σεβαστοῖς πλημμελοῦντα). Kaja Harter-Uibopuu discusses this inscription in the context of offenses such as *asebeia* or *hierosylia* and notes the following regarding possible punishments for these acts: "Während die *asebeia* auf jeden Fall den Ausschluß aus der Kultgemeinschaft als Folge einer Verurteilung nach sich zog, werden auf die *hierosylia* noch strengere Strafen, etwa die Aberkennung aller Bürgerrechte oder sogar die Todesstrafe gestanden haben." In "Bestandsklauseln und Abänderungsverbote: Der Schutz zweckgebundener Gelder in der späthellenistischen und kaiserzeitlichen Polis," *Tyche* 28 (2013): 51–96 (92). These Greek parallels illustrate how the Qumranic understanding of "guilt" fits within the broader Hellenistic milieu.
97 Literally, "avengers of vengeance."
98 J. A. Loader, "The Model of the Priestly Blessing in 1QS," *JSJ* 14.1 (1983): 16–17.

themes outlined in the blessings mirror the negative ones in the curses.⁹⁹ The liturgical nature of these blessings and curses is borne out by the conclusion of this subsection with the exhortation that everyone is to proclaim, "Amen, amen" (1QS 2:10, אמן אמן).¹⁰⁰

Another feature of this insider-outsider boundary is the way in which the Qumran community guards itself against dangers that lie at the margins, particularly when potential members move from the outside to the inside. According to Mary Douglas, this movement is one type of social pollution that could endanger a community.¹⁰¹ The period of initiation is dangerous since the candidate remains in a liminal space that is neither fully inside nor outside the boundaries of the group.¹⁰² 1QS 2:25–3:12 addresses this uncertain period with bountiful language about purity and pollution. It promotes a new understanding among potential members while reinforcing the same among those already within. The auditor is presented with an imaginary vision of refusing the precepts of the Qumran community, and is "made to realize that it is only by subscribing to this instruction that he can obtain the knowledge necessary for purity."¹⁰³ This narrative technique, therefore, encourages the formation of a particular mindset among auditors, to equate submission to the community as submission to God.¹⁰⁴

Third, the members are taught that the community is the sole custodian over God's precepts, and to deviate from its teachings results in exclusion, if not worse. Members were expected to demonstrate right discernment concerning divine wisdom and knowledge, and a prospective member would be continually tested regarding " his understanding and deeds" (לשכלו ולמעשיו, 1QS 6:14). The pure meal of the congregation remains barred to the initiate until the first year is completed without blemish *and* until "he has been examined concerning

---

99 For examples: all good things vs. all wicked, guilty deeds; preservation from all evil vs. destruction by vengeful avengers; enlightenment vs. darkness; divine favor vs. no mercy; life vs. eternal fire; gracious countenance vs. angry countenance; and peace vs. no peace.
100 This conclusion of curses with "Amen (amen)" may be derived from a similar tradition in the Hebrew Bible: Num 5:22; Deut 27:15–26; Neh 5:13.
101 Mary Douglas, *Purity and Danger: An Analysis of Concepts of Pollution and Taboo* (London: Routledge, 1966), 122–124.
102 The person in this marginal state is dangerous because his/her status is "indefinable" (Douglas, *Purity and Danger*, 96). The following analysis of 1QS is drawn from Conway, "Toward a Well-Formed Subject."
103 Conway, "Toward a Well-Formed Subject," 115.
104 See, for example, 1QS 3:5–6, "Unclean, unclean, shall he be all the days that rejects the laws of God, refusing to be disciplined in the community of God's council."

his spirit and deeds" (לרוחו ומעשו, 1QS 6:17). The incentive to demonstrate correct knowledge of the precepts and to follow them is provided by the community's hierarchical structure. 1QS 5:23–24 commands: "they shall examine their spirit (רוחם) and deeds yearly, so that each man may be advanced in accordance with his understanding and perfection of way, or moved down in accordance with his distortions."[105] The sectarians' concern for right discernment was also tied to their purity concerns, most notable in their rule to deny individuals under probation the right to share his knowledge and counsel with other members (1QS 8:24–25).

4.5.3 *Excursus:* Spirit in the Qumran Community

As seen in several primary texts, "spirit" is an important term in Qumran ideology, particularly as it relates to the sectarians' concern for purity. The use of רוח in the Dead Sea Scrolls is not uniform, and attending to the various uses of this term will illuminate points of comparison between how "spirit" functions in Qumran and in Pauline discourse as it occurs in 1 Corinthians.

The most well-known passage from Qumran regarding "spirit" is the Treatise on the Two Spirits in 1QS 3:13–4:26. This is the longest extant discussion at Qumran regarding "spirit," though scholars have argued that this passage should not be read as "*the* definitive summary of the community's ideology."[106] The treatise is striking for the way in which it depicts the presence of both good and evil powers in the world that can influence humankind.[107] According to 1QS 4:20–23, hu-

---

[105] See also 1QHᵃ 17:15–16: "One man may be more righteous than another, one person may be more wiser than his fellow, the flesh may be more honored than one made of clay, and one spirit may be stronger than another spirit (ורוח מרוח תגבר)."
[106] Jörg Frey, "Different Patterns of Dualistic Thought in the Qumran Library. Reflections on their Background and History," in *Legal Texts and Legal Issues: Proceedings of the Second Meeting of the International Organization for Qumran Studies Cambridge 1995*, ed. M. Bernstein, F. García Martínez, and J. Kampen (Leiden: Brill 1997), 290 (emphasis added). For the purposes of the foregoing discussion, however, it is not important whether or not the Treatise—or any other sectarian text analyzed here for that matter—represents *the* Qumran view of spirit. What is important is that these texts represent *one* or *several* ancient Jewish perspective(s) about the spirit and the existence of such discussions alone suffices as valuable evidence for present comparative analysis.
[107] Other contemporaneous Jewish sources believed likewise. E.g. T. Ben. 3:3 ("If the spirits of Beliar seek to oppress you with wicked tribulation"); T. Dan 1:7–8 ("And one of the spirits of Beliar worked in me, saying 'Take this sword and kill Joseph with it … This is the spirit of anger"); Jubilees 10:1 ("impure demons began to mislead Noah's grandchildren … to destroy them); 10:3 ("may the wicked spirits not rule them"); 11:4 ("the spirits of the savage ones were helping and

mans share in both the good spirit of truth and the evil spirit, an internal struggle within every human being:[108]

> [20]Then God will purify by his truth all the works of man and refine for himself the sons of man. He will utterly destroy the spirit of deceit (רוח עולה) from the veins of [21]his flesh. He will purify him by the Holy Spirit (ברוח קודש) from all ungodly acts and sprinkle upon him the Spirit of Truth (רוח אמת) like waters of purification, (to purify him) from all the abominations of falsehood and from being polluted [22]by a spirit of impurity (ברוח נדה), so that upright ones may have insight into the knowledge of the Most High and the wisdom of the sons of heaven, and the perfect in the Way may receive understanding. For those God has chosen for an eternal covenant, [23]and all the glory of Adam shall be theirs without deceit. All false works will be put to shame.

Jörg Frey rightly observes: "there can be little doubt that contemporary readers saw an angelic reality behind the two spirits, as is especially suggested by the fact that the 'spirits' are later called 'Prince of Light' and 'Angel of Darkness'" in 1QS 3:20–21.[109] Here, the Holy Spirit is not coterminous with any one individual or with the larger community, but acts as an external power that performs two deeds.[110]

---

misleading [them] so that they would commit sins, impurities, and transgression"); 12:20 ("Save me from the power of the evil spirits"); 19:28 ("may the spirits of Mastema not rule over you and your descendants"); 1QapGen 20:26 ("this plague and the spirit of purulent evils"); T. Sol. 18. See Hermann Lichtenberger, "Demonology in the Dead Sea Scrolls and the New Testament," in *Text, Thought, and Practice*, 267–280.

108 Translation adapted from Frey, "Different Patterns," 251. See also 4Q186 (4QHoroscope) 1ii:5–8 that describes the constitution of a human being: "And his thighs are long and slender, and his toes are slender and long ... His spirit has six parts in the house of light and three in the house of darkness."

109 Frey, "Different Patterns," 251. See Devorah Dimant, "The Demonic Realm in Qumran Sectarian Literature," in *Gut und Böse in Mensch und Welt: philosophische und religiöse Konzeptionen vom Alten Orient bis zum frühen Islam*, ed. Heinz-Günther Nesselrath and Florian Wilk (Tübingen: Mohr Siebeck, 2013), 103–117. 1QH^a 5:32 states: "and a perverted spirit ruled him" (ורוח נעוה משלה בו). See also 11Q5 19:15.

110 Émile Puech, "L'Esprit Saint à Qumrân," *LASBF* 49 (1999): 286: "Une même réalité se cache dans l'expression 'esprit de vérité' (*rwḥ ʾmt*) en 1QH VIII 24 [= XVI 6], 1QS IV 21 ou encore 1QS III 6–8 qui y ajoute un esprit de droiture et d'humilité (*rwḥ ywšr wʿnwh*). Ces qualifications de l'esprit de Dieu rejoignent celles du Ps 143:10 ou de Ne 9:20 à propos du 'bon esprit,' expression tout à fait parallèle à 'esprit saint' de Ps 51:12–13." There is also 1QS 3:6–9 where the lines between the human spirit, the spirit in the community, and the spirit of God are blurred. Jörg Frey suggests that "[t]hese distinctions are clearer in Paul" ("Paul's View of the Spirit in the Light of Qumran," in *The Dead Sea Scrolls and Pauline Literature*, ed. Jean-Sébastien Rey [Leiden: Brill, 2014], 237–260 [256]), but I problematize this conclusion in my discussion of 1 Corinthians 5 in chapter 3.

First, it acts as God's purifying agent: God will destroy the deceitful and polluting spirit dwelling within the human being and the Holy Spirit will purify the person from all impurity (4:20–22).[111] The use of the verb זקק with human objects recalls the refinement of precious metals in the Hebrew Bible, along with its implied use of fire.[112] This is not an insignificant detail since in 1 Corinthians, Paul too envisages a future when precious metals—along with other building materials—will be refined by fire (on 1 Cor 3:5–17, see chapter 2.2).

Second, the Spirit acts as a medium of divine revelation at Qumran: a strong contrast is made between truth/wisdom and falsehood/deceit, the former only available to the "upright ones" (4:22, ישרים). Divine knowledge is shown through the Holy Spirit only to those chosen by God (see 1 Cor 2:6–16) while other spirits can lead the people of God astray.[113] The fragmentary text, 4Q560, is notable for its description of the negative influence of "spirits." It reads:

> [1:1]Beelzebub, to you ... ²an evil visitant, a demon ... ³I adjure you all who enter into the body, the male wasting-demon and the female wasting-demon ... ⁴I adjure you by the name of YHWH, 'He who removes iniquity and transgression.' O fever and chills and chest pain ... ⁵and forbidden to disturb by night in dreams or by day in sleep, the male shrine-spirit and the female shrine-spirit ... ²:⁵And I, O spirit ... ⁶I adjure you, O spirit.[114]

This text clearly shows an understanding that spirits have supernatural power and influence over human bodies, such that even diseases can manifest themselves.[115] Another important factor in this magic formula is the connection be-

---

111 Purity as God's end goal is evident in the employment of various verbs for God's actions: ברר(4:20, "to purify" or "to purge"); זקק (4:20, "to refine"); and טהר (4:21, "to be clean" or "to purify").
112 E.g., Ps 12:6; Job 28:1; 1 Chr 28:18; and 29:4. It also occurs once in Mal 3:3 to describe the coming of God to his temple, when he will refine Levites like gold and silver. In both contexts (metals and Levites), the use of fire is implied. See 1 Cor 3:12–15.
113 1QS 4:3–6a names various positive attributes such as humility, compassion toward their own members, purity that detests idols, and faithful stewardship of the mysteries, and concludes: "these are the counsels of the spirit (אלה סודי רוח) to the sons of truth in this world" (4:6b). Then 4:9–11 lists "the ways of the spirit of falsehood" (ולרוח עולה) as greed, wickedness, pride, deceit, cruelty, uncleanness, and so on.
114 4Q560 1i:1–5, ii:5–6. For transcription and translation, see Douglas L. Penney and Michael O. Wise, "By the Power of Beelzebub: An Aramaic Incantation Formula From Qumran (4Q560)," *JBL* 113 (1994): 631–632.
115 Penney and Wise, "By the Power," 642: "The last words of line 4 designate diseases. Two are well attested in other texts, while the third has a number of precedents. Their appearance together here, as in the considerably earlier Akkadian and later Aramaic texts, places their interpretation as demonic diseases beyond debate. Both the earlier and later literatures spell out

tween preservation from demons and forgiveness from transgressions. Unfortunately, the exact mechanics of this connection are not described, but somehow the two are directly related: to be forgiven from sins is to be preserved from demons and vice versa.[116]

In the Hodayot, the author acknowledges that at a base level—that is, prior to God's intervention—the human being remained a source of impurity and negatively affected by "a spirit of error ... without understanding" (1QH[a] 9:24–25; also 5:30–31).[117] This sordid state leads the author to pray, "I entreat you with the spirit that you have placed in me

(ברוח אשר נתתה בי) that you make your kindness to your servant complete forever, cleansing me by your holy spirit (לטהרני ברוח קודשך) and drawing me nearer by your good favor" (8:29–30).[118] There are two distinct features of this entreaty: (1) the spirit enables the author to pray,[119] and (2) the spirit begins the cleansing process in the present. Just as in 1QS, God's spirit imparts knowledge to the chosen.[120]

4QInstruction is another text that describes the role of various spirits in the life of the Qumran community.[121] 4Q417 1i:13–18 shows how people are endowed with a spirit and how certain individuals are excluded from divine revelation:[122]

> [13]And you, [14]O understanding one, inherit your reward ... [15]engraved is the decree by God, against all iniquities of the sons of perdition, and a book of memory is written before him,

---

explicitly the demonic etiology of these very diseases." They also note that beyond these magic texts, similar idea of the connection between demons/diseases found in Matt 8:15 (+ pars.).
116 See also 11QApPs[a] 5:4–6:3 and 11QPs[a] 19:1–18 that invoke the name of God against demons and spirits while asking for forgiveness of sins in the same context.
117 Another fragmentary text (4Q438 4ii:5) makes God's intervention even more explicit: "You have removed from me the spirit of destruction (רוח מחיתה) and you have clothed me with the spirit of salvation (רוח ישועות)."
118 Carol Newsom observes one of preferred locutions in the Hodayot is "the spirit that you have placed in me" (see 1QH[a] 4:29; 5:36; 8:20, 29; 20:15; 21:34). See Carol A. Newsom, "Flesh, Spirit, and the Indigenous Psychology of the *Hodayot*," in *Prayer and Poetry in the Dead Sea Scrolls and Related Literature: Essay sin Honor of Eileen Schuller on the Occasion of Her 65th Birthday*, ed. J. Penner, K. M. Penner, and C. Wassen (Leiden: Brill, 2012), 344.
119 See Rom 8:26; 1 Cor 14:15.
120 1QH[a] 6:36: "And as for me, your servant, you have favored me with the spirit of knowledge (ברוח דעה) to choose truth." The connection between the spirit of God and purity or knowledge is also noted in 1QH[a] 6:24; 20:14–15; 1QS 3:6–9.
121 The following analysis will refer to each text by their specific manuscript number, but the readers should be aware that technically, these fragmentary scrolls all belong to the larger work known as 4QInstruction.
122 See 4Q416 1:12 (+ par. in 4Q418 2+2a–c:4); 4Q417 1i:17; and 4Q418 81+81a:2. See also 1QH[a] 5:30–31.

> ¹⁶for those who keep His word, and this is the vision of meditation ... And He made humanity, a people with a spirit (עם רוח) ... ¹⁷and no longer is the vision given to a spirit of flesh (לרוח בשר) because it did not distinguish ¹⁸between good and evil according to the judgment of his spirit.¹²³

The author emphasizes the fact that all humanity was created with a spirit. The problem occurs when some stray from the truth and are no longer given God's vision. In turn, this affects the quality of their spirit such that it is called a "spirit of flesh." Benjamin Wold concludes: "the beginning point is 'spirit' and when not maintained becomes a 'spirit of flesh.'"¹²⁴ The fate that awaits the "spirit of flesh" is portrayed in the eschatological judgment scene of 4Q416 1:10–14:

> ¹⁰From heaven he will judge over the work of wickedness. But all the sons of his truth will be favorably accepted ... ¹¹And all those who polluted themselves in it [wickedness] will be afraid ... ¹²And every spirit of flesh will be stripped (ויתערעו כל רוח בשר) ... ¹³And every iniquity will come to an end forever and the period of truth will be completed ¹⁴in all the periods of eternity, for he is the God of truth.

The text portends the spirit's eventual destruction.¹²⁵

4QInstruction reveals a somewhat different reflection about spirit(s) from that observed in the Community Rule and in the Hodayot, since the author of the former text considers the "spirit" from an internal perspective, as an entity already existing *within* the individual that could be transformed from either a neutral or positive state to a negative one. In a second fragment, the author acknowledges that it is even possible to diminish or exchange the spirit, as ways to corrupt the spirit: "And with your words do not diminish your spirit (אל תמעט רוחכה) and for wealth do not exchange your holy spirit (אל תמר רוח קודשכה) because there is no price that is equal to it" (4Q416 2ii:6–7). One's handling of

---

123 For the interpretation of the Hebrew phrase in line 16, see Benjamin Wold, "'Flesh' and 'Spirit' in Qumran Sapiential Literature as the Background to the Use in Pauline Epistles," *ZNW* 106.2 (2015): 262–279, esp. 265–267.
124 Wold, "'Flesh' and 'Spirit,'" 267.
125 Matthew J. Goff suggests that the verb יתערעו should be read as a hithpalpel of ערר: "The Word in this *binyan* refers to the destruction of Babylon's walls in Jer 51:58. The verb in 4QInstruction denotes the obliteration of the fleshly spirit." In *4QInstruction* (Atlanta: Society of Biblical Literature, 2013), 52. Elsewhere he writes: "The death of this spirit is ordained by God." Idem, "Being Fleshly or Spiritual: Anthropological Reflection and Exegesis of Genesis 1–3 in 4QInstruction and First Corinthians," in *Christian Body, Christian Self: Concepts of Early Christian Personhood*, ed. Clare K. Rothschild and Trevor W. Thompson (Tübingen: Mohr Siebeck, 2011), 44.

words and money had direct impact on the purity or pollution of the spirit.¹²⁶ Another text, the Damascus Document, contains a list of sexual transgressions in CD 5:6b–11a begun by the statement, "they also defile the sanctuary" (6b, וגם מטאים הם את המקדש), and a screed against the sectarians' opponents in 5:11b–19 that observes: "And they also have defiled their holy spirit" (11b, וגם את רוח קדשיהם טמאו). This passage suggests that one's sexual purity is closely tied to the purity of the sanctuary and the Holy Spirit.¹²⁷

Finally, the vulnerability of the spirit—and therefore, the need to maintain or preserve it—is noted in several instances that the scrolls mention weighing out or discerning the spirit of others. Émile Puech suggests that this interest in the spirit's integrity is perhaps related to the temple:

> Dans sa marche à la perfection, la Communauté ainsi constituée se présente comme le temple saint réunissant le saint et le saint de saints (1QS IX 3–6), tel un temple d'hommes où la louange tient lieu d'offrandes (voir 4Q174 1–2,2–6). Ce temple, foundation de l'esprit saint, qui a remplacé les sacrifices par la consécration de pierres vivantes à la louange divine, annonce en quelque sorte le temple de l'Esprit Saint de la Communauté chrétienne (1 Co 3:16ss; 6:19). Mais l'homme peut profaner son esprit saint, ainsi que l'ont fait la plupart des guides religieux du people qui ont péché en menant une vie non conforme aux décrets de l'alliance et qui ont profané le sanctuaire (CD V 6–15). Et l'auteur du passage de donner une série de recommandations à observer afin que les membres de la Communauté évitent toute forme d'iniquité et ne profanent ainsi leur esprit saint (CD VI 11-VII 6, 4Q270 2 ii 11).¹²⁸

This 'series of recommendations,' for example, can be seen in a fragment of 4Q415 that asserts each member "will be measured according to their spirits" (4Q415 11:7) and in another fragment that proscribes control over a woman's spirit, as if it could be a threat otherwise (4Q415 9:8; also 4Q416 2iv:6–8). Also, the Damascus Document stipulates that each member will be judged in the holy council "according to his spirit" (CD 20:24) and the Community Rule enforced probation upon "the one whose spirit deviates from the truth of the Yahad" (1QS 7:18).¹²⁹

---

126 See also 4Q416 2iii:5–6 that forbids the borrowing of money from untrustworthy sources because the possibility of corrupting one's spirit (line 6: ורוחכה אל תחבל). CD 6:11–7:6 provides a series of laws that members must abide by, and warns each person "not defile his holy spirit" (7:3–4, ולא ישקץ איש את רוח קדשיו).
127 See also 4QMMT B:48–49: "For all the sons of Israel are responsible to guard themselves against all defiling union and (thus) show reverence for the sanctuary."
128 Puech, "L'Esprit Saint à Qumrân," 289.
129 See also 1QS 5:20–21, 24 ("they shall investigate their spirit"); 6:16–17 ("he must not touch the pure food ... before they examined his spirit and works"); 9:14–15 ("to weigh each person's spirit"). See Robert. W. Kvalvaag, "The Spirit in Human Beings in Some Qumran Non-Biblical

4.5.4 Penalties for Transgressions

Given the above discussions of Qumran as sacred space and the presence of spirit(s) in their midst, how did the sectarians deal with those who transgressed their laws and/or boundaries? What types of punishments were meted out against those who might imperil the community with their impurities and sins? The previous section examined the blessings and curses pronounced upon certain groups in the Community Rule (1QS 2:2–9). A few verses prior, the author asserts that the present period is the time of "Belial's dominion" (1:18, ממשלת בליעל), heightening the perception that evil is lurking.[130] The curses contain an onslaught of imprecations heaped upon those who might turn away from the community at this critical period. They call for transgressors to be handed over to "avengers of vengeance" so that they might meet "destruction" (2:6). Those destined for destruction will find no mercy and there will be no one to atone for their sins (2:7–8). The ambiguities of the visitation by destruction and the impossibility of atonement recall similar motifs found in other ancient inscriptions within sacred spaces (see chapter 3). In the discussion of the "spirit" in Qumran, the connection between one's state of sinfulness and the vulnerability to attacks by demons or spirits was made clear, and it is possible that a similar idea underlies the warning here that apostates will find no atonement.

The Qumran community espoused a multi-layered approach towards transgressors regarding their exclusion and/or expulsion. Minor infractions such as lying about one's property, addressing a fellow member with a stubborn or impatient attitude, or speaking out in anger against a priest entailed a one-year exclusion from the pure meal of the congregation (1QS 6:24–27, 7:2–3). A person who deviates from the truth but repents faces two years of probation: the first year prohibits taking part in the pure meal of the congregation and the second year prohibits taking part in the pure drink (1QS 7:18–20). Other misdeeds such as deliberate lies or failure to care for another member would yield a penance for

---

Texts," in *Qumran Between the Old and New Testaments*, ed. Frederick H. Cryer and Thomas L. Thompson (Sheffield: Sheffield Academic Press, 1998), 159–180.

130 See also 4Q286 7ii:2–4 (par. 4Q287 6:2–4): "Cursed be Belial in his hostile plan, and he is cursed for his guilty authority. And cursed are all the spirits of his lot in their wicked plan, and they are cursed for the plans of their unclean impurity." See 4Q174 f1–2i:7–9: "As for what He said to David, 'I will give you rest from all your enemies,' this is that He will give them rest from all the children of Belial who cause them to stumble in order to destroy them ... just as they came with a plan of Belial in order to cause the children of light to stumble, and to plot against them wicked plans so that they might be caught by Belial through their guilty error."

various lengths of time (1QS 7:3–5).[131] In severe cases, the community instituted immediate expulsion with no possibility of rehabilitation or acceptance. See the following cases: to misspeak "the holy name of God" (1QS 6:27, שם הנכבד) for whatever reason; to slander the community (1QS 7:16–17); to "grumble" against the teachings of the Yaḥad (1QS 7:17[132]); to act against the congregation with the backsliding of "his spirit" (1QS 7:22–24[133]). The expulsion was final to the degree that if any member shared food or property with the expelled, he too would be put out of the community (1QS 7:25).

In the Damascus Document, there is a striking imagery of judgment against the transgressor:

> [19:32]And this is the judgment against anyone who despises the commandments of God and abandons them to follow their own heart … [35]They will not be counted among the council of the people … [20:3]This is the man 'who is melted in the midst of a furnace' [Ezek 22:21]. When his deeds become evident, he will be expelled from the congregation [4]as one whose lot had never fallen among those taught by God … [7]let no one share either wealth or work with such a one, [8]for all the holy ones of the Most High have cursed him.

The Ezekiel citation that describes the refining fire is used here to describe the process of *revealing* the transgressor as dross. The same motif found in 1QS 4:20–23 to describe the process of *purifying* followers of God (see above) occurs in CD to show that some did not belong to the community. The conclusion of this expulsion ceremony also prohibits contact with the expelled (4Q269 16:12–15). 11Q19 also warns against profaning the temple, lest it lead to the death penalty:

> [35:4] Every person … who is not [5] a priest will be put to death, and every person who … enters [6] it and he is not dressed with the holy vest[ments] … [7] must also be put to death. They are not to pro[fane the tem]ple of their God, incurring [8] a sin punishable by death (עוון אשמה למות).

---

131 For a list of offenses and the various lengths of penance, see 1QS 7:5–18.
132 The verb used here (לין) is not a common term in the Dead Sea Scrolls or the Hebrew Bible. In the latter, it occurs most frequently in the wilderness narratives, and is translated in the LXX by the (δια)γογγύζω verb family. Paul recalls the wilderness narrative with the only Pauline use of γογγύζω (2x) in 1 Cor 10:10.
133 1QS 7:23, ושבה רוחו. This punishment only applies to a senior member of the community (1QS 7:22). This likely shows that expectations were different between members based on their years of membership; younger members could face punishments and probations, but there remained for them the possibility of acceptance. Senior members, however, were apparently held to a higher standard. But see also 1QS 8:21–23 that suggests that *anyone* who transgresses the commandments intentionally or deceitfully will be permanently expelled.

The scroll then exhorts the auditors to maintain the perpetual sanctity of the temple.

4.6 Summary of Evidence from Jewish Contexts

Beginning with the Genesis narrative with the Garden of Eden, ancient Israelite and early Jewish conceptions of sacred spaces are marked by their recognition that it is the presence of God that sets a particular space apart from the rest. In the Garden, God "walked" among humankind (Gen 3:8); in the exodus narrative, God marked the tabernacle with his presence in the ark of the covenant (Exod 25:22); in Jerusalem, the placement of the same ark in the holy of holies (1 Kgs 8:6–11; 9:3); and in Qumran, God's spirit was available in their midst (e.g. 1QS 3:7). Simply put, without the presence of God, the space was not sacred.

Similar to the role of divine *dynamis* in Greek and Roman sacred spaces, there are several instances in Israelite and Jewish sources when a transgression either at the margins of a sacred space or within the sacred space itself led to severe punishments, including death. But compared to the punishments found in Greek and Roman sources, there are far fewer accounts of simple and minor punishments (e.g., monetary or food rations). Since every culture maintains its own symbolic system with its accompanying discourse of risks and problems regarding purity, it is at the places of multicultural encounter that this becomes most problematic.[134] That is to say, the potential for conflict and danger is most acute when a community remains proximate to another long-standing, established religious culture with its own competitive symbolic world, its own deities, and its own rituals. Given Qumran's separatist and ascetic nature, one may have expected that the sectarians would have been the strictest with regard to boundaries and behaviors, but it is notable that it is at Qumran where there are records of more lenient punishments for transgressions. Because Qumran remained more insulated against outside intrusions that could be damaging to their purity system, the need to bear down so harshly against transgressors seems somewhat diminished.[135] In contrast, the Jerusalem temple was situated in a city located within a Roman-controlled province, likely filled with citizens of various religious persuasions—and therefore, of dangerous degrees

---

[134] Douglas, *Purity and Danger*, 122.
[135] It is important to distinguish between Qumran's punishments for transgressions and its halakhic regulations for purity (the latter, is at times, recognized to be quite strict). See Paul Heger, "Stringency in Qumran?" *JSJ* 42 (2011): 188–217.

of pollution. For Jews to be lenient within such a context would have brought great peril to the purity of their sacred space.

Also, among Diaspora Jews, Philo being exemplary, there is a move towards a preference for a portable tabernacle as opposed to a fixed location of the temple in Jerusalem. This was due in part to Philo's criticism of "the city" and the dangers posed therein. Such flexibility in where God can encounter God's people is even more pronounced in Paul, where there is not even a physical tabernacle to be carried and constructed by God's people. It is difficult to conclude firmly whether this move towards portability was an impulse within early Judaism broadly defined—including Paul himself. Nevertheless, it is a significance shift from ancient Israelite religion that previously emphasized a specific built structure to Philo's example that preferred a less fixed structure as the dwelling place of God.

Clearly, one of the most important data gleaned from Qumran is the conceptual shift where the community itself is described in architectural terms as the temple of God. Israelite and Jewish sources have consistently maintained a line between sacred spaces marked out by YHWH God and the community that surrounded it, but at Qumran, the same line is not as clearly demarcated.[136] This is a new development within early Judaism, though the evidence from the Scrolls is ambiguous with regard to expectations about the physical temple. The sectarians criticized the temple in some respects, but did not break completely with Jerusalem, maintaining a hope that the temple—whether the current one in Jerusalem or another in the eschaton—would be renewed. Some texts still acknowledged the importance of the temple cult as an ideal, even as they disparaged the current state of the Jerusalem temple.[137]

In contrast to Greek and Roman sacred spaces, there are fewer examples of Israelite or Jewish sanctuaries serving as places of healing.[138] Because access to

---

136 See George J. Brooke, "The Visualisation of the Sacred at Qumran," in *Sibyls, Scriptures, and Scrolls: John Collins at Seventy*, ed. J. Baden, H. Najman, and E. Tigchelaar (Leiden: Brill, 2017), 1:226–240. In later Jewish periods, there is also what Steven Fine calls the "templization" of the synagogue, where Temple motifs are applied to these structures. I purposely do not discuss synagogues in this chapter because the sources postdate Paul by many centuries and their conceptuality of "temple" is formulated in light of the vacuum of a temple-less Judaism. For discussion, see Steven Fine, *This Holy Place: On the Sanctity of the Synagogue during the Greco-Roman Period* (Notre Dame: University of Notre Dame Press, 1997), esp. 41–59.
137 See Kapfer, "Relationship between the Damascus Document and the Community Rule."
138 There are, however, literary accounts of *prayers* for deliverance or protection said within the temple grounds or towards the temple: 2 Sam 22:7; 2 Kgs 1:2; 2 Chr 20:5–17; Isa 37:14–20; Ps 18:6; 20:1–3; 28:2; 1 Macc 7:36–38; 2 Macc 3:15–22; 10:25–27; 3 Macc 1:16; 2:1; Jdt 4:9–13; Josephus, *Ant.* 9.8–9; *J.W.* 5.517. What divides this Jewish evidence apart from the Greek/Roman

Israelite and Jewish sanctuaries was severely limited compared to Greek and Roman temples, the former did not become popular destinations for incubation and healing like the latter (see the accounts of Aelius Aristides). It is, however, implied in the available Israelite and Jewish temple discourse that the outside world is filled with harmful entities such as contagions, demons, diseases, and death, while within the community and temple one can find benefits such as holiness, God's spirit, life, and well-being.[139]

Finally, from the Hebrew Bible to the Dead Sea Scrolls, there is a display of extreme caution regarding the levels of purity required to partake in meals. This is most explicit at Qumran with its detailed regulations surrounding the "pure meal" and "pure drink" (משקה הרבים and טהרת הרבים). 1QS 6:13–21 is a good example of upholding a probationary period for new members so that they might attain the necessary level of purity before gaining access to the pure meal/drink of the community. The perpetual importance of meals in this community is also noted in several texts that visualize future meals that are filled with abundance and attended by a messianic figure.[140] Purity was an important topic of concern for temples throughout the Mediterranean, and the Qumran community likewise adopts the same posture.

In conclusion, the Jewish material demonstrates a close proximity to Paul's view of power and peril within the community as sacred space. This is most apparent in Qumran, where the first paradigm shift occurs: from an external discourse about the temple in the Hebrew Bible to an internalized discourse where the community is sometimes described to be coterminous with a type of temple. This idea is not fully developed at Qumran and remains a point of con-

---

ones is the actual event or encounter of power: the prayer texts above do not tend to relay the events afterwards (i.e. did the deity in fact display his *dynamis* on their behalf?) but the Greek and Roman evidence—especially the inscriptions—find their genesis in the fact that a divine power was made manifest. See Hector Avalos, *Illness and Health Care in the Ancient Near East: The Role of the Temple in Greece, Mesopotamia and Israel* (Atlanta: Scholars Press, 1995), passim.

139 See the discussion regarding impurity/death and purity/life in Milgrom, *Leviticus 1–16*, 766–768. Milgrom argues that impurity and the demonic is internalized in humankind in Israelite religion. This might be true for the ancient Israelite tradition that he is analyzing, but the above Qumran texts show otherwise. See Hannah K. Harrington, "Keeping Outsiders Out: Impurity at Qumran," in *Defining Identities: We, You, and the Other in the Dead Sea Scrolls. Proceedings of the Fifth Meeting of the IOQS in Groningen*, ed. Florentino García Martínez and Mladen Popović (Leiden: Brill, 2008), 187–203.

140 See 1QH^a 16:5–14; 1QSa 2:17–22; 4Q88 9:8–14; 4Q504 f1–2iv:2–14; 4Q521 2ii+4:6–13. The citations from 4Q88 and 4Q521 emphasize the idea that the poor and hungry will be fed/satisfied.

tention among some scholars of the Dead Sea Scrolls. In whatever case, Paul's statement in 1 Corinthians is without a doubt the most explicit form of imputation of temple imagery upon a gathering of religious adherents.

5 Temple Discourse in 1 Corinthians

How can interpreters account for Paul's language and conceptions in 1 Corinthians 5:1–13, 10:1–22, and 11:17–34, especially in relation to community as temple? Chapter 2 was an exegetically thick analysis of these three sections of Paul's first letter to the Corinthians, showing that the sections can be read in conversation and suggesting that the best way to read them is through an awareness of temple discourse from the ancient Mediterranean world. Chapters 3 and 4 drew upon an array of available evidence, in order to visualize the Greek, Roman, and Jewish milieux that shaped Paul's ideas concerning the Corinthian assembly. The following review will begin first by answering broader questions about temples, other sacred spaces/sanctuaries, and their relevance for reading Paul, then turn to addressing more specific issues that pertain to the situation in Corinth. The goal is to arrive at a more finely-tuned understanding of Paul's views about the nature of the Corinthian assembly.

5.1 Broad Outlines

Paul's words in 1 Corinthians 3:16 evoke a common motif in both the ancient Mediterranean and Near Eastern worlds: temples housed the presence of the gods in the midst of humankind, and they functioned as the primary places or spaces where one encountered the gods.[1] Human-divine interactions within sacred spaces, however, were never simply benign events: supplicants sought to receive divine benefits, but temples and other sanctuaries also provoked fear and threatened danger, especially against those who entered unworthily or transgressed certain regulations within the sacred space.[2] Just as entering the private residence of one belonging to a higher socio-economic or political status would oblige entrants to follow certain protocols, much more so was the case for those entering temples and other sanctuaries.[3]

---

[1] Tony Spawforth, *The Complete Greek Temples* (London: Thames & Hudson, 2006), 74–91.
[2] Michael B. Hundley, *God in Dwellings: Temples and Divine Presence in the Ancient Near East* (Atlanta: Society of Biblical Literature, 2013), 9.
[3] Hundley, *God in Dwellings*, 10: "Because the space belongs to another, a guest would never think to regulate the inhabitant's rules; he or she would instead follow those rules willingly. Ancient Near Eastern temples functioned similarly." While Hundley's study focuses on temples from ANE context, his comments would be just as apt for sanctuaries found throughout the ancient Mediterranean world. For temple as house of a god, see Walter Burkert, "The Meaning and Function of the Temple in Classical Greece," in *Temple in Society*, ed. Michael V. Fox (Winona

Various features marked sacred spaces as different from profane spaces. As examples: the marble or limestone *horoi* served as boundary markers for Greek sanctuaries,[4] walls set apart the tabernacle during the exodus, and a partition encircled the inner part of the sanctuary at Jerusalem. Feigning ignorance of such boundaries provided no relief for transgressors since the various literary and material accounts analyzed in chapters 3 and 4 demonstrate clearly that it was up to each individual to recognize when she or he entered a sacred space. The accounts of recorded punishments are legion and to my knowledge, none grant exemptions to a person who transgressed while ignorant of the laws.

If Paul conceived of the Corinthian assembly in terms of sacred space—and expected the Corinthians to subscribe to the same belief—then texts such as 1 Corinthians 5:1–13, 10:1–22, and 11:17–34 should be read in light of other ancient discourses on temples and sacred spaces. Indeed, if the concept of Corinthian assembly as temple was an essential part of Paul's teaching, then this idea is critical for interpreting texts thereafter that show how Paul thought about the Corinthians. Moreover, this study also highlights the importance of the religious experience of visitors to temples and other sanctuaries, i.e. the power and peril that one encountered when entering such spaces.

This study aimed to answer several fundamental questions about ancient religious experience: what was the significance of temples and other sanctuaries in the first place? What did people hope to gain from visitations to sacred spaces? What kind of experiences did people expect to have *within* a sacred space? Why is the maintenance of boundaries surrounding a sacred space such an important dimension of religion in the ancient world? This project addressed these questions by focusing not simply on secondary reflections about Paul's rhetoric, but on primary issues concerning the Corinthians' own experience of visiting temples. Christfried Böttrich rightly observes concerning temples: "Er bezeichnet kein neutrales Terrain, sondern den *Einfluß- und Machtbereich der Gottheit.*"[5]

Lake, IN: Eisenbrauns, 1988), 27–47, esp. 29–31. Gregory Stevenson observes in *Power and Place: Temple and Identity in the Book of Revelation* (Berlin: Walter de Gruyter, 2001), 42: "Both Greeks and Romans felt free to use the same terminology for their temples that they used for their own homes (*aedes, domus,* οἶκος)."

[4] See the relevant discussion in chapter 3 and for one set of material evidence of ὅρος τεμένος, see *IG* IV 29–38 (Aegina, late 5th BCE).

[5] Christfried Böttrich, "'Ihr seid der Tempel Gottes'. Tempelmetaphorik und Gemeinde bei Paulus," in *Gemeinde ohne Tempel: Zur Substituierung und Transformation des Jerusalemer Tempels und seines Kults im Alten Testament, antiken Judentum und frühen Christentum*, ed. B. Ego et al. (Tübingen: Mohr Siebeck, 1999), 416 (emphasis added).

5.2 Specific Issues

It is now possible to compare and contrast Paul's understanding of the Corinthian assembly to other gathered groups and sacred spaces from the ancient Mediterranean. The Qumran sectarians' views on temple, spirit, use of Scripture, and punishments best approximate the way that Paul conceives of the community in Corinth. Although the Hebrew Bible provided the overarching symbolism for Paul and the sectarians, they both take the notion of sacred space one step further by applying it to a gathering of religious adherents. The following subsections describe in greater detail the features that contribute to Paul's overall view of the Corinthian assembly.

5.2.1 Location of the Temple: Corinth

Paul does not exhort the Corinthians to escape to the wilderness as a potential place to establish God's temple or to create other extreme measures that would permanently insulate the assembly from contact with foreign deities and their concomitant cultic functions.[6] In fact, Paul assumes that the Corinthians will inevitably rub shoulders with followers of other deities and come in contact with their foods, rituals, and idols (1 Cor 8:1–13; 10:1–22; 12:1–3). He explicitly notes in 1 Cor 5:10 that the Corinthian assembly should not "go out of the world" (ἐκ τοῦ κόσμου ἐξελθεῖν). Paul's dilemma, therefore, is how to carefully delimit the boundaries of the Corinthian assembly within the polytheistic context of a Hellenistic city.

The literary, archaeological, and epigraphical evidence indicate that the Greek city of Corinth was destroyed by the Roman general Lucius Mummius in 146 BCE due to the city's participation in the Achaean League's revolt. Roman

---

6 There is, however, the difficult passage of 2 Corinthians 6:14–7:1 that has a long history of scholarly debate. Paul asserts in 2 Cor 6:16, "But what agreement does the temple of God have with idols? For we are the temple of the living God (ἡμεῖς γὰρ ναὸς θεοῦ ἐσμεν ζῶντος)." For an older but measured reading of this passage, see Nils A. Dahl, "A Fragment and Its Context: 2 Corinthians 6:14–7:1," in *Studies in Paul: Theology for the Early Christian Mission* (Minneapolis: Augsburg Publishing, 1977), 62–69. While some scholars have opted for a non-Pauline interpolation, the external evidence from the manuscript tradition makes such an option highly speculative. The present study, however, helps make better sense of this passage in 2 Cor as more Pauline than usually assumed. See also Vahrenhorst, *Kultische Sprache*, 206–215; David A. DeSilva, "Measuring Penultimate Against Ultimate Reality: An Investigation of the Integrity and Argumentation of 2 Corinthians," *JSNT* 52 (1993): 41–70.

colonists resettled Corinth as *Colonia Laus Iulia Corinthiensis* in 44 BCE.[7] By the time Paul visited the city of Corinth, it boasted a number of vibrant sanctuaries that sometimes blurred the line between what is "Roman" and "Greek" as well as what was "public" versus "private" religion.[8] The evidence points to a city that was, as Paul notes negatively throughout his Corinthian correspondence, filled with "idols" along with the potential for one to engage in "idolatry."[9] From a more neutral perspective, it is at least certain that religious architecture dotted the landscape of Corinth and that both private and public religion was an essential part of life in this city.[10] For example, during his travel through Corinth, Pau-

---

[7] Pausanias, *Descr.* 7.15.1–16.8; Strabo, *Geogr.* 8.6.23; Diodorus Siculus, *Bib. hist.* 32.4.5, 27.1–3; Polybius, *Hist.* 39.2; Livy, *Perioch.* 52.4; Velleius Paterculus, *Hist.* 1.13.1; Cicero, *Agr.* 2.87; *Verr.* 2.1.55; Dio Cassius, *Hist. rom.* 43.50.4; *CIL* I² 626 (Rome, ca. 144 BCE); 628 (Nursia, ca. 146 BCE); 629 (Parma, ca. 146 BCE). For the discussion of the archaeological evidence, see Elizabeth R. Gebhard and Matthew W. Dickie, "The View from the Isthmus, ca. 200 to 44 B.C.," *Corinth, The Centenary: 1896–1996*, ed. Charles K. Williams II and Nancy Bookidis, Corinth XX (Princeton: The American School of Classical Studies at Athens, 2003), 261–278, esp. 266–277.

[8] Nancy Bookidis, "The Sanctuaries of Corinth," in *Corinth, The Centenary*, 247–259; idem, "Religion in Corinth: 146 BCE to 100 CE," in *Urban Religion in Roman Corinth*, ed. D. N. Schowalter and S. J. Friesen (Cambridge: Harvard University Press, 2005), 141–64; Mary E. Hoskins Walbank, "The Cults of Roman Corinth: Public Ritual and Personal Belief," in *Roman Peloponnese III: Society, Economy and Culture Under the Roman Empire: Continuity and Innovation*, ed. A. D. Rizakis and C. E. Lepenioti (Athens: Research Institute for Greek and Roman Antiquity, 2010), 357–376. See, however, recent publications that argue for an appreciation of the "Roman" character of divinities and temples present at Corinth. Jon Michael Frey, "The Archaic Colonnade at Ancient Corinth: A Case of Early Roman Spolia," *AJA* 119.2 (2005): 147–175; Barbette Stanley Spaeth, "Greek Gods or Roman? The Corinthian Archaistic Blocks and Religion in Roman Corinth," *AJA* 121.3 (2017): 397–423. Betsey A. Robinson rightly highlights the fact that scholarship has tended towards opposites: continuity versus break or memory versus forgetfulness/confusion with regard to Corinth's Greek heritage. She argues instead for a more nuanced approach that appreciates the hybrid characteristic of Corinth. In *Histories of Peirene: A Corinthian Fountain in Three Millennia* (Princeton: American School of Classical Studies at Athens, 2011), 179. The numismatic evidence implies a similar strategy from the part of the Corinthian authorities. See the coinage relating the Pegasos myth in Bradley J. Bitner, "Coinage and Colonial Identity: Corinthian Numismatics and the Corinthian Correspondence," in *The First Urban Churches 1: Methodological Foundations*, ed. J. R. Harrison and L. L. Welborn (Atlanta: Society of Biblical Literature, 2015), 151–187 (esp. 175–79).

[9] See the frequency of εἴδωλ- terms in the undisputed Pauline letters: Rom 2:22; 1 Cor 5:10, 11; 6:9; 8:1, 4, 7, 10; 10:7, 14, 19; 12:2; 2 Cor 6:16; Gal 5:20; 1 Thess 1:9.

[10] Much of the activity could be found in the Roman Forum that encompassed a vast open space of over 15,300 m². Michael C. Hoff, "Greece and the Roman Republic: Athens and Corinth from the Late Third Century to the Augustan Era," in *A Companion to the Archaeology of the Roman Republic*, ed. Jane Derose Evans (Chicester, West Sussex: UK: Wiley Blackwell, 2013), 559–77. The forum was situated on a shallow valley outlined by the Hellenistic South Stoa to

sanias recorded numerous sanctuaries throughout the city along with the statues of Athena, Heracles, Hermes, Poseidon, and other deities that could be found throughout.[11]

The socio-religious landscape of Corinth was such that inhabitants of the city would have been fully engaged in a variety of voluntary associations, not least in the various cultic groups. There was great fluidity and permeability in the way that a person interacted with the various deities and rituals that existed in the private and public arenas. Transgressions could result in fines or some other punishment, but none of these cultic groups and sacred spaces maintained the kind of strict exclusivity that Paul envisioned for the Corinthians. One could potentially be a member of several associations, take part in their respective cult rituals, and remain in good standing before the members and patron deities of each association or temple. The numerous sanctuaries within the city are where one expected to have contact with the gods and participate in their sacrifices.

Different from both Paul and other Hellenistic associations in Corinth, the Qumran sectarians located their community in an entirely different place. They removed themselves from contact with others and believed that such measures were required to maintain proper access to God. 1QS 8:13 exhorts: "they [the sectarians] will separate from within the dwelling of the men of sin to go to the wilderness (למדבר), in order to prepare there His way" (see also 1QS 9:19). The citation from Isaiah 40:3 that follows in 1QS 8:14 suggests that the sectarians expected encounters with God to occur in the wilderness, away from other dwelling places of humankind. An important component of their "preparation" for theophany was scriptural interpretation: "the way of the Lord" (דרך ייי) from 1QS 8:14 is interpreted as expounding the law in 1QS 8:15.[12] In other texts, the sectarians called themselves "the returnees of the wilderness" (4Q171 f1 3:1, שבי המדבר) and the "exiled of the wilderness" (1QM 1:2, גולת המדבר). To the sectarians, the location of their community beyond the usual places of human habitation was key to their existence and religious experience.

---

the south and the Archaic Temple to the north, both buildings which were part of the early renovations in the Roman colony. Walbank, "Cults of Roman Corinth," 360.
11 Book 2 of *Descriptions of Greece*.
12 The author continues in 1QS 8:14–16: "As it is written, 'In the wilderness, prepare the way of ****, make straight in the desert a highway for our God.' This is the interpretation of the law which He commanded through the hand of Moses for obedience, with all that has been revealed from age to age, and according to what the prophets have revealed through his Holy Spirit." See 5.2.4 below for discussion on "scripture" in Paul, Qumran, and Hellenistic sources.

Similarly, Philo espoused a suspicious attitude towards temples housed within the walls of a city. Philo viewed such places to be filled with corruption and temptation, liable not only to affect God's people but even God's own dwelling place. This belief underlies Philo's preference—and possibly that of Stephen in Acts[13]—for a portable tabernacle that exists beyond the walls of any city. Paul, like Philo, recognizes the dangers inherent within the city, though Paul takes the portability concept in a different direction by mapping God's temple unto the people themselves. In contrast to Philo, Paul also firmly rooted the Corinthian assembly as the temple of God in the city of Corinth itself.

5.2.2 Inclusion and Exclusion

In light of the religious atmosphere of Corinth, Paul could have followed the way of the Qumran sectarians and suggest that the community establish itself beyond the city. This would have eliminated several issues raised by the character of the city of Corinth, such as the engagement with other cults, contact with polluting foods, or entering into shameful relationships. Nevertheless, Paul does not suggest leaving the city (1 Cor 5:10). Paul founds the group in Corinth, exhorts them to view themselves as the temple of God, and provides them with specific guidelines on how to maintain the sanctity of their assembly, all within close proximity to other physical temples, religious symbols, and cultic activities. Paul could also have followed the way of other Hellenistic associations by creating flexibility in the membership requirements of the Corinthian community.[14] That is, the

---

[13] See chapter 4.3.
[14] I have specifically shied away from framing this project as a comparative analysis of the Corinthians and other Hellenistic associations in the vein of Kloppenborg, Ascough, Harland, and others because that is precisely not the goal of this project. I am interested in the larger question of *Paul's* view of the Corinthian assembly as a place of power (positive and negative). The various secondary literature cited regarding ancient associations tend to focus on the *internal* constitution of group(s) such as the leadership structures, economic systems, group size, and occupations. I am also not interested in pursuing the genealogical questions criticized by Jonathan Z. Smith in *Drudgery Divine* (Chicago: University of Chicago Press, 1990) or in establishing conclusions that assert the superiority of the Corinthian assembly over other cultic associations in antiquity. The best measured statement, given the evidence, may be from John S. Kloppenborg himself, who asserts: "I will argue that Graeco-Roman associations are 'good to think with', not necessarily because we must assume that Christ groups were typical associations, but because we have rich data from ancient associations that can generate heuristic questions for interrogating the data from Christ groups." In "Membership Practices in Pauline Christ Groups," *EC* 4 (2013): 187.

Corinthians could have been allowed to participate in multiple θίασοι or *collegia* and their associated rituals, and be allowed to remain upstanding members of God's temple. The relevant passages from 1 Corinthians, however, show that Paul regards this to be an untenable position.

From a social-anthropological perspective, Paul's view of the Corinthian assembly can be understood as one positioned high on the group/grid matrix as defined by Mary Douglas.[15] He envisions strong social cohesion among members ("group") and high levels of obligation that an individual retains towards the group ("grid"). Encompassing all of this is Paul's view of the Corinthian assembly as an exclusive entity that stands apart in this regard from all other temples and related cultic associations in Corinth. Simultaneously, however, this sacred space is highly inclusive, at least with respect to those who form the materials of this temple structure. The Corinthians gathered *together*, expelled impure agents from the group (1 Cor 5:2, 5, 13) *together*, and participated in meals *together*, all the while excluding others—that is, other substances of consumption (1 Cor 10:20–21) and other (disqualified) consumers of the substance (1 Cor 5:11).[16] This process of vetting *who* can consume the meal and *what* can be consumed is emphasized by Paul in all three sections of the letter and is one that recalls sacred laws concerning Hellenistic temples.[17] While ancient temples and cultic associations shared many of the above characteristics, the level of exclusivity marks Paul's exhortations as distinct among these parallels. This does not mean, however, that Paul's way of constructing a group of religious adherents was utterly unique, since the available evidence has clearly shown various internal similarities between the Corinthians, other Christ groups, and Hellenistic associations.[18] Recognizing this exclusivity in Paul can help make sense of another

---

15 Mary Douglas, *Natural Symbols: Explorations in Cosmology* (New York: Routledge, 2003 [1970]), 57–71.
16 Wayne A. Meeks calls this exclusivity, "perhaps the strangest characteristic of Christianity, as of Judaism, in the eyes of the ordinary pagans." In *The First Urban Christians: The Social World of the Apostle Paul*, 2nd ed. (New Haven: Yale University Press, 2003 [1983]), 160.
17 See the language of "judgment" (κριν-) and "approval" (δοκιμ-) regarding meal eating in 1 Cor 5:12; 10:15; and 11:28–31. In Greek temple inscriptions regarding "approval" (δοκιμ-) see chapter 3.2.3. The term, δοκιμασία, was also used in Greek political discourse concerning who was fit to be accepted into office. See Gabriel Adeleye, "The Purpose of the *Dokimasia*," *GRBS* 24.4 (1983): 295–306.
18 In contrast to the older "pneumatic consensus" that asserted that Christ groups—including the Corinthians—lacked any organization structures common in other Hellenistic associations, numerous recent works have shown that ecclesial structures of early Christian communities can be mapped unto the framework of other associations in the Hellenistic world. These studies should be commended for illuminating important topics as social organization, economics, and

passage in the Corinthian correspondence, namely, 2 Corinthians 6:14–7:1. This passage has often been read as a non-Pauline interpolation, but the present study has shown that such naming of elements incompatible with the "temple of God" fits with Paul's views of the Corinthian assembly from 1 Corinthians.[19]

5.2.3 Divine Spirit and Power

The divine spirit dwelling among and within the Corinthians is a highly particular form of spirit manifestation in antiquity, especially as it occurs in temple discourse. There are certainly other accounts from the ancient Mediterranean world that talk about the possibility of ecstatic speech, the cosmic *pneuma*, and other encounters with spirit(s), but in these accounts, the spirit tends to be either localized in one individual temporarily or described as a permanent characteristic of the cosmos without reference to a specific deity or sacred

---

hierarchy/leadership. It is no longer necessary, therefore, to subscribe to a strict *either/or* dichotomy in considering Christ groups among other cultic associations in the ancient Mediterranean (i.e. either Christ groups were entirely akin to other associations or they were not). The phrase "pneumatic consensus" is taken from Richard Last, *The Pauline Church and the Corinthian Ekklēsia: Greco-Roman Associations in Comparative Context* (Cambridge: Cambridge University Press, 2016), 5. Other recent scholarship includes e.g., John S. Kloppenborg and Richard S. Ascough, *Greco-Roman Associations: Texts, Translations, and Commentary. I. Attica, Central Greece, Macedonia, Thrace* (Berlin: Walter de Gruyter, 2011); Philip A. Harland, *Greco-Roman Associations: Texts, Translations, and Commentary. II. North Coast of the Black Sea, Asia Minor* (Berlin: Walter de Gruyter, 2014); Richard S. Ascough, "What Are They *Now* Saying about Christ Groups and Associations?" *CBR* 13 (2015): 207–244.

Influential proponents of the older model are Rudolf Sohm (*Kirchengeschichte im Grundriss* [Leipzig: E. Ungleich, 1894]) and Adolf von Harnack (*Die Mission und Ausbreitung des Christentums in den ersten drei Jahrhunderten* [Leipzig: J.C. Hinrichs, 1902]). For example, Sohm asserts: "Es bedarf nicht notwendig eines besonderen Amtsträgers. Sie sind alle geborene Diener am Wort und sollen es sein!" (*Kirchengeschichte im Grundriss*, 28). Harnack, in his chapter that names Christianity as a religion of the Spirit and power, observes that while other religions and cults may have ecstatic experiences, visions, or (anti-)demonic manifestations, "allein für keine von ihnen ist ims eine solche Fülle von Erscheinungen überliefert wie hier [i.e. in Christianity]" (*Die Mission und Ausbreitung*, 175). Longer citations from the English translations of Sohm and Harnack are in Last, *Pauline Church*, 6. Within English scholarship, Last names Wayne A. Meeks (*The First Urban Christians: The Social World of the Apostle Paul*, 2nd ed. [New Haven: Yale University Press, 2003 [1983]) as most influential.

19 Vahrenhorst, *Kultische Sprache*, 209: "Schon im 1 Kor hatte Paulus die Gemeinde (bzw. den Leib des einzelnen Gemeindegliedes) als Tempel Gottes bezeichnet und die notwendigen Konsequenzen, die zum Schutz der Heiligkeit dieses Tempels zu ziehen sind, dargestellt ... Um notwendige Trennungen geht es auch hier."

space.[20] The evidence from ancient temple discourse also highlights the distinctively Pauline connection between spirit, temple, and assembly, and on this point, the closest approximation is the community at Qumran.

At Qumran, the Holy Spirit and other spirits play important roles in the self-understanding of the community as well as in their religious experience. They understood the world to be inhabited by a variety of spirits, benevolent and malevolent, and one must take care as not to be negatively influenced by the latter type of spirits. The Holy Spirit performs revelatory and purifying acts upon members of the community (1QS 4:20–22; 1QH^a 6:36; also 1 Cor 2:10–14; 3:17; 5:5; 6:11). One's individual spirit could be at risk depending on one's level of purity (4Q416 2ii:6–7), and even the sanctuary and the Holy Spirit could be defiled by certain sexual transgressions (CD 5:6–15; see 1 Cor 5:1–13). These various similarities to Pauline discourse need not mean that Paul was influenced by the sectarians' views on s/Spirit or vice versa, but it does prove that this manner of reflection on the religious experience of the Holy Spirit and other spirits within a communal setting was not wholly unprecedented in antiquity. Martin Vahrenhorst rightly observes that while the Qumran community is a valid analogy to the Corinthian assembly, the direct connection between temple and presence of God's spirit occurs only in Paul.[21]

The Corinthian assembly as temple of God also implies a specific form of divine presence. The "Einwohnungsmotiv" derived from 1 Corinthians 3:16 makes clear that Paul envisions a permanent divine presence among the Corinthians and not just God's temporary habitation.[22] This divine presence manifests itself specifically through the Holy Spirit that is said to dwell among the Corinthians. Divine Spirit is also essential for linking the idea of the community as temple to Paul's body language. In 1 Corinthians 12, Paul describes the various roles of the

---

[20] See Gen 41:38; Exod 28:3; Ezek 37:4–6; Mic 3:8; Sir 39:6–8; Wis 1:5–8; LAB 28:6; 62:2; Philo, *Her.* 264–5; *Opif.* 135; Plutarch, *Def. orac.* 432D–E; Cicero, *Nat. d.* 2.19; Alexander of Aphrodisias, *Mixt.* 216.14–17; Seneca, *Ep.* 41.2; See Dale B. Martin, *Biblical Truths: The Meaning of Scripture in the Twenty-first Century* (New Haven: Yale University Press, 2017), 223–226.; Troels Engberg-Pedersen, *Cosmology and Self in the Apostle Paul: The Material Spirit* (Oxford: Oxford University Press, 2010), 19–22. Even Philo in *On Giants* 19 cites Genesis 6:3 as justification for the idea that the spirit of God can only remain temporarily with human beings. See also *Gig.* 28: "And so though the divine spirit (πνεῦμα θεῖον) may remain awhile in the soul, it cannot remain there."
[21] Martin Vahrenhorst, *Kultische Sprache in den Paulusbriefen*, WUNT 230 (Tübingen: Mohr Siebeck, 2008), 149.
[22] Böttrich, "'Ihr seid der Tempel Gottes,'" 416: "Durch dieses Einwohnungsmotiv wird deutlich, daß es dabei nicht um die naïve Annahme einer begrenzten Behausung, sondern um das Bewußtsein besonderer Gottesgegenwart geht."

Spirit that energizes the members of the community and notes in verse 13, "For in one Spirit we all were baptized into one body, whether Jews or Greeks, whether slave or free, and we all were made to drink of the one Spirit."

In one sense, the spirit of God dwelling among the people is similar to the motif of God's presence among the Israelites in the Hebrew Bible. But this idea is reconfigured significantly. The Israelites are never described as being the structure that housed God's presence. In another sense, it is also akin to how Hellenistic worshippers understood the relationship between temples and divine presence, i.e. that the deities manifested themselves within the confines of these sacred spaces, through images or through other mediums. There too, however, the mechanism is not exactly the same as that envisioned by Paul since the Corinthian assembly *itself* constitutes the temple structure (1 Cor 3:9, 16–17).

Paul's understanding of divine spirit in the community at Corinth is striking for the way in which he articulates the connection between spirit and power as well as the vulnerability of the divine spirit among the Corinthians. Chapter 2 showed import of the threat of the display of God's "power" in 1 Cor 10:22 as well as the result of unworthy consumption of the bread and cup in 1 Cor 11:27 which Origen later named as ἡ τοῦ ἄρτου δύναμις (*Comm. Matt.* 10.25). Furthermore, there is Paul's imagery of the destruction of the temple in 1 Cor 3:16–17 and of the concern for the preservation of the s/Spirit in 1 Cor 5. All of these details from 1 Corinthians 5, 10, and 11 point to the importance of ensuring the continued presence of God's spirit and power within the Corinthian assembly. Moreover, the presence of the Holy Spirit is essential since it makes certain the Corinthians' proximity to God.[23] The Spirit is necessary such that it manifests itself among the assembly in demonstrable ways: what Paul calls the ἀπόδειξις of the Spirit and power (1 Cor 2:4); divine revelation (2:10–13); other divine benefits (2:14; 12:4–11); and salubrity (11:17–34[24]).

While scholarly discussions of Paul's view of the Spirit often focus on *individual* possessions of divine spirit, it is equally important to acknowledge the *corporate* dimension of divine presence that is noted first of all in 1 Cor 3:16–17 and in the three passages analyzed in chapter 2.[25] These two facets of

---

[23] Michael Wolter, "Der heilige Geist bei Paulus," in *Heiliger Geist*, ed. Martin Ebner et al. (Neukirchen-Vluyn: Neukirchener, 2011), 95: "Durch den Geistbesitz wird Nähe zu Gott hergestellt."
[24] See the relevant discussion in chapter 2.
[25] For all his helpful work in problematizing the dichotomies that exist in scholarly discourse vis-à-vis Paul's view of *pneuma* (e.g., Jewish vs. Hellenistic; apocalyptic vs. philosophical; immaterial vs. material), Troels Engberg-Pedersen fails to avoid the dichotomy I note here on individual vs. corporate dimension of *pneuma*. See his "The Material Spirit: Cosmology and Ethics in

Paul's discussions about spirit vis-à-vis the Corinthian assembly should not be pitted against the other, but understood to exist in dynamic relationship. For example, in 1 Corinthians 5, Paul blurs the lines between what may be perceived as individual spirit and the corporate Spirit that dwells within the community.[26]

To return to Paul's view of the divine spirit in light of other sacred spaces in antiquity, it is again clear that the Qumran community presents itself as a helpful analogy. Both Paul and the sectarians view the Spirit as an agent of positive experience for members of the community (e.g. divine revelation). Both recognize the plurality of spirits that can influence human beings: on the one hand, the Holy Spirit, and on the other hand, an impure or worldly spirit.[27] Both describe the vulnerable presence of God's spirit in the midst of the community and enact certain standards of purity in order to ensure the continued presence of this divine spirit. An important dimension of this legislation is the call to "examine" the spirit or things of the spirit.[28] The community can thus be described as מקדש אדם at Qumran and the ναὸς θεοῦ at Corinth because the presence of God is maintained through their proximity to the divine spirit that resides among them. A distinctive feature in Paul's view, however, is the blurred line between the spirit that belongs to an individual and the Spirit that inhabits the community.[29]

5.2.4 Use of Scripture

In seeing the community as a temple with its specific boundaries, Paul is unique in his use of scriptural texts to convey this perspective. There are various inscrip-

---

Paul," *NTS* 55 (2009): 179–197. He asserts that "the Corinthians literally become God's holy temple ... a single body energized by the single *pneuma*" (190) but does not explain what this means at the *corporate* level.

26 John Levison understands Paul's use of *pneuma* along similar lines in his interpretation of 1 Cor 6:19 in "The Spirit and the Temple," 206.

27 See 1 Cor 2:12; 1QS 4:20–23; 4Q417 1i:13–18; 4Q560 1i:1–2i:6.

28 See 1 Cor 2:14–15; 14:24, 29; CD 20:24; 1QS 5:20–21, 24; 6:16–17; 9:14–15; 4Q415 11:7.

29 John R. Levison, *Filled With the Spirit* (Grand Rapids: Eerdmans, 2009), 298: "By crossing the border between individual and community, the metaphor of the spirit-filled temple returns us to the fundamental Corinthian failure, which Paul addressed when he first adopted the metaphor in 3:16–17 ... They fail to grasp that the church as a whole, as a living temple, is filled communally in a way that transcends or, more emphatically, relativizes individual experience, that draws an indispensable relationship between the individual and the community." See also Vahrenhorst, *Kultische Sprache*, 149: "Eine direkte Verbindung beider Motive (Tempel und Gegenwart des Geistes) stellen die Qumrantexte jedoch nirgends her."

tional remnants from temples and sanctuaries in the Hellenistic world, but none of them evince an appeal to an established authority, be it oral or written, to ensure proper behavior within the limits of sacred spaces. This may not be particularly surprising since Greeks and Romans did not appear to hold any body of text as scripture or canon anywhere near to the degree as those within the Jewish tradition.[30] As the classicist Michael H. Jameson rightly observed, "[in Greek religion] what the priest controlled was access to space rather than knowledge."[31]

Granted such differences between Jewish and Hellenistic religious traditions, it is still striking that Paul adopts the language and narrative of scripture to shape the Corinthians' knowledge and access regarding the sacred. Although the Corinthians' experiences of sacred places and objects were likely conditioned by the Hellenistic religious landscape of a highly pluralistic city that was Corinth, Paul relays a particular way of thinking about sacred space and behavior by drawing from Exodus.[32] In 1 Corinthians 5:1–13, 10:1–22, and 11:17–34— the only places in the entire letter that Paul refers to the exodus tradition—Paul describes the Corinthians' encounters with power and peril, a tradition intimately

---

30 The exception here may be Homer, but as far as I can tell, no temple or sacred space in Greek and Roman contexts employ Homeric poems as the grounds or explanation for maintaining the sanctity of a particular sanctuary. For discussion on the reception of Homer, see the relevant essays in Maren R. Niehoff, ed., *Homer and the Bible in the Eyes of Ancient Interpreters* (Leiden: Brill, 2012). See Duncan MacRae, *Legible Religion: Books, Gods, and Rituals in Roman Culture* (Cambridge: Harvard University Press, 2016) that nuances this view further for late Republican Roman religion. Even in the cases noted by MacRae, however, earlier texts cited by later authors do not come close to forming an ideology of sacred space that we see in Paul. This need not mean that Greek and Roman religions had no systems in place that propagated beliefs and practices, but rather it was far more fluid and contextual than might have been possible under a religion dependent on a set of writings. It is well known that Greek religion had an intimate connection between the λεγόμενα (the things spoken) and the δρώμενα (the things done).
31 Michael H. Jameson, "The Spectacular and the Obscure in Athenian Religion," in *Cults and Rites in Ancient Greece: Essays on Religion and Society*, ed. Allaire B. Stallsmith (Cambridge: Cambridge University Press, 2014), 288. Originally published in S. Goldhill and R. Osborne, eds., *Performance Culture and Athenian Democracy* (Cambridge: Cambridge University Press, 1998), 321–40. Jameson cites Walter Burkert who argued: "Greek religion might almost be called a religion without priests: there is no priestly caste as a closed group with fixed tradition, education, initiation, and hierarchy, and even in the permanently established cults there is no *disciplina*, but only usage, *nomos*." In *Greek Religion: Archaic and Classical*, trans. John Raffan (Malden: MA: Blackwell Publishing, 1985), 95.
32 This again contrasts with the Greek system, which Jameson provocatively names as the "lack of articulateness in an otherwise very articulate culture." In "Sacred Space and the City: Greece and Bhaktapur," in *Cults and Rites*, 302–15 (310). He attributes this in part to "the absence of a clerical class or caste and *of sacred texts requiring exegesis*" (emphasis added).

tied to accounts of God's presence among Israelites through the tabernacle. Moreover, for Paul, Exodus plays an important function in his understanding of the formation and experience of the Corinthian assembly.

Paul's way of framing the Corinthians as inheritors of the Israelite tradition is surprising since a group such as the Qumran community would have been far more justified in naming the Israelites from Exodus as "all our fathers" (1 Cor 10:1, οἱ πατέρες ἡμῶν πάντες) rather than the Corinthians, who were primarily pagan or Gentile by origin (1 Cor 12:2). To be sure, the appellation "all our fathers" is one that Paul himself provides, but his unapologetic way of connecting the narrative from scripture to the contemporary situation in Corinth implies that this was an accepted part of Paul's teaching. The analysis of Exodus in 1 Cor 5:1–13, 10:1–22, and 11:17–34 in chapter 2 showed Paul incorporating the story of Exodus in sequential order for a particular purpose: to describe the Corinthians' encounter with power during the formative period of the community.

Numerous texts from the collection at Qumran also demonstrate the vitality of scriptural interpretation for the sectarians. Indeed, the wilderness motif provided an important foundational narrative for the community at Qumran.[33] For example, the Temple Scroll employs the purity rule from Deut 23:10–11 for controlling access to the temple:

> No man who has a nocturnal emission is to enter any part of my temple (כול המקדש) until three complete days have passed. He must wash his clothes and bathe on the first day; on the third he must again wash and bathe; then, after the sun has set, he may enter the temple (המקדש). They are not to enter my temple while unclean, for that would defile it (ולוא יבואו בנגדת טמאתמה אל מקדשי וטמאו).[34]

This is an interesting interpretation since Deut 23:10–11 uses the term "camp" (מַחֲנֶה) not temple and stipulates a half-day ban from entering the temple rather than the three days observed in the Temple Scroll.[35]

The scrolls often identify the community by using the term, "camps" (מחנות), the same organizational term used to describe the Israelites during their wander-

---

33 Alison Schofield, "The Wilderness Motif in the Dead Sea Scrolls," in *Israel in the Wilderness: Interpretations of the Biblical Narratives in Jewish and Christian Traditions*, ed. Kenneth E. Pomykala (Leiden: Brill, 2008), 37–53.
34 11Q19 45:7–10.
35 Deut 23:10–11, "If one of you becomes unclean due to a nocturnal emission, he shall go outside the camp (למחנה). He must not come within the camp (המחנה). When evening comes, he shall wash himself with water, and when the sun has set, he may come back into the camp (המחנה)." Baruch M. Bokser suggests the extension of the days is influenced by Exod 19:10–15. In "Approaching Sacred Space," *HTR* 78.3 (1985): 282.

ings in the wilderness.[36] Like Paul, the importance of Exodus in the collection of writings at Qumran is undeniable: there are also eighteen fragmentary manuscripts that show that Exodus was read and copied thoroughly.[37] Different from Paul, however, the Qumran community uses the Exodus story to interpret and authorize their current dwelling in the wilderness, but does not use the same narrative to inform the continued maintenance of boundaries. This fact is notable when considering the genre of writings at Qumran that employ Exodus. Most of the extant texts are either copied manuscripts of Exodus or rewritten/parabiblical texts. Important texts for communal behavior, such as 1QS and CD, are not part of the aforementioned writings that engage in interpretations of Exodus.

5.2.5 Penalties for Transgressions

Another distinctive feature of Paul's understanding of the Corinthian assembly is his warning concerning the punishments for transgressions. It should be noted, however, that Paul is not wholly unique in his way of dealing with transgressors of sacred objects or spaces in antiquity. The point that makes him rather distinctive is not the *amount* or degree of punishments prescribed against offenders but the *account* or warrant for who is to be punished in the first place. In other words, it is more instructive to consider *the who* in punishments rather than *the what* as one reflects upon Paul's instructions to the Corinthians. Chapters 3 and 4 have shown that in many other cases, the sole target of punishments was the individual offender.

Greek and Roman sanctuaries legislated against errant visitors with various kinds of horizontal—that is, enacted by human agents—punishments: monetary fines up to a thousand drachma; exclusion or prevention from taking part in cultic activities; and physical punishment such as whipping or flogging. There are also vertical punishments such as the gods' rejection of sacrifices; inability to atone for one's ἁμαρτία; encountering divine δύναμις; supernatural disasters; and curses.[38] The offenses that incurred the above punishments ranged from

---

[36] E.g., CD 7:6; 9:11; 10:23; 12:23; 14:3; 1QM 3:5; 4:9; 4Q266 f11:17; 4Q270 f7 ii:14; Num 1:52; 2:3, 10, 17, 32.

[37] Sidnie White Crawford, "Exodus in the Dead Sea Scrolls," in *The Book of Exodus: Composition, Reception, and Interpretation*, ed. Thomas B. Dozeman, Craig A. Evans, and Joel N. Lohr (Leiden: Brill, 2014), 320.

[38] See chapter 3 for analysis of both horizontal and vertical punishments.

simple misdeeds such as wearing improper clothing, to far more serious crimes, such as mishandling sacred objects, incest, and prevaricating on sacred grounds.

The literary and material evidence concerning ancient temples show that *the what* Paul describes in 1 Corinthians 5:1–13, 10:1–22, and 11:17–34 regarding punishments reflects the general response seen in ancient parallels. In 1 Corinthians 5, Paul instructs the assembly to hand over the offender to Satan (5:5) and concludes with the image of purging the evil that recalls the language from Deuteronomy (5:13). These statements suggest physical punishment, possibly even death, meted out against the transgressor. In 1 Corinthians 10, Paul recounts the striking down of the Israelites in the wilderness (10:1–11) and refers to ὁ ὀλοθρευτής (10:10) in relationship to partaking of sacrificial foods. In 1 Corinthians 11, Paul describes the physical maladies and death (11:30) that befell some who participated in the Lord's meal.

In 1 Corinthians, Paul indicates the possibility that transgressions committed by one individual put the entire group at risk. Thus, Paul outlines strict rules about ridding the Corinthian assembly from such dangerous agents. Paul relays the solemn process of handing over the incestuous man to Satan (1 Cor 5:3–6), "so that the Spirit may be preserved" and employs the metaphor of yeast (i.e. the offender) leavening the dough (i.e. the group). He also recalls stories from the Israelite exodus such as the bronze serpent from Num 21 and of Baal worship from Num 25 as examples when death came upon the people (1 Cor 10:6–10). It is possible that the wilderness stories recount punishments meted out only against transgressors, but Paul's employment of these examples serve to highlight the *corporate* consequences of misdeeds rather than simply their ramifications for *individuals*. Even Paul's account of the weakness and death associated with the Lord's supper in 1 Cor 11:17–34 does not single out individual offenders as the only ones in the Corinthian assembly to experience physical ailments.[39]

Paul's descriptions concerning punishments for offenses would have been perfectly intelligible to the Corinthians in degree, though his exhortations are re-

---

[39] Commentators tend to agree with this assessment of the situation described in 1 Corinthians 11:30. See, for examples, Hans Conzelmann, *1 Corinthians: A Commentary on the First Epistle to the Corinthians* (Philadelphia: Fortress Press, 1975), 203n155 ("He does not accuse the individual sick people, but the community: it is sick."); Gordon D. Fee, *The First Epistle to the Corinthians*, NICNT (Grand Rapids: Eerdmans, 1987), 565 ("Most likely Paul does not see the judgment as a kind of 'one for one,' that is, the person who has abused another is the one who gets sick. Rather, the whole community is affected by the actions of some."); Joseph A. Fitzmyer, *First Corinthians: A New Translation with Introduction and Commentary*, AB 32 (New Haven: Yale University Press, 2008), 447 ("He may have the Corinthian church as a whole in mind, for it is sick, and the unworthy reception of the Eucharist allows such destructive forces to afflict it.").

markable for the way that they connect individual actions to the larger group. Even concerning the degree of punishments, however, Paul's approach towards transgressors remained far more punitive than other laws related to sacred spaces. Monetary fines and temporary exclusions were commonplace for individuals who mishandled sacred things or misbehaved within the boundaries of sacred spaces. But in the three sections of 1 Corinthians, Paul does not prescribe such types of punishments. The danger remained more imminent and complete than could be addressed by the payment of coins or temporary banishment. There is evidence in all three sections of the letter that improper behavior led to permanent expulsion or even death (1 Cor 5:5, 13; 10:6–10, 21; 11:29–30).

In summary, the distinctive aspect in Paul's account is the scope, that is, the belief that individual member's actions can negatively affect the integrity, purity, and health of the larger whole. Such an idea is possible because Paul maps unto the Corinthian assembly the framework of the temple of God (1 Cor 3:16–17), which also includes within this discourse the body language that follows in 1 Cor 12. These images make it impossible to separate the actions—and their consequences—of one member of the community from those of the larger assembly. The corruption of one column in a temple cannot be interpreted apart from the integrity of the larger structure, and the disease of one part of the body cannot be separated from the health of the entire body. In contrast, within other ancient accounts concerning sacred spaces, an individual's actions and their consequences need not—indeed, cannot—be transferred to the group associated with that space, since the latter remained external to and separate from the members. In other words, the sanctuary consistently stood as the buffer or intermediary between one person to another. If a person committed an offense, she or he made amends in order to protect the integrity of the temple or sanctuary. At this moment, the potential pollutant cannot imperil other visitors to the temple. For Paul, since the members themselves *are* the temple of God, the transgressions of a single member of the assembly immediately put others of this assembly (= temple) at risk of pollution and harm.

A final related point is the meal that takes place within the gathered assembly where physical well-being, communal wholeness, and divine presence come together. These meals signal the community's "participation in a greater energy field" during a dedicated time and within a particular space, and they may even highlight punishments meted out against offenders.[40] Paul prohibits the trans-

---

[40] Luke Timothy Johnson, *Religious Experience in Earliest Christianity: A Missing Dimension in New Testament Studies* (Minneapolis: Fortress Press, 1998), 165. Paul is not utterly unique in thinking about possible punishments associated with the meal, as other parallel accounts can be found in Josephus, *J.W.* 2.143 and 1QS 7:2–5 (noted in Johnson, *Religious Experience*,

gressor from participating in the meal (1 Cor 5:11), admonishes the Corinthians for failing to distinguish the table of the Lord and the table of demons (1 Cor 10:20–22), and notes the harmful consequences of their misconduct regarding the Lord's supper (1 Cor 11:20, 27–30).

5.2.6 Presence of Christ

The most important characteristic of the Corinthian assembly as temple concerns the presence of Christ noted in 1 Corinthians 5:1–13, 10:1–22, and 11:17–34. More specifically, the divine presence manifests itself through the paschal tradition that is found in all three sections of the letter.[41] This tradition serves to highlight the immediate presence of Christ within the Corinthian assembly. The Qumran sectarians imagined a distant future when the messiah would come once again in their midst, but in Corinth, the messiah was already present through the Spirit and through the Lord's table. In the Corinthian assembly, the divine presence of Christ can be experienced in various ways: through their evocation of Jesus's name and power to protect the presence of the Spirit in their midst (1 Cor 5:3–5), through Christ who has been among his people since the time of the exodus (1 Cor 10:4), and through their present participation in the table of the Lord and the Lord's supper (1 Cor 10:16–22; 11:17–34). This space is distinguished as temple not only by the Corinthians' ritual activities, but by Christ himself.[42]

Paul's use of the exodus tradition and the references made to Christ are critical for connecting the Corinthians to a rich heritage that stretches back centuries and for creating a parallel between the story of the Israelites and their relationship to YHWH and the Corinthians and their relationship to Christ. The Holy Spirit is that which gives life to the assembly and is the medium through whom the Corinthians experience the presence of God in their midst. Sanctuaries and temples all over the Mediterranean also boasted the presence of their own re-

---

166n112 and 170n123, respectively). In these sources, however, it is the decreased rations or complete exclusion from nourishment that is understood to be the punishment. In 1 Corinthians 11:17–34, Paul takes the additional step of thinking about the consumption of the meal as somehow effecting punishment upon members of the assembly.
41 See Carla Swafford Works, *The Church in the Wilderness: Paul's Use of the Exodus Tradition*, WUNT II/379 (Tübingen: Mohr Siebeck, 2014), 160–63. It should be noted here that Works focuses primarily on 1 Cor 5 and 10.
42 This dual sacralization of the Corinthian assembly renders the bifurcation created by Mircea Eliade and Jonathan Z. Smith unnecessary (see discussion in chapter 1).

spective gods, but nowhere else is the presence of divine spirit and the structure of the temple so closely tied to the people themselves. Christ himself literally nourishes this assembly through his body and blood, and he is named as the foundation of this temple (1 Cor 3:10–12).[43] Just as the Israelites drank from Christ (1 Cor 10:4), so now the Corinthians partake of his body (1 Cor 10:16–17; 11:23–28).

5.3 Constructing Temple in 1 Corinthians

Concerning the symbolic importance of temples in the book of Revelation, Gregory Stevenson writes:

> As a mediator of divine presence on earth, the temple provided access to divine power—power to protect, to deal vengeance and retribution, to judge, and to establish victory. The perception that a temple offered access to divine power is what motivated individuals to supplicate at temples, to pray for victory, healing, and deliverance ... To be cut off from one's temple was to be cut off from access to power.[44]

The present study shows that Paul operated under similar assumptions, though taking a step further since he regards the Corinthian assembly itself to be the temple of God. This idea was emphasized in Paul's teaching among the Corinthians, as can be implied in Paul's expectation of the Corinthians to affirm his position. A further implication is that the ethical or moral instructions found in 1 Corinthians 5:1–14:40 should not be read apart from the community as temple motif found in 1 Cor 3:16–17.[45]

Paul's statements about the permanent expulsion of the incestuous offender, the dangers of consuming certain foods (which already contains within its conceptual domain, the temple grounds, where such foods were distributed), and the errors during the Lord's supper all make better sense when read in light of temple discourse in antiquity. That is, Paul assumes the identity of the Corinthi-

---

[43] The permanent nature of Christ's presence through the spirit is one that Paul emphasizes in his second letter to the Corinthians. See the use of the term, ἀρραβών, in 2 Cor 1:22; 5:5.
[44] Stevenson, *Power and Place*, 279.
[45] Margaret Mitchell has already convincingly argued that 1 Cor 1:10–4:21 should not be read without reference to the rest of the letter and vice versa, particularly with respect to the theme of factionalism. See *Paul and the Rhetoric of Reconciliation: An Exegetical Investigation of the Language and Composition of 1 Corinthians* (Louisville: Westminster/John Knox Press, 1991), passim. In the same way, the relevance for temple discourse in reading 1 Cor 5:1–13, 10:1–22, and 11:17–34 should not be bracketed out.

an assembly as a place of power and peril, and he exhorts the Corinthians to follow rules regarding purity and communal activities that parallel regulations found in other sacred spaces throughout the ancient Mediterranean. According to Paul, the Corinthian assembly is not a static entity that was established once for all time, but it remains liable to corruption and danger from external forces.[46] Moreover, the gathering of the Corinthians as the temple of God allow them to participate in divine power that was made available to them, most notably in the Lord's supper, the Holy Spirit, and pneumatic powers that are endowed upon those belonging to this assembly.

By shaping the Corinthians' understanding of their gathering as the temple, Paul is able to address important issues at Corinth regarding boundaries, meals, and spiritual power. Since the community *is* the temple of God, access to the assembly must be restricted. And as Paul notes in 1 Cor 5:12, the group must carefully vet those who are *inside* this community: "Is it not those inside you are to judge? (οὐχὶ τοὺς ἔσω ὑμεῖς κρίνετε;)" Their communal meal represented something more powerful than the typical Greek *symposium* or Roman *convivium*. It is true that scholars have detected similarities in 1 Corinthians with other Hellenistic dining activities in form, but the significance of the paschal tradition and experience of the meal noted in 1 Corinthians 5:1–13, 10:1–22, and 11:17–34 are not exhausted by these ancient parallels. Divine power, which exists within the meal, is made available only in community, and is one that corresponds to the kind of powers experienced by visitants to temples in antiquity. The exhortations found in 1 Corinthians 5:1–13, 10:1–22, and 11:17–34 are not just ethical imperatives that may help the Corinthians fight against *stasis* in Corinth, but are prescriptions towards essential behaviors and boundaries that must be maintained towards the construction of a pure ναὸς τοῦ θεου.

---

46 Despite my general agreement with Christfried Böttrich's study, he is wrong on this particular point when he writes: "Während Pflanzung und Bauwerk durch die Umschreibung mit den entsprechenden Verben vor allem die Dynamik eines anhaltenden Wachstumsprozesses ausdrücken, hat die Rede vom Tempel hier *eher statischen Charakter* und läßt an etwas bereits Abgeschlossenes denken." In "'Ihr seid der Tempel Gottes'. Tempelmetaphorik und Gemeinde bei Paulus," in *Gemeinde ohne Tempel: Zur Substituierung und Transformation des Jerusalemer Tempels und seines Kults im Alten Testament, antiken Judentum und frühen Christentum*, ed. B. Ego et al. (Tübingen: Mohr Siebeck, 1999), 415 (emphasis added). This is one important result of my study; in Paul's estimation, the Corinthian assembly as the temple of God is not a static entity and therefore it remains vulnerable to corruption or destruction if members did not take care to maintain boundaries and regulations.

6 Conclusion

At the outset, the study suggested that 1 Corinthians 5:1–13, 10:1–22, and 11:17–34 can and indeed should be read in conversation, particularly as these passages unpack the important concept of the Corinthians as the temple of God emphasized by Paul in 1 Cor 3:16–17. The present study made use of historical and anthropological tools without eschewing a phenomenological approach that takes into account the experience of Paul and the Corinthians vis-à-vis the temple of God. The passages analyzed describe the importance of the communal meal that mediated the presence of Christ when they gathered together, and showed the way in which access to meals—the Lord's or otherwise—must be carefully guarded and discerned so as not to bring the community into contact with powers that might harm its members. Such experiences of divine presence and consumption of sacrificial meals are essential religious phenomena tied to temples in antiquity. For Paul, the Corinthians as temple meant that it is the locus where members can experience the power of God in a variety of ways. But as temple, they also remained vulnerable to dangerous consequences for transgressions.

Paul's temple discourse draws upon an array of established ideas about sacred spaces and their location as places of power and peril. But in several ways Paul departs from his contemporaries. The second chapter of this project focused specifically on the three passages of Paul's letter to the Corinthians that contain a host of themes relating to the Corinthians as the temple of God. The third and fourth chapters analyzed ancient comparanda to show that Paul's use of temple discourse in the specific manner that he does is quite unprecedented within the ancient Mediterranean context. To be sure, there were hints of this temple concept present at Qumran, but it is nowhere near as developed as it is in Paul. Also, in comparison to his contemporaries, Paul is far more punitive regarding transgressions and remains innovative in the way that he merged the idea of temple and community into one unified concept that informed his idea about how this community can flourish. The distinctive quality of Paul's exhortations, however, cannot be detected without the broad survey of the ancient Mediterranean evidence. Furthermore, the idea of power cannot be understood simply horizontally as a cipher for a social concept or problem that existed among the Corinthians such as divisions or the failure to share one's food. Rather, it is an important descriptor of experiences within temples throughout the ancient Mediterranean world. Additionally, the threat of harmful powers is clear and present such that the Corinthians must watch out, lest they become susceptible to malevolent forces.

This is a more nuanced understanding of how Paul incorporates the assembly as temple concept in 1 Corinthians 5:1–13, 10:1–22, and 11:17–34. It should now be clear that "temple" is just as a major organizing principle for Paul as "body." The temple motif that was introduced in 1 Corinthians 3:16–17 underlie these later passages where Paul envisions the community not as a static entity but as a fragile temple, even a vulnerable one, that must be protected if the Corinthians are to come together as a holy people to properly participate in the Lord's meal. Paul tells the Corinthians in 3:17b that "God's temple is holy, and you are that temple" (ὁ γὰρ ναὸς τοῦ θεοῦ ἅγιός ἐστιν, οἵτινές ἐστε ὑμεῖς). The purity of the temple must be maintained, and thus Paul calls upon the Corinthians to maintain strict boundaries and to behave in accordance with their purified status in 1 Cor 5:1–13, 10:1–22, and 11:17–34.

The Corinthian assembly is the temple where members experienced divine presence in the form of the Holy Spirit and the Lord's supper. As temple in Corinth, the assembly vies for distinction among a host of other sanctuaries in the city, and unlike supplicants to other temples, the Corinthians must adhere themselves solely to Jesus Christ and to the foods provided by him and for him. Paul is not interested primarily in developing a spiritualization of the temple-concept or even in providing a veiled critique of the Jerusalem cult. For Paul, the Corinthians as the temple of God meant that they constitute a new building formed with new materials. The members of this assembly are themselves these materials, as they are now joined together as the ναὸς τοῦ θεοῦ. Being the temple of God did not mean that it is established once-for-all, but this structure has upkeep, maintained strict boundaries that must not be transgressed, and remained liable to corruption and even to destruction. The reality of both power and peril inherent in temples is one that Paul incorporates skillfully in his first letter to the Corinthians as he constructs the temple of God in Corinth.

Bibliography

B.1 Primary Sources

Achilles Tatius. *Leucippe* and *Clitophon*. Translated by S. Gaselee. LCL 45. Cambridge: Harvard University Press, 1969.
Aelian. *Historical Miscellany*. Translated by N. G. Wilson. LCL 486. Cambridge: Harvard University Press, 1997.
Aelian. *On Animals, Books 6–11*. Translated by A. F. Scholfield. LCL 448. Cambridge: Harvard University Press, 1959.
Aelius Aristides. *The Complete Works*. Translated by C. A. Behr. 2 vols. Leiden: Brill, 1981–1986.
Aeschines. *Speeches*. Translated by C. D. Adams. LCL 106. Cambridge: Harvard University Press, 1919.
Aeschylus. *Oresteia: Agamemnon. Libation-Bearers. Eumenides*. Translated by Alan H. Sommerstein. LCL 146. Cambridge: Harvard University Press, 2009.
Aeschylus. *Persians. Seven against Thebes. Suppliants. Prometheus Bound*. Translated by Alan H. Sommerstein. LCL 145. Cambridge: Harvard University Press, 2009.
Andocides. *Minor Attic Orators: Antiphon. Andocides*. Translated by K. J. Maidment. LCL 309. Cambridge: Harvard University Press, 1941.
Antiphon. *Minor Attic Orators: Antiphon. Andocides*. Translated by K. J. Maidment. LCL 309. Cambridge: Harvard University Press, 1941.
Apollodorus. *The Library: Books 3.10–End. Epitome*. Translated by James G. Frazer. LCL 122. Cambridge: Harvard University Press, 1921.
Appian. *Roman History: The Civil Wars, Books 3.27–5*. Translated by Horace White. LCL 5. Cambridge: Harvard University Press, 1913.
Aristophanes. *Birds. Lysistrata. Women at the Thesmophoria*. Edited and translated by Jeffrey Henderson. LCL 179. Cambridge: Harvard University Press, 2000
Aristophanes. *Clouds. Wasps. Peace*. Edited and translated by Jeffrey Henderson. LCL 488. Cambridge: Harvard University Press, 1998.
Aristophanes. *Frogs. Assemblywomen. Wealth*. Edited and translated by Jeffrey Henderson. LCL 180. Cambridge: Harvard University Press, 2002.
Artemidorus. *Artemidorus'* Onericritica: *Text, Translation, and Commentary*. Daniel E. Harris-McCoy. Oxford: Oxford University Press, 2012.
Athanasius. *The Letters of Saint Athanasius Concerning the Holy Spirit*. Translated by C. R. B. Shapland. New York: Philosophical Library, 1951.
Athenaeus. *Learned Banqueters*. 8 vols. Edited and translated by S. Douglas Olson. Cambridge: Harvard University Press, 2007–2012.
Aulus Gellius. *Attic Nights: Books 1–5*. Translated by J. C. Rolfe. LCL 195. Cambridge: Harvard University Press, 1927.
Cato. *On Agriculture*. Translated by W. D. Hooper. LCL 283. Cambridge: Harvard University Press, 1934.
Catullus. *Catullus. Tibullus. Pervigilium Veneris*. Translated by F. W. Cornish. LCL 6. Cambridge: Harvard University Press, 1913.
Cicero. *On the Commonwealth* and *On the Laws*. Edited and translated by James E. G. Zetzel. Cambridge: Cambridge University Press, 1999.

Cicero. *On the Nature of the Gods. Academics.* Translated by H. Rackham. LCL 268. Cambridge: Harvard University Press, 1933.
Cicero. *On the Republic. On the Laws.* Translated by Clinton W. Keyes. LCL 213. Cambridge: Harvard University Press, 1928.
Cicero. *The Verrine Orations, Volume I.* Translated by L. H. G. Greenwood. LCL 221. Cambridge: Harvard University Press, 1928.
Cicero. *Pro Archia. Post Reditum in Senatu. Post Reditum ad Quirites. De Domo Sua. De Haruspicum Responsis. Pro Plancio.* Translated by N. H. Watts. LCL 158. Cambridge: Harvard University Press, 1923.
Demosthenes. *Orations.* Translated by J. H. Vince, C. A. Vince, A. T. Murray, and N. J. De Witt. 7 vols. Cambridge: Harvard University Press, 1926–1949.
Diodorus Siculus. *Library of History.* Translated by C. H. Oldfather, Charles L. Sherman, C. Bradford Welles, Russel M. Geer, and Francis R. Walton. 12 vols. Cambridge: Harvard University Press, 1933–1967.
Dio Chrysostom. *Orations.* Translated by J. W. Cohoon and H. Lamar Crosby. 5 vols. Cambridge: Harvard University Press, 1932–1951.
Dionysius of Halicarnassus. *Roman Antiquities.* Translated by Earnest Cary. 7 vols. Cambridge: Harvard University Press, 1937–1950.
Edelstein, Emma J. and Ludwig Edelstein. *Asclepius: A Collection and Interpretation of the Testimonies.* 2 vols. Baltimore: The Johns Hopkins Press, 1975 [1945].
Epictetus. *Discourses: Books 1–2.* Translated by W. A. Oldfather. LCL 131. Cambridge: Harvard University Press, 1925.
Epictetus. *Discourses: Books 3–4. Fragments. The Encheiridion.* Translated by W. A. Oldfather. LCL 218. Cambridge: Harvard University Press, 1928.
Epiphanius of Salamis. *The Panarion of Epiphanius of Salamis, Books II and III. De Fide.* 2nd rev. ed. Translated by Frank Williams. Leiden: Brill, 2013.
Eunapius. *Philostratus: Lives of the Sophists. Eunapius: Lives of the Philosophers.* Translated by Wilmer C. Wright. LCL 134. Cambridge: Harvard University Press, 1921.
Euripides. *Bacchae. Iphigenia at Aulis. Rhesus.* Edited and translated by David Kovacs. LCL 495. Cambridge: Harvard University Press, 2003.
Euripides. *Children of Heracles. Hippolytus. Andromache. Hecuba.* Edited and translated by David Kovacs. LCL 485. Cambridge: Harvard University Press, 1995.
Euripides. *Cyclops. Alcestis. Medes.* Edited and translated by David Kovacs. LCL 12. Cambridge: Harvard University Press, 1994.
Euripides. *Helen. Phoenician Women. Orestes.* Edited and translated by David Kovacs. LCL 11. Cambridge: Harvard University Press, 2002.
Euripides. *Suppliant Women. Electra. Heracles.* Edited and translated by David Kovacs. LCL 9. Cambridge: Harvard University Press, 1998.
Euripides. *Trojan Women. Iphigenia among the Taurians. Ion.* Edited and translated by David Kovacs. LCL 10. Cambridge: Harvard University Press, 1999.
Galen. *Hygiene: Books 1–4.* Edited and translated by Ian Johnston. LCL 535. Cambridge: Harvard University Press, 2018.
Galen. *Hygiene: Books 1–5. Thrasybulus. On Exercise with a Small Ball.* Edited and translated by Ian Johnston. Cambridge: Harvard University Press, 2018.
Galen. *Method of Medicine.* Translated by Ian Johnston. 3 vols. LCL 516–518. Cambridge: Harvard University Press, 2011.

Galen. *On the Natural Faculties*. Translated by A. J. Brock. LCL 71. Cambridge: Harvard University Press, 1916.

Galen. *On the Parts of Medicine: On Cohesive Causes. On Regimen in Acute Diseases, in Accordance with the Theories of Hippocrates*. Edited and translated by M. Lyons, H. Schoene, K. Kalbfleisch, J. Kollesch, D. Nickel, and G. Strohmaier. Berlin: Akademi-Verlag, 1969.

Galen. *On the Usefulness of the Parts of the Body*. Translated by Margaret Tallmadge May. 2 vols. Ithaca, NY: Cornell University Press, 1968.

Herodotus. *The Persian Wars*. Translated by A. D. Godley. LCL 117–120. Cambridge: Harvard University Press, 1920–1925.

Hesiod. *Theogony. Works and Days. Testimonia*. Edited and translated by Glenn W. Most. LCL 57. Cambridge: Harvard University Press, 2007.

Hippocrates. *Ancient Medicine. Airs, Waters, Places. Epidemics* (1 and 3). *The Oath. Precepts. Nutriment*. Translated by W. H. S. Jones. LCL 147. Cambridge: Harvard University Press, 1923.

Hippocrates. *Prognostic. Regimen in Acute Diseases. The Sacred Disease. The Art. Breaths. Law. Decorum. Physician* (Ch. 1). *Dentition*. Translated by W. H. S. Jones. LCL 148. Cambridge: Harvard University Press, 1923.

Homer. *Iliad*. Translated by A. T. Murray. 2 vols. LCL 170–171. Cambridge: Harvard University Press, 1924–1925.

Homer. *Odyssey*. Translated by A. T. Murray. 2 vols. LCL 104–105. Cambridge: Harvard University Press, 1919.

Homeric Hymns. Homeric Apocrypha. Lives of Homer. Translated by Martin L. West. LCL 496. Cambridge: Harvard University Press, 2003.

Hunt, Arthur S. and Campbell C. Edgar. *Select Papyri. Volume I: Private Documents*. LCL 266. Cambridge: Harvard University Press, 1932.

Isocrates. *To Demonicus. To Nicocles. Nicocles or the Cyprians. Panegyricus. To Philip. Archidamus*. Translated by George Norlin. LCL 209. Cambridge: Harvard University Press, 1928.

Josephus. *Jewish Antiquities*. Translated by H. St. J. Thackeray et al. LCL. Cambridge: Harvard University Press, 1930–1965.

Josephus. *The Jewish War*. Translated by H. St. J. Thackeray. LCL. Cambridge: Harvard University Press, 1927–1928.

Josephus. *The Life. Against Apion*. Translated by H. St. J. Thackeray. LCL. Cambridge: Harvard University Press, 1926.

Juvenal. *Juvenal and Persius*. Edited and translated by Susanna Morton Braund. LCL 91. Cambridge: Harvard University Press, 2004.

Livy. *History of Rome*. Translated by F. G. Moore, et al. LCL. Cambridge: Harvard University Press, 1919–2018.

Lysias. *Lysias*. Translated by W. R. M. Lamb. LCL 244. Cambridge: Harvard University Press, 1930.

Macrobius. *Saturnalia*. Edited and translated by Robert A. Kaster. LCL 510–512. Cambridge: Harvard University Press, 2011.

Menander. *Aspis. Georgos. Dis Exapaton. Dyskolos. Encheiridion. Epitrepontes*. Edited and translated by W. G. Arnott. LCL 132. Cambridge: Harvard University Press, 1979.

Menander. *Samia. Sikyonioi. Synaristosai. Phasma. Unidentified Fragments*. Edited and translated by W. G. Arnott. LCL 460. Cambridge: Harvard University Press, 2000.
Ovid. *Fasti*. Translated by James G. Frazier. Revised by G. P. Goold. LCL 253. Cambridge: Harvard University Press, 1931.
Pausanias. *Descriptions of Greece*. Translated by W. H. S. Jones et al. LCL. 5 vols. Cambridge: Harvard University Press, 1918–1935.
Petronius. *Satyricon. Apocolocyntosis*. Translated by Michael Haseltine and W. H. D. Rouse. Revised by E. H. Warmington. LCL 15. Cambridge: Harvard University Press, 1913.
Philo. Translated by F. H. Colson et al. 10 vols. LCL. Cambridge: Harvard University Press, 1929–1962.
Philostratus. *Apollonius of Tyana*. Edited and translated by Christopher P. Jones. 2 vols. LCL 16–17. Cambridge: Harvard University Press, 2005.
Pindar. *Nemean Odes. Isthmian Odes. Fragments*. Edited and translated by William H. Race. LCL 485. Cambridge: Harvard University Press, 1997.
Plato. *Charmides. Alcibiades. Hipparchus. The Lovers. Theages. Minos. Epinomis*. Translated by W. R. M. Lamb. LCL 201. Cambridge: Harvard University Press, 1927.
Plato. *Lysis. Symposium. Gorgias*. Translated by W. R. M. Lamb. LCL 166. Cambridge: Harvard University Press, 1925.
Plautus. *Casina. The Casket Comedy. Curculio. Epidicus. The Two Menaechmuses*. Edited and translated by Wolfgang de Melo. LCL 61. Cambridge: Harvard University Press, 2011.
Plautus. *The Little Carthaginian. Pseudolus. The Rope*. Edited and translated by Wolfgang de Melo. LCL 260. Cambridge: Harvard University Press, 2012.
Pliny the Elder. *Natural History*. Translated by H. Rackham. LCL. Cambridge: Harvard University Press, 1938–1963.
Plutarch. *Lives*. Translated by Bernadotte Perrin. 11 vols. LCL. Cambridge: Harvard University Press, 1914–1926.
Plutarch. *Moralia*. Translated by F. C. Babbitt et al. 17 vols in 16. LCL. Cambridge: Harvard University Press, 1927–2004.
Polybius. *The Histories*. Translated by W. R. Paton and S. Douglas Olson. 6 vols. LCL. Cambridge: Harvard University Press, 2010–2012.
Porphyry. *On Abstinence from Killing Animals*. Translated by Gillian Clark. London: Bloomsbury, 2000.
Proclus (*Chrestomathia* II). *Homeric Hymns. Epic Cycle. Homerica*. Translated by Hugh G. Evelyn-White. LCL 57. Cambridge: Harvard University Press, 1936.
Ps.-Aristotle. *Metaphysics: Books 10–14. Oeconomica. Magna Moralia*. Translated by Hugh Tredenick. LCL 287. Cambridge: Harvard University Press, 1935.
Quintus Curtius Rufus. *History of Alexander*. Translated by J. C. Rolfe. 2 vols. LCL 368–368. Cambridge: Harvard University Press, 1946.
Sallust. *The War with Catiline. The War with Jugurtha*. Translated by J. C. Rolfe. Revised by John T. Ramsey. LCL 116. Cambridge: Harvard University Press, 2013.
Seneca. *Epistles*. Translated by Richard M. Gummere. LCL 75–77. Cambridge: Harvard University Press, 1917–1925.
Sophocles. *Ajax. Electra. Oedipus Tyrannus*. Edited and translated by Hugh Lloyd-Jones. LCL 20. Cambridge: Harvard University Press, 1994.
Sophocles. *Antigone. The Women of Trachis. Philoctetes. Oedipus at Colonus*. Edited and translated by Hugh Lloyd-Jones. Cambridge: Harvard University Press, 1994.

Statius Papinius. *Silvae*. Edited and translated by D. R. Shackleton Bailey. Revised by Christopher A. Parrott. LCL 206. Cambridge: Harvard University Press, 2015.
Strabo. *Geography*. Translated by H. L. Jones. 8 vols. LCL. Cambridge: Harvard University Press, 1917–1932.
Suetonius. *Lives of the Caesars*. Translated by J. C. Rolfe. 2 vols. LCL. Cambridge: Harvard University Press, 1914.
Tacitus. *Annals* and *Histories*. Translated by M. Hutton et al. LCL. Cambridge: Harvard University Press, 1914–1937.
Tryphiodorus. *Oppian. Colluthus. Tryphiodorus*. Translated by A. W. Mair. LCL 219. Cambridge: Harvard University Press, 1928.
Valerius Maximus. *Memorable Doings and Sayings*. Edited and translated by D. R. Shackleton Bailey. 2 vols. LCL 492–493. Cambridge: Harvard University Press, 2000.
Virgil. *Eclogues. Georgics. Aeneid: Books 1–6*. Translated by H. R. Fairclough. Revised by G. P. Goold. LCL 63. Cambridge: Harvard University Press, 1999.
Virgil. *Aeneid: Books 7–12*. Translated by H. R. Fairclough. Revised by G. P. Goold. LCL 64. Cambridge: Harvard University Press, 2001.
Xenophon. *Memorabilia. Oeconomicus. Symposium. Apology*. Translated by E. C. Marchant. LCL 168. Cambridge: Harvard University Press, 2013.

B.2 Commentaries

B.2.1 Ancient to Pre-Modern

Aquinas, Thomas. *Commentary on the Letters of Saint Paul to the Corinthians*. Edited by J. Mortensen and E. Alarcón. Translated by F. Larcher, E. Mortensen, and D. Keating. Lander, WY: The Aquinas Institute for the Study of Sacred Doctrine, 2012.
Barclay, John M.G. *Flavius Josephus: Translation and Commentary, Volume 10. Against Apion*. Edited by Steve Mason. Leiden: Brill, 2007.
Bray, Gerald. *1–2 Corinthians*. Ancient Christian Commentary on Scripture VII. Downers Grove, IL: InterVarsity Press, 1999.
Calvin, John. *Commentary on the Epistle of Paul the Apostle to the Corinthians*. Translated by J. Pringle. 2 vols. Grand Rapids: Eerdmans, 1948.
Kovacs, Judith L., ed. *1 Corinthians: Interpreted by Early Christian Commentators*. Grand Rapids: Eerdmans, 2005.
Locke, John. *A Paraphrase and Notes on the Epistles of St Paul to the Galatians, 1 and 2 Corinthians, Romans, Ephesians*. Edited by A. W. Wainwright. 2 vols. Oxford: Clarendon, 1987.
Origen. *Commentary on the Epistle to the Romans, Books 6–10*. Translated by Thomas P. Scheck. FC. Washington, D.C.: Catholic University of America Press, 2002.
Origen. *Commentary on the Gospel of John, Books 1–10*. Translated by R. E. Heine. FC 80. Washington, D.C.: Catholic University of America Press, 1989.
Origen. *Homilies on Genesis and Exodus*. Translated by R. E. Heine. FC 71. Washington, D.C.: Catholic University of America Press, 1982.
Theodore of Mopsuestia. *Commentary on the Eucharist and Liturgy*. In A. Mingana, *Woodbrooke Studies*. Vol. 6. Cambridge: W. Heffer & Sons, Ltd., 1933.

B.2.2 Modern

Barrett, C. K. *A Commentary on The First Epistle to the Corinthians*. 2nd edition. London: Adam & Charles Black, 1971 (1968).

Bovon, François. *Luke 3: A Commentary on the Gospel of Luke 19:28–24:53*. Minneapolis: Fortress Press, 2012.

Bruce, F. F. *1 and 2 Corinthians*. London: Oliphants, 1971.

Bruce, F. F. *The Epistles to the Colossians, to Philemon, and to the Ephesians*. NICNT. Grand Rapids: Eerdmans, 1984.

Ciampa, Roy E. and Brian S. Rosner. *The First Letter to the Corinthians*. PNTC. Grand Rapids: Eerdmans, 2010.

Collins, Raymond F. *First Corinthians*, Sacra Pagina 7. Collegeville, MN: The Liturgical Press, 1999.

Conzelmann, Hans. *Der erste Brief an die Korinther*. KEK 5. Göttingen: Vandenhoeck & Ruprecht, 1969. English translation: *1 Corinthians: A Commentary on the First Epistle to the Corinthians*. Philadelphia: Fortress Press, 1975.

Craigie, Peter C. *The Book of Deuteronomy*. NICOT. Grand Rapids: Eerdmans, 1976.

Dunn, James D. G. *The Epistles to the Colossians and to Philemon*. NIGTC. Grand Rapids: Eerdmans, 1996.

Fee, Gordon D. *The First Epistle to the Corinthians*. NICNT. Grand Rapids: Eerdmans, 1987. Updated version published in 2014.

Fisk, Bruce N. *First Corinthians*. Louisville, KY: Geneva Press, 1998.

Fitzmyer, Joseph A. *First Corinthians: A New Translation with Introduction and Commentary*. AB 32. New Haven: Yale University Press, 2008.

Garland, David E. *1 Corinthians*. BECNT. Grand Rapids: Baker Academic, 2003.

Green, Joel B. *The Gospel of Luke*. NICNT. Grand Rapids: Eerdmans, 1997.

Hays, Richard B. *1 Corinthians*. Interpretation. Louisville: John Knox, 1997.

Héring, Jean. *La première épître de Saint Paul aux Corinthiens*. Neuchâtel: Delachaux & Niestlé, 1949.

Horsley, Richard A. *1 Corinthians*. ANTC. Nashville: Abingdon Press, 1998.

Johnson, Luke Timothy. *Hebrews: A Commentary*. NTL. Louisville: Westminster John Knox Press, 2006.

Keener, Craig S. *1–2 Corinthians*. NCBC. Cambridge: Cambridge University Press, 2005.

Kremer, Jacob. *Der Erste Brief an die Korinther*. Regensburger Neues Testament. Regensburg: Friedrich Pustet, 1997.

Lietzmann, Hans. *An die Korinther I–II*. Tübingen: Verlag von J.C.B. Mohr, 1949.

Lightfoot, J. B. *Saint Paul's Epistles to the Colossians and to Philemon*. London: Macmillan, 1890 [1875].

Lindemann, Andreas. *Der Erste Korintherbrief*. Tübingen: Mohr Siebeck, 2000.

Matera, Frank J. *Romans*. Grand Rapids: Baker Academic, 2010.

Meyers, Carol. *Exodus*. NCBC. Cambridge: Cambridge University Press, 2005.

Milgrom, Jacob. *Leviticus 1–16: A New Translation with Introduction and Commentary*. New York: Doubleday, 1991.

Milgrom, Jacob. *Leviticus 17–22: A New Translation with Introduction and Commentary*. New York: Doubleday, 2000.

Moffatt, James. *The First Epistle of Paul to the Corinthians*. London: Hodder & Stoughton, 1938.

Montague, George T., SM. *First Corinthians*. Grand Rapids: Baker Academic, 2011.
Moo, Douglas J. *The Epistle to the Romans*. NICNT. Grand Rapids: Eerdmans, 1996.
Moo, Douglas J. *The Letters to the Colossians and to Philemon*. PNTC. Grand Rapids: Eerdmans, 2008.
Murphy-O'Connor, Jerome. *1 Corinthians*. Wilmington, DE: Michael Glazier, 1979.
Orr, William F. and James A. Walther. *1 Corinthians*. New York: Doubleday, 1976.
Perkins, Pheme. *First Corinthians*. Paideia. Grand Rapids: Baker Academic, 2012.
Robertson, A. and A. Plummer. *A Critical and Exegetical Commentary on the First Epistle of St. Paul to the Corinthians*. ICC. New York: Scribner's Sons, 1911; 2nd ed. 1914; repr. 1975.
Schmeller. Thomas. *Der zweite Brief an die Korinther. Teilband 1, 2Kor 1,1–7,4*. EKK 8/1. Neukirchen-Vluyn: Neukirchener Theologie, 2010.
Schmiedel, Paul W. *Die Briefe an die Thessalonicher und an die Korinther*. HKNT 2.1 Tübingen: J. C. B. Mohr [Paul Siebeck], 1893.
Schottroff, Luise. *Der erste Brief an die Gemeinde in Korinth*. Stuttgart: Verlag W. Kohlhammer, 2013.
Schrage, Wolfgang. *Der Erste Brief an die Korinther*. EKKNT 7/1–4. Zurich: Benzinger, 1991–2001.
Schwartz, Daniel R. *2 Maccabees*. Berlin: Walter de Gruyter, 2008.
Senft, Christophe. *La première Épître de Saint-Paul aux Corinthiens*. Neuchâtel: Delachaux & Niestlé, 1979.
Thiselton, Anthony. *The First Epistle to the Corinthians: A Commentary on the Greek Text*. NIGTC. Grand Rapids: Eerdmans, 2000.
Weiss, Johannes. *Der Erste Korintherbrief*. Göttingen: Vandenhoeck & Ruprecht, 1910.
Zeller, Dieter. *Der erste Brief an die Korinther*. KEK 5. Göttingen: Vandenhoeck & Ruprecht, 2010.

B.3 Secondary Literature

Adeleye, Gabriel. "The Purpose of the *Dokimasia*." *GRBS* 24.4 (1983): 295–306.
Alcock, Susan E. and Robin Osborne, eds. *Placing the Gods: Sanctuaries and Sacred Space in Ancient Greece*. New York: Oxford University Press, 1994.
Aldrete, Gregory S. *Daily Life in the Roman City: Rome, Pompeii and Ostia*. Westport, CT. Greenwood Press, 2004.
Alikin, Valeriy. "Eating the Bread and Drinking the Cup in Corinth: Defining and Expressing the Identity of the Earliest Christians." Pages 119–130 in *Mahl und religiöse Identität im frühen Christentum*. Edited by Matthias Klinghardt and Hal Taussig. Tübingen: Francke, 2012.
Allegro, John M. "Fragments of a Qumran Scroll of Eschatological *Midrashim*." *JBL* 77.4 (1958): 350–354.
Amzallag, Nissim and Mikhal Avriel. "Responsive Voices in the *Song of the Sea* (Exodus 15:1–21)." *JBQ* 40.4 (2012): 211–224.
Andersson, P. and B.-A. Roos. "On the psychology of Aelius Aristides." *Eranos* 95 (1997): 26–38.
Ascough, Richard S. "What Are They *Now* Saying about Christ Groups and Associations?" *CBR* 13 (2015): 207–244.

Atkinson, Kenneth and Jodi Magness. "Josephus's Essenes and the Qumran Community." *JBL* 129.2 (2010): 317–342.
Avalos, Hector. *Illness and Health Care in the Ancient Near East: The Role of the Temple in Greece, Mesopotamia and Israel*. Atlanta: Scholars Press, 1995.
Baden, Joel, Hindy Najman, and Eibert Tigchelaar, eds. *Sibyls, Scriptures, and Scrolls: John Collins at Seventy*, 2 vols. Leiden: Brill, 2017.
Balch, David L. and Annette Weissenrieder, eds. *Contested Spaces: Houses and Temples in Roman Antiquity and the New Testament*. Tübingen: Mohr Siebeck, 2012.
Barclay, John M.G. "Thessalonica and Corinth: Social Contrasts in Pauline Christianity." *JSNT* 47 (1992): 49–74.
Barclay, John M.G. *Jews in the Mediterranean Diaspora: From Alexander to Trajan (323 BCE– 117 CE)*. Edinburgh: T&T Clark, 1996.
Barth, Karl. *Die Auferstehung der Toten. Eine akademisch Vorlesung über I Kor. 15*. München: Chr. Kaiser, 1924. English translation: *The Resurrection of the Dead*. Translated by H. J. Stenning. London: Hodder and Stoughton, 1933.
Bauks, Michaela. "Sacred Trees in the Garden of Eden and Their Ancient Near Eastern Precursors." *Journal of Ancient Judaism* 3.3 (2012): 267–301.
Baumgarten, Joseph M. "Exclusions from the Temple: Proselytes and Agrippa I." *JJS* 33 (1982): 215–225.
Baur, Ferdinand Christian. *Paul: The Apostle of Jesus Christ*. Translated by Eduard Zeller. 2nd ed. London: Williams & Norgate, 1876.
Bauspieß, Martin, Christof Landmesser, and David Lincicum, eds. *Ferdinand Christian Baur und die Geschichte des frühen Christentums*. Tübingen: Mohr Siebeck, 2014.
Bayliss, Grand D. *The Vision of Didymus the Blind: A Fourth-Century Virtue-Origenism*. Oxford: Oxford University Press, 2015.
Beale, G. K. *The Temple and the Church's Mission: A Biblical Theology of the Dwelling Place of God*. Downers Grove, IL: InterVarsity Press, 2004.
Becker, Jürgen. "Die Gemeinde als Tempel Gottes und die Tora." Pages 9–25 in *Das Gesetz im frühen Judentum und im Neuen Testament: Festschrift für Christoph Burchard zum 75. Geburtstag*. Edited by Dieter Sänger and Matthias Konradt. Göttingen: Vandenhoeck & Ruprecht, 2006.
Beek, Leon ter. "Divine Law and the Penalty of *Sacer Esto* in Early Rome." Pages 11–29 in *Law and Religion in the Roman Republic*. Edited by Olga Tellegen-Couperus. Leiden: Brill, 2012.
Beeley, Christopher A. *The Unity of Christ: Continuity and Conflict in Patristic Tradition*. New Haven: Yale University, 2012.
Behr, C. A. *Aelius Aristides and the Sacred Tales*. Amsterdam: Adolf M. Hakkert, 1968.
Behr, C. A. *The Complete Works*. 2 vols. Leiden: Brill, 1981–1986.
Bell, Catherine. *Ritual: Perspectives and Dimensions*. Oxford: Oxford University Press, 1997.
Bendlin, Andreas. "Purity and Pollution." Pages 178–189 in *A Companion to Greek Religion*. Edited by D. Ogden. Oxford: Wiley-Blackwell, 2007.
Benedict, James. "The Corinthian Problem of 1 Corinthians 5:1–8." *Brethren Life and Thought* 32.2 (1987): 70–73.
Best, Ernest. *One Body in Christ: A Study in the Relationship of the Church to Christ in the Epistles of the Apostle Paul*. London: SPCK, 1955.
Bickerman, Elias J. "The Warning Inscription of Herod's Temple." *JQR* 37.4 (1947): 387–405.

Bitner, Bradley J. "Coinage and Colonial Identity: Corinthian Numismatics and the Corinthian Correspondence." Pages 151–187 in *The First Urban Churches 1: Methodological Foundations*. Edited by J. R. Harrison and L. L. Welborn. Atlanta: Society of Biblical Literature, 2015.

Black, Matthew. *The Scrolls and Christian Origins: Studies in the Jewish Background of the New Testament*. London: Nelson, 1961.

Blue, Bradley B. "The House Church at Corinth and the Lord's Supper: Famine, Food Supply, and the *Present Distress*." *CTR* 5 (1991): 221–239.

Bockmuehl, Markus. "The Personal Presence of Jesus in the Writings of Paul." *SJT* 70.1 (2017): 39–60.

Boers, Hendrikus W. "Apocalyptic Eschatology in I Corinthians 15: An Essay in Contemporary Interpretation." *Int* 21.1 (1967): 50–65.

Bokser, Baruch M. "Approaching Sacred Space." *HTR* 78.3 (1985): 279–299.

Bonner, Campbell. "Some Phases of Religious Feeling in Later Paganism." *HTR* 30.3 (1937): 119–140.

Bookidis, Nancy. "The Sanctuaries of Corinth." Pages 247–259 in *Corinth, The Centenary: 1896–1996*. Edited by Charles K. Williams and Nancy Bookidis. Corinth XX. Princeton: The American School of Classical Studies at Athens, 2003.

Bookidis, Nancy. "Religion in Corinth: 146 BCE to 100 CE." Pages 141–164 in *Urban Religion in Roman Corinth*. Edited by D. N. Schowalter and S. J. Friesen. Cambridge: Harvard University Press, 2005.

Böttrich, Christfried. "'Ihr seid der Tempel Gottes'. Tempelmetaphorik und Gemeinde bei Paulus." Pages 411–425 in *Gemeinde ohne Tempel: Zur Substituierung und Transformation des Jerusalemer Tempels und seines Kults im Alten Testament, antiken Judentum und frühen Christentum*. Edited by B. Ego et al. Tübingen: Mohr Siebeck, 1999.

Bowersock, G. W. *Greek Sophists and the Roman Empire*. Oxford: Clarendon, 1969.

Bradley, Mark, ed. *Rome, Pollution and Propriety: Dirt, Disease and Hygiene in the Eternal City from Antiquity to Modernity*. Cambridge: Cambridge University Press, 2012.

Bradley, Mark. "Approaches to pollution and propriety." Pages 11–40 in *Rome, Pollution and Propriety: Dirt, Disease and Hygiene in the Eternal City from Antiquity to Modernity*. Edited by M. Bradley. Cambridge: Cambridge University Press, 2012.

Brendel, Otto J. "Two Fortunae, Antium and Praeneste." *AJA* 64.1 (1960): 41–47.

Brenneman, Laura L. "Corporate discipline and the people of God: a study of 1 Corinthians 5.3–5." Ph.D. diss., University of Durham, 2005.

Bromiley, Geoffrey W., ed. *International Standard Bible Encyclopedia*. 4 vol. Grand Rapids: Eerdmans, 1979–1988.

Brooke, George J. "Miqdash Adam, Eden and the Qumran Community." Pages 285–301 in *Gemeinde ohne Tempel = Community Without Temple: zur Substituierung und Transformation des Jerusalemer Tempels und seines Kults im Alten Testament, antiken Judentum und frühen Christentum*. Edited by B. Ego, A. Lange, and P. Pilhofer. Tübingen: Mohr Siebeck, 1999.

Brouwer, H. H. J. *Bona Dea: The Sources and a Description of the Cult*. Leiden: Brill, 1989.

Brown, Alexandra R. "The Gospel Takes Place: Paul's Theology of Power-in-Weakness in 2 Corinthians." *Int* 52.3 (1998): 271–285.

Brown, Derek R. "The God of This Age: Satan in the Churches and Letters of the Apostle Paul." PhD diss., University of Edinburgh, 2011.
Brown, Peter. *The Making of Late Antiquity*. Cambridge: Harvard University Press, 1978.
Bruun, Christer and Jonathan Edmonson, eds. *The Oxford Handbook of Roman Epigraphy*. Oxford: Oxford University Press, 2015.
Buber, Martin and Franz Rosenzweig. *Die Schrift und ihre Verdeutschung*. Berlin: Im Shocken Verlag, 1936.
Bultmann, Rudolf. "Karl Barth, "Die Auferstehung der Toten.'" *Theologische Blätter* 5 (1926): 1–14. English translation: "Karl Barth, *The Resurrection of the Dead*." Pages 66–94 in *Faith and Understanding I*. Translated by Louise Pettibone Smith. London: SCM Press, 1969.
Bultmann, Rudolf. *Theology of the New Testament*. Translated by Kendrick Grobel. 2 vols. Baylor: Baylor University Press, 2007.
Burkert, Walter. *Greek Religion: Archaic and Classical*. Translated by J. Raffan. Malden, MA: Blackwell Publishing, 1985.
Burkert, Walter. "The Meaning and Function of the Temple in Classical Greece." Pages 27–47 in *Temple in Society*. Edited by Michael V. Fox. Winona Lake, IN: Eisenbrauns, 1988.
Bussières, Marie-Pierre. "Les *quaestiones* 114 et 115 de l'Ambrosiaster ont-elles été influencées par l'apologétique de Tertullien?" *Revue de Études Augustiniennes* 48 (2002): 101–130.
Campbell, Barth. "Flesh and Spirit in 1 Cor 5:5: An Exercise in Rhetorical Criticism of the NT." *JETS* 36.3 (1993): 331–342.
Castelli, Elizabeth A. "Interpretations of Power in 1 Corinthians." *Semeia* 54 (1991): 197–222.
Castelli, Elizabeth A. *Imitating Paul: A Discourse of Power*. Louisville: Westminster John Knox Press, 1991.
Cerfaux, Lucien. *The Church in the Theology of St. Paul*. Translated by G. Webb and A. Walker. New York: Herder and Herder, 1963.
Chaniotis, Angelos. "Greek Ritual Purity: From Automatisms to Moral Distinctions." Pages 123–139 in *How Purity Is Made*. Edited by P. Rösch and U. Simon. Wiesbaden: Harrassowitz Verlag, 2012.
Charles, Ronald. "The Report of 1 Corinthians 5 in Critical Dialogue with Foucault." *Journal for Cultural and Religious Theory* 11.1 (2010): 142–158.
Charlesworth, James H. ed. *The Old Testament Pseudepigrapha*. 2 volumes. Peabody, MA: Hendrickson Publishers, 1983.
Chong, Joong Ho. "The Song of Moses (Deuteronomy 32:1–43) and the Hoshea-Pekah conflict." Ph.D. diss., Emory University, 1990.
Chow, John K. *Patronage and Power: A Study of Social Networks in Corinth*. JSNTSS 75. Sheffield: JSOT, 1992.
Clements, Ruth A. and Daniel R. Schwartz, eds. *Text, Thought, and Practice in Qumran and Early Christianity: Proceedings of the Ninth International Symposium of the Orion Center for the Study of the Dead Sea Scrolls and Associated Literature, Jointly Sponsored by the Hebrew University Center for the Study of Christianity, 11–13 January, 2004*. Leiden: Brill, 2009.
Clinton, Kevin. "A Law in the City Eleusinion Concerning the Mysteries." *Hesperia* 49.3 (1980): 258–288.

Cole, Susan G. *Landscapes, Gender, and Ritual Space: The Ancient Greek Experience.* Berkeley: University of California Press, 2004.
Collier, Gary D. "'That We Might Not Crave Evil': The Structure and Argument of 1 Corinthians 10.1–13." *JSNT* 55 (1994): 55–75.
Collins, Adela Yarbro. "The Function of 'Excommunication' in Paul." *HTR* 73 (1980): 251–263.
Collins, John J. "Reinventing Exodus: Exegesis and Legend in Hellenistic Egypt." Pages 52–62 in *For a Later Generation: The Transformation of Tradition in Israel, Early Judaism, and Early Christianity.* Edited by R. A. Argall, B. Bow, and R. Werline. Harrisburg, PA: Trinity Press International, 2000.
Connor, W. R. "'Sacred' and 'Secular': Ἱερὰ καὶ ὅσια and the Classical Athenian Concept of the State." *Ancient Society* 19 (1988): 161–188.
Conway, Colleen M. "Toward a Well-Formed Subject: The Function of Purity Language in the Serek Ha-Yahad." *JSP* 21 (2000): 103–120.
Cooley, Alison E. *The Cambridge Manual of Latin Epigraphy.* Cambridge: Cambridge University Press, 2012.
Coppens, J. C. "The Spiritual Temple in the Pauline Letters and Its Background." Pages 53–66 in *Studia Evangelica VI: Papers Presented to the Fourth International Congress on New Testament Studies Held at Oxford.* Edited by E. A. Livingstone. Berlin: Akademie-Verlag, 1973.
Cornelius, Izak. "Paradise Motifs in the 'Eschatology' of the Minor Prophets and the Iconography of the Ancient Near East." *JNSL* 14 (1988): 41–83.
Crawford, Matthew R. "Scripture as 'One Book': Origen, Jerome, and Cyril of Alexandria on Isaiah 29:11." *JTS* 64.1 (2013): 137–153.
Cross, F. L. and E. A. Livingstone. *Oxford Dictionary of the Christian Church.* 3rd ed. Oxford: Oxford University Press, 2005 (1997).
Dahl, Nils A. "A Fragment and Its Context: 2 Corinthians 6:14–7:1." Pages 62–69 in *Studies in Paul: Theology for the Early Christian Mission.* Minneapolis: Augsburg Publishing, 1977.
Dahl, Nils A. "Paul and the Church at Corinth." Pages 40–61 in *Studies in Paul: Theology for the Early Christian Mission.* Minneapolis: Augsburg Publishing, 1977.
Davidson, Richard. "Earth's First Sanctuary: Genesis 1–3 and Parallel Creation Accounts." *AUSS* 53.1 (2015): 65–89.
Davies, Jason P. *Rome's Religious History: Livy, Tacitus and Ammianus on their Gods.* Cambridge: Cambridge University Press, 2004.
Deissmann, Adolf. *Light from the Ancient Near East: The New Testament Illustrated by Recently Discovered Texts of the Graeco-Roman World.* Translated by Lionel R. M. Strachan. Peabody, MA: Hendrickson, 1995.
DelCogliano, Mark, Andrew Radde-Gallwitz, and Lewis Ayres, trans. and eds. *Works on the Spirit: Athanasius and Didymus.* Yonkers, NY: St. Vladimir's Seminary Press, 2011.
DeMaris, Richard E. "Contrition and Correction or Elimination and Purification in 1 Corinthians 5?" Pages 39–50 in *The Social Sciences and Biblical Translation.* Edited by Dietmar Neufeld. Atlanta: Society of Biblical Literature, 2008.
DeSilva, David A. "Measuring Penultimate against Ultimate Reality: An Investigation of the Integrity and Argumentation of 2 Corinthians." *JSNT* 52 (1993): 41–70.
Dijkhuizen, Peter. "The Lord's Supper and Ritual Theory: Interpreting 1 Corinthians 11:30 in Terms of Risk, Failure, and Efficacy." *Neot* 50.2 (2016): 446–476.

Dimant, Devorah. "4QFlorilegium and the Idea of the Community as Temple." Pages 165–189 in *Hellenica et Judaica: Hommage à Valentin Nikiprowetzky*. Edited by André Caquot, et al. Leuven: Peeters, 1986.
Dimant, Devorah. "The Demonic Realm in Qumran Sectarian Literature." Pages 103–117 in *Gut und Böse in Mensch und Welt: philosophische und religiöse Konzeptionen vom Alten Orient bis zum frühen Islam*. Edited by Heinz-Günther Nesselrath and Florian Wilk. Tübingen: Mohr Siebeck, 2013.
Dobschütz, E. Von. *Die urchristlichen Gemeinden*. Leipzig: J. C. Hinrichs, 1902.
Donfried, Karl P. "Justification and Last Judgment in Paul." *Int* 30.2 (1976): 140–152.
Douglas, Mary. *Purity and Danger: An Analysis of Concepts of Pollution and Taboo*. London: Routledge, 1966.
Douglas, Mary. *Natural Symbols: Explorations in Cosmology*. New York: Routledge, 2003 [1970].
Douglas, Mary. "Deciphering a Meal." *Daedalus* 101.1 (1972): 61–81.
Downs, David J. "Pauline Ecclesiology." *PRSt* 41.3 (2014): 243–255.
Dozeman, Thomas B. *God at War: Power in the Exodus Tradition*. Oxford: Oxford University Press, 1996.
Dozeman, Thomas B. *Commentary on Exodus*. Grand Rapids: Eerdmans, 2009.
Duval, Yves-Marie. *L'affaire Jovinien. D'une crise de la société romaine à une crise de la pensée chrétienne à la fin due IVe et au début du Ve siècle*. Roma: Institutum Patristicum Augustinianum, 2003.
Ego, Beate, Armin Lange, and Peter Pilhofer, eds. *Gemeinde ohne Tempel = Community Without Temple: zur Substituierung und Transformation des Jerusalemer Tempels und seines Kults im Alten Testament, antiken Judentum und frühen Christentum*. Tübingen: Mohr Siebeck, 1999.
Ehrensperger, Kathy. *Paul and the Dynamics of Power: Communication and Interaction in the Early Christ-Movement*. LNTS 325. London: T&T Clark, 2007.
Eliade, Mircea. *The Sacred and the Profane: The Nature of Religion*. Translated by Willard R. Trask. New York: Harcourt, 1959.
Elgvin, Torleif. "Temple Mysticism and the Temple of Men." Pages 227–242 in *The Dead Sea Scrolls: Texts and Context*. Edited by C. Hempel. Leiden: Brill, 2010.
Ellis, E. Earle. *Paul's Use of the Old Testament*. Grand Rapids: Eerdmans, 1957.
Elsner, Jas and Ian Rutherford, eds. *Pilgrimage in Graeco-Roman and Early Christian Antiquity: Seeing the Gods*. Oxford: Oxford University Press, 2005.
Engberg-Pedersen, Troels. "The Material Spirit: Cosmology and Ethics in Paul." *NTS* 55 (2009): 179–197.
Engberg-Pedersen, Troels. *Cosmology and Self in the Apostle Paul: The Material Spirit*. Oxford: Oxford University Press, 2010.
Faraone, Christopher A. "The Agonistic Context of Early Greek Binding Spells." Pages 3–32 in *Magika Hiera: Ancient Greek Magic and Religion*. Edited by Christopher A. Faraone and Dirk Obbink. Oxford: Oxford University Press, 1991.
Fascher, Erich. "Dynamis." *RAC* 4 (1959): 415–458.
Fee, Gordon D. *God's Empowering Presence: The Holy Spirit in the Letters of Paul*. Peabody, MA: Hendrickson, 1994.
Feeney, Denis. *Literature and Religion at Rome: Cultures, Contexts, and Beliefs*. Cambridge: Cambridge University Press, 1998.

Fehr, Burkhard. "The Greek Temple in Early Archaic Period: Meaning, Use and Social Context." *Hephaistos* 14 (1996): 165–191.
Feyel, Christophe. *Dokimasia: La place et le role de l'examen préliminaire dans les institutions des cités grecques*. Nancy: ADRA, 2009.
Fine, Steven. *This Holy Place: On the Sanctity of the Synagogue during the Greco-Roman Period*. Notre Dame: University of Notre Dame Press, 1997.
Fishbane, Michael. *Text and Texture: A Literary Reading of Selected Texts*. Oxford: Oneworld, 1998 (1979).
Foster, Paul. "Echoes without Resonance: Critiquing Certain Aspects of Recent Scholarly Trends in the Study of the Jewish Scriptures in the New Testament." *JSNT* 38.1 (2015): 96–111.
Fotopoulos, John. "Paul's Curse of Corinthians: Restraining Rivals with Fear and *Voces Mysticae* (1 Cor 16:22)." *NovT* 56 (2014): 275–309.
Foucault, Michel. *Discipline and Punish: The Birth of the Prison*. Translated by Alan Sheridan Smith. Harmondsworth: Penguin, 1977.
Foucault, Michel. *The History of Sexuality*, Vol. 1: *Introduction*. Translated by Robert Hurley. New York: Vintage, 1980.
Foucault, Michel. *Power/Knowledge: Selected Interviews and Other Writings, 1972–1977*. Edited by Colin Gordon. Translated by Colin Gordon et al. New York: Pantheon, 1980.
Foucault, Michel. "The Subject and Power." Pages 208–226 in *Michel Foucault: Beyond Structuralism and Hermeneutics*. By Hubert L. Dreyfus and Paul Rabinow. Chicago: University of Chicago Press, 1982.
Fox, Michael V., ed. *Temple in Society*. Winona Lake, IN: Eisenbrauns, 1988.
Frank, Tenney. "On the Stele of the Forum." *CP* 14.1 (1919): 87–88.
Freedman, David Noel, ed. *The Anchor Bible Dictionary*. 6 vols. New York: Doubleday, 1992.
Frayer-Griggs, Daniel. "Neither Proof Text nor Proverb: The Instrumental Sense of διά and the Soteriological Function of Fire in 1 Corinthians 3.15." *NTS* 59 (2013): 517–534.
Frey, Jörg. "Different Patterns of Dualistic Thought in the Qumran Library. Reflections on their Background and History." Pages 275–335 in *Legal Texts and Legal Issues: Proceedings of the Second Meeting of the International Organization for Qumran Studies Cambridge 1995*. Edited by M. Bernstein, F. García Martínez, and J. Kampen. Leiden: Brill 1997.
Frey, Jörg. "Paul's View of the Spirit in the Light of Qumran." Pages 237–260 in *The Dead Sea Scrolls and Pauline Literature*. Edited by Jean-Sébastien Rey. Leiden: Brill, 2014.
Frey, Jon Michael. "The Archaic Colonnade at Ancient Corinth: A Case of Early Roman Spolia." *AJA* 119.2 (2005): 147–175.
Garland, David E. "Paul's Apostolic Authority: The Power of Christ Sustaining Weakness (2 Corinthians 10–13)." *RevExp* 86.3 (1989): 371–389.
Gärtner, Bertil. *The Temple and the Community in Qumran and the New Testament*. SNTSMS 1. Cambridge: Cambridge University Press, 1965.
Gebhard, Elizabeth R. and Matthew W. Dickie. "The View from the Isthmus, ca. 200 to 44 B.C." Pages 261–278 in *Corinth, The Centenary: 1896–1996*. Edited by Charles K. Williams II and Nancy Bookidis. Corinth XX. Princeton: The American School of Classical Studies at Athens, 2003.
Geljon, Albert-Kees. "Didymus the Blind: Commentary on Psalm 24 (23 LXX): Introduction, Translation, and Commentary." *VC* 65.1 (2011): 50–73.

George, Mark K., ed. *Constructions of Space IV: Further Developments in Examining Ancient Israel's Social Space*. London: Bloomsbury, 2013.
Goff, Matthew J. "Being Fleshly or Spiritual: Anthropological Reflection and Exegesis of Genesis 1–3 in 4QInstruction and First Corinthians." Pages 41–59 in *Christian Body, Christian Self: Concepts of Early Christian Personhood*. Edited by Clare K. Rothschild and Trevor W. Thompson. Tübingen: Mohr Siebeck, 2011.
Goff, Matthew J. *4QInstruction*. Atlanta: Society of Biblical Literature, 2013.
Goffinet, Emile. *L'utilisation d'Origène dans le commentaire des Psaumes de Saint Hilaire de Poitiers*. Louvain: Publications universitaries, 1965.
Gourevitch, M and D. Gourevitch. "Le cas Aelius Aristide ou mémoire d'un hystérique au 2e siècle." *Information psychiatrique* 44 (1968): 897–902.
Gräbe, Petrus J. *The Power of God in Paul's Letters*. WUNT II/123. Tübingen: Mohr Siebeck, 2000.
Grimes, Ronald L. *Rite out of Place: Ritual, Media, and the Arts*. Oxford: Oxford University Press, 2006.
Gruben, Gottfried. *Griechische Tempel und Heiligtümer*. München: Hirmer, 2001.
Gruber, Margareta M. *Herrlichkeit in Schwachheit: Eine Auslegung der Apologie des Zweiten Korintherbriefs 2 Kor 2,14–6,13*. Würzburg: Echter, 1998.
Grundmann, Walter. *Der Begriff der Kraft in der neutestamentlichen Gedankenwelt*. Stuttgart: W. Kohlhammer, 1932.
Gupta, Nijay K. "Which 'Body' Is a Temple (1 Corinthians 6:19)? Paul beyond the Individual/Communal Divide," *CBQ* 72.3 (2010): 518–536.
Haar Romeny, Bas ter. "Procopius of Gaza and His Library." Pages 173–190 in *From Rome to Constantinople: Studies in Honour of Averil Cameron*. Edited by H. Amirav and B. ter Haar Romeny. Leuven: Peeters, 2007.
R. J. Hankinson, ed. *The Cambridge Companion to Galen*. Cambridge: Cambridge University Press, 2008.
Harland, Philip A. *Greco-Roman Associations: Texts, Translations, and Commentary. II. North Coast of the Black Sea, Asia Minor*. Berlin: Walter de Gruyter, 2014.
Harnack, Adolf von. *Die Mission und Ausbreitung des Christentums in den ersten drei Jahrhunderten*. Leipzig: Hinrichs, 1902.
Harrington, Hannah K. "Purity and the Dead Sea Scrolls—Current Issues." *CBR* 4.3 (2006): 397–428.
Harter-Uibopuu, Kaja. "Bestandsklauseln und Abänderungsverbote: Der Schutz zweckgebundener Gelder in der späthellenistischen und kaiserzeitlichen Polis." *Tyche* 28 (2013): 51–96.
Hatzfeld, Jean. "Inscriptions de Panamara." *BCH* 51 (1927): 57–122.
Havener, Ivan. "A Curse for Salvation—1 Corinthians 5:1–5." Pages 334–344 in *Sin, Salvation, and the Spirit: Commemorating the Fiftieth Year of The Liturgical Press*. Edited by Daniel Durken. Collegeville, MN: The Liturgical Press, 1979.
Hays, Richard B. *Echoes of Scripture in the Letters of Paul*. New Haven: Yale University Press, 1989.
Heckel, Ulrich. *Kraft in Schwachheit: Untersuchungen zu 2. Kor 10–13*. WUNT II/56. Tübingen: Mohr Siebeck, 1993.
Heger, Paul. "Stringency in Qumran?" *JSJ* 42 (2011): 188–217.

Hendel, Ronald S. "Sacrifice as a Cultural System: The Ritual Symbolism of Exodus 24,3–8." *ZAW* 101.3 (1989): 366–390.

Hoff, Michael C. "Greece and the Roman Republic: Athens and Corinth from the Late Third Century to the Augustan Era." Pages 559–577 in *A Companion to the Archaeology of the Roman Republic*. Edited by Jane Derose Evans. Chicester, West Sussex: UK: Wiley Blackwell, 2013.

Hoffmann, Adolf. "The Roman Remodeling of the Asklepieion." Pages 41–49 in *Pergamon: Citadel of the Gods*. Edited by Helmut Koester. Harrisburg, PA: Trinity Press International, 1997.

Hogeterp, Albert L.A. *Paul and God's Temple: A Historical Interpretation of Cultic Imagery in the Corinthian Correspondence*. Leuven: Peeters, 2006.

Holladay, Carl R. *Fragments from Hellenistic Jewish Authors*. 4 vols. Chico, CA; Atlanta: Scholars Press, 1983–1996.

Holladay, Carl R. "Spirit in Philo of Alexandria." Pages 341–363 in *The Holy Spirit and the Church according to the New Testament: Sixth International East-West Symposium of New Testament Scholars, Belgrade, August 25 to 31, 2013*. Edited by Predrag Dragutinovic, Karl-Wilhelm Niebuhr, and James Buchanan Wallace, with Christos Karakolis. WUNT I/354. Tübingen: Mohr Siebeck, 2016.

Holland, Louise Adams. "Qui Terminum Exarasset." *AJA* 37.4 (1933): 549–553.

Hollander, Harm W. "The Idea of Fellowship in 1 Corinthians 10.14–22." *NTS* 55.4 (2009): 456–470.

Holmberg, Bengt. *Paul and Power: The Structure of Authority in the Primitive Church as Reflected in the Pauline Epistles*. Philadelphia: Fortress Press, 1980.

Holmes, Brooke. "Aelius Aristides' Illegible Body." Pages 81–113 in *Aelius Aristides between Greece, Rom, and the Gods*. Edited by W.V. Harris and B. Holmes. Leiden: Brill, 2008.

Horst, Pieter W. van der. "The Great Magical Papyrus of Paris (PGM IV) and the Bible." Pages 173–183 in *A Kind of Magic: Understanding Magic in the New Testament and its Religious Environment*. Edited by Michael Labahn and Bert J. L. Peerbolte. London: T&T Clark, 2007.

Horst, Pieter W. van der. "Jewish–Greek epigraphy in antiquity." Pages 215–228 in *The Jewish–Greek Tradition in Antiquity and the Byzantine Empire*. Edited by James K. Aitken and James Carleton Paget. Cambridge: Cambridge University Press, 2014.

Horster, Marietta. "Religious Landscape and Sacred Grounds: Relationships between Space and Cult in the Greek World." *Revue de l'histoire des religions* 227.4 (2010): 435–458.

Hughes, Julie. *Scriptural Allusions and Exegesis in the Hodayot*. Leiden: Brill, 2006.

Hundley, Michael B. *God in Dwellings: Temples and Divine Presence in the Ancient Near East*. Atlanta: Society of Biblical Literature, 2013.

Hundley, Michael B. "Before YHWH at the Entrance of the Tent of Meeting: A Study of Spatial and Conceptual Geography in the Priestly Texts." *Zeitschrift für die Alttestamentliche Wissenschaft* 123.1 (2011): 15–26.

Hunter, David G. "Fourth-Century Latin Writers: Hilary, Victorinus, Ambrosiaster, Ambrose." Pages 302–317 in *The Cambridge History of Early Christian Literature*. Edited by Frances Young, Lewis Ayres, and Andrew Louth. Cambridge: Cambridge University Press, 2004.

Israelowich, Ido. *Society, Medicine and Religion in the Sacred Tales of Aelius Aristides*. Leiden: Brill, 2012.

Jacobsen, Anders-Christian, ed. *Origeniana Undecima: Origen and Origenism in the History of Western Thought. Papers of the 11th International Origen Congress, Aarhus University, 26–31 August 2013.* Leuven: Peeters, 2016.

Jacobson, Howard. *The Exagoge of Ezekiel.* Cambridge: Cambridge University Press, 1983.

Jameson, Michael H. *Cults and Rites in Ancient Greece: Essays on Religion and Society.* Edited by Allaire B. Stallsmith. Cambridge: Cambridge University Press, 2014.

Jamir, Lanuwabang. *Exclusion and Judgment in Fellowship Meals: The Socio-historical Background of 1 Corinthians 11:17–34.* Eugene: OR: Pickwick Publications, 2016.

Jenkins, Claude. "Origen on 1 Corinthians." *JTS* 9 (1908): 231–247; 353–372; 500–514.

Jenkins, Claude. "Origen on 1 Corinthians." *JTS* 10 (1909): 29–51.

Johnson, Luke Timothy. *Religious Experience in Earliest Christianity: A Missing Dimension in New Testament Studies.* Minneapolis: Fortress Press, 1998.

Johnson, Luke Timothy. *Among the Gentiles: Greco-Roman Religion and Christianity.* New Haven: Yale University Press, 2009.

Johnson, Luke Timothy. *The Writings of the New Testament: An Interpretation.* 3rd ed. Minneapolis: Fortress Press, 2010.

Johnson, Luke Timothy. "Life-Giving Spirit: The Ontological Implications of Resurrection." *Stone-Campbell Journal* 15.1 (2012): 75–89.

Johnson, Luke Timothy. *Contested Issues in Christian Origins and the New Testament: Collected Essays.* Leiden: Brill, 2013.

Kajava, Mika. "Religion in Rome and Italy." Pages 397–419 in *The Oxford Handbook of Roman Epigraphy.* Edited by C. Bruun and J. Edmondson. Oxford: Oxford University Press, 2015.

Kapfer, Hilary Evans. "The Relationship between the Damascus Document and the Community Rule: Attitudes toward the Temple as a Test Case." *DSD* 14 (2007): 152–177.

Karlsson, Gustav. "Formelhaftes in Paulusbriefen?" *Eranos* 54 (1956): 138–141.

Käsemann, Ernst. "Sätze Heiligen Rechts im Neuen Testament." *NTS* 1 (1954/55): 248–260.

Käsemann, Ernst. *New Testament Questions of Today.* Translated by W. J. Montague. London: SCM Press, 1969.

Keech, Dominic. "John Cassian and the Christology of Romans 8,3." *VC* 64 (2010): 280–299.

Kilde, Jeanne Halgren. *Sacred Space: An Introduction to Christian Architecture and Worship.* Oxford: Oxford University Press, 2008.

Kimble, Jeremy M. "'That His Spirit May be Saved': Church Discipline as a Means to Repentance and Perseverance." Ph.D. diss., Southeastern Baptist Theological Seminary, 2013.

Kirk, Alexander N. "Building with the Corinthians: Human Persons as the Building Materials of 1 Corinthians 3.12 and the 'Work' of 3.13–15." *NTS* 58.4 (2012): 549–570.

Klauck, Hans-Josef. *Ancient Letters and the New Testament: A Guide to Context and Exegesis.* Translated by Daniel P. Bailey. Baylor: Baylor University Press, 2006.

Klawans, Jonathan. *Impurity and Sin in Ancient Judaism.* Oxford: Oxford University Press, 2000.

Klawans, Jonathan. "The Essene Hypothesis: Insights from Religion 101." *DSD* 23 (2016): 51–78.

Klein, Anja. "Hymn and History in Ex 15: Observations on the Relationship between Temple Theology and Exodus Narrative in the Song of the Sea." *ZAW* 124.4 (2012): 516–527.

Klinzing, Georg. *Umdeutung des Kultus in der Qumrangemeinde und im Neuen Testament.* Göttingen: Vandenhoeck & Ruprecht, 1971.
Kloppenborg, John S. "Membership Practices in Pauline Christ Groups." *EC* 4 (2013): 183–215.
Kloppenborg, John S. and Richard S. Ascough. *Greco-Roman Associations: Texts, Translations, and Commentary. I. Attica, Central Greece, Macedonia, Thrace.* Berlin: Walter de Gruyter, 2011.
Knowles, Michael P. "'The Rock, His Work is Perfect': Unusual Imagery for God in Deuteronomy XXXII." *VT* 39.3 (1989): 307–322.
Koch, Dietrich-Alex. *Die Schrift als Zeuge des Evangeliums. Untersuchungen zur Verwendung und zum Verständnis der Schrift bei Paulus.* BHT 69. Tübingen: Mohr Siebeck, 1986.
Koet, Bart J. "The Old Testament Background to 1 Cor 10,7–8." Pages 607–615 in *The Corinthian Correspondence.* Edited by R. Bieringer. Leuven: Leuven University Press, 1996.
Korner, Ralph J. *The Origin and Meaning of Ekklēsia in the Early Jesus Movement.* Leiden: Brill, 2017.
Kvalvaag, Robert. W. "The Spirit in Human Beings in Some Qumran Non-Biblical Texts." Pages 159–180 in *Qumran Between the Old and New Testaments.* Edited by Frederick H. Cryer and Thomas L. Thompson. Sheffield: Sheffield Academic Press, 1998.
Lanci, John R. *A New Temple for Corinth: Rhetorical and Archaeological Approaches to Pauline Imagery.* Studies in Biblical Literature 1. New York: Peter Lang, 1997.
Lanfer, Peter Thacher. *Remembering Eden: The Reception History of Genesis 3:22–24.* Oxford: Oxford University Press, 2012.
Langdon, Merle K. "Mountains in Greek Religion." *CW* 93.5 (2000): 461–470.
Lauterbach, Jacob Z. *Mekhilta De-Rabbi Ishmael: A Critical Edition, Based on the Manuscripts and Early Editions, with an English Translation, Introduction, and Notes.* 2 volumes. Philadelphia: The Jewish Publication Society, 2004.
Layton, Richard A. "Propatheia: Origen and Didymus on the Origin of the Passions." *VC* 54.3 (2000): 262–282.
Layton, Richard A. *Didymus the Blind and His Circle in Late-Antique Alexandria: Virtue and Narrative in Biblical Scholarship.* Urbana: University of Illinois Press, 2004.
Lee, Michelle V. *Paul, the Stoics, and the Body of Christ.* Cambridge: Cambridge University Press, 2006.
Lennon, Jack J. "Pollution, religion and society in the Roman World." Pages 43–59 in *Rome, Pollution and Propriety: Dirt, Disease and Hygiene in the Eternal City from Antiquity to Modernity.* Edited by M. Bradley. Cambridge: Cambridge University Press, 2012.
Lennon, Jack J. *Pollution and Religion in Ancient Rome.* Cambridge: Cambridge University Press, 2014.
Levison, John R. "The Spirit and the Temple in Paul's Letters to the Corinthians." Pages 189–215 in *Paul and His Theology.* Edited by Stanley E. Porter. Leiden: Brill, 2006.
Levison, John R. *Filled With the Spirit.* Grand Rapids: Eerdmans, 2009.
Lewis, George, trans. *The Philocalia of Origen, A Compilation of Selected Passages from Origen's Works Made by St. Gregory of Nazianzus and St. Basil of Caesarea.* Edinburgh: T&T Clark, 1911.
LiDonnici, Lynn R. *The Epidaurian Miracle Inscriptions: Text, Translation and Commentary.* Atlanta: Scholars Press, 1995.

Lietzmann, Hans. *Mass and Lord's Supper: A Study in the History of Liturgy.* Translated by D. H. G. Reave. Introduction and supplementary essay by R. D. Richardson. Leiden: Brill, 1953.

Lim, Kar Yong. "Paul's Use of Temple Imagery in the Corinthian Correspondence: The Creation of Christian Identity." Pages 189–205 in *Reading Paul in Context: Explorations in Identity Formation: Essays in Honour of William S. Campbell.* Edited by Kathy Ehrensperger and J. Brian Tucker. London: T&T Clark, 2010.

Lim, Kar Yong. *Metaphors and Social Identity Formation in Paul's Letter to the Corinthians.* Eugene, OR: Pickwick Publications, 2017.

Lim, Timothy H. "'Not in Persuasive Words of Wisdom, But in the Demonstration of the Spirit and Power.'" *NovT* 29.2 (1987): 137–149.

Lincicum, David. "Philo on Phinehas and the Levites: Observing an Exegetical Connection." *BBR* 21.1 (2011); 43–50.

Liu, Yulin. *Temple Purity in 1–2 Corinthians.* Tübingen: Mohr Siebeck, 2013.

Llewelyn, Stephen R. and Dionysia van Beek. "Reading the Temple Warning as a Greek Visitor." *JSJ* 42 (2011): 1–22.

Loader, J. A. "The Model of the Priestly Blessing in 1QS." *JSJ* 14.1 (1983): 11–17.

Lupu, Eran. *Greek Sacred Law: A Collection of New Documents (NGSL).* 2nd ed. Leiden: Brill, 2009.

MacArthur, S. D. "'Spirit' in Pauline Usage: 1 Corinthians 5.5." Pages 249–256 in *Studia biblica 1978, III: Papers on Paul and Other New Testament Authors.* Edited by E. A. Livingstone. Sheffield: JSOT Press, 1980.

MacRae, Duncan. *Legible Religion: Books, Gods, and Rituals in Roman Culture.* Cambridge: Harvard University Press, 2016.

Magness, Jodi. *The Archaeology of Qumran and the Dead Sea Scrolls.* Grand Rapids: Eerdmans, 2002.

Magness, Jodi. "Were Sacrifices Offered at Qumran? The Animal Bone Deposits Reconsidered." *Journal of Ancient Judaism* 7 (2016): 5–34.

Malina, Bruce J. and John J. Pilch. *Social Science Commentary on the Letters of Paul.* Minneapolis: Fortress Press, 2006.

Marinatos, Nanno and Robin Hägg, eds. *Greek Sanctuaries: New approaches.* London: Routledge, 1993.

Markschies, Christoph. "Ambrosius und Origenes: Bemerkungen zur exegetischen Hermeneutik zweier Kirchenväter." Pages 545–570 in *Origeniana Septima: Origenes in den Auseinandersetzungen des 4 Jahrhunderts.* Edited by W. A. Bienert and U. Kühneweg. Louvain: Leuven University Press, 1999.

Martens, Peter W. "Interpreting Attentively: The Ascetic Character of Biblical Exegesis According to Origen and Basil of Caesarea." Pages 1115–1121 in *Origeniana Octava: Origen and the Alexandrian Tradition.* Edited by L. Perrone. Leuven: Leuven University Press, 2003.

Martens, Peter W. *Origen and Scripture: The Contours of the Exegetical Life.* Oxford: Oxford University Press, 2012.

Martin, Dale B. *The Corinthian Body.* New Haven: Yale University Press, 1995.

Martin, Dale B. "When Did Angels Become Demons?" *JBL* 129.4 (2010): 657–677.

Martin, Dale B. *Biblical Truths: The Meaning of Scripture in the Twenty-first Century.* New Haven: Yale University Press, 2017.

Martin, Troy W. "Paul's Pneumatological Statements and Ancient Medical Texts." Pages 105–126 in *The New Testament and Early Christian Literature in Greco-Roman Context: Studies in Honor of Davie E. Aune.* Edited by John Fotopoulos. Leiden: Brill, 2006.

Martínez, Florentino García and Eibert J.C. Tigchelaar, eds. *The Dead Sea Scrolls Study Edition.* Leiden: Brill, 1999.

Martínez, Florentino García and Mladen Popović, eds. *Defining Identities: We, You, and the Other in the Dead Sea Scrolls. Proceedings of the Fifth Meeting of the IOQS in Groningen.* Leiden: Brill, 2008.

McDonald, Bruce A. "Spirit, Penance, and Perfection: The Exegesis of I Corinthians 5:3–5 from A.D. 200–451." Ph.D. diss., The University of Edinburgh, 1993.

McDonough, Sean M. "Competent to Judge: The Old Testament Connection Between 1 Corinthians 5 and 6." *JTS* 56.1 (2005): 99–102.

McGowan, Andrew. *Ascetic Eucharists: Food and Drink in Early Christian Ritual Meals.* Oxford: Clarendon Press, 1999.

McKelvey, R. J. *The New Temple: The Church in the New Testament.* Oxford: Oxford University Press, 1969.

McLean, B. H. *An Introduction to Greek Epigraphy of the Hellenistic and Roman Periods from Alexander the Great down to the Reign of Constantine (323 B.C.–A.D. 337).* Ann Arbor: University of Michigan Press, 2011.

McNicol, Allan J. "The Eschatological Temple in the Qumran Pesher 4QFlorilegium 1:1–7." *Ohio Journal of Religious Studies* 5.2 (1977): 133–141.

Meeks, Wayne A. "'And Rose up to Play': Midrash and Paraenesis in 1 Corinthians 10:1–22." *JSNT* 16 (1982): 64–78.

Meeks, Wayne A.. *The First Urban Christians: The Social World of the Apostle Paul.* 2nd ed. New Haven: Yale University Press, 2003 (1983).

Meritt, Benjamin Dean, ed. *Corinth 8.1. Greek Inscriptions: 1896–1927.* Cambridge: Harvard University Press, 1931.

Michenaud, G. and J. Dierkens. *Les rêves dans les "Discours sacrés" d'Aelius Aristide: Essai d'analyse psychologique.* Brussels: Université de Mons, 1972.

Mitchell, Margaret M. *Paul and the Rhetoric of Reconciliation: An Exegetical Investigation of the Language and Composition of 1 Corinthians.* Louisville: Westminster/John Knox Press, 1991.

Mizzi, Dennis and Jodi Magness. "Was Qumran Abandoned at the End of the First Century BCE?" *JBL* 135.2 (2016): 301–320.

Mody, Rohintan Keki. "The Relationship Between Powers of Evil and Idols in 1 Corinthians 8:4–5 and 10:18–22 in the Context of the Pauline Corpus and Early Judaism." Ph.D. diss., University of Aberdeen, 2008.

Mommsen, Th., ed. *The Digest of Justinian.* Berlin: Weidmann, 1868; repr. with English trans. Edited by A. Watson. Philadelphia: University of Pennsylvania Press, 1985.

Moses, Robert E. "Physical and/or Spiritual Exclusion? Ecclesial Discipline in 1 Corinthians 5." *NTS* 59 (2013): 172–191.

Moule, C. F. D. "Sanctuary and Sacrifice in the Church of the New Testament." *JTS* 1 (1950): 29–41.

Moule, C. F. D. "A Reconsideration of the Context of *Maranatha*." *NTS* 8 (1960): 307–310.

Murphy-O'Connor, Jerome. "1 Corinthians 5:3–5." *RB* 84.2 (1977): 239–245.

Murphy-O'Connor, Jerome. *Keys to First Corinthians: Revisiting the Major Issues.* Oxford: Oxford University Press, 2009.

Mylonopoulos, Joannis. "Divine Images *Versus* Cult Images. An Endless Story about Theories, Methods, and Terminologies." Pages 1–20 in *Divine Images and Human Imaginations in Ancient Greece and Rome.* Edited by Joannis Mylonopoulos. Leiden: Brill, 2010.

Naiden, F. S. *Smoke Signals for the Gods: Ancient Greek Sacrifice from the Archaic through Roman Periods.* Oxford: Oxford University Press, 2013.

Naidu, Ashish J. *Transformed in Christ: Christology and the Christian Life in John Chrysostom.* Eugene, OR: Pickwick Publications, 2012.

Newsom, Carol A. *The Self as Symbolic Space: Constructing Identity and Community at Qumran.* Leiden: Brill, 2004.

Newsom, Carol A. "Flesh, Spirit, and the Indigenous Psychology of the *Hodayot*." Page 339–354 in *Prayer and Poetry in the Dead Sea Scrolls and Related Literature: Essays in Honor of Eileen Schuller on the Occasion of Her 65th Birthday.* Edited by J. Penner, K. M. Penner, and C. Wassen. Leiden: Brill, 2012.

Newton, Michael. *The Concept of Purity at Qumran and in the Letters of Paul.* Cambridge: Cambridge University Press, 1985.

Niehoff, Maren R., ed. *Homer and the Bible in the Eyes of Ancient Interpreters.* Leiden: Brill, 2012.

Nielsen, Helge Kjaer. "Paulus' Verwendung des Begriffes Δύναμις. Eine Replik zur Kreuzestheologie." Pages 137–158 in *Die Paulnische Literatur und Theologie.* Edited by Sigfried Pedersen. Göttingen: Vandenhoeck & Ruprecht, 1980.

Friedrich Nötscher, "Heiligkeit in den Qumranschriften." *Revue de Qumran* 2 (1959–60): 163–181.

Økland, Jorunn. *Women in Their Place: Paul and the Corinthian Discourse of Gender and Sanctuary Space.* London: T&T Clark, 2004.

Ostmeyer, Karl-Heinrich. "Satan und Passa in 1. Korinther 5." *ZNW* 5.9 (2002): 38–45.

Parker, Robert. *Miasma: Pollution and Purification in Early Greek Religion.* Oxford: Oxford University Press, 1983.

Penney, Douglas L. and Michael O. Wise. "By the Power of Beelzebub: An Aramaic Incantation Formula From Qumran (4Q560)." *JBL* 113 (1994): 627–650.

Petsalis-Diomidis, Alexia. *Truly Beyond Wonders: Aelius Aristides and the Cult of Asklepios.* Oxford: Oxford University Press, 2010.

Petzl, Georg. "Die Beichtinschriften Westkleinasiens." *Epigraphica Anatolica* 22 (1994): article occupies entire volume.

Pitkänen, Pekka. "Temple Building and Exodus 25–40." Pages 255–280 in *From the Foundations to the Crenellations: Essays on Temple Building in the Ancient Near East and Hebrew Bible.* Edited by Mark J. Boda and Jamie Novotny. Münster: Ugarit-Verlag, 2010.

Pitkänen, Pekka. *Central Sanctuary and Centralization of Worship in Ancient Israel: From the Settlement to the Building of Solomon's Temple.* Piscataway, NJ: Gorgias Press, 2003.

Platt, Verity J. *Facing the Gods: Epiphany and Representation in Graeco-Roman Art, Literature, and Religion.* Cambridge: Cambridge University Press, 2011.

Polaski, Sandra Hack. *Paul and the Discourse of Power.* Sheffield: Sheffield Academic Press, 1999.

Porten, Bezalel and Ada Yardeni. *Textbook of Aramaic Documents from Ancient Egypt, Volume 1: Letters*. Jerusalem: Hebrew University, 1986.
Prümm, Karl. "Dynamis in griechisch-hellenisticher Religion und Philosophie als Vergleichsbild zu göttlicher Dynamis im Offenbarungsraum." *ZKT* 83 (1961): 393–430.
Puech, Émile. "L'Esprit Saint à Qumrân." *LASBF* 49 (1999): 283–298.
Rabello, A. M. "The 'Lex de Templo Hierosolymitano', Prohibiting Gentiles from Entering Jerusalem's Sanctuary." *Christian News From Israel* 21 (1970–71): 3.28–32 and 4.28–32.
Radde-Gallwitz, Andrew. "The Holy Spirit as Agent, not Activity: Origen's Argument with Modalism and its Afterlife in Didymus, Eunomius, and Gregory of Nazianzus." *VC* 65.3 (2011): 227–248.
Ramelli, Ilaria, L. E. "Origen's Anti-Subordinationism and its Heritage in the Nicene and Cappadocian Line." *VC* 65.1 (2011): 21–49.
Ramelli, Ilaria, L. E. "Spiritual Weakness, Illness, and Death in 1 Corinthians 11:30." *JBL* 130.1 (2011): 145–163.
Ramelli, Ilaria, L. E. "The *Dialogue of Adamantius:* A Document of Origen's Thought? (Part Two)." StPatr 56 (2013): 227–273.
Ramelli, Ilaria, L. E. "Origen in Augustine: A Paradoxical Reception." *Numen* 60 (2013): 380–307.
Regev, Eyal. "Abominated Temple and a Holy Community: The Formation of the Notions of Purity and Impurity in Qumran." *Dead Sea Discoveries* 10.2 (2003): 243–278.
Regev, Eyal. "Temple and Righteousness in Qumran and Early Christianity: Tracing the Social Difference Between the Two Movements." Pages 63–87 in *Text, Thought, and Practice in Qumran and Early Christianity: Proceedings of the Ninth International Symposium of the Orion Center for the Study of the Dead Sea Scrolls and Associated Literature, Jointly Sponsored by the Hebrew University Center for the Study of Christianity, 11–13 January, 2004*. Edited by Ruth A. Clements and Daniel R. Schwartz. Leiden: Brill, 2009.
Renberg, Gil H. "Public and Private Places of Worship in the Cult of Asclepius at Rome." *Memoirs of the American Academy in Rome* 51/52 (2006/7): 87–172.
Ridder, A. de and A. Choisy. "Devis de Livadie." *BCH* 20 (1896): 318–335.
Rice, Joshua. *Paul and Patronage: The Dynamics of Power in 1 Corinthians*. Eugene, OR: Pickwick Publications, 2013.
Rigsby, Kent J. *Asylia: Territorial Inviolability in the Hellenistic World*. Berkeley: University of California Press, 1996.
Rives, James B. *Religion in the Roman Empire*. Malden, MA: Blackwell Publishing, 2007.
Robinson, Betsey A. *Histories of Peirene: A Corinthian Fountain in Three Millennia*. Princeton: American School of Classical Studies at Athens, 2011.
Roebuck, Carl. *Corinth XIV: The Asklepieion and Lerna*. Princeton: The American School of Classical Studies at Athens, 1951.
Röhser, Günther. "Vorstellungen von der Präsenz Christi im Ritual nach 1Kor 11,17–34." Pages 131–158 in *Mahl und religiöse Identität im frühen Christentum*. Edited by Matthias Klinghardt and Hal Taussig. Tübingen: Francke, 2012.
Romano, Irene Bald. "Early Greek Cult Images and Cult Practices." Pages 127–134 in *Early Greek Cult Practice: Proceedings of the Fifth International Symposium at the Swedish Institute at Athens, 26–29 June, 1986*. Edited by R. Hägg, N. Marinatos, and G. C. Nordquist. Stockholm: Svenska Institutet i Athen, 1988.

Rosner, Brian S. "Temple and Holiness in 1 Corinthians 5." *TynBul* 42.1 (1991): 137–145.
Rosner, Brian S. "'ΟΥΧΙ ΜΑΛΛΟΝ ΕΠΕΝΘΗΣΑΤΕ': Corporate Responsibility in 1 Corinthians 5." *NTS* 38 (1992): 470–473.
Rosner, Brian S. "'Stronger than He?' The Strength of 1 Corinthians 10:22b." *TynBul* 43.1 (1992): 171–179.
Rosner, Brian S. *Paul, Scripture, and Ethics: A Study of 1 Corinthians 5–7*. Grand Rapids: Baker, 1999.
Rosner, Brian S. "Deuteronomy in 1 and 2 Corinthians." Pages 118–135 in *Deuteronomy in the New Testament*. Edited by Maarten J. J. Menken and Steve Moyise. London: T&T Clark, 2007.
Runia, David T. "The Idea and the Reality of the City in the Thought of Philo of Alexandria." *JHI* 61.3 (2000): 361–379.
Rüpke, Jörg. *Die Religion der Römer: Eine Einführung*. München: Verlag C. H. Beck, 2001.
Rüpke, Jörg. *Religion in Republican Rome: Rationalization and Ritual Change*. Philadelphia: University of Pennsylvania Press, 2012.
Sanders, E. P. *Jesus and Judaism*. Philadelphia: Fortress Press, 1985.
Sanders, E. P. *Paul and Palestinian Judaism: A Comparison of Patterns of Religion*. Philadelphia: Fortress Press, 1977.
Savage, Timothy B. *Power Through Weakness: Paul's Understanding of the Christian Ministry in 2 Corinthians*. SNTSMS 86. Cambridge: Cambridge University Press, 1996.
Schatkin, Margaret A. "The Influence of Origen Upon St. Jerome's Commentary on Galatians." *VC* 24 (1970): 49–58.
Schatkin, Margaret A. "The Origenism of St. John Chrysostom in the West: From St. Jerome to the Present" Pages 125–137 in *Origeniana Undecima: Origen and Origenism in the History of Western Thought. Papers of the 11th International Origen Congress, Aarhus University, 26–31 August 2013*. Edited by Anders-Christian Jacobsen. Leuven: Peeters, 2016.
Scheid, John. "Sacrifices for Gods and Ancestors." Pages 263–271 in *A Companion to Roman Religion*. Edited by J. Rüpke. Oxford: Blackwell, 2007.
Schiffman, Lawrence H. "Community Without Temple: The Qumran Community's Withdrawal from the Jerusalem Temple." Pages 267–284 in *Gemeinde ohne Tempel = Community Without Temple: zur Substituierung und Transformation des Jerusalemer Tempels und seines Kults im Alten Testament, antiken Judentum und frühen Christentum*. Edited by B. Ego, A. Lange, and P. Pilhofer. Tübingen: Mohr Siebeck, 1999.
Schiffman, Lawrence H. "Qumran Temple? The Literary Evidence." *Journal of Ancient Judaism* 7.1 (2016): 71–85.
Schlosser, Jacques, ed. *Paul et l'unité des chrétiens*. Leuven: Peeters, 2010.
Schmitz, Otto. "Der Begriff ΔΥΝΑΜΙΣ bei Paulus: Ein Beitrag zum Wesen urchristlicher Begriffsbildung." Page 139–167 in *Festgabe für Adolf Deissmann zum 60. Geburtstag 7. November 1926*. Edited by K. L. Schmidt. Tübingen: J. C. B. Mohr, 1926.
Schneider, Sebastian. "Glaubensmängel in Korinth: Eine neue Deutung der 'Schwachen, Kranken, Schlafenden,' in 1 Kor 11,30." *Filologia Neotestamentaria* 9 (1996): 3–19.
Schofield, Alison. *From Qumran to the Yaḥad: A New Paradigm of Textual Development for The Community Rule*. STDJ 77. Leiden: Brill, 2009.
Schröder, Heinrich O. *Galeni in Platonis Timaeum commentarii fragmenta*. CMG 1 Leipzig: B. G. Teubner, 1934.

Schüssler Fiorenza, Elisabeth. "Cultic Language in Qumran and in the NT." *CBQ* 38.2 (1976): 159–177.
Schwartz, Daniel R. "The Three Temples of 4QFlorilegium." *RevQ* 10 (1979): 83–91.
Schwartz, Daniel R. *Agrippa I: The Last King of Judaea*. Tübingen: Mohr Siebeck, 1990.
Schwartz, Daniel R. "Humbly Second-Rate in the Diaspora? Philo and Stephen on the Tabernacle and the Temple." Pages 81–89 in *Envisioning Judaism: Studies in Honor of Peter Schäfer on the Occasion of his Seventieth Birthday*. Edited by R. S. Boustan et al. Tübingen: Mohr Siebeck, 2013.
Schwarz, Sarah L. "Demons and Douglas: Applying Grid and Group to the Demonologies of the Testament of Solomon." *JAAR* 80.4 (2012): 909–931.
Schwiebert, Jonathan. "Table Fellowship and the Translation of 1 Corinthians 5:11." *JBL* 127.1 (2008): 159–164.
Segal, Peretz. "The Penalty of the Warning Inscription from the Temple of Jerusalem." *Israel Exploration Journal* 39 (1989): 79–84.
Sellew, Philip. "Achilles or Christ? Porphyry and Didymus in Debate over Allegorical Interpretation." *HTR* 82.1 (1989): 79–100.
Shillington, V. George. "Atonement Texture in 1 Corinthians 5.5." *JSNT* 71 (1998): 29–50.
Smit, Peter-Ben. "Ritual Failure, Ritual Negotiation, and Paul's Argument in 1 Corinthians 11:17–34." *JSPL* 3.2 (2013): 165–193.
Smith, David Raymond. *'Hand This Man Over to Satan': Curse, Exclusion and Salvation in 1 Corinthians 5*. LNTS 386. London: T&T Clark, 2008.
Smith, Dennis E. *From Symposium to Eucharist: The Banquet in the Early Christian World*. Minneapolis: Fortress Press, 2003.
Smith, Jonathan Z. *To Take Place: Toward Theory in Ritual*. Chicago: University of Chicago Press, 1987.
Smithals, Walter. *Die Gnosis in Korinth: Eine Untersuchung zu den Korintherbriefen*. Göttingen: Vandenhoeck & Ruprecht, 1956.
Smyth, Herbert Weir. *Greek Grammar*. 1916. Revised by Gordon M. Messing. Cambridge: Harvard University Press, 1956.
Sohm, Rudolf. *Kirchengeschichte im Grundriss*. Leipzig: E. Ungleich, 1894.
South, James T. "A Critique of the 'Curse/Death' Interpretation of 1 Corinthians 5.1–8." *NTS* 39 (1993): 539–561.
Spaeth, Barbette Stanley. "Greek Gods or Roman? The Corinthian Archaistic Blocks and Religion in Roman Corinth." *AJA* 121.3 (2017): 397–423.
Spawforth, Tony. *The Complete Greek Temples*. London: Thames & Hudson, 2006.
Spencer, William David. "The Power in Paul's Teaching (1 Cor 4:9–20)." *JETS* 32.1 (1989): 51–61.
Staab, Karl. *Pauluskommentare aus der Griechischen Kirche*. Münster: Aschendorffschen, 1933.
Stamper, John W. *The Architecture of Roman Temples: The Republic to the Middle Empire*. Cambridge: Cambridge University Press, 2005.
Stanley, Christopher D. *Paul and the Language of Scripture: Citation technique in the Pauline Epistles and Contemporary Literature*. SNTSMS 69. Cambridge: Cambridge University Press, 1992.
Steaniw, Blossom. *Mind, Text, and Commentary: Noetic Exegesis in Origen of Alexandria, Didymus the Blind, and Evagrius Ponticus*. Frankfurt am Main: Lang, 2010.

Stevenson, Gregory. *Power and Place: Temple and Identity in the Book of Revelation.* Berlin: Walter de Gruyter, 2001.

Swarup, Paul. *The Self-Understanding of the Dead Sea Scrolls Community: An Eternal Planting, A House of Holiness.* London: T&T Clark, 2006.

Talbott, Rick F. *Jesus, Paul, and Power: Rhetoric, Ritual and Metaphor in Ancient Mediterranean Christianity.* Eugene, OR: Cascade Books, 2010.

Thiessen, Matthew. "'The Rock Was Christ': The Fluidity of Christ's Body in 1 Corinthians 10.4." *JSNT* 36.2 (2013): 103–126.

Thome, Gabriele. "Crime and Punishment, Guilt and Expiation: Roman Thought and Vocabulary." *Acta Classica* 35 (1992): 73–98.

Thraede, Klaus. "Schwierigkeiten mit 1Kor 5,1–13." *ZNW* 103.2 (2012): 177–212.

Tiller, Patrick A. "The 'Eternal Planting' in the Dead Sea Scrolls." *DSD* 4.3 (1997): 312–335.

Travlos, John. *Pictorial Dictionary of Ancient Athens.* London: Thames and Hudson, 1971.

Trebilco, Paul. "Epigraphy and the Study of Polis and *Ekklēsia* in the Greco-Roman World." Pages 89–109 in *The First Urban Churches 1: Methodological Foundations.* Edited by James R. Harrison and L. L. Welborn. Atlanta: Society of Biblical Literature, 2015.

Tuckett, Christopher M. "Paul, Scripture and Ethics: Some Reflections." *NTS* 46.3 (2000): 403–424.

Vahrenhorst, Martin. *Kultische Sprache in den Paulusbriefen.* WUNT 230. Tübingen: Mohr Siebeck, 2008.

VanderKam, James C. *The Book of Jubilees.* Louvain: Peeters, 1989.

Walbank, Mary E. Hoskins. "The Cults of Roman Corinth: Public Ritual and Personal Belief." Pages 357–376 in *Roman Peloponnese III: Society, Economy and Culture Under the Roman Empire: Continuity and Innovation.* Edited by A. D. Rizakis and C. E. Lepenioti. Athens: Research Institute for Greek and Roman Antiquity, 2010.

Wan, Sze-kar. *Power in Weakness: Conflict and Rhetoric in Paul's Second Letter to the Corinthians.* Harrisburg, PA: Trinity Press International, 2000.

Wardle, Timothy. *The Jerusalem Temple and Early Christian Identity.* WUNT II/291. Tübingen: Mohr Siebeck, 2010.

Wassen, Cecilia. "What Do Angels Have against the Blind and the Deaf? Rules of Exclusion in the Dead Sea Scrolls." Pages 115–129 in *Common Judaism: Explorations in Second-Temple Judaism.* Edited by Wayne O. McCready and Adele Reinhartz. Minneapolis: Fortress Press, 2008.

Wassen, Cecilia. "Visions of the Temple: Conflicting Images of the Eschaton," *SEÅ* 76 (2011): 41–59.

Watson, Francis. "Scripture in Pauline Theology: How Far Down Does It Go?" *Journal of Theological Interpretation* 2.2 (2008): 181–192.

Watson, Francis. *Paul and the Hermeneutics of Faith.* London: T&T Clark, 2004.

Weber, Max. *Economy and Society: An Outline of Interpretive Sociology.* Edited by G. Roth and C. Wittich. Translated by E. Fischoff et al. 2 vols. Berkeley: University of California Press, 1978.

Weiss, Johannes. *Earliest Christianity: A History of the Period A.D. 30–150.* Translated by F. C. Grant. 2 vols. New York: Harper & Brothers, 1959.

Wells, Jack. "Impiety in the Middle Republic: The Roman Response to Temple Plundering in Southern Italy." *CJ* 105.3 (2010): 229–243.

Wenham, Gordon J. "Sanctuary Symbolism in the Garden of Eden Story." Pages 399–404 in *I Studied Inscriptions from Before the Flood: Ancient Near Eastern, Literary, and Linguistic Approaches to Genesis 1–11*. Edited by Richard S. Hess and David Toshio Tsumura. Winona Lake, IN: Eisenbrauns, 1994.

Wenham, Gordon J. *Genesis 16–50*. Dallas, TX: Word Books, 1994.

Wenschkewitz, Hans. *Die Spiritualisierung der Kultusbegriffe: Tempel, Priester und Opfer im Neuen Testament*. Leipzig: E. Pfeiffer, 1932.

Whitfield, Bryan J. *Joshua Traditions and the Argument of Hebrews 3 and 4*. BZNW 194. Berlin: De Gruyter, 2013.

Wickkiser, Bronwen L. *Asklepios, Medicine, and the Politics of Healing in Fifth-Century Greece: Between Craft and Cult*. Baltimore: The Johns Hopkins University Press, 2008.

Wiles, Gordon P. *Paul's Intercessory Prayers: The Significance of the Intercessory Prayer Passages in the Letters of St Paul*. Cambridge: Cambridge University Press, 1974.

Winter, Bruce W. "Secular and Christian Responses to Corinthian Famines." *TynBul* 40.1 (1989): 86–106.

Wise, Michael O. "4QFlorilegium and the Temple of Adam." *RevQ* 15.1–2 (1991–92): 103–132.

Wissowa, Georg. *Religion und Kultus der Römer*. 2nd ed. München, C.H. Beck, 1912.

Wold, Benjamin. "'Flesh' and 'Spirit' in Qumran Sapiential Literature as the Background to the Use in Pauline Epistles." *ZNW* 106.2 (2015): 262–279.

Wolter, Michael. "Der heilige Geist bei Paulus." Pages 93–119 in *Heiliger Geist*. Edited by Martin Ebner et al. Neukirchen-Vluyn: Neukirchener, 2011.

Woyke. Johannes. *Götter, "Götzen," Götterbilder: Aspekte einer paulinischen "Theologie der Religionen"*. Berlin: De Gruyter, 2005.

Yadin, Y. "A Midrash on 2 Sam. Vii and Ps. I–ii (4Q Florilegium)." *Israel Exploration Journal* 9.2 (1959): 95–98.

Zaas, Peter S. "'Cast Out the Evil Man from Your Midst' (1 Cor 5:13b)." *JBL* 103.2 (1984): 259–261.

Zeitlin, S. "The Warning Inscription of the Temple." *JQR* 38.1 (1947): 111–116.

Index of Ancient Citations

1 Clement
38:2	102
57:4	3

1 Enoch
10:8	93
10:16	174
10:24–26	174
12:4	93
16:1	93
24:2–5	164
25:3	164
25:5	164
25:6	164
69:12	83
84:6	174
90:28–29	171
93:2–5	174

2 Baruch
4:2–6	171

Achilles Tatius
Leucippe et Clitophon
3.25.6–7	124

Acts of John
29	37

Aelian
De natura animalium
3.47	33
9.33	119, 147

Varia historia
3.43	116

Aelius Aristides
Hieroi Logoi
2.5	147
2.7	148
2.69	147
2.70	148
4.14	148
4.29	151
4.53	151
5.37	152

Orationes
1.1	150
1.37	149
1.87	149
1.167	149
1.190	150
1.191–193	149
1.322	150
1.330	149
1.338	149
1.341	149
1.363	149
1.364	149
1.373	149
1.404	149
2.52	149
2.201	152
2.379	150
2.411	149
3.97	149
3.100	150
3.218	149
3.245	149
3.252	149
3.265–266	150
3.270	149
3.276	150
3.285	149
3.290	150
3.310	149
3.327	150
3.392	149
4.19	150
7.1	149
9.46	149
16.11	149
16.31	152
17.5–6	150
17.10–11	149
17.16	150
18.1	150
18.6	149
22	149
23.57	150
24.16–17	149
24.42	150

24.48–50	152	49.8	148
24.52	150	**Aeschines**	
26.2	150	De falsa legatione	
26.104–105	150	87	131
26.108–109	149	In Ctesiphonem	
27.39	150	121	127
28.2	150	In Timarchum	
28.45–50	150	67	129
28.109	150	**Aeschylus**	
28.127	147	Agamemnon	
28.156	150	1501	135
29.4	149 f.	1508	135
29.7	152	Choephori	
29.14	152	566	83
30.1	149	Persae	
30.28	149	354	83, 135
33.2	150	Prometheus vinctus	
33.17	150	517	102
33.19	147	Septem contra Thebas	
33.20	150	181–202	127
34.59–60	150	700	116
35.1–2	150	812	83
36.104	150	**Alexander of Aphrodisias**	
37	150	On Mixture and Growth	
38.2	150	216.14–17	203
38.42	150	**Ambrose of Milan**	
39.5	150	De fuga saeculi	
40	150	2.8	64
40.12	149	De officiis ministrorum	
41	150	3.18.109	64 f.
42	150	De paenitentia	
42.2	150	1.13	64
42.4	150	2.2	64
42.5	150	**Ambrosiaster**	
42.6	150	In Epistulas ad Corinthios I	
42.12	150	5:5	69
42.14	150	10:26	82
43.7–15	150	**Andocides**	
43.17	150	On His Return	
43.18	149	2.15	126
43.256	150	On the Mysteries	
45	145	110	126
45.16–17	150	124–129	33
45.19	150	**Antiphon**	
45.26–27	145	On the Murder of Herodes	
45.33	150	82	116
46.1–4	150		

Apocalypse of Abraham
25.1–6   166
27.3–7   166
Apollonius of Rhodes
Argonautica
2.87   22
3.410   22
3.496   22
3.1303   22
Appian
Bella civilia
4.6.44   102
5.1.4   144
5.1.7   144
Hannibalica
56   141
Apuleius
Metamorphoses
10.2–12   33
Aristophanes
Aves
850   116
958–59   116
Ecclesiazusae
6.111   102
Lysistrata
1129–1131   116
Pax
948–62   116
Plutus
633–747   118
Ranae
327–35   116
385   116
404–12   116
Thesmophoriazusae
331–51   131
Vespae
121–23   118
Aristotle
Categoriae
9a.2   22
De coloribus
793a   37
Historia animalium
634b   102

Artemidorus
Onirocritica
2.34   139
4.20   33
Athanasius
Apologia ad Constantium
7.14   135
Epistula ad Serapionem de more Arii
4.13   59
Epistulae ad Serapionem
1.4   70
Epistulae festales
3   37
6   37
Athenaeus
Deipnosophistae
13.67   129
Augustine
Epistulae
93.7   64
Expositio in epistulam ad Galatas
32.9–10   64
Sermones
82.13   76
Aulus Gellius
Noctes atticae
4.9.9   138
Barnabas
12:2   74
19:7   74
Basil of Caesarea
Asceticon magnum
1.29   4
2.133   4
Enarratio in prophetam Esaiam
13.261   64
Epistulae
188.7   64
Homiliae in Psalmos
17.7   64
Regulae morales
6.72   64
11.3   4
Cato
De agricultura
132   146
134   146

Catullus
64.403–8	143
74	33
88–9	33
90	33

Chrysippus
Frag. mor. 233.5   22
Fragmenta logica et physica
fr. 1105	37

Cicero
De divinatione
1.121	7

De haruspicum responso
9	7
19	138

De Lege agraria
2.87	198

De legibus
2.15	138
2.19	138 f.
2.19–24	7
2.21	140
2.22	140, 143
2.24	138 f.
2.25	139 f.
2.26	141
2.41	140
2.44	140

De natura deorum
1.81	139
2.3	138
2.19	203
2.28	7
2.71	139
3.2	138

De republica
2.25–27	139

In Verrem
2.1.55	198
2.4.99–101	139

Pro Cluentio
14–15	33

Clement of Alexandria
Eclogae propheticae
49.2	39

Paedagogus
1.6	22
2.2.33	54
3.1	22

Stromateis
1.1.10.5	101
1.11	22
2.11	22
2.13	59
3.3.12	129
4.22	37
5.1.13	116
5.14.132	128
6.7	37
7.7	22

Clement of Rome
Epistulae de virginitate
1.7.2	53
1.11	22

Codex Theodosianus
3.12.1	33

Cyril of Alexandria
Contra Julianum
9.310	116

Damascus Document
3.7–13	41
3.21–4.1	173

De recta in Deum fide
2.825d–826b	65

Demosthenes
Adversus Androtionem
78	116

De falsa legatione
19.71	131

De symmoriis
25.5	54

In Aphobum
3.7.4	54

In Neaeram
86	127

Didache
4:10	74
10:6	87

Didymus the Blind
Fragmenta in Epistulam ii ad Corinthios
2:10	64

Fragmenta in Psalmos
416	101
417	101

De Spiritu Sancto
3	70
15	70

Dio Cassius
Historiae romanae
41.61.1–4	176
42.26.1–4	176
43.50.4	198
58.22	33

Dio Chrysostom
De aegritudine
11.3	102

De regno
3.97	120
3.137	102
4.29	102

De virtute
32	128

Defensio
1–2	129

Diodorus Siculus
Bibliotheca historica
1.88.4	124
3.13.3	102
3.47.2	129
4.22.3	129
4.71.1	102
4.84.4	132
5.46.7	122
10.27.1	54
11.89.1	131
11.89.3	132
11.89.5	132
13.18.6	102
14.114.6	96
15.49	132
15.80.5	96
16.27.1–2	176
17.41.7–8	121
19.108.6	96
20.33.5	33
23.13.1	129
32.4.5	198
32.27.1–3	198

Diogenes Laertius
2.142	113

Diognetus
10:5	102

Dionysius of Halicarnassus
Antiquitates romanae
1.87.2	136
2.10.3	137
2.18.1–3	138
2.20	135
2.20.2	129
2.74.3	137
3.1.2	136
7.12.3	102
7.68.3	102
8.50.3	128
12.9	145

Epictetus
Diatribai
1.14.11–17	83
3.13.21	102
3.22.53	83
3.26.23	102

Enchiridion
48.2	102

Epiphanius
Panarion
42.11–12	39
66.86.2	68
66.86.7–10	69

Eunapius
Vitae sophistarum
472	135

Euripides
Alcestis
119–20	116

Bacchae
199	129 f.

Electra
979	135

Hecuba
807	102

Helena
1337	135

Heraclidae
807	102

Hercules furens
1234	135

Hippolytus
  33
  316–7   117
Ion
  1314–19   126
Iphigenia aulidensis
  1514   83
  1568–69   116
Medea
  807   102
Orestes
  1104   54
  1604   117
Phoenissae
  1556   135
Troades
  941   135

Eusebius
Commentarius in Psalmos
  38:8–12   64
  58:16   4
Demonstratio evangelica
  1.3.10   161
Historia ecclesiastica
  6.2   66
  7.11.12   52
  7.32.16–19   32
Praeparatio evangelica
  3.17   22
  13.13   128

Evagrius
Tractatus ad Eulogium
  7   135

Ezekiel the Tragedian
  150–192   32
  171   36
  189   36
  241   3

Festus
De verborum significatu
  5 L   137
  184 L   136
  260 L   137
  422 L   137
  423 L   137

Gaius
Institutiones
  1.59   33
  1.61   33
  1.63   33
  2.1–10   7

Galen
Ad Thrasybulum utrum medicinae sit an gymnastices hygenie 102
De consuetudinibus 102
De methodo medendi
  2.91K   102
  2.103K   102
  8.544K   102
  9.621K   102
  9.626KK   102
  12.824K   102
De naturalibus facultatibus
  3.4.153   102
De sanitate tuenda
  1.8.20   118
De temperamentis
  3   102
De usu partium   102
In Hippocratis de acutorum morborum victu
                 102

Genesis Rabbah
  16.5   155
  21.8   155

Gregory Nazianzus
Orationes
  6.3   22

Herodotus
Historiae
  1.19.2–3   116
  1.159   176
  2.38–39   124
  5.61   114
  5.72   126
  5.87.2   83
  6.81–82   116
  6.111   102
  7.141   128
  8.53.14   96
  9.31   102
  9.69.13   96
  9.76.1   96

Hesiod
Opera et dies
  238–45   131

314	83		

Hilary of Poitiers
Tractatus super psalmos
51	64
59	64
68	64

Hippocrates
De aere, aquis, locis
22.8–13	118

De morbo sacro
4.40–50	117
4.54–60	116
15	83

De ratione victus in morbis acutis
9.13	102
9.29	102

Epidemiae
2.3.11	102

History of the Rechabites
8.2	3

Homer
Iliad
1.317	120
4.227	22
6.297–310	116
8.166	83
16.506	22

Odyssey
1.60–69	116
3.273–75	116
3.440–441	116
4.499–511	132
6.162–69	156
6.293–94	156
13.184–87	116

Horace
Carmina
2.13.1	7

Hyginus
Fabulae
116	132

Hym. Hom. Herm.
4.322	120

Iamblichus
De vita pythagorica
31.210	33

Ignatius
To Polycarp
4.3	22

To the Ephesians
13.1	3
20.2	85

To the Magnesians
12.1	22

To the Philadelphians
7.1	74
8.1	59

To the Smyrnaeans
6.1	22

To the Trallians
4.1	22
7.1	22

Isocrates
Aegineticus
20	102

Archidamus
31	116, 127

Areopagiticus
73	83

De bigis
33	102

Panathenaicus
9	102

Plataicus
6.111	102

Jerome
Adversus Jovinianum
1.8	64

Adversus Rufinum
2.7	64

Altercatio Luciferiani et orthodoxi seu dialogus contra Luciferianos
5	64

Commentariorum in Joelem
2:25–27	64

De viris illustribus
61	66
75	66

Epistulae
39	66
51	4

John Cassian
Conlationes
22.5	101

John Chrysostom
Ad populum Antiochenum de statuis
5.4	102

Ad Stagirium a daemone vexatum
1.3	64, 102

Ad Theodorum lapsum
1.8	64

Adversus Judaeos
8.6–7	64

De decem millium talentorum debitore
5	102

De diabolo tentatore
1.8	102
2	59

De laudibus sancti Pauli apostoli
3	65
6	65

De Lazaro
3	102

De mutatione nominum
3.1	65

De paenitentia
1.3	65

De sanctis martyribus
3	102

Epistulae ad Olympiadem
2.3	65

Expositiones in Psalmos
141	4
142	102

Homiliae in epistulam ad Colossenses
1	54

Homiliae in epistulam ad Hebraeos
5	102

Homiliae in epistulam ad Philippenses
9	102

Homiliae in epistulam ad Romanos
13.6	65

Homiliae in epistulam i ad Corinthios
3.5	22
6	23
15.3	54
15.4–9	64 f.
23	4

Homiliae in epistulam ii ad Corinthios
15.2	65

Homiliae in Joannem
38.1	65
57.3	64

Homiliae in Mattaeum
9.2	64

In illud: Habentes eundem spiritum
3	102

Josephus
Antiquitates judaicae
1.43	129
2.312–3	32
3.45	102
3.248	32
3.249	36
3.274	34
3.321	36
4.181	129
4.217	129
4.309	54
5.308	102
6.150	129
6.181	102
7.81	163
8.42–46	93
8.251	129
9.8–9	192
9.173	129
11.59–63	175
11.109–10	32
11.282	3
12.357	129
14.213–216	164
14.231–232	164
15.417	169
15.418–420	169
20.216–218	175

Bellum judaicum
2.10	32
2.138–140	180
2.143	210
3.62	102
3.110	102
3.523	102
4.62	102
4.489	102

5.35	3	**Livy**	
5.193–194	169	Ab urbe condita	
5.404	96	1.45	7, 144
5.517	192	3.18.10	7
5.526	102	3.55	144
5.549	99	3.57.2	135
6.122–5	169	5.13.4–8	145
6.299–300	178	5.40.59	145
6.415	102	6.33.4–6	176
Contra Apionem		7.2.2	141
2.102	169	22.56	139
2.102–7	169	24.20	136
Vita		26.30	141
10–12	180	26.31	141
Jubilees		27.16	141
1:10	165	29.8	142
1:16–17	165	29.10	141
1:28	171	29.14	141
3:10–13	165	29.18	142, 164
3:12	174	29.19	142
8:19	165, 174	29.21	142
10:1	183	31.12	142
10:3	183	34.6.15	139
11:4	183	40.37	141
12:20	184	40.40	150
19:28	184	42.3	142
23:21	165	44.1	138
30:13–15	165	45.39	138
33:1–13	34	Periochae	
48:12–19	32	52.4	198
49:1–13	32	**Lysias**	
Justin Martyr		Against Andocides	
Apologia		11.1	129
i 25	129	**Macrobius**	
Dialogus cum Tryphone		Saturnalia	
10.3	161	1.23.13	146
14.2	37	3.3.2	144
23.4	161	3.7.3	144
Juvenal		**Martial**	
Satirae		4.16	33
6.50–51	139	**Menander**	
6.133–4	33	Dyskolos	
Liber antiquitatum biblicarum		440	116
28:6	203	**On the Origin of the World**	
62:2	203	107	93
Lives of the Prophets			
4.7	3		

Oppian
Halieutica
1.570	22
2.325	22
2.545	22

Origen
Commentarii in evangelium Joannis
1.10	23
13.18	52

Commentarii in Romanos
6.6.5–6	60, 66

Commentarium in evangelium Matthaei
10.25	85, 204
12.5	37
16.8	62, 66
17.14	62

Commentarius in Canticum
2.8	38

Contra Celsum
3.64	22
5.8	22
6.2	23

De principiis
1.2	23
1.62	23
3.68	23

Epistula ad Gregorium Thaumaturgum 63
Fragmenta ex commentariis in epistulam i ad Corinthios
24.93	66
24.93.1–19	61
24.93.9–11	64
24.93.12–13	63
24.93.18	64
24.93.19	63

Fragmenta in Jeremiam
48	66
48.7	62

Fragmenta in Psalmos
37:4	66
118:121	62

Homiliae in Exodum
5	38
7.3–4	4
9.4	53

Homiliae in Ezechielem
3.8	66

Homiliae in Jeremiam
1.3	62
1.3–4	66
19.14	62

Homiliae in Leviticum
14.4	66

Homiliae in Numeros
7.2	38
21.1	4

Homiliae in Psalmos
37 1	59
37 1.2	60, 66

Philocalia
14	63
27.8	62

Scholia in Apocalypsem
30.39	62

Ovid
Fasti
4.353–60	145
6.249–68	145

Metamorphoses
3.512	135
8.742–3	135
13.761	135

Pausanias
Graeciae descriptio
1.20.7	132
2	199
2.7.7–8	118
2.32.6	118
3.15.7	121
3.15.11	121
4.25.5–6	144
5.21.5	116
5.26.2	118
6.20.3	114
7.15.1–16.8	198
8.30.2	113
8.31.5	113
8.36.3	113
8.38.6	113
8.41.8–9	118
9.19.7	123
9.22.1–2	118
9.25.10	129
9.38.5	121

10.13.8	116	66	2
10.38.13	119	81	36

Petronius
Satyricon
60	146

Philo
De Abrahamo
234	96

De congressu eruditionis gratia
106	32
143	37
162	36

De decalogo
2–10	167

De ebrietate
101	37
101–3	167
189	37
222	99

De gigantibus
19	203
28	203

De migratione Abrahami
25	32
69	168
92	170

De opificio mundi
31	37
135	203

De sacrificiis Abelis et Caini
63	32

De somniis
2.74	37
2.134	37

De specialibus legibus
1.315–16	168
2.145–9	32
2.148	106
3.12–21	34
3.126	38
4.126–130	97

De virtutibus
30	54
43	96
136	99

De vita contemplativa
19–20	168

De vita Mosis
1.302	38
2.34	166
2.71–73	166
2.74	168
2.170–2	38
2.214	167
2.255	96
2.273	38

Hypothetica
7.13	2

In Flaccum
122	167

Legatio ad Gaium
184	170
198	170
212	170
222	96

Legum allegoriae
1.88	37
2.34	3
3.138	99

Quaestiones et solutiones in Exodum
1.4	32
2.28	47

Quis rerum divinarum heres sit
255	32
98	37
192	32
264–5	203

Quod deterius potiori insidari soleat
113	99

Philostratus
Vita Apollonii
1.10	116

Vitae sophistarum
2.9	147

Pindar
Pythionikai
55	102

Plato
Apologia
40a	83

Gorgias
507a–b	115

Hipparchus
  229a   115
Leges
  4.716b–717a   140
  838a–39a   33
Phaedo
  66a   37
  81c   37
Symposium
  211e   37

Plautus
Curculio
  260–69   139
Poenulus
  449–56   139

Pliny the Elder
Naturalis historia
  2.26   140
  24.102   120
  28.5   138
  29.1.4   118
  31.24   143

Plutarch
Agesilaus
  9.3   129
  27.2   102
Alcibiades
  19–22   126
Alexander
  24.3–4   121
Cato Minor
  35.7   129
De defectu oraculorum
  10   83
  432D–E   203
  437B   123
De E apud Delphos 152
De Iside et Osiride 152
  25   83
  363B–C   124
De sera numinis vindicta
  560E   116
De superstitione
  1–14   152
Demetrius
  38   33

Fabius Maximus
  22.5   141
Galba
  16.1–2   144
Lysander
  8.4   129
Marius
  39.6   128
Moralia
  267D   114
  1128B–1130E   152
Non posse suaviter vivi secundum Epicurum
  1101E–F   121
  1102 A–B   121
Otho
  3.1   144
Quaestiones romanae et graecae
  109   89
Quaestionum convivialium libri IX
  614D–615C   146
  635C   102
  745A   118
Septem sapientium convivium
  8   83
  149D   128
Themistocles
  13   127

Polybius
Historiae
  3.112.6   138
  4.35.4   122
  39.2   198

Polycarp
To the Philippians
  6.1   102
  11.4   59

Porphyry
De abstinentia
  2.19   116

Prayer of Azariah
  1:16   166
  1:31   166

Proclus
Chrestomathia II   132

(Ps.)-Apollodorus
Epitome
  6.6   132

Ps.-Aristotle
Oeconomica
  1352a   129
Pseudo-Phocylides
  179–80   34
Quintus Curtius Rufus
Historiae Alexandri Magni
  4.3.19–22   121
  8.2.19   33
Quintus Smyrnaeus
Fall of Troy
  14.530–640   132
Revelation of Adam
  7.13   93
Sallust
Bellum catalinae
  12   138
Seneca
Epistulae morales
  41.2   203
  95.50   140
Phaedra
  165–6   34
  165–73   33
Sibylline Oracles
  5.304   3
  5.422–427   171
Silius Italicus
Punica
  10.432–33   176
Socrates Scholasticus
Historia ecclesiastica
  4.19.3   135
  7.38.28   135
Sophocles
Antigone
  999–1022   116
  1238   22
Elektra
  637–59   116
  882   54
Oedipus coloneus
  788   135
Oedipus tyrannus   33
  445   54
  828   83

Philoctetes
  8–11   116
  1326–28   131
  1420   54
Trachiniae
  1023–30   83
Statius Papinius
Silvae
  1.5.23–26   143
  3.1.138   145
Strabo
Geographica
  3.3.7   102
  5.3.13   143
  8.6.23   198
  16.1.20   102
Suetonius
Divus Augustus
  35.2–3   147
Domitianus
  22   143
Gaius Caligula
  24   143
Galba
  15.1   144
Nero
  28   143f.
  49.2   144
  56   135
Tacitus
Annales
  6.19   33
  6.49   33
  12.7   33
  13.58   136
  14.2   143
  14.22   143f.
Historiae
  1.20   144
  1.78   144
  3.72   144
  4.45   34
  5.13   178
Targum Neofiti
Numbers
  21:6   99

Targum Onqelos
Leviticus
16:1   161

Targum Pseudo-Jonathan
Numbers
21:6   99

Tertullian
De pudicitia
13.22   68
13.24 – 26   67
13.25   70
14.1 – 3   68
14.16   34

Testament of Benjamin
3:3   183
6:5   37
9:1 – 5   165

Testament of Dan
1:7 – 8   183

Testament of Judah
6:5   3
7:3   3

Testament of Levi
5:1   165
8:16   83
9:9 – 10   166
13:7   3
14:5 – 15:2   166
14:7 – 8   22
16:1 – 5   166
18:4   93

Testament of Moses
5:3   166

Testament of Reuben
1:6 – 10   34
3:10   34
3:14 – 15   34
4:6   3

Testament of Solomon
18   184
18:1   93
18:40   93

Testimony of Truth
70   93

Theodore of Mopsuestia
Commentary on the Eucharist and Liturgy   71

Theodoret of Cyrus
De incarnatione Domini
6   135
Interpretatio in epistulam i ad Corinthios
5:5   72
Interpretatio in epistulam ii ad Corinthios
2:11   135
Interpretatio in epistulam ii ad Thessalonicenses
2:3   135
Interpretatio in epistulam ii ad Timotheum
2:3   135
Interpretatio in Ezechielem
13:16   135
Interpretatio in xii prophetas minores
Zach 3:1 – 6   135

Theophrastus
Characteres
23.4   54

Thucydides
4.97   115
4.126.4   102
5.46   54
6.28 – 29   126
7.48.1   102
7.75.3   102

Tryphiodorus
The Taking of Ilios
647 – 48   132

Valerius Maximus
Factorum ac dictorum memorabilium libri IX
2.1.2   145

Varro
De lingua latina
6.30   7

Velleius Paterculus
Historiae
1.13.1   198

Vergil
Aeneid
1.723 – 56   146
2.217 – 20   144
6.258 – 9   7
7.648   135
Eclogae
4.11 – 14   7

Xenophon
Cyropaedia
1.4.6	102
3.3.64	96

Memorabilia
1.4.6	102
2.2.13	116
2.6.12	102

Xenophon of Ephesus
1.5.6–8	116

1Q14
f8	179

1QapGen
14:13–17	174
20:26	184

1QH^a
4:29	186
5:30–31	186
5:32	184
5:36	186
6:24	186
6:36	186, 203
8:20	186
8:29	186
8:29–30	186
8:30	177
9:24–25	186
10:12	173
14:16	178
15:10	177
15:11–12	173
16	173
16:5–14	193
16:13	177
17:15–16	183
20:14–15	186
20:15	177, 186
21:34	186
23:33	177

1QM
1:2	199
3:5	208
4:9	208
7:10	173
12:2	173
17:2	173

1QpHab
8:8–13	179
9:4–12	179
12:6–10	179
12:7–9	179
12:9–10	179

1QS
1:18	189
2:1–2	180
2:2	180
2:2–9	189
2:4–5	180
2:5	180
2:6	189
2:7–8	189
2:10	182
2:25–3:12	182
3:5–6	182
3:6–9	184, 186
3:7	177, 191
3:13–4:26	183
3:20–21	184
3:25	173
4:3–6	185
4:9–11	185
4:20–22	185, 203
4:20–23	183, 190, 205
4:21	177
4:22	185
5:2	173
5:5–6	172
5:9	173
5:20–21	188, 205
5:21	173, 180
5:23	180
5:23–24	183
5:24	188, 205
6:13–21	193
6:14	179, 182
6:16	180
6:16–17	188, 205
6:17	180, 183
6:18	180
6:19–20	180
6:20	180
6:22	180
6:24–27	189

6:27	190	3:22	173
7:2–3	189	4:28	174
7:2–5	210	**3Q15**	
7:3–5	190	11:7	174
7:5–18	190	**4Q88**	
7:16–17	190	9:8–14	193
7:18	188	**4Q164**	
7:18–20	189	f1:1–5	175
7:22	190	**4Q171**	
7:22–24	190	f1 3:1	199
7:23	190	**4Q174**	
7:25	190	f1–2i:7–9	189
8:4–10	172 f.	f1–2ii:17	173
8:5	173 f.	**4Q186**	
8:5–6	174	1ii:5–8	184
8:6	175	**4Q249c**	
8:6–7	174	1:5	173
8:7	173	**4Q249e**	
8:8	173	f1 i–3:8	173
8:9	173, 175	**4Q249 f**	
8:9–10	175	f1–3:2	173
8:10	174	**4Q249 g**	
8:13	199	f1–2:1	173
8:14	199	f3 7:13	173
8:14–16	199	**4Q258**	
8:15	199	2:1	173
8 :16	177	6:2	173 f.
8:21–23	190	6:4	173
8:24–25	183	7:4	173
9:3–6	172	7:7	173
9:4–5	174	**4Q259**	
9:6	174	2:14	174
9:7	173	2:16	173
9:14–15	188, 205	2:17	174
9:19	199	**4Q266**	
11:8	173 f.	2:3	173
1QSa		2:19	173
1:2	173	f11:17	208
1:12	173	**4Q267**	
1:23	173	f5 3:8	173
1:24	173	**4Q269**	
2:3	173	16:12–15	190
2:3–9	177	**4Q270**	
2:13	173	f7 ii:14	208
2:17–22	193	**4Q279**	
1QSb		f5 4	173
2:22–24	177		

Index of Ancient Citations

4Q286		**4QMMT**	178
7ii:2–4	189	B:48–49	188
4Q287		C:7–8	179
6:2–4	189	**11Q5**	
4Q320		19:15	184
f4 iii	174	**11Q11**	83, 93
4Q366		**11Q20**	
f3 ii:20–22	179	5:25	173
4Q390		**11QApPs**[a]	
f1–3	173	5:4–6:3	186
4Q397		**11QPs**[a]	
f6 13:14	173	19:1–18	186
4Q403		**CD**	
f1 i:41	173 f.	1:3–5	179
f1 i:44	174	2:12	177
4Q415		4:15–18	179
9:8	188	5:6–7	179
11:7	188, 205	5:6–11	188
4Q416		5:6–15	203
1:10–14	187	5:11–19	188
1:12	186	6:11–7:6	188
2ii:6–7	187, 203	6:11–17	179
2iii:5–6	188	6:16–17	179
2iv:6–8	188	7:6	208
4Q417		9:11	208
1i:13–18	186, 205	10:23	208
1i:17	186	12:23	208
4Q418		13:11	180
81+81a:2	186	14:3	208
2+2a–c:4	186	20:24	188, 205
f81 10–14	174	**Songs of the Sabbath Sacrifice** 178	
4Q438		**Temple Scroll**	
4ii:5	186	22:5	173
4Q500	174	29:2–10	177
4Q504		34:4–8	190
f1–2iv:2–14	193	34:13	173
4Q521		45:7–10	207
2ii+4:6–13	193	45:10	177
4Q560		45:12–14	177
1i:4–5	185	46:9–12	177
1i:1–2i:6	205	46–47	174
ii:5–6	185	47:3–6	177
4QFlor	179	47:11	177
f1 2i:6	173, 175	51:7–9	177
4QInstruction[a]		52:15–16	177
f81 4	174	53:9–10	177
		56:5	177

66:12	34	12	131
		33	134
b. Eruvin		35	129
104b	169	69	131
b. Pesahim		71	131
3b	169	106	129
b. Sanhedrin		107	135
54a	34	109	135
103b	33	**CID**	
b. Yevamot		1.10	123
13a	34	33	134
6b	160	**CIL**	
m. Arakhin		I^2 366	125, 137
2.6	175	I^2 626	198
m. Berakhot		I^2 628	198
9.5	160	I^2 629	198
m. Bikkurim		I^2 2872	125
3.3	175	VI 68	134
m. Kelim		VI 32323	145
1.8–9	169	XIV 2112	147
m. Kerithot		**CMRDM**	
1.1	34	42	130
m. Pesahim		77	130
5.7	175	80	131
m. Sanhedrin		**CPJ**	
7.4	34	1.129	171
9.1	34	3.1449	170
m. Sukkah		**F. Delphes III,3**	
5.4	175	383	124
m. Tamid		**Halikarnassos**	
7.3	175	6	124
m. Yevamot		**IC**	
1.3	34	II xvi	128
Mekilta Exodus		**IDelos**	
12:21–24	37	500	124
Sifra Qedoshim		504	124
7.9	160	505	124
t. Sanhedrin		**IEph**	
10.1–2	34	1a.2	132
y. Sanhedrin		**IG**	
7.6	34	II^2 244	124
		II^2 1322	122
BGU		II^2 1328	125
1.250	124	II^2 1361	122
523	134	II^2 1365	102, 114, 116, 127
BIWK		II^2 1366	127
1	131	II^2 1368	126

II² 1369	122, 127	*ISmyrna*	
II² 1635	127	573	163
II² 1670	124	603	123
II² 1678	124	*IStratonikeia*	
II² 1933	122	22	122
II² 2499	125	25	122
II² 4964	113	29	122
II² 13200	127	33	122
III App. 108	56	35	122
IV 29–38	196	255	122
IV² 1.94–95	118	*IvP* III	
IV² 1.121	118, 119	161	118
IV² 1.122	118, 119	*LGS*	
IV² 1.258	118	161	118
VII 3073	124	*Livadie*	
VII 3074	124	1	124, 125
XI⁴ 1296	131	*LSAM*	
XII⁵ 647	123	12	114
XII⁶ 1:172	122	17	131
XIV 645	125	18	114
XIV 1389	135	19	128
IGUR		20	114, 131
III.1155	135	28	181
IIasos		29	114, 128
247	181	35	114, 157
IJO		51	114
1:Ach62	164	52B	127
IK		68	114
57.5	133, 134	75	131
57.167	126	84	131
57.168	126	*LSCG*	
57.169	126	36	125
57.170	126	37	125, 127
57.172	126	53	117, 126, 127
IKibyra		55	114, 127
1.82	134	65	114, 115, 120, 123, 125, 126, 127
1.83	134	69	113
ILS		82	114
3846	134	84	125, 127
3847	134	86	128
4912	137	91	125
4913	136	95	114
ILydiaHM		109	114
85	129	110	114
Iscr. di Cos		111	125
178	127	116	125

121	113	**P. Oxy.**	
122	127	110	145
124	114	523	145
136	114, 115, 125	1484	145
137B	127	1485	122
139	114	**SEG**	
148	125	8.169	169
150 A	125	11.314	112, 113
150B	125	11.336	112
171	114	19.427	115
LSS		27.30	161
34	114	28.421	116
36	125	28.1568	129
49	113, 114	31.122	125, 126
53	125	35.1157	135
54	114	35.1158	132
56	114	36.1221	114
59	114	37.1001	128
60	114	38.1236	129
75	114	43.710	117
81	125	50.1352bis	117
82	115	55.981	123
91	114, 125	60.891	116
106	114	**Syll.³**	
108	114, 115, 116	601	138
115 A	118	611	138
118	114	725	164
119	114	**TAM**	
128	113, 125	V.1 159	128
NewDocLyd		V.1 179a	129
51	132	V.1 179b	129
83	143	V.1 238	130
85	135	V.1 317	129
OGIS		V.1 460	130
228	163	V.1 509	131
598	169	V 1539	132
P. Gen.			
1.32	124		

Index of Bible Citations

Genesis
1–3	155
2:9	156
2:15	155
2:17	156
3:8	155, 191
3:16–19	156
3:24	155 f.
6:3	177
9:25–27	90
15:1	157
17:4	160
17:14	160
19:3	36
20:9	160
28:11–19	156
35:22	33
41:38	203
46:2	157
49:4	33

Exodus
3:5	156
3:12	155
5:1	37
7:16	156
12	159
12:6	35
12:8	36
12:14	37
12:15	35 f., 160
12:18	36
12:19	29, 35, 160
12:19–20	35
12:20	36
12:21	29, 35
12:22	37
12:23	3 f., 37, 99
12:34	36
12:39	36
12:43–45	159
12:48	159
13:3	35
13:6–8	35 f.
13:7	29, 35
13:21	29
13:21–22	38
14:19–22	38
14:22	29
15:1–21	39
15:24	98
16:2	29, 39
16:2–12	98
16:4–35	29, 38
16:27–28	89
17:1–7	38 f.
17:3	98
17:6	29
20:24	159
22:19	3, 161
23:14	37
23:14–17	159
23:15	162
24:2	43
24:3–8	159
24:8	29, 40, 42 f.
24:9	159
24:11	42
24:15	42
25:22	191
27:9–15	157
27:13–16	156
28:3	203
29:1	157
29:18	175
29:25	175
29:41	175
29:42–46	158
30:33	160
30:34–38	120
30:38	160
31:1–11	157
31:3	157
31:4	26
31:13	161
31:14	160
32:1–5	158

32:6	29, 38, 98	17:4	160
32:10	158	17:9	160
32:25–29	38	17:10	160
32:26–28	158	17:14	160
32:35	158	18:7–8	34
33:3	158	18:21	160
33:9	42	18:24–28	160
33:16	158	18:29	160
34	158	19:8	160
34:18	36	19:12	160
34:20	162	19:30	160
35:31	158	20:2–3	161
35:31–33	26	20:3	160
35:32	26	20:5	160
35:35	26	20:6	160
36:24	156	20:10–21	161
37:21	26	20:11	34
39:42	156	20:17	160
40:34	38, 159	20:18	160
40:36–37	42	21:6	160
40:38	38	21:8	161
Leviticus		21:15	161
1:9	175	21:23	161
1:13	120, 175	22:2	160
2:12	175	22:3	160
4:3	160	22:4	159
4:13	181	22:6	159
4:22	181	22:9	160 f.
5:3	181	22:10	159
5:4	181	22:12–13	159
5:15	159	22:16	161
5:19	181	22:32	160 f.
7:6–36	84	23:4–8	31
7:20	160	23:6	36
7:21	160	23:39	37
7:25	160	23:41	37
7:27	160	26:2	160
8:35	161	26:12	155
10:1	161	27:29	161
10:2	161	Numbers	
10:6	160 f.	1:51	161
10:6–9	161	1:52	208
10:12	36	1:52–53	161
10:12–15	84	2:1–34	161
15:31	160 f.	2:3	208
16:2	161	2:10	208
16:13	161	2:17	208

2:32	208	18:9	181
3:4	161	18:17	175
3:8	156	18:21	156
3:10	161	18:22	162
3:38	161	18:32	162
4:3–4	161	19:13	162
4:5–15	161	19:20	89, 160, 162
4:16–17	161	20:1–13	39
4:18	3	21	209
4:19–20	162	21:4–7	98
4:28	156	21:4–9	39
4:33	156	25	161, 209
5:3	162	25:1–9	39, 98
5:6	181	25:1–15	38
5:22	182	26:61	161
6:24–26	180	28:2	155
8:19	156, 161	28:16–25	31
8:26	156	28:17	36
9:1–15	31	29:12	37
9:11	36	31:19	162
9:13	160	33:3	31
9:15	159	Deuteronomy	
9:15–17	38	1:27	90
11:1	161f.	5	92
11:4–34	97	12:1–7	92
11:33	158	13:1–5	92
12:6	157	16:1–8	31
12:14	162	16:2	35
12:15	162	16:3	36
13:18	102	16:3–4	35
14:2	98	16:15	37
14:6	39	16:16	162
14:16	39, 96	17:2–7	92
14:27–29	98	17:7	89, 92
14:36	98	17–18	92
15:3	175	18:1–4	84
15:24	175	19:15–21	92
15:30	160	19:16–19	92
15:35	162	21:18–21	92
15:36	162	22	92
16:24–27	89	23:1	34
17:13	162	23:10–11	207
18:1	162	23:10–14	162
18:3	162	23:15	155
18:5	161	24:7	92
18:6	156	27:15–26	182
18:7	162	27:20	34, 90

28:45	90	13:34	3
28:58–61	158	18:24–26	56
31:14–15	81	2 Kings	
32	80	1:2	192
32:1–4	81	2:24	56
32:10–14	81	5	54
32:15–18	81	5:11	56
32:19–27	81	23:9	36
32:28–30	81	23:21–23	31
32:30	81	1 Chronicles	
32:31–33	81	5:1	33
32:34–36	81	6:32	156
32:36	82	13:5	162
32:37–38	81 f.	13:9	162
32:39–43	81	13:10	162 f.
Joshua		15:13	163
3:10	3	23:2–5	175
5:10–15	31	23:24	156
7:25	3	28:13	156
Judges		28:18	185
2:14	90	29:4	185
6:21	36	2 Chronicles	
16:13	102	19:11	175
1 Samuel		20:5–17	192
2:10	102	23:19	178
4:3	162	30	31
4:7	162	35:1–19	31
4:10–11	162	1 Esdras	
4:21–22	162	1:47–55	166
5:2–12	162	8:69	34
6:3	162, 181	9:2	34
6:4	181	2 Esdras	
6:17	181	10:6	34
6:19	158	4 Ezra	
30:15	90	10:21–22	166
30:16	37	10:51–56	171
2 Samuel		14:29–30	41
6:2	162	Ezra	
6:6	162	6:16–18	175
6:7	162 f.	6:19–22	31
7:6–7	155	9:7	90
16:20–2	33	Nehemiah	
22:7	192	5:13	182
1 Kings		Esther	
6:23–28	156	16:21	3
8:6–11	191	Judith	
9:3	191	2:3	3

4:9–13	192		12:28	96
7:14	96		13:6	3
7:25	96		15:27	96
8:15	3		3 Maccabees	
9:7–13	165		4:2, 3	3
11:15	3		6:30, 34	3
14:4	96		1:16	192
Tobit			2:1	192
1:4	165		4:20	23
3:4	90		5:5	3
3:8	83		6:21	3
3:17	83		4 Maccabees	
6:8	83		1:33	99
6:14–17	83		1:35	99
8:3	83		3:19	23
13:10	165		4:9	129
13:12	165		10:15	3
14:5	171		Psalms	
1 Maccabees			5:10	181
1:44–59	163		11:4	158
2:40	3		12:6	185
4:41–54	163		18:6	158, 192
7:17	163		20:1–3	192
7:36–38	192		23:1	82
15:22–23	164		24:3–6	178
2 Maccabees			27:4	158
1:7	163		28:2	192
1:8	163		41:5	37
1:9	163		43:6	56
1:18	163		48:9	158
2:29	26		51:11	177
3:7	163		53:3	56
3:12	163		65:4	158
3:15–22	192		68:21	181
3:24	164		75:11	37
3:28	164		77:18–19	98
3:31	164		77:48	90
3:32–33	164		77:56–58	98
3:34–36	164		78	41
3:37–39	164		78:15–20	39
4:14	129		90:6	83
5:6	163		95:5	83
5:8	163		105	41, 98
5:26	96		105:25	98
6:12	3		117:18	90
10:25–27	192		123:8	56
11:11	96		135	41

136	41	4:24	93
Proverbs		5:1–13	83
1:26	3	8:1	3
1:27	3	8:9–13	166
14:9	181	15:5	3
21:7	3	17:24	3
22:22	102	17:36	93
31:5	102	Hosea	
31:9	102	4:15	181
Job		6:7	129
1:13–19	94	7	76
2:1–8	94	7:8	76
2:6	93	9:6	3
28:1	185	10:2	181
36:15	102	13:16	181
Wisdom of Solomon		Amos	
1:5–8	203	2:7b	34
1:12	3	Micah	
1:14	3	3:8	203
7:25	37	Obadiah	
11:4	39	13	3
12:17–18	82	Nahum	
14:30	129	2:1	37
16:1–14	99	Habakkuk	
16:6	99	1:11	181
18:5–25	31	Haggai	
18:13	3	2:4–5	177
18:20–25	99	2:9	171
18:25	3, 99	2:22	3
Sirach		Zechariah	
7:35	102	9:11	42
18:30	99	14:16	37
23:6	99	14:18	37
23:23	33	14:19	37
24:1–4	166	Malachi	
25:24	156	1:7–12	83
26:9	33	1:8	102
38:27	26	3:3	185
39:6–8	203	3–4	9
39:30	3	Isaiah	
50:1–20	175	3:3	26
Psalms of Solomon		6:1–3	178
1:8	166	13:21–22	83
2:3	166	20:2	157
2:12–13	166	24:6	181
4:12	3	28:16	173
4:22	93	30:29	37

Index of Bible Citations

34:14	83
37:14–20	192
44:3	177
48:21	39
54:11–12	175

Jeremiah
2:3	181
2:30	3
5:6	3
22:7	3
28:55	3
31:3	3
31:8	3
31:32	3
32:31	3
32:36	3
38:31	42
39:40	42
50:7	181
51:5	181

Lamentations
2:7	178

Ezekiel
6:14	3
11:22	178
14:16	3
20:1–31	41
22:4	181
22:10–11	33
23:28	90
36:25–27	177
37:4–6	203
37:26–28	171
39:29	177
40:1–43:12	171
44:1	156
44:14	156
44:16	83
44:29	181
45:21	31, 36

Daniel
1:10	102
1:17	157
10:1	34

Matthew
4:12	90
5:4	34
5:25	90
6:24	129
8:15	186
8:28	94
9:32	94
10:4	90
10:17	90
10:21	90
12:22	94
14:14	102
17:18	94
17:22	90
18:34	90
20:18	90
20:19	90
24:9	90
25:43	102
25:44	102
26:2	90
26:15	90
26:45	90
27:26	90

Mark
1:12	74
1:13	93
5:2	94
5:5	94
6:5	102
6:13	102
9:17	94
9:20	74
9:31	90
10:33	90
13:9	90
13:12	90
14:12	35
14:41	90
15:15	90
16:18	102

Luke
8:17	132
8:27	94
9:39	94
9:44	90
10:9	102
12:58	90

13:16	93 f.	**Romans**	
18:32	90	1:7	88
20:20	90	1:11	72
21:12	90	1:13	30
21:16	90	1:17	153
22:3	93	2:4	129
22:7	35	2:22	198
24:7	90	2:24	153
24:20	90	3:4	153
John		3:10	153
1:29	35	4:10	48
1:36	35	4:12	40
6:31	41	4:16	40
6:48–50	41	4:17	153
6:63	74	5:5	53
8:44	94	5:12–17	156
13:2	90	6:3	40
13:27	93	6:11	61
19:16	90	6:12–13	95
19:36	35	6:16	30
Acts		8:9	53
2:4	74	8:14	53
3:6	56	8:16	74
3:11–16	40	8:26	74, 186
4:7–10	56	8:36	153
4:9	102	9:1	53
5:1–11	94	9:10	40
5:3	93	9:13	153
5:15	102	9:22	48
5:16	102	9:33	153
5:27–32	40	10:15	153
7	40	11:2	30
7:23–51	41	11:8	153
8:3	90	11:23	48
8:18	74	11:25	30
8:29	74	11:26	153
10:10	74	11:29	72
10:38	94	12:6	72
11:12	74	12:11	53
12:4	90	12:19	153
13:13–17	40	13:1–2	48
15:1–11	40	14:11	153
16:18	56	15:3	153
22:4	90	15:9	153
22:12–16	40	15:21	153
26:1–8	40	**1 Corinthians**	
26:18	93	1:2	88

Index of Bible Citations — 269

1:5–7	22	3:17	27, 75, 179, 203
1:7	72	3:19	153
1:9	49, 87	3:21–23	24
1:10–4:21	24	4:6	22, 153
1:11	22	4:6–8	24
1:11–17	24	4:17–18	22
1:12	23	4:18	22
1:12–13	22	4:19	22
1:13	22, 40	4:19–20	24
1:14	40	4:21	48
1:15	40	5	7, 204
1:16	40	5:1	32, 34
1:17	40	5:1–5	62, 95
1:18	22–24, 47	5:1–13	2–4, 7, 13, 19–21, 24, 26 f., 32, 38, 61, 87, 95, 104, 107, 152 f., 179, 203, 211, 214
1:19	153		
1:22–25	23		
1:24	24, 47	5:1–14:40	24
1:26	22, 41, 48	5:2	22, 34, 89, 201
1:26–31	24	5:3	51–53
1:31	153	5:3–5	55, 211
2:4	23, 47, 204	5:3–6	209
2:4–5	22	5:4	24, 49, 54
2:5	24, 47	5:4–5	93
2:6–16	185	5:5	3, 48, 54, 58, 61, 74, 90, 100, 106, 201, 203, 209 f.
2:9	153		
2:10	48	5:6	30
2:10–13	204	5:6–8	29, 35, 76
2:10–14	203	5:6–11	95
2:11–12	48	5:7	30, 35 f., 40
2:12	22, 48, 205	5:7–8	12, 29, 105, 108
2:12–14	24	5:8	3, 36 f., 79, 95
2:14	48, 204	5–8	7
2:14–15	205	5:9–11	76
2:16	79	5:10	197 f., 200
3:1–9	24	5:10–11	76
3:5–17	25, 28, 185	5:11	29, 92, 95, 105, 198, 201, 211
3:9	24, 26, 79, 173, 204	5:12	92, 201, 213
3:10–12	212	5:12–13	76
3:10–17	9	5:13	89 f., 201, 209 f.
3:12	26	6:1–11	24
3:12–15	185	6:2	30
3:13	132	6:3	30
3:13–15	26	6:9	30, 198
3:16	25, 27, 29 f., 48, 53, 171, 173, 195	6:11	48, 203
		6:12–13	81
3:16–17	1, 4, 12, 21, 24, 26, 49, 75, 107, 110, 204, 210, 212, 214	6:12–20	6 f., 24
		6:14	24

6:15	28, 30	10:16–21	29
6:16	30	10:16–22	211
6:16–17	74	10:17	77, 79
6:17	53, 77	10:18	12, 41, 83, 87
6:19	4, 12, 28, 30, 48, 77, 205	10:18–22	84
7:1–38	6	10:19	80, 198
7:1–40	24	10:19–20	81
7:5	93	10:20	81
7:7	72	10:20–21	87, 201
7:34	48, 53	10:20–22	211
7:40	48	10:21	80, 82, 98, 210
8:1	22, 79, 198	10:21–22	81, 83
8:1–11:1	24	10:22	78 f., 81 f., 98, 204
8:4	198	10:23	81
8:7	198	10:26	82
8:9	41	10:28	81
8:10	198	10:32	88
9:9	153	11:2–16	24
9:13	30	11:16	79
9:24	30	11:17	2
10:1	30, 38, 40, 42, 207	11:17–18	49
10:1–4	81, 97	11:17–29	103
10:1–11	209	11:17–34	2–4, 7, 13, 19–21, 24, 26 f.,
10:1–13	78		29, 40, 85, 88, 100, 104 f.,
10:1–22	2–4, 7, 13, 19–21, 26 f., 29,		107, 131, 152 f., 179, 204,
	88, 104 f., 107, 152 f., 160,		209, 211, 214
	179 f., 211, 214	11:18	2
10:2	38, 40	11:19	132
10:2–5	97 f.	11:20	2, 49, 104–106, 211
10:3	38	11:20–30	210
10:4	38 f., 42, 83, 86, 211 f.	11:22	44, 88, 103, 129
10:4–20	103	11:23–26	42
10:5	38, 97	11:23–27	108
10:5–10	81	11:23–28	212
10:6	97, 99	11:25	29, 42
10:6–10	83, 209 f.	11:27	30, 43, 85, 87, 108, 204
10:7	30, 38 f., 98, 153, 158, 198	11:27–30	211
10:7–10	95	11:28–31	201
10:8	38, 79, 98	11:29	103, 108
10:9	30, 38 f., 79, 83, 98	11:30	3, 43, 85, 100, 102 f., 105,
10:10	38, 98 f., 190, 209		209
10:11	99	11:32	62, 79
10:12	41	11:33	2
10:14	78, 81, 198	11:33–34	49
10:15	201	11:34	2
10:16	30, 49, 80, 83, 86 f., 108	12	210
10:16–17	83, 212	12:1	30

12:1–10	49	16:22	56, 87
12:1–13	49	2 Corinthians	
12:1–31	24	1:1	88
12:2	198, 207	1:8	30
12:3	48, 50, 53	1:11	72
12:4	72	1:22	212
12:4–11	204	2:5–11	61
12:6	48	2:11	93
12:9	72	3:3	53
12:12–27	49	3:17	48, 74
12:13	40, 49, 53, 204	4:2	95
12:23	79	5:5	212
12:27	28	6:6	53
12:28	72	6:9	62
12:30	72	6:14–7:1	197, 202
12:31	72	6:15	180
13:1–13	24	6:16	4, 75, 197 f.
13:4	22	8:15	153
13:12	79	9:9	153
14:1–25	24	10:2	54
14:1–40	2	10:4	48
14:14	48	10:7	41
14:15	53, 186	10:8	48
14:16	53	10:10	94, 102
14:20–25	2	10:11	54
14:21	153	11:4	93
14:23	2, 50	11:9	54
14:24	205	12:7	93 f.
14:25	50, 132	12:10	48
14:26	2, 49	12:21	34
14:26–33	2	13:2	54
14:26–40	24	13:3	48
14:29	205	13:10	48, 54
15	48	Galatians	
15:1–58	24	1:2	88
15:19	79	3:5	48
15:21	156	3:10	153
15:24	48	3:13	153
15:29	40	3:27	40
15:45	153	4:18	54
16:1–4	25	4:20	54
16:1–24	25	4:22	153
16:5–12	25	4:27	153
16:10	41	5:6	48
16:13–18	25	5:9	36
16:18	48	5:15	41
16:19–24	25	5:20	198

Ephesians
1:1	88
2:19–22	26, 75
4:27	95
5:3	32
5:15	41
6:4	99

Philippians
1:1	88
1:10	37
1:19	53
3:2	41
4:13	48

Colossians
1:2	88
1:5–6	54
2:5	51, 53
2:8	41
2:18	22
2:21	95

1 Thessalonians
1:1	88
1:5	53
1:9	198
2:13	48
2:18	93
4:13	30
5:3	3
5:14	102

2 Thessalonians
1:1	88
1:9	3
2:9	93
3:10	95
3:14	76

1 Timothy
1:2	88
1:20	63, 93
4:14	72
5:15	93
6:9	3
1:19b–20	62

2 Timothy
1:2	88
1:6	72
2:25	62

Titus
1:4	88
2:12	62
3:10	99

Philemon
1	88
6	48

Hebrews
2:14	94
3:7–19	41
11:28	3

James
2:21	40
4:5	74

1 Peter
1:19	35
2:4–8	26

1 John
5:6	74
5:8	74

Revelation
2:7	74
2:10	94
2:11	74
2:17	74
2:29	74
3:6	74
3:13	74
3:22	74
5:6	35
5:9	35
5:12	35
12:9	93
12:11	35
14:13	74
20:2	93
22:17	74
22:20	87

Index of Names

Ascough, Richard   13, 116, 200, 202
Avalos, Hector   193
Barclay, John M.G.   81, 169f.
Barrett, C.K.   4, 21, 28, 39, 51f., 54f., 57, 63, 68, 75, 103
Barth, Karl   24, 57
Baur, F. C.   22
Beale, G. K.   9
Becker, Jürgen   10
Behr, C. A.   145, 147f., 216
Bell, Catherine   1f., 15
Blum, Jason   17f.
Boers, Hendrikus   24
Bookidis, Nancy   198
Böttrich, Christfried   9f., 27, 196, 203, 213
Brooke, George   9
Brown, Peter   148
Bultmann, Rudolf   24, 48, 52, 63, 68
Burkert, Walter   111, 115, 176, 195, 206
Calvin, John   33, 53, 55, 90, 97
Castelli, Elizabeth   45f.
Cerfaux, Lucien   49
Chaniotis, Angelos   117f.
Cole, Susan   111
Collins, Adela   56, 62
Collins, Raymond F.   61, 100
Conzelmann, Hans   4, 21, 23f., 34f., 40, 47, 52–54, 57, 75, 78, 83, 90, 95, 97, 99, 209
Crawford, Sidnie White   208
Dahl, Nils   23, 197
Deissmann, Adolf   46, 56
Dimant, Devorah   9, 174, 178, 184
Donfried, Karl   57
Douglas, Mary   6f., 15f., 104, 159, 182, 191, 201
Dozeman, Thomas   37, 41, 44
Dunn, James D. G.   51
Eliade, Mircea   1, 17, 211
Engberg-Pedersen, Troels   203f.
Faraone, Christopher   56

Fee, Gordon   4, 21, 23, 25, 28, 33–35, 39f., 47, 51–55, 57–59, 61, 63, 71, 75, 79, 84, 86f., 92, 95, 97, 99, 105, 209
Feyel, Christophe   123
Fiorenza, Elisabeth Schüssler   9
Fitzmyer, Joseph   4, 28, 33–35, 39f., 43, 51–58, 61, 68, 78, 83, 95, 97, 100f., 209
Fotopoulos, John   56, 83, 90, 103
Fox, Michael   111
Frey, Jörg   183f.
Gärtner, Bertil   8, 171, 174f.
Gräbe, Petrus   45, 47f.
Gupta, Nijay   28
Harnack, Adolf   202
Hays, Richard   21, 29, 41, 57, 61f., 68, 74f., 79f., 83, 91, 95, 97, 100
Hogeterp, Albert   10, 21, 172
Holladay, Carl   30, 32, 47, 154
Horsley, Richard   57, 79, 97
Hundley, Michael   13, 110, 157, 195
Jameson, Michael   153, 206
Jeremias, Joachim   36
Johnson, Luke Timothy   18, 23, 41, 48, 74, 87f., 99, 104, 119, 149f., 152, 210
Käsemann, Ernst   75
Kilde, Jeanne   2
Klauck, Hans-Josef   52
Klawans, Jonathan   15, 17, 159, 179f.
Klinzing, Georg   9, 172
Kloppenborg, John   200
Korner, Ralph   3
Kovacs, Judith   61f.
Kugel, James   13
Lanci, John   10, 21, 172
Lanfer, Peter   156
Last, Richard   202
Lee, Michelle   28
Lennon, Jack   15, 133, 140, 143
Levison, John   28, 205
LiDonnici, Lynn   118f.
Lietzmann, Hans   21, 33, 55, 57, 104f.
Lim, Kar Yong   10f.

Lindemann, Andreas   2, 21, 54, 58, 62, 70
Liu, Yulin   10, 16
Lupu, Eran   113
Markschies, Christoph   66
Martens, Peter   62, 66
Martin, Dale   6–8, 28, 83, 103 f., 203
Martin, Troy   103
Martínez, Florentino García   172, 177, 183, 193
McGowan, Andrew   105
McKelvey, R. J.   8, 21, 39
Meeks, Wayne   21, 80 f., 84, 96 f., 201 f.
Meyers, Carol   30, 39, 43, 157
Milgrom, Jacob   15 f., 159–161, 176, 178, 193
Mitchell, Margaret   11, 24, 28, 36, 77 f., 97, 212
Moo, Douglas   51, 53
Moule, C. F. D.   8, 90
Murphy-O'Connor, Jerome   21, 54 f.
Newsom, Carol   171, 173, 186
Newton, Michael   10, 177, 180
Neyrey, Jerome   6–8, 16
Økland, Jorunn   1, 10, 21, 44
Parker, Robert   15, 110
Ramelli, Ilaria   65 f., 100–103
Regev, Eyal   15, 178 f.
Rigsby, Kent   163
Röhser, Günther   84–86
Rosner, Brian   12, 28, 45, 55 f., 77, 79 f., 82, 89, 91, 97, 179
Runia, David   168
Rüpke, Jörg   136 f., 146
Sanders, E. P.   10, 171
Schatkin, Margaret   65 f.
Scheid, John   14, 146
Schiffman, Lawrence   9, 172, 175, 178
Schmiedel, Paul   24
Schofield, Alison   173
Schottroff, Luise   4, 55, 57
Schrage, Wolfgang   2, 21, 42 f., 52, 58, 103
Schwarz, Sarah   93
Smit, Peter-Ben   15, 21, 104
Smith, David Raymond   61, 68, 90, 95
Smith, Dennis   120
Smith, Jonathan Z.   1, 16, 18, 112, 200, 211
Spawforth, Tony   195
Stevenson, Gregory   171, 176, 196, 212
Thiselton, Anthony   21, 25, 52, 58, 63
Vahrenhorst, Martin   12, 27 f., 83, 87, 89, 95 f., 105, 197, 202 f., 205
VanderKam, James   165
Walbank, Mary   198 f.
Wardle, Timothy   10, 175
Wassen, Cecilia   172, 174, 178
Watson, Francis   33, 91, 97, 99
Weiss, Johannes   21, 24, 39, 51 f., 83, 97
Weissenrieder, Annette   10, 111
Wenschkewitz, Hans   8 f.
Wolter, Michael   204
Works, Carla   40, 84, 97, 100, 211
Zeller, Dieter   23, 26, 30, 40, 43, 80, 84, 87, 95, 97, 99 f.

Index of Subjects

Asclepius   115, 117, 118, 119, 134, 148, 150
body language   6, 8, 203, 210
death   3, 17, 19, 43, 61, 77, 85, 90, 92–94, 98–99, 100–104, 108, 126, 132, 137, 140, 156, 161, 162, 169–170, 190, 209
destroyer   3f., 19, 37, 38, 99, 135, 160
destruction   3, 17, 38, 61–68, 75, 81, 84, 90, 94, 95, 96–99, 128, 131, 140, 151, 160, 189, 204, 213
divine power   1, 2, 43, 44, 48, 49, 51, 77, 86, 93, 107, 117–119, 120, 133–145, 147–151, 193, 212, 213
epigraphy   1, 12, 13, 14, 27, 110, 151
exodus tradition   4, 29f., 35f., 38, 68, 80, 108, 153, 206, 211
field   7, 25, 173
garden   26, 155f., 164, 174
Garden of Eden   9, 155f., 165, 191
inscriptions   4, 14, 75, 102, 110f., 161, 164, 168–170, 181, 189, 193, 201
Jerusalem   8, 9, 10, 11, 12, 21, 28, 154, 162, 163, 164, 166, 168, 169, 170, 174, 175, 178, 179, 191, 192, 196, 215
material culture   13f., 154, 181
meals   2, 3, 31, 42–44, 50, 82–83, 85–87, 94, 95–96, 97, 103, 104–106, 107, 108, 120–122, 145–146, 159, 180, 189, 193, 201, 210, 213, 214
medical tradition   102, 103, 117, 118, 134, 147f.
Passover   4, 19, 31f., 35–37, 95, 105f., 108, 159
pollution   7f., 14, 16, 68, 83, 109f., 117, 127, 133, 137f., 142f., 151, 162, 165, 182, 188, 192, 210
power of God   22, 24, 47, 78, 88, 163f., 214
punishment   27, 35, 43, 59, 64f., 67, 89, 126, 128, 130, 132, 140, 143, 151f., 154, 156, 158, 160f., 164f., 169, 176, 190, 199, 208f., 211

purity   4, 7, 10, 14–16, 36, 37, 68, 77, 115–116, 131, 138–139, 144, 155, 159, 161, 166–167, 171, 176–179, 182, 183, 185, 188, 191, 193, 203, 210, 215
Qumran   8–10, 27, 154, 171–191, 192, 193, 197, 199, 200, 203, 205, 207, 208, 211, 214
religious experience   13, 17–18, 85, 86, 133, 145, 147–151, 196, 199, 203
ritual   1, 2, 3, 7, 14, 15, 19, 43, 50, 85, 87, 104, 105, 109, 115, 116, 119–124, 145–147, 157, 211
spirit   13, 19, 22, 23, 26, 28, 45, 47–49, 50, 51, 52, 53, 54, 55, 57, 58–73, 74, 75, 76, 77, 87, 88, 89, 93, 94, 95, 96, 103, 106, 107, 157, 158, 173, 177, 179, 183–188, 189, 190, 191, 193, 197, 202–205, 209, 211, 212, 213, 215
tabernacle   26, 31, 37f., 42, 44, 107f., 155–162, 166, 168, 191f., 196, 200, 207
temple
– healing   94, 113, 118–120, 134f., 147f., 150, 164, 192f., 212
– of Asclepius   115, 118
– sanctuary   39, 75, 89, 105, 110, 112–120, 123–127, 131f., 135f., 139, 142, 160–162, 164–166, 168f., 173–179, 188, 196, 203, 206, 210
– temenos   110f., 113, 132, 157
temple discourse   4f., 8, 11–13, 18, 21, 25, 27–29, 31, 110, 151, 155, 193, 195, 202, 212, 214
temple of God   1f., 4, 11f., 21, 25f., 28–31, 38, 42, 44f., 50, 75f., 84, 88, 96, 99, 104–107, 109, 168, 171, 173, 192, 197, 200, 202f., 210, 212–215
– spiritualization   8f., 11
– substitution   8–11, 21, 38, 178

www.ingramcontent.com/pod-product-compliance
Lightning Source LLC
Chambersburg PA
CBHW031802220426
43662CB00007B/492